UNDERSTANDING

FINANCE

UNDERSTANDING
FINANCE
MONEY, CAPITAL, AND INVESTMENTS

KAREN D. HALPERN

South Puget Sound Community College
Olympia, Washington

Upper Saddle River, New Jersey 07458

Library of Congress Cataloging-in-Publication Data

Halpern, Karen D.
    Understanding finance: money, capital, and investments /
    Karen D. Halpern
        p. cm.
        Includes index.
    ISBN 0-13-093354-6
    1. Finance. 2. Money. 3. Capital. 4. Investments. I. Title.

HG173.H3 2004
332—dc21   2002192998

Editor-in-Chief: Stephen Helba
Director of Production and Manufacturing: Bruce Johnson
Executive Editor: Elizabeth Sugg
Editorial Assistant: Cyrene Bolt de Freitas
Marketing Manager: Leigh Ann Sims
Managing Editor—Production: Mary Carnis
Manufacturing Buyer: Ilene Sanford
Production Liaison: Denise Brown
Full Service Production/Composition: Emily Bush/ Carlisle Publishers Services

Director, Image Resource Center: Melinda Reo
Manager, Rights and Permissions: Zina Arabia
Interior Image Specialist: Beth Brenzel
Cover Image Specialist: Karen Sanatar
Image Permission Coordinator: Carolyn Gauntt
Design Director: Cheryl Asherman
Design Coordinator: Christopher Weigand
Cover Design: Joe Sengotta
Cover Printer: Phoenix Color
Printer/Binder: Courier Westford

Credits and acknowledgments borrowed from other sources and reproduced, with permission, in this textbook appear on appropriate page within text.

Pearson Education Ltd.
Pearson Education Singapore Pte. Ltd.
Pearson Education Canada, Ltd.
Pearson Education—Japan
Pearson Education Australia Pty. Limited
Pearson Education North Asia Ltd.
Pearson Educación de Mexico, S.A. de C.V.
Pearson Education Malaysia Pte. Ltd.

10 9 8 7 6 5 4 3
ISBN 0-13-093354-6

*This book is dedicated to
my beloved Nicholas and Katie,
without whose love, support, encouragement, and patience
it would never have been written.*

BRIEF CONTENTS

CONTENTS

PART II CORPORATE FINANCE

CHAPTER 9

WORKING CAPITAL MANAGEMENT: THE MANAGEMENT OF SHORT-TERM ASSETS   182

CHAPTER 10

CAPITAL BUDGETING   209

APPENDIX A

TIME VALUE OF MONEY CHARTS **309**

APPENDIX B

MACRS DEPRECIATION SCHEDULES **317**

INDEX **319**

PREFACE

This book grew out of the finance and business math classes that I teach at South Puget Sound Community College in Olympia, Washington. For years, students in the business math class would ask for more than the basic math computations that we did in class. They also wanted more than just the accounting statements that they were learning about in the principles of accounting classes taught by my colleagues. The students would ask about the following "what" and "why" questions:

- Why does the bond price change?
- What happens if I buy stock and the price falls?
- Why did the stock market go up today?
- Just what did the Fed do? And how do I interpret the speech that the chairman made?
- Why do companies offer low financing rates? And why is it not offered on the car that I really want?
- How would I decide which mortgage was better?
- I'm buying a business. How do I know how much to pay for it?
- The business I really, really, really want to buy is losing money but I *know* I can fix it. Right?
- Our small business needs more funding if we're going to expand. What should we do?
- We need a small business loan. What bank should we go to? What type of financing is available?
- What do I use these present value tables for? Why would I set up a sinking fund? Oh, and just what *is* a sinking fund?

I didn't have time to answer those questions and teach math so I proposed to our college that we offer a finance class, but not personal finance or the kind of corporate finance that a huge multinational corporation would use. We needed something that local businesses could get their hands on and work with. We needed something for the horticulture student who was starting a landscape business and the food service students who would eventually open a bakery downtown. It had to be rigorous but practical, grounded in what we consider "real" business, that is, small- and medium-size companies, the kind that keep large and small towns humming with economic vitality.

Over the years I've taught as much from the questions and knowledge in the classroom and the experiences that my students have had, as I have from a book. I hope when you use this book, that you will be able to use it as the framework upon which you model your own experiences. In order to get full value from an education, you have to be an active participant.

For that reason, while there are chapter-ending questions and problems, much of the benefit of the book could come from examining the term paper topics and project suggestions that you will also find at the end of each chapter. Although they fall at the end of the chapters, there might be some value in exploring them before you embark on the course so that you can develop an idea that will tie all the loose ends of finance together.

This is a basic book, designed to give you an introduction to the fascinating world of finance. I have to confess that my personality will come through as you read it. Finance is serious business. It is the means of obtaining the funds necessary to open a business, run it, and help it grow. But there are also some wonderful stories in finance. As you go through the book, I'll share some of them with you.

Finance is also an ever-changing field. You'll notice that many of the boxes within the text contain what were, at the time I wrote this, relatively current events. As you read the book, also read the newspaper or a business magazine. Bring current issues into the classroom for discussion or debate. Examine policies that are being made by the Board of Governors of the Federal Reserve System. Look at financing decisions that affect you such as interest rates offered by banks and the availability of financing for durable goods such as equipment or vehicles. Examine how those outward signs indicate changes in the economy and business strategy of the companies offering them.

Oh, remember to think, analyze, and ask questions. That's how you will learn.

TO THE STUDENT

The files on the CD-ROM are meant to support and supplement the information in this textbook. There is a text file for each chapter that provides the learning objectives, formatted with space so that you can print the document and use it when you are taking class notes. The terms used within the chapter are listed and defined. There are also additional exercises that are meant to stimulate classroom discussion or opportunities for further consideration. Your teacher may want to use these as essay questions on a test so it wouldn't be a bad idea to take a look at them before that date!

In addition, there are a few Excel files which provide the templates for worksheets you will find in this text. Try playing with them and see if they help you make your own financial analyses.

Enjoy!

ACKNOWLEDGMENTS

This book would not have been possible without the help and encouragement of many people. First, I should thank my students who complained about the books I made them buy. They kept telling me I could do better, so they are the first to get credit for this project.

Emmie San Nicolas and Lucinda Noreen were unflagging in their encouragement and support. Their smiles and faith in me helped immeasurably. My accounting colleague, Lance Avery, provided much needed accounting advice (although the errors are mine—not his). Ben Ferguson provided moral support and a critical eye. Richard Wadley, President of the Board of Trustees of South Puget Sound Community College, read the chapter on risk and provided valuable insights and references.

A special thanks to manuscript reviewers Chris K. McDaniel, Nash Community College, North Carolina; Kenneth R. Osterling, Aims College, Colorado; Jacquelyn Blakely, Tri-County Technical College, South Carolina.

Thanks to all of you. I couldn't have done it without you.

CHAPTER

1

INTRODUCTION: WHAT IS FINANCE?

LEARNING OBJECTIVES

1. Describe finance and how it relates to economics and accounting.

2. Understand how financial managers work with others in the firm.

3. Identify the three areas of finance.

4. Compare profit and value.

5. Describe the three forms of business organization.

6. Discuss the challenges faced by small business managers.

7. Understand the types of legal and ethical issues involved in finance.

Finance is one of the key functions of business. In the simplest terms, the finance manager is responsible for planning, obtaining, and managing the funds necessary to maintain the operations of the business. Many businesses fail, not because they do not have an excellent product or service, but because the managers did not pay careful attention to the financing needs of the organization. Business history is full of stories of inventors who had groundbreaking products or ideas but were unable to sustain a business due to financial pressures.

The field of finance draws from several disciplines, chief among them are accounting and economics. While it is helpful to have some knowledge of accounting to work in finance, the two are different. Accountants draw up statements that describe what has already occurred in a business; in that sense, accounting statements are historic documents even if they are examining a relatively short and recent period of time such as the previous month's income statement. The income statement does not predict the firm's future earnings or expenses, therefore, it is not a planning document. Finance managers, on the other hand, should be planning for the future. Their work is tied directly to the corporate mission and strategic goals. Is the company planning a major expansion in the next two years? If so, how is it going to obtain the funds necessary to pay for that expansion? It is the responsibility of the finance manager to integrate corporate goals into an action plan.

1

<$\langle$ **Looking Back** $\rangle$>

Preston Thomas Tucker was a visionary. He dreamed of producing a car that was safe, reliable, and stylish. Shortly after the end of World War II, Tucker founded The Tucker Corporation. Americans were eager to buy new automobiles and Tucker thought that he could provide the first completely new automobile in years.

Tucker arranged to lease a factory in a suburb of Chicago, but before he could have full access to the plant he had to raise $15 million. He would also need to hire skilled laborers and purchase raw materials. The expenses were astronomical.

Rather than cede control of his company to wealthy investors, Tucker tried to finance the firm by selling dealer franchises, stock, and preselling automobile accessories, but it wasn't enough to finance full-scale production.

The Securities and Exchange Commission and the Justice Department charged Tucker and some of his associates with fraud in connection with his financing efforts. In the end, all of the men were acquitted, but by then the factory had been closed and the firm was bankrupt. There was only one model year, 1948, and a total of 51 cars were produced.

One of the Tucker cars belongs to the Smithsonian Institution and can be seen at the Blackhawk Museum in Danville, California.

To learn more:

www.si.edu/resource/faq/nmah/tucker.htm
www.hfgmv.org
www.tuckerclub.org

Movie:
Tucker, the Man and His Dream. 1988, Paramount.

Book:
Pearson, Charles T. *The Indomitable Tin Goose: The True Story of Preston Tucker and his Car.*

In addition to understanding accounting principles, the finance manager should have some knowledge of economics. Every business is affected by interest rates, the level of consumer spending, unemployment figures, and inflation. A finance manager does not have to be an economist, anymore than an accountant, however an understanding of the relationships between economic factors and business activity within the firm's industry is important when formulating future investment plans.

Finance is often seen as a very mathematical field, and it does require that managers have computational skills. But even more important is the manager's ability to communicate effectively and integrate information from many different sources. Finance managers are boundary-spanning agents who communicate the firm's internal goals and objectives to potential lenders and investors. Finance managers will find themselves working closely with marketing and production managers, human resource professionals, and attorneys within the firm as well as bankers, vendors, and investors outside the firm. Written and oral presentation skills are very important.

Toolbox

Here are several points to remember when you are making a business presentation.

Your audience doesn't have much time. What you want to communicate must be clear from the outset. Does the firm need working capital financing or is it looking to acquire another company? The shorter and more to the point you are, the more attention you will garner.

Know where you are going. Use an outline so that you are sure to cover the salient points.

Make the presentation appropriate to the audience. Be careful not to use acronyms that are specific to your industry if the listener or reader would not understand them. Don't assume that everyone shares your level of knowledge about your firm, the industry, or your financial situation.

Written documents and presentations should be easy to read. The text should be printed on good quality white paper using a simple font in 10 or 12 point type. It is possible to use fancy typefaces and cute illustrations. Resist the temptation. If the document is too cluttered you will distract from the serious message that you wish to convey.

Spelling and grammar count. Spelling errors, incomplete sentences, and lack of punctuation create a poor impression. Don't rely upon the software package to catch your mistakes. As helpful as the spelling and grammar features are, they will not catch all of the mistakes.

Write confidently; don't beat around the bush. Your presentation should convince the audience to invest in your business, lend you money, or buy your product. If you do not convey confidence, your audience will not be likely to have any either.

Be honest. Being confident does not mean glossing over potential risks. Discuss any economic, business, or financial challenges and describe how the firm intends to address them.

Have someone else look over your draft. You know what you want to say but did you say it clearly? Did you make assumptions that need to be explained? Did you wander from the point?

Provide visual representations when appropriate. Graphs, charts, and diagrams can break up the look of a document and allow the audience to see the information in another way. If you are talking about the increase in sales, provide a graph showing sales volume over a period of time. Pie charts are a good way to demonstrate the percent of sales by product line. Be sure that the charts illustrate what is in the text of the presentation. Otherwise they will merely be a distraction.

(continued)

(continued)

Make a good first and last impression. The cover of a written document can include a copy of the company logo or slogan but should not be flashy or distracting. The title page or cover letter should include an easy way for the recipient to contact you or the firm. Be sure to close on a positive note.

THE THREE AREAS OF FINANCE

There are three main areas of finance: Money and Financial Institutions, Corporate Finance, and Investments. This book separates the areas because they represent very different aspects of the field.

The first section, Money and Financial Institutions (Chapters 2, 3, 4, and 5), addresses the basic building blocks of an economy. Money is anything generally accepted as a unit of exchange, and financial institutions are the mechanisms by which exchange can occur. Without a strong monetary system, economies cannot grow. Nor can they expand without the help of financial institutions that transfer money from savers to investors.

The second section, Corporate Finance (Chapters 6 through 11), reviews the relationship between accounting and finance and provides financial planning tools. Break-even analysis, pricing, and profit calculations are important not just for marketing and production departments but because they influence the types of assets and liabilities that a firm may acquire (Chapter 7). The process of budgeting and forecasting (Chapter 8) should alert the finance manager to the cash needs of a business. Revenue and profit forecasts allow the manager to match monthly cash inflows with expenditures and decide how to make up for shortfalls or how to benefit from excess cash (Chapter 9). If the firm has a need for a large piece of equipment, it must decide whether to buy or lease the equipment and how to finance it (Chapter 10). When the firm is growing through acquisition or reducing its size by divesting portions of its current operations, the capital structure of the organization may change dramatically (Chapter 11). This section addresses these strategically important issues and gives the manager tools with which to plan ahead.

One firm's need for cash is another's opportunity for income. The third section, Investments (Chapters 12 through 14), examines the types of capital structure: selling equity (ownership) in the firm versus incurring debt with a separate chapter on mortgage financing. The choices are examined from two perspectives: that of the company that needs money and from the viewpoint of the investor.

Most of the examples we will look at concern profit-making enterprises, however, financial controls and planning may be even more essential for not-for-profit organizations that depend on donor contributions. As an example, the local food pantry receives much of its financial support and food donations during the last few months of the year when contributors are moved by holiday spirit, however, the demand for services continues throughout the year as do expenses for rent, utilities, and the sundries necessary to operate. The staff,

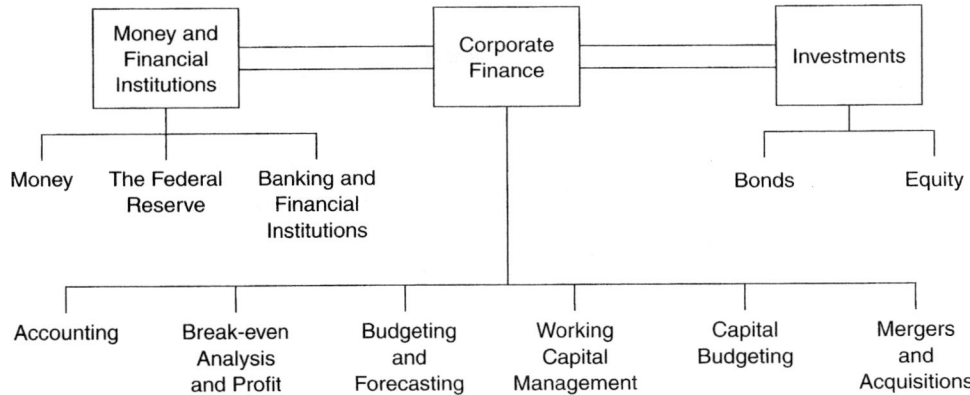

The three areas of finance described in this book.

whether volunteer or paid, must allocate scarce resources during periods where demand exceeds the level of contributions and recognize the cyclical nature of cash inflows and in-kind donations.

PROFIT VERSUS VALUE

The goal of most organizations is to generate a profit through the wise investment of productive resources. There are five main types of resources utilized by businesses: natural resources, human resources, capital, entrepreneurship, and knowledge.

- Natural resources are items that are useful in their natural state. Natural resources can be extracted from the earth such as coal or they can be an agricultural commodity like corn or wheat. Timber is a resource whether it is cut from naturally occurring forests or from commercial tree farms.
- Human resources are the employees of the firm. The productive value of human resources encompasses both the physical work of assembly line workers and the inventiveness of research scientists.
- Capital is not synonymous with cash. In this definition, capital includes technology, tools, and factories; it is the engineered components of production as opposed to the naturally occurring ones. Because capital also refers to the funds necessary to finance the operation, the term can be confusing.
- Entrepreneurship is the willingness to accept the risk inherent in a business venture. Traditionally, we have used the word entrepreneur to designate the originator of a small business, however, today the term has expanded to include the risk taking within a firm that allows it to launch new products or envision significant change within an industry.
- Knowledge is the result of experimentation and collaboration. It has also been described as the collective intelligence of an organization, the ideas or experiences that stay within a working group even as the personnel vary.

By definition, **profit** is the amount left over after expenses are subtracted from income. Some organizations try to increase profit merely by slashing expenses, arguing that lower expenses will, by default, lead to higher returns. In the short term, the strategy may increase profits. A more balanced, long-term approach is a focus on creating added value. **Value** is the customer's perception of the balance between the positive characteristics of the product and its price. Investments that improve the quality of the product or reduce the cost of manufacturing will improve profits if the firm has accurately gauged its market. The finance manager should be sensitive to the cost-benefit relationship of investments, not just their effect on expenses.

THE THREE FORMS OF BUSINESS STRUCTURE

The form that a business takes can influence its access to capital. The three most common forms of business organization are sole proprietorships, partnerships, and corporations. Each has its own advantages and disadvantages.

The **sole proprietorship** is the easiest to form. In many states, the business owner simply buys a business license, registers the business name, and begins operation. Some industries have supervisory boards: restaurants must pass inspection by the health department, contractors often have to post a bond, but the firm can begin operations as soon as the owner completes relatively simple paperwork. The profits of a proprietorship are reported to the Internal Revenue Service on the owner's individual tax return.

The ease of forming a proprietorship is offset by some of the difficulties the owner faces. If the business sustains losses rather than profit, the owner is personally liable for the debts of the firm. The owner is also personally responsible for any judgments rendered against the company. Liability insurance is available for small businesses, but that does not absolve the owner of responsibility for awards that go beyond the insurance coverage. Because the owner has unlimited liability for the losses and debts of the business, many find it difficult to obtain financing for their firms, especially when the firm is new.

Another consideration in forming a proprietorship is that the business ends with the death or retirement of the owner. Legally the business and the owner are one and the same. If the business is thriving, the owner may be able to sell the location, inventory, and good name of the firm, but the new owner will have to create a new business entity.

If two or more people join together to organize a business, it is a **partnership**. Although partnerships can be informal, it is best to have a written partnership agreement that delineates the scope of work and the responsibility of the partners. The initial investment and shares of ownership, the division of profits or losses, and the methods for leaving or dissolving the partnership should all be part of the agreement.

A partnership is similar to a sole proprietorship in that the owners have unlimited financial liability. Liability is not proportional: each partner has unlimited personal liability for all of the debts of the partnership regardless of the initial investment made or their role within the firm. Partnerships often find it easier to borrow money because there are more personal assets that the lender can attach if the firm defaults on the loan. However, financing is still difficult.

Some partnerships have two different types of partners: general partners and limited partners. General partners are involved in the day-to-day operation of the business and retain unlimited liability. Limited partners are investors who provide capital to the business and earn an agreed-upon share of the profits, but their liability is limited to the amount of their investment in the firm. A firm can have all general partners and no limited partners, but a firm cannot have all limited partners. If all of the owners want to separate their personal assets from the firm, they must form a corporation.

The third major form of business is a corporation. A **corporation** is considered a legal entity with rights and responsibilities under the law. In order to form a corporation, the owners of the business must set rules for governing the actions of the corporation and draw up a document called the articles of incorporation. If the corporation will only be doing business in one state, it files the articles of incorporation in that state and receives a charter that grants the firm legal standing in that state. If the firm intends to do business nationwide, it will choose a state in which to register and specify that it intends to do business across state lines.

The corporation has a legal identity separate from that of its owners. In a small corporation, the owners may very well continue to manage the firm, however, as the company grows larger, there is a practical as well as legal separation between ownership and management. In order to protect the owners' interests, all corporations are required to have a Board of Directors. The duty of the board is to represent the owners in major decisions facing the firm. We will discuss the election of directors in Chapter 14, but the key point is that ownership has become separate from management.

As a separate legal entity, corporations have to pay income taxes on the revenue they earn. If the firm chooses to distribute some of the profits to the owners in the form of dividends, the dividends are taxed again as personal income of the owners. A common complaint is that stockholders are subject to "double taxation" because the profits of the firm are taxed twice: once at the corporate tax rate and once when the shareholder pays personal income tax. This "double taxation" only occurs if dividends are paid. If the profits are reinvested in the firm, they are only taxed once. The penalty of double taxation is outweighed by

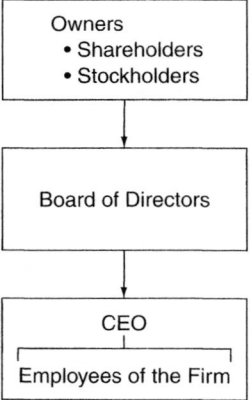

The organizational structure of a large corporation. Shareholders elect the Board of Directors who, in turn, oversee the CEO and other employees of the firm.

Toolbox

> Many states have a variety of rules for forming small business partnerships and corporations if the intent of the owners is to operate only within that state. Laws vary by state, so it is important to check the laws in your area.
>
> Many state and local agencies provide advice for the small business owner. For example, the state of Washington has created a brochure entitled *Operating a Business in Washington State: A Business Resource Guide* that is a result of collaboration between the Department of Licensing, the Department of Revenue (taxation), the Office of the Secretary of State, and other interested state agencies. It provides advice on forming different types of organizations, how to obtain licenses, how to pay taxes, and how to register as an employer in the state. It also has a section on "Getting Advice" and another on "Getting Financial Help."
>
> Check with your state to see if a similar brochure is available.

the financial protection that is afforded by incorporation. The firm itself is liable for its debts, not the owners. If a firm declares bankruptcy, the most an investor could lose is the money that was used to purchase shares of stock.

Many corporations are large businesses with many managers. As companies grow in size and complexity, the separation of ownership and management becomes more marked. Ownership in a corporation can be transferred from one party to another, and the presence of professional managers assures that the firm will continue regardless of the identities of the individual owners. This also means that dissolving a corporation is not as simple as closing the doors and pulling down the blinds.

BUSINESS SIZE AND ITS RESOURCES

The form of a business can influence its ability to raise funds, but money is not the only resource that may be scarce. The larger the business, the more specialized the functions can become. In most medium or large businesses, the **Chief Financial Officer (CFO)** directs the financial activities of the firm. The CFO supervises a Controller and a Treasurer. The **Controller** is primarily responsible for accounting. The **Treasurer's** department is usually responsible for cash management, investments, financial planning, and funds acquisition. A multibillion-dollar corporation has a staff of financial specialists; career paths can include cash management, investing, negotiating and structuring loans, or analyzing acquisitions. Firms with this depth of specialization can take advantage of sophisticated financing opportunities.

A small firm may have one person who does all of the finance as well as the accounting. In a sole proprietorship, the owner might wear all of the hats: sales manager, purchasing agent, chief financial officer, and night janitor. When time is at a premium, the owner may look outside the firm for financial advice. Many communities have economic development agencies or small

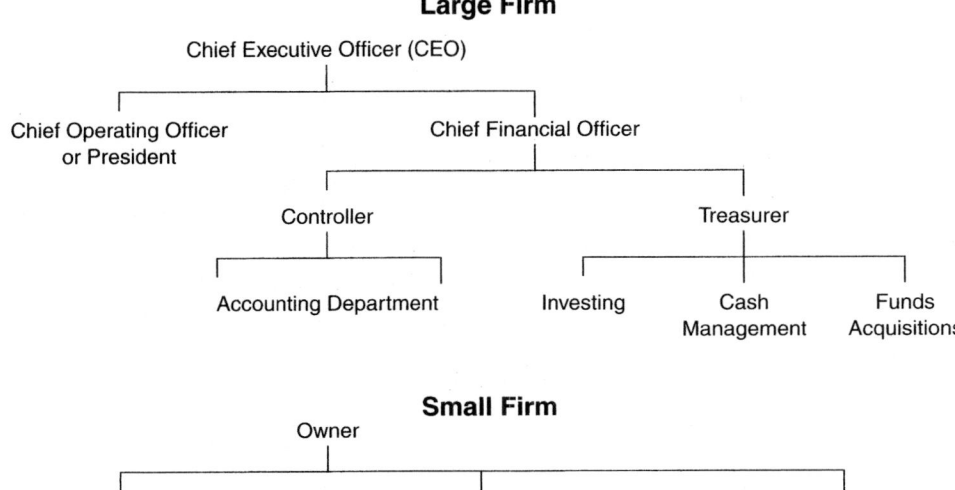

In a large firm, the CEO supervises a staff of specialists who concentrate their efforts in a specific area of expertise such as operations, marketing, or finance. In the smaller company, employees must be generalists and wear several hats.

business assistance centers that will provide advice and guidance. Business bankers and public accounting firms are also sources of information.

LEGAL AND ETHICAL ISSUES

Whether or not a firm has **stockholders,** each business has stakeholders. **Stakeholders** are people who have a "stake" in the success of the organization. Stakeholders include employees, vendors, customers, lenders, and even members of the community in which the company does business. In general, the business has a legal and ethical responsibility to serve the needs of stakeholders. This would include properly disposing of hazardous waste, providing a safe workplace, and not engaging in predatory pricing. Among other things, the finance

---

Ethics in Finance

- Honest financial statements
- The push to demonstrate short-term income growth
- Responsibility to shareholders and investors

These are a few of the many ethical issues in finance.

manager has what is referred to as a **fiduciary responsibility.** That means he or she is responsible for accurately depicting the financial condition of the firm, not engaging in legal but misleading accounting practices, and divulging all risk factors that might influence the present or future security of an investment in the firm.

Beginning in late 2001, the business world was rocked by repeated examples of financial irresponsibility, if not outright fraud. Enron collapsed when it was discovered that the firm had transferred debt to what were financial entities in so-called off balance sheet transactions. The apparent goal of the transactions was to hide the amount of debt that Enron had acquired, thus making the company look more profitable. At this point, Enron has not been found guilty of fraud, however, both the corporation and many of its senior executives are under investigation by the federal government and, by the time you read this, may very well have been indicted or tried.

The accounting firm, Arthur Andersen, that had audited Enron's financial statements was convicted of obstruction of justice for destroying documents related to its work for Enron, which had been requested by the Securities and Exchange Commission. Andersen's license to practice accounting was revoked in several states after it was found guilty and as a result, it has ceased to exist as an ongoing business.

In June 2002, financial markets were further rocked when WorldCom, the parent company of phone company MCI, announced that it had misstated its income statement by nearly $4 billion. An income statement describes the relationship between revenue earned in a certain period and the expenses that relate to that revenue. In theory, any excess revenue can be applied as the firm sees fit. For example, if the company earned more on telephone service than it cost to provide that service, WorldCom would have had internally generated funds available to expand its operations. Those excess funds would also have been able to support interest payments on additional debt if WorldCom felt that it needed to borrow more than it could generate from its earnings. By classifying certain operating expenses as capital expenses (costs associated with long-term investments or business expansion), the firm had shown a profit where none actually existed. WorldCom's restatement of its income statement eliminated approximately 15 months of previously claimed profits and drastically changed the financial picture of the corporation. A misstatement of this magnitude is not a simple "mistake"; thus the Securities and Exchange Commission has charged the company and its officers with fraud.

Unfortunately, these do not appear to be isolated cases. In recent years, investors and managers have lost sight of the importance of long-term corporate growth and focused instead on short-term earnings. With the spotlight trained only on quarterly profits, there has been a temptation to make the firm's earnings match or exceed expectations each and every quarter. That is not always possible; some quarters may be disappointing. But in their drive to succeed, some executives and some companies have not only used "aggressive" accounting but have betrayed their fiduciary responsibilities and defrauded investors, lenders, and their own employees.

Congress and the Securities and Exchange Commission are calling for hearings, sanctions, and new regulations in the wake of these incidents. What must happen, however, is for a culture of financial responsibility to take hold. Financial managers must accurately report the health of their business, even if that includes bad news. Investors and lenders should accept that not all companies will show dramatic increases in profit each and every quarter. Stockholders must learn to take a longer view of investments rather than sell stock at the first sign of a dip in business. Until these changes take place, there will be continuing temptation to trim corners and exaggerate successes.

THEORY AND PRACTICE

In this book, we will look at basic financial theories and hypothetical applications. Most of the "companies" named in the text are purely fictional. They have simplified financial statements that were created to illustrate a specific point. As you move through each chapter, you will be able to put the various components of finance into perspective and, if you choose, you will be able to decipher what you need from even the most complex financial statements.

In order to do that, you will have to learn to ask questions and accept that there may not be one good answer. There may not even be much of an answer at all. Business is filled with a lot of "what-ifs": What if we change the price of our product? How would that affect profits? What if we bought a new piece of equipment that allowed us to double production as well as lower the price per item? Would we be able to sell enough to cover the cost of the machine? What if there is a recession? Will we be able to collect accounts receivable fast enough to cover our own expenses? Will we even be able to collect? One of the things you will notice is that there are lists of questions sprinkled throughout the text that are never answered. The point is not to answer those specific questions but to learn to ask them.

Finance is a rapidly changing field and a text cannot address events that will occur after it is written. For that reason, many of the chapters contain side-bars giving addresses for Internet sites, which provide a wealth of information, news, and recently published articles and opinion pieces. The addresses and content were accurate at the time this book was written but, given the fast pace of change, some may have disappeared by the time you read this.

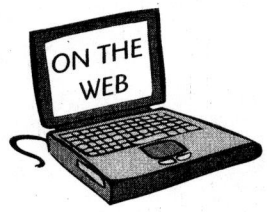

There are many sites on the Internet that can provide financial information. Some of the sites listed here are commercial and others provide access to information collected by various governmental agencies. The list is by no means exhaustive, but it will give you a place to start looking for general information. As with any other Internet search, be careful to consider the source of the information you find. Is the content provider an unbiased data collection service such as the Census Bureau or a commercial site that might have an economic incentive in providing advice or information?

There are many more Internet sites than could possibly be included in this box. The ones listed below were chosen in order to illustrate possibilities, not to exclude other valuable resources. Other sites will be described in following chapters.

(continued)

(continued)

Government Sites:

The United States Department of Commerce (*www.doc.gov*) provides information about export assistance including grants, programs for economic development, and industrial information. The Bureau of the Census (*www.census.gov*) falls under the Department of Commerce and provides statistics on a wide range of subjects such as housing units, population growth and migration, and county business patterns.

The Bureau of Labor Statistics (*www.bls.gov*) page contains economic information, hourly earnings by areas and occupation, productivity statistics, and information about producer prices. It also provides an inflation calculator.

The Small Business Administration (*www.sbaonline.sba.gov*) offers advice for small business owners.

There are many other sites that provide statistical information, both from the federal government and state and local agencies. These four provide a good start and include links to other federal agencies.

Search Engines and Portals:

Many of the popular search engines such as *www.yahoo.com* have sections devoted specifically to business. Another resource is *www.ceoexpress.com*, which has segmented its site into topics including one called Business Research that provides links to various other Web sites.

Business Magazines:

Many business magazines provide not only content from the printed magazine but business tools including spreadsheets, financial calculators, and learning modules. One of the great benefits of these sites is that the content is continually updated with news, information, and analysis of changes in the economy and business practices. The sites listed below are sponsored by general business magazines.

www.businessweek.com
www.cfo.com
www.forbes.com
www.fortune.com
www.inc.com
www.money.com
www.smartmoney.com

(continued)

(continued)

Small Business:

Small businesses face challenges that are different from major corporations. These sites are sponsored by magazines that specialize in small business. The articles and tools provide advice geared toward entrepreneurs and small- to medium-size firms.

www.chamberbiz.com
www.bizmove.com
www.morebusiness.com
www.entreworld.com
www.entrepreneur.com

Many colleges and universities have small business development centers. To find them, search for words such as "family business," "small business," or "entrepreneur" and specify that the site end in .edu. Also, contact your local community or junior college for classes in your area.

You will find that I have included bits of history and trivia throughout the book. Finance is serious business. In the very first paragraph of this chapter, I wrote that many businesses fail because they do not have adequate financing. But finance can also be fascinating and curious. As you read the text, don't ignore the boxes. That's where you'll find more than just numbers.

 **Book Report**

Millionaire: The Philanderer, Gambler, and Duelist Who Invented Modern Finance
By Janet Gleeson, New York: Simon and Schuster, 1999.

The title alone should be enough to get you reading! This is the biography of John Law, a Scottish banker born in 1671. Law was intrigued by games of chance, in part because of the mathematical challenge they posed. He amassed a fortune through gambling but saw more opportunity in finance.

(continued)

(continued)

European economies were cash poor as a result of years of warfare and high taxes. Law proposed creating banks that would issue paper money backed by securities such as land. He was ahead of his time, separating the idea of money as a unit of exchange from the intrinsic value of the gold or silver in coins.

Law got his chance to put his theories to the test in 1717 in France where he established a national bank and later the Mississippi Company, which was given the right to trade between France and Louisiana. To underwrite the venture, Law issued shares of stock at an original selling price of 500 livres. He already had introduced the idea of paper currency, which acted as receipts for gold on deposit at the national bank. Unfortunately, speculative fever struck. Demand for shares in the Mississippi Company rose and more paper currency was printed with which investors could buy shares. By 1719 the price of the stock was up to 1,000 livres, and by the end of the year it had reached 10,000 livres.

Inflation soared. Merchants began to demand gold instead of the now-suspect paper currency. Stock prices softened and citizens clamored to exchange their paper currency for familiar gold and silver coins. There were riots in Paris, the value of shares in the Mississippi Company crashed, and Law was arrested. In 1720, France ended the experiment with paper money and did not reintroduce it for 80 years.

The book is fascinating, both because of the man whose life it profiles, as well as for the description of a stock market ascent that was not supported by rational investment. The Mississippi Company was not the first example of highly speculative investment nor would it be the last.

TERMS TO KNOW

Finance	Corporation	Treasurer
Profit	Stockholders	Controller
Value	Stakeholders	Fiduciary
Sole proprietorship	Chief Financial	responsibility
Partnership	Officer (CFO)	

TERM PAPERS AND PROJECTS

1. Choose a financial current event at the beginning of the term and follow the story throughout the period. Try to determine which aspects of finance are most relevant to the story.
2. Send for the annual report of a company that interests you or contact a local company. Use that company as the example when you examine the different aspects of finance.

REVIEW QUESTIONS

1. What are the basic responsibilities of a financial manager? Why should the finance manager be familiar with accounting and economics?
2. What are the three main areas of finance?
3. Give a brief description of the main types of resources used by businesses.
4. What is profit and how is it determined?
5. Name and describe the three most common forms of business organizations.
6. What are the two basic types of partnerships? How do they differ?

2

KEY FINANCIAL CONCEPTS

LEARNING OBJECTIVES

1. Describe the concept of time value of money.

2. Distinguish between simple interest and compound interest.

3. Distinguish between present value and future value.

4. Calculate the future value (or maturity value) of an investment using compound interest.

5. Calculate present value of a future lump sum value.

6. Describe the benefit of setting up a sinking fund.

7. Calculate sinking fund principal payments.

8. Understand the difference between an annuity due and an ordinary annuity.

9. Compute the present value of an annuity.

10. Calculate the future value of a stream of payments (an annuity).

11. Describe the various forms of investment risk.

12. Distinguish between diversifiable and systematic risk.

A bird in the hand is worth two in the bush.
A penny saved is a penny earned.
90 days, same as cash.

What do all these sayings have in common? Each recognizes that there is a value in having money in the present rather than in the future. Except for rare historical periods of deflation, the money that one has in one's pocket today purchases more than the identical amount of money would next year or, more significantly, 5 years from now. **Time value of money** captures two related concepts: money that we have now, in the present, can be invested, which should result in having more in the future. The investment we make can either be in the form of investing in productive assets such as equipment or it can be placed in an interest-bearing investment such as a savings account. In either case, the amount of money we have now should be used to yield more in the future.

THE TIME VALUE OF MONEY

Several economic factors influence the value of our money, both in the present and in the future. For example, inflation, the increase in the cost of goods and services in an economy, shrinks the buying power of today's dollars. When the cost of energy to heat your home increases, it leaves less money for the purchase of other items. If this inflation continues over time, and your earnings do not increase, you will have suffered a loss of purchasing power. However, if your income increases at a rate faster than inflation, your real purchasing power will have increased.

Finance managers are interested in mentally moving money between the present and the future. Money that the firm has today should not be left idle or it will lose real value. It should be put to work earning interest or creating income for the firm. Companies also need to plan for future investment in new technology or equipment. Although the actual cash outlay may come at some point in the future, finance managers need to prepare for the expenditure, which requires decision making in the present.

We usually describe changes in the value of money in percentage terms. The local newspaper may report that the inflation rate is expected to be 2.45% this year. The cost of energy has increased at an annual rate of 30% this year. The average wage increase in 2001 for skilled workers in Smith County was 3.25%. Notice that each of the descriptions contains a percentage (a rate) and a time period.

One way of looking at the time value of money is to ask "What is this investment worth to me today? How else could I employ the same funds and have the same return?" The time value of money depends on its alternate uses. For example, Cole Property Management has a small apartment complex near the local university. The building is smaller than the other units they own, and the firm has decided that it is not cost effective for them to manage that size property. They have received two purchase offers: the Applegate Company has offered $1,300,000, payable immediately. Cole received a purchase offer of $1,500,000 from Gilbert Properties, but the terms of the purchase are staggered: $500,000 in 6 months, a second payment of $500,000 at the end of the year, and the final $500,000 in 18 months. If Cole wants the higher price, they will not receive the final payment for a year and a half. Is this a good deal? The answer depends on what Cole could do with the $1,300,000 that Applegate is offering. Among the considerations are the amount of interest Cole could earn on the money, the rate of inflation, and whether they could reinvest the proceeds in an apartment complex that more closely matches their preferred properties. Later in the chapter, we will determine which purchase offer Cole should accept.

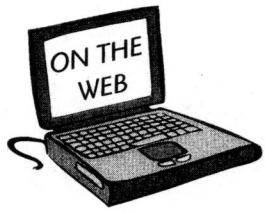

The Bureau of Labor Statistics (www.bls.gov/) uses census data to calculate the effect of inflation. The **consumer price index (CPI)** describes the change in price of a market basket of consumer goods. Eight major groups of expenditures are measured:

> Food and beverages
> Housing
> Apparel
> Transportation
> Medical care
> Recreation, which also includes durable goods such as televisions
> Education and communication
> Other goods and services such as tobacco, haircuts, and other personal services

Also included in the measurement are user fees for things such as water and sewage charges, sales tax, and automobile registration fees.

The consumer price index is important in part because it is used as an overall economic indicator. It can be used as the benchmark when setting up an escalator clause in a contract. For example, a union might negotiate a labor contract that increases wages in line with the increase in the CPI.

Because the CPI measures an average market basket, it does not necessarily reflect the inflation experienced by a single consumer. Still, it is interesting to use the CPI to move prices from "old" advertisements into the present and examine the effect of inflation. You can find the inflation calculator at the Bureau of Labor Statistics Web page.

FUTURE VALUE

Future value describes the amount of money one could expect to have (or owe) in the future when today's value of the money is known. The future value includes total amount of principal along with the accumulated interest earned. The future value can also be referred to as the maturity value.

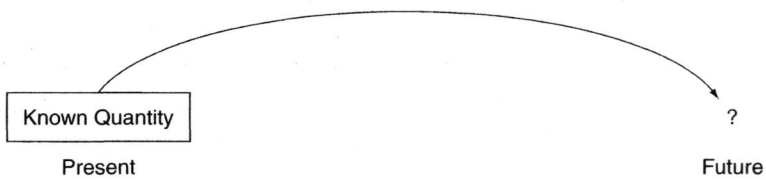

The future value is the value of today's principal and all of the interest it earns over the course of the investment.

Stop and Think

Teachers have agreed to a 3-year contract that will give them a 3% raise each year of the contract. The average teacher's pay is $34,725 per year. What will be the new average at the end of the 3-year contract?

When Andrew was 3 years old, his grandparents opened a $500 savings account that earns 6% compounded daily. How much will it be worth in 15 years when Andrew goes to college?

In both cases, we know that the amounts will have increased over time, but what will they actually be worth? We'll see the answers at the end of this section.

Most of us are familiar with the concept of interest: money that is paid by a borrower as a fee for having the current use of money and earned by the lender for assuming the risk of that loan. **Simple interest** is expressed as an annual percentage even if the period of the loan is not exactly a year. The formula for simple interest calculation is

$$I = PRT$$

where

I = Interest earned
P = Principal (the amount borrowed/loaned)
R = Rate of interest (expressed as an annual percentage rate)
T = Time of the loan (expressed as some component of a year)

If Sally borrowed $500 at 8% for 1 year, the simple interest would be

$$I = PRT$$
$$I = \$500 \times 8\% \times 1$$
$$I = \$40$$

The maturity value of the investment, the amount that Sally has to repay on the due date, would be $540, which represents the original amount borrowed (P) as well as the interest owed (I). The **maturity value** is merely another name for the future value of an investment.

$$MV = P + I$$
$$MV = \$500 + \$40$$
$$MV = \$540$$

If Sally required the money for only 6 months, the formula would be

$$I = PRT$$
$$I = \$500 \times 8\% \times \tfrac{6}{12}$$

The time component has changed to 6/12 or 6 months of a 12-month year. The simple interest payment on the loan would be only $20, or half the amount in the first example. In this case, the maturity value is $520(MV = P + I).

Loans can be taken for longer than a single year. Sally is in college and does not expect to be able to repay the $500 for 3 years. Using simple interest the maturity value, or future value, of her loan is:

$$I = PRT$$
$$I = \$500 \times 8\% \times 3$$
$$I = \$120$$
$$MV = \$500 + \$120$$
$$MV = \$620$$

Simple interest calculations can be performed quickly on any basic calculator. Unfortunately, simple interest loans are not common in the business world. In most cases, lenders charge compound interest. In **compound interest,** interest is posted to the account or charged to the loan at regular intervals. This requires some adjustments to the formula we have been using.

Let's say the same borrower required a $500 loan, however the lender charged 8% interest compounded quarterly. The time period of the loan remains one year, however during that year the interest will be calculated and posted to the account quarterly, four times during the year. Let's see what effect that would have on Sally.

After the first quarter, the lender would need to calculate interest.

$$I = PRT$$

where

P = $500
R = 8%
T = $\frac{1}{4}$ of the year

$$I = \$500 \times 8\% \times \frac{1}{4}$$
$$I = \$10$$

That interest is added to the principal, which means that at the end of the second quarter, P has increased. The interest charge for the second quarter is

$$I = PRT$$

where

P = $510
R = 8%
T = $\frac{1}{4}$

$$I = \$510 \times 8\% \times \frac{1}{4}$$
$$I = \$10.20$$

In the second quarter of the loan, the interest has increased $.20. We can calculate the quarterly interest charges and the total amount owed for the balance of the loan by following the pattern we have already established.

Third installment:

$$I = PRT$$

where

P = $520.20
R = 8%
T = $\frac{1}{4}$

$$I = \$520.20 \times 8\% \times \tfrac{1}{4}$$
$$I = \$10.40 \text{ (rounded)}$$

Fourth installment:

$$I = PRT$$

where

P = $530.60
R = 8%
T = $\frac{1}{4}$

$$I = \$530.60 \times 8\% \times \tfrac{1}{4}$$
$$I = \$10.61 \text{ (rounded)}$$

When the final interest charge is added to the loan, the borrower will repay $541.21. The maturity value (MV) is the original principal (P) plus the four quarterly interest charges (I). The price to the borrower of the compound interest is $1.21 over the course of the year. While that may seem small, think about the difference if the loan had been $5,000 or $500,000. The effects of compounding become far more costly.

The method we have used to calculate compound interest is both tedious and imprecise. By the third period, we were forced to round even though we had used a whole interest rate that could easily be divided into its periodic equivalent. Imagine if we had used 8.27% compounded daily. The loan would have required 365 separate calculations, which is not a good use of time and would have inevitably resulted in significant rounding errors.

There are many tools available that will provide exact interest calculations. For simplicity's sake, we will rely on tables that can be found in Appendix A. There are two that will give us the future value of an investment: compound interest chart (A-1) and daily compound interest chart (A-2). Notice that both of the charts give the maturity value of the investment—both the original principal and the earned interest are included in the factor.

Toolbox

Even using the charts in Appendix A can be tedious. Many software programs include basic financial formulas including future value and present value. Some of the programs, such as Excel, are designed for widespread use, while others are developed on a proprietary basis for specific clients such as a bank or auto dealer's lending subsidiary. If your job requires that you perform frequent future value calculations, you should invest in an appropriate software package and learn its idiosyncrasies. Each of them has its own syntax and assumptions embedded within the program, but once you are familiar with the format, calculations become far simpler and quicker.

Compound Interest Chart

The compound interest chart allows a single calculation to be performed for an investment with any number of compounding periods (subject to the limitations of the chart). The values in the table provide the maturity value (P + I) of the investment. Thus, the effect of the four calculations we made above can be re-created in a single transaction. But to do so, we will need to adjust our original formula slightly.

$$MV = P + I$$
$$I = PRT$$

where

P = \$500
R = 8%
T = 1 year
Compounded quarterly

Now look at the chart in Appendix A-1. The left-hand column reads "n^*". The asterisk explains that n is the number of compounding periods. To calculate n, you must multiply the time period of the loan (T) by the number of compounding periods per year. In this example n = 1 year × 4 quarters = 4. However, if we do not also adjust the interest rate to its periodic equivalent, we will be quadrupling the interest owed. The lender may appreciate that, however the borrower most certainly will not. The interest rate (R) must be divided into quarterly units of 2%, expressed as i.

The new format would be expressed as

$$MV = P \times TV(n,i)$$

where

P = \$500
i = 8% ÷ 4 quarters = 2%
n = 1 year × 4 quarters = 4

Follow down the far left column until you find the correct value for *n*. Read across the top row until you find the value for *i*. At the intersection of the two is a factor (or table value: TV), which when multiplied by the principal will give you the maturity value of the investment. The table value bundles together the interest and rate components of the simple interest formula. Rather than multiply the principal by two numbers, the compound interest table allows you to use one factor that includes both the interest rate and time.

$$MV = \$500 \times 1.08243$$
$$MV = \$541.22 \text{ (rounded)}$$

The use of the chart simplified the process of calculating compound interest and, except for the effect of rounding in both problems, produced the same result. The compound interest chart can be used to estimate the future value of an investment with periodic interest payments. However, the compound interest chart does not allow you to reduce interest to a daily rate. For that reason, there is a second compound interest chart in Appendix A.

Daily Compound Interest Chart

The daily compound interest chart is simple to use. The left-hand column indicates the length of the loan in terms from days to years. The top row provides the annual interest rate. At the intersection of the row and column, you will find a number, the factor (or table value), which when multiplied by the principal will give you the maturity value of the loan. This chart does not require you to adjust the time (T) component to reflect the compounding period, therefore, you will not adjust the annual interest rate.

Let's say our $500 loan now carries 8% interest compounded daily.

$$MV = P \times TV \ (T,R)$$

where

P = $500
R = 8%
T = 1 year
Compounded daily

$$MV = \$500 \times 1.08328$$
$$MV = \$541.64$$

Since each chart gives us the maturity value of the investment, we can compare the effect of compounding on the interest charged to the borrower.

Simple interest:	$540.00
Compounded quarterly:	$541.22
Compounded daily:	$541.64

Stop and Think

Teachers have agreed to a 3-year contract that will give them a 3% raise each year of the contract. The average teacher's pay is $34,725 per year. What will be the new average at the end of the 3-year contract?

Note: Because the teachers get a raise at the end of each school year, the compounding period will be annual (once per year).

$$MV = P \times TV(n,i)$$

where

P = $34,725
i = 3% ÷ 1 period = 3%
n = 3 years × 1 period = 3
Compounded annually

$$MV = \$34,725 \times 1.09273$$
$$MV = \$37,945.05$$

When Andrew was 3 years old, his grandparents opened a $500 savings account that earns 6% compounded daily. How much will it be worth in 15 years when Andrew goes to college?

$$MV = P \times TV(R,T)$$

where

P = $500
R = 6%
T = 15 years
Compounded daily

$$MV = \$500 \times 2.45942$$
$$MV = \$1,229.71$$

As the frequency of compounding increases, so does the interest owed on the loan. Let's return to the questions at the beginning of this section.

In the preceding problems, we knew what the interest rate was: the teachers' contract was a legal document and we assumed that the savings account would always earn 6%. Sometimes firms have to estimate what they will earn on an investment. For example, property situated on the banks of the Puget Sound, with a view of Mount Rainier to the east, the Olympic Mountains on the north, and spectacular sunsets over the water, will increase in value over time because that type of parcel is a scarce commodity. To estimate the future value, the developer could estimate the yearly increase in value of comparable properties. The interest rate, or in this case growth rate, would reflect the uniqueness of the investment and the near impossibility of duplicating it. However, there is no guarantee that the past rate of growth will continue into the future just as there is no guarantee that interest rates will remain constant over time. Future value calculations make assumptions about continuity that may or may not remain accurate throughout the life of the investment.

Future value computations are often used to calculate the effect that inflation will have on a firm's future investments. We assume that the future value of an investment will be higher than its present cost. That is not always an accurate perception.

Just For Fun

My grandfather was an amateur painter. When he framed a picture, he often used newspaper between the drawing and the backing of the frame. When I reframed an old picture, I found an advertisement dated Sunday, January 31, 1960.

The style of the 40-year-old gas range and oven looks odd to me. The cooking surface has four burners and a backsplash that looks like the one on my washing machine. The "king-size superoven" looks tiny to me. It takes up about a quarter of the space at the top left-hand side immediately below the burners. The ad boasts that this range, with its separate pullout broiler, is so advanced that even the oven and broiler light without matches!

Budget-conscious homemakers were urged to rush to the store and buy the range, which was on sale for $169.88.

There have undoubtedly been improvements in energy efficiency and product design but not the same type of radical technological advances in stoves and ovens, as we have seen in other products such as typewriters, word processors, and computers. Because of that, we can more easily compare prices between 1960 and 2001 ovens.

What would the budget-conscious homemaker expect to pay for a gas range if we applied the consumer price index? Using the Bureau of Labor Statistics CPI calculator (www.bls.gov/) and bringing the price to its 2001 equivalent, I would have to pay $1,081.71 for a gas range. However, a quick phone call to the local home improvement store resulted in a quote of $399 for a comparable product. How can this be?

The CPI estimates the change in price for a "market basket" of consumer goods. It does not take into account the effect of technological innovation, lower manufacturing costs due to increased worker productivity, a change in price for basic commodities, and other factors of production that might relate to a single item such as an oven or washing machine. The disparity that we see between the expected price and the actual 2001 price represents the value gained through innovation. In real terms, the price of the oven fell compared with prices in general.

(continued)

(continued)

   When using time value of money calculations, whether you are using the consumer price index or trying to estimate the amount your firm needs to save for a future investment, it is important to consider more than just inflation. The price of money, the lost opportunity of not having cash in hand, may be offset by the improvements to be gained through investment in technology or innovation.

   Think about the changes in automobiles in the past 40+ years. The same newspaper had an advertisement for a brand new 1960 Mercury, 2-door Monterey Sedan, factory equipped for only $2,495.00. The CPI inflation calculator tells me that the car should sell for $14,961.57 in 2001 dollars. Just for fun, try to find an example of a 1960s car and then go to a local auto dealer. See what sort of technology you could buy today for slightly less than $15,000 and compare it to that 1960s car, if you can find one!

PRESENT VALUE

In some cases, we know how much we will need in the future to buy an item. In essence, we know the maturity value. If we put the money away today in an interest-bearing savings account, the interest earned will help defray the cost of the item we plan to purchase. We know the interest rate we will earn and the length of time we can leave the money in the investment account. What we do not know is the **present value,** or the principal component. How much do we need today in order to purchase the item in the future?

   In order to move that future desired amount (the maturity value) into present-day dollars, we turn to the present value chart (A-3).

   This chart looks very much like the compound interest chart. It, too, has a column labeled n, which corresponds to the number of compounding periods, and an interest rate (i), which is the periodic interest rate. An inspection of the table values shows that unlike the compound chart, the table values are all less than 1.0. This makes sense since we are solving for the present value of an investment, the principal component only, and we

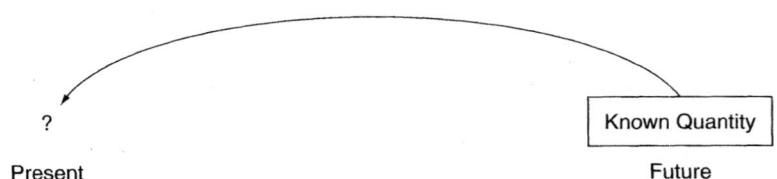

When the firm knows the future value (maturity value) that it requires, it can calculate the present value, or principal, that must be invested at a certain rate of return in order to reach the desired maturity value.

> *The factors in the present value table are in decimal form. If you converted them to percents, they would express the percent of the maturity value that must be invested today. The complement (100% − the table value) is the percent of the final investment that is earned interest.*

know the future value, which is the principal as well as the interest earned. You would not want to invest more money in a savings account than you received in the future, would you?

$$PV = MV \times TV(n,i)$$

where

PV = The present dollar amount that needs to be invested (in other words, the principal)
MV = The maturity value that we desire
i = The annual interest rate ÷ the number of compounding periods
n = The number of years × the number of compounding periods

Notice again that the table value combines the interest rate and the time period into one factor.

Sam's parents estimate that in 5 years from now they will need $5,000 to pay the first year of tuition at the state college Sam is interested in attending. How much must they invest today in a 5-year certificate of deposit that offers 6% compounded monthly?

$$PV = MV \times TV(n,i)$$

where

MV = $5000
i = 6% ÷ 12 months = 0.5%
n = 5 years × 12 months = 60

$$PV = MV \times TV(n,i)$$
$$PV = \$5,000 \times 0.74137$$
$$PV = \$3,706.85$$

Remember that the difference between the $3,706.85 that Sam's parents invested and the $5,000 that they estimate they will need is the value of the interest they have earned during the 5 years ($1,293.15). For purposes of this chapter, we are going to disregard any taxes that might be owed on interest income. In future chapters, we will look at the tax implications of investment income.

Both the compound interest and present value tables assume that there is a single transaction. A specific amount is deposited in an investment account and

Stop and Think

How do we know for sure that an investment will return a set amount of income or interest?

We have assumed that interest rates will remain constant over a relatively long period of time. In the example of the teachers' pay, the contract called for a specific rate of increase in each of 3 years, so we can use that figure with assurance. The other examples imply that the interest rate earned at the time of the investment will continue throughout its entire life. Unfortunately, there is no guarantee that the interest rate on savings accounts will remain constant in perpetuity. If the firm is valuing an investment such as a piece of property that will be held for future sale, the annual rate of return is even more difficult to assess.

The best strategy for choosing a discount rate (or an expected rate of return) is to use historical averages, if they exist, and adjust for current economic conditions that may influence those averages. An astute financial manager should construct several possible values for a single investment (conservative, realistic, and optimistic), which would allow for a range of possible future values. The discount rate used to determine each value should be stated, along with the assumptions that influenced the choice of rate.

earns interest until the maturity value is reached or a loan is negotiated to be due in full at some future date. In these instances we know the current value and are seeking the future (or compound) value. Perhaps we know the amount of a future expenditure and want to invest now (the present value) so that the money is available when needed. In both cases a lump sum is deposited. Interest may be posted as periodic payments, but the investment itself is not periodic.

INVESTING OVER TIME

As the amount of money required by the firm increases, the firm's ability to make lump sum investments diminishes. The firm begins to utilize a variety of payment plans, each of which takes advantage of interest earned but spreads payments over the length of the investment.

Lucinda wants to buy the gymnastics studio that she has managed for the past several years. She knows that the owners are contemplating retirement 5 years from now and are interested in selling the business. If she starts now, she hopes to save enough money for a sizeable down payment on the business. Lucinda has estimated that she will need $50,000 five years from now. The calculations we have performed thus far assume that Lucinda can invest a lump sum today at some agreed-upon interest rate. Assume that Lucinda can earn 6% compounded quarterly.

$$PV = MV \times TV(n,i)$$

where

$$MV = \$50{,}000$$
$$i = 6\% \div 4 = 1\tfrac{1}{2}\%$$
$$n = 5 \text{ years} \times 4 \text{ quarters} = 20$$

$$PV = \$50{,}000 \times 0.7424704$$
$$PV = \$37{,}123.52$$

Although her investment will earn interest of \$12,876.48, in order to have the \$50,000 down payment in 5 years time, Lucinda would already have to have amassed more than \$37,000. That may not be practical. She needs to begin investing now, in smaller increments, in order to meet her goal.

SINKING FUND

A firm can set up a savings account, called a **sinking fund,** into which it makes periodic payments and earns interest. After the payments have been made and interest posted, the firm will have reached the desired maturity value of that investment. If the firm is setting up a sinking fund (savings account) for some future use, it needs to calculate the present value of the payments that will result in attaining the desired maturity value. The funds that are immediately deposited will earn interest throughout the life of the investment, while later deposits will earn interest from the time that they are added to the fund.

Once again, the sinking fund chart resembles the charts we have seen earlier. There is a column labeled n, which corresponds to a number of compounding periods, and a row at the top that gives the periodic interest rate (i). The intersection of the two columns provides a table value that is multiplied times the desired maturity value. Note that the table values are very small, even smaller than the values in the present value table. The sinking fund chart (A-4) assumes that the deposits are made at the same interval that interest is compounded. In the real world, that may not be accurate: a firm may be able to add to the savings vehicle at any time with interest credited on specific dates. However, for the sake of simplicity, we will allow the previous assumption to stand.

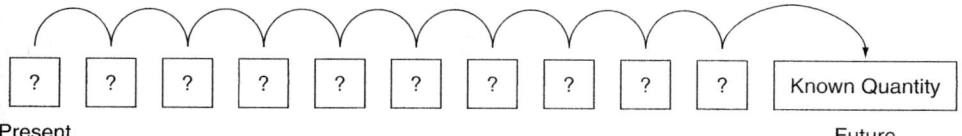

In some cases the firm has a desired maturity value in mind, however, the single sum is not readily available. A sinking fund, or savings account, allows the firm to save in increments and earn interest to attain its longer-term goal.

When we solve an equation using the sinking fund chart, we know the final maturity value that we desire. What is unknown are the principal payments that need to be made in order to attain that maturity value.

Lucinda needs to have $50,000 in 5 years. Her bank offers the 6% compounded quarterly rate for lump sum deposits or quarterly deposits. Lucinda calculates her quarterly payments:

$$SF = MV \times TV(n,i)$$

where

MV = $50,000
$i = 6\% \div 4 \text{ quarters} = 1\frac{1}{2}\%$
$n = 5 \text{ years} \times 4 \text{ quarters} = 20$

$$SF = MV \times TV(n,i)$$
$$SF = \$50,000 \times 0.0432457$$
$$SF = \$2,162.29 \text{ (rounded)}$$

Each payment will earn interest, just as the lump sum investment earned interest, but the timing of the investment allows Lucinda to make smaller and perhaps more affordable payments.

Stop and Think

How much total interest will Lucinda earn on her sinking fund payments? If Lucinda makes 20 payments of $2162.29 each, her total principal investment will be

$$\$2,162.29 \times 20 = \$43,245.80$$

By definition, the sinking fund account will be worth $50,000, which means that Lucinda has earned

$$\$50,000 - \$43,245.80 = \$6,754.20 \text{ in interest.}$$

The interest earned on the sinking fund is less than she would have earned had she invested a lump sum, however, the sinking fund allows her to spread payments over time and may cause less disruption to her cash flow.

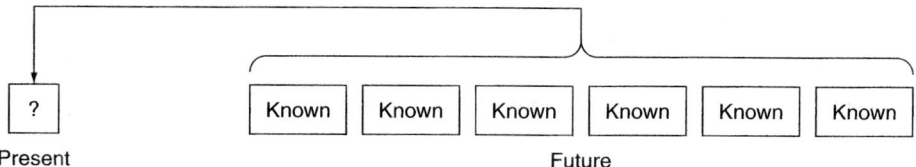

What sum would have to be invested today in order to yield a stated stream of future payments? That is the present value of an annuity.

ANNUITIES

The root word of annuity is *anno,* which means year. **Annuities** are a series of payments, usually of equal amounts and in specific intervals, which earn interest. The investment interval does not have to be a year; it can be monthly, quarterly, or even biweekly. It is possible to use the compound value and future value charts we have already looked at to determine a future value of a stream of payments, but the value of each payment would have to be calculated individually, which requires more work than necessary. Instead, we use annuity charts that are also found in Appendix A.

The value of annuities is influenced by whether the payments are made at the beginning or end of a compounding period. The principal in an annuity due is invested at the beginning of the compounding period and begins earning interest at that time. The first payment of an annuity that compounds monthly will have accumulated 12 interest payments by the end of the first year. By contrast, an ordinary annuity allows payments to be made at the end of a compounding period. The first payment does not earn interest until the second compounding period because there was no principal invested until the conclusion of the compounding period. After 1 year, the first monthly payment will have received 11 additions of interest.

PRESENT VALUE OF AN ANNUITY

Many states have lotteries in order to fund state services. Most lotteries promise to pay the jackpot in 20 or 25 annual installments. The lottery commission needs to determine what portion of ticket revenue needs to be invested now to fund the future payments of lottery winnings and what portion can be used for other purposes. The commission knows the value of each payment that will be made; it needs to determine the present value of that stream of expenditures.

Let's assume that the jackpot was $1,000,000 and there will be 25 annual payments made at the beginning of the year. Each payment will be $40,000 ($1,000,000 ÷ 25). We know the value of each payment that will be made; we need to determine the amount of money invested today that will allow us to make those guaranteed payments. We will use the chart for the present value of an annuity due (A-5).

$$PV(a) = A \times TV(n,i)$$

where

PV(a) = the present lump sum value that needs to be invested (in other words, the principal)

A = the value of each annuity payment

i = the periodic interest rate

n = the number of compounding periods

    Assume that the lottery commission can invest funds at 5% compounded annually.

$$PV(a) = A \times TV(n,i)$$

where

A = $40,000

n = 25 years × 1 payment per year

i = 5% × 1 payment per year

$$PV(a) = \$40,000 \times 14.7986$$
$$PV(a) = \$591,944$$

    For a present investment of $591,944, the lottery commission can guarantee that it will have sufficient capital to fund 25 yearly payments of $40,000 each. Whatever revenue it earned in excess of the present value of the annuity can be directed to some other use.

    Another use for the present value of an annuity chart is to determine the present value of income that a firm will receive over a period of time. Remember the apartment complex that Cole Property Management wanted to sell? Gilbert Properties would like to acquire the building and has offered to pay the entire asking price, however, they wish to stagger the payments over 18 months, making three payments of $500,000 each at the end of 6-month intervals. Cole has another offer for cash to be paid immediately, however, the second buyer is only offering $1,300,000 for the apartment building. In order to compare the two offers, Cole Property Management needs to have a present value for the stream of payments that Gilbert Properties is offering. Cole assumes that it could earn 6% compounded semiannually if it had the cash in hand. Gilbert's payments will be made at the end of the period, thus it is an ordinary annuity and we will use the present value of an ordinary annuity chart (A-6).

$$PV(a) = A \times TV(n, i)$$

where

A = $500,000

i = 6% ÷ 2 = 3%

n = 18 months ÷ 6-month compounding period = 3

$$PV(a) = \$500,000 \times 2.8266$$
$$PV(a) = \$1,413,300$$

The equation tells us that if Cole received $1,413,300 today, it would be the same as receiving the semiannual payments from Gilbert. The cash offer Cole received was only $1,300,000, which is less than the present value of the stream of payments; therefore Cole should accept Gilbert's offer.

The present value of Gilbert's offer would change, however, if Cole could find an alternative investment that paid more than the 6% assumed in the previous example. Suppose that Cole could invest today and earn 12% compounded semiannually.

$$PV(a) = \$500,000 \times 2.6730$$
$$PV(a) = \$1,336,500$$

Gilbert's offer is still better than the cash offered by the Applegate Company, however, the difference between the two is less. If Applegate can be convinced to increase their offer to $1,340,000, Cole Property Management should take the cash.

Another Way of Saying It. . .

Another term for the present value of an annuity is **discounted cash flow.** The value of the cash inflows has been discounted by the interest rate that could have been earned had the firm had the cash.

FUTURE VALUE OF AN ANNUITY

When we calculated sinking fund payments, we were looking for the principal payment, which when augmented with interest would yield a known future value. Sometimes the principal payment and rate of interest are known, however, the future value of that investment is not known.

Alexander and Adams is a partnership. In order to protect the firm from loss should one of the partners die, the partnership has purchased a life insurance policy. The partners could buy a term insurance policy; at the end of term the policy would expire and there would be no residual (cash) value. However, the partners would also like to set up a savings vehicle. The insurer has offered a universal policy that includes a guaranteed death benefit as well as a cash

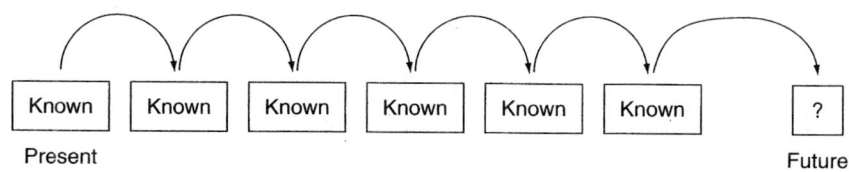

The maturity value of steady payments, each earning a stated rate of interest, is the future value of an annuity.

value component. Alexander and Adams's policy states that $100 of each monthly premium is credited toward the cash value of the policy and will earn 4% compounded quarterly. Although they do not intend to cash out the policy, Alexander and Adams want to be able to calculate the cash value of the annuity. They know the value of each principal payment and the interest earned. Since payments are being made at the beginning of each month, it is an annuity due and Alexander and Adams will use the future value of an annuity due chart (A-7).

$$FV(a) = A \times TV(n, i)$$

where

$FV(a)$ = the future value of a stream of known payments
A = the value of each payment
i = the periodic interest rate
n = the number of compounding periods

After 5 years, the cash value of Alexander and Adams's policy is

$$FV(a) = A \times TV(n,i)$$

where

$A = \$100$
$i = 4\% \div 4 \text{ quarters} = 1\%$
$n = 5 \text{ years} \times 4 \text{ quarters} = 20$

$$FV(a) = \$100 \times 22.2392$$
$$FV(a) = \$2,223.92$$

Alexander and Adams have made 20 payments that decreased the balance in their checkbook by a total of $2,000, however, the cash value of the insurance policy is $2,223.92. The difference is the value of the interest they have received.

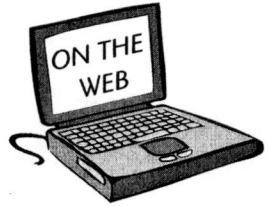
ON THE WEB

In calculating the present value of a stream of future earnings, we have been comparing the value of different investment options. There has been no assumption that the stream of income would actually be converted into present-day cash. However, there are firms that are involved in what is called the "cash flow industry" that do buy future earnings streams.

(continued)

(continued)

In order to find some of these firms, I went to a search engine and asked it to find sites having to do with lottery payments. The list below includes the firms that I found after one quick search. Each of the firms promises to purchase a variety of income: lottery and casino winnings, owner-held real estate contracts, insurance settlements, and military pensions, among other things. The seller is encouraged to fill out an on-line form that describes the stream of payments, and each of these firms promises to respond with a purchase offer.

http://integrityfunding.net
http://structured-settlements.org
www.drw.com
www.discovery-funding.com
www.stanfordservices.com
www.eastbaymortgage.com
www.fredcoutts.com
www.rp-capital.com
www.annuity-mort-purchase.com

I have to confess that the Web addresses for the next two companies appealed to the marketer in me. The addresses are easy to remember and express very clearly what the business is about!

www.money-now.net
www.webuypayments.com

Since you would know the value of the periodic payments you were receiving and the firm's cash offer, you could calculate the discount rate that they had used to construct their purchase price by rearranging the terms in the present value of annuity formula.

$$PV(a) = A \times TV(n, i)$$

becomes

$$\frac{PV(a)}{A} = TV(n, i)$$

To find the discount rate using the charts in Appendix A, you would go to the row that described the number of payments remaining and follow that line across the chart until you found a value closest to PV(a)/A.

It would be interesting to know if the discount rate varies depending on the type of income stream, for example, lottery winnings versus personal injury insurance settlements.

RISK AND RETURN

Calculating the value of financial investments at any given point in time requires making assumptions about the economic conditions that will exist in the future. As a result, many of the decisions that are made are based on the best guess of the forecaster and may or may not turn out exactly as planned. We call this uncertainty **risk.** Risk is neither positive nor negative. The word

 **Book Report**

Against the Gods: The Remarkable Story of Risk
    By Peter L. Bernstein, New York: John Wiley and Sons, Inc., 1998.

The title of this fascinating book alludes to the fact that until the Renaissance, the gods were given credit or blame for any occurrence that could not be predicted with complete certainty. The sun rose in the east but what was the chance that it would rain on any given day? Many explanations were offered but until very recently (in historical terms), there was no framework to describe the range of chances that existed. Now the local weather report will predict what percent likelihood there is that it will rain. The higher the percentage, the more likely it is that current atmospheric conditions will result in rainfall. The prediction describes what is expected to happen today based on patterns that have been established over time. The ability to provide a glimpse of the future within some degree of certainty provided a significant perceptual shift.

Mr. Bernstein begins his book by reminding us that gambling has been present, in some form or another, for as long as we have recorded history. And yet, gamblers did not have a system for determining the likelihood of success for each wager. A good result was often attributed to Lady Luck or the Fates, while a run of bad luck might be blamed on the interference of a not-so-benign deity. Modern-day gamblers may still practice this logic, but they have far more sophisticated predictors at their disposal.

The book moves from gambling as exemplified by games of chance to the idea that one could predict a community's mortality rate given statistics collected over a length of time. Being able to predict life expectancy allowed the growth of the insurance industry. Without a system of risk management, pricing of policies would be based on whim, not science, and the chances of financial ruin would be high.

The book's later chapters describe some of the more complex risk management strategies that have been employed such as futures, options, and derivatives. This section becomes more complicated, but it is well worth the effort. Probability and statistics were never this intriguing when I was in school!

does not indicate that all of the decisions will adversely affect an investment. The "risk" in falling interest rates is that a borrower may be able to renegotiate a loan and receive a lower interest rate. For the borrower the "risk" has been positive. For the lender, who is receiving less interest income, the risk is perceived to be negative. Risk itself is a neutral concept.

Investors and business owners are compensated for taking risks by the rate of **return** that they receive on their investment. Treasury notes issued by the United States government are considered virtually risk-free, and their return is low compared to other investments. Lending money to a bankrupt company is very risky, and the return that the investor would require is commensurately high.

The compensation, or return, that investors require varies between investments because the level of risk varies. One type of risk can occur due to the effect of management decisions. For example, a firm might decide to increase its leverage by using a higher proportion of debt financing than equity. If sales revenue decreases, interest charges become a higher percentage of the firm's operating earnings and more sharply reduce its net income. Risk is also influenced by market conditions unrelated to the firm issuing the security. In a period of high inflation, bonds that have a lower coupon rate (interest rate) will be less valuable, regardless of the business strength of the issuing corporation. The interest rate, even in the absence of other information, has made the bond less desirable.

There are several specific types of risk that investors should consider when calculating the expected return of an asset.

Liquidity risk describes the possible inability to liquidate an asset at fair market value. U. S. savings bonds can be cashed in at any bank in town during normal banking hours. There is no liquidity risk. On the other hand, the owner of a restaurant may find it more difficult to sell the building and equipment. Although the land and equipment can be carried on a balance sheet at some fair market value, there is no guarantee that the owner will find a buyer who is interested in obtaining precisely that location and mix of equipment. Even if the potential purchaser wishes to open another restaurant at the same location, the type of food to be prepared may necessitate investment in different equipment, which reduces the value of the existing property below its theoretical market value. The longer it would take to sell the asset, the higher its liquidity risk.

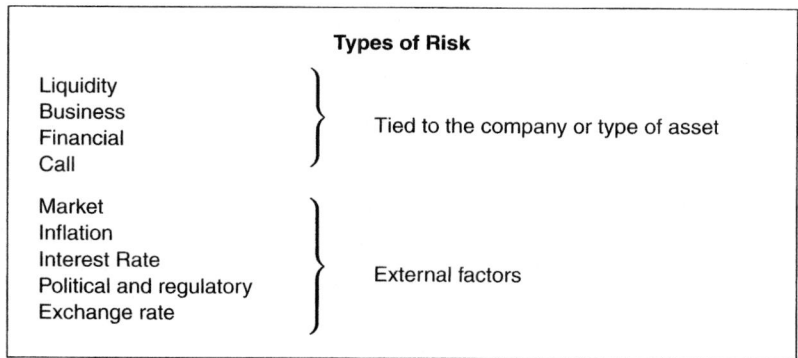

There are many types of financial risk, not all of which can be avoided by the prudent investor.

Business risk describes the type of uncertainty that is a result of the firm's operations. It can be as a result of industry changes or the decisions of an individual firm. For example, after years of growth, the personal computer market is slowing. The number of individuals who own personal computers has increased markedly over the years, so there are not as many new customers available. In addition, consumers do not perceive a need to upgrade their computers as frequently as a new model can be engineered. In order to stimulate sales, personal computer manufacturers are reducing prices, which in turn, lowers profit margins. Business risk can increase across an industry but at varying rates for participants within that industry, depending on how they adjust to market conditions. Business risk can also occur as a result of strategic decisions made by individual companies within a more stable industry. The decision not to extend store hours may cost a retailer revenue that then flows to a rival merchant. Business risk has increased as a result of the choice not to stay open later.

Financial risk is related to the amount of debt that a company issues. As the firm becomes more highly leveraged, its risk increases. Leverage describes the amount of debt a firm has in contrast to its equity, or the owners' investment in the firm. In a growing economy the risk due to leverage may not be as apparent, however, if sales revenue decreases, the proportion of interest expense to operating income will increase. In addition to interest, the firm may also be required to make periodic principal payments that decrease its working capital. The more highly leveraged the firm, the more risk there is that the firm may not be able to repay its debts.

Firms can assume debt by borrowing from a bank or by issuing bonds. Each bond issued has terms that the borrower must meet and these are spelled out in an indenture. We will discuss bonds and indentures in more detail in Chapter 13. Among the options available to the bond issuers is the right to call in the bonds under specified circumstances. A company would choose to call in their bonds if they could retire higher-priced debt and replace it with lower interest loans or bonds. **Call risk** is the risk to bondholders that the bond may be called by the issuer before maturity. In that case, the investor does not receive the interest payments that were expected. Although the principal has been repaid in full, the investor may not be able to realize as high a rate of return without increasing the risk of the substitute investment.

These first types of risk are closely tied to the type of asset or specific company that issued the securities. To some degree, these types of risk are known and can be managed. The investor can choose to purchase a callable bond, knowing the risk involved, and will demand a higher coupon rate to compensate for the call risk. Companies with higher financial risk will be required to offer higher coupon rates on their bonds to offset the risk the investor is taking. In each of these cases, the risk is considered diversifiable risk. The type of assets within an investment portfolio can be balanced, or diversified, to include both high- and low-risk holdings.

Other sources of risk result from broader-based economic or social changes that affect a wide variety of businesses and are considered systematic or undiversifiable risks.

Market risk is associated with overall market movements. For many years, it appeared that the stock market could only increase in value. However in 2001, the stock markets lost value across the board. Even if a corporation had sound business strategies and limited debt, the value of stock plummeted. Bond values were also affected by consumer confidence rather than just the underlying creditworthiness of the issuing firm. Some analysts claim to have the ability to predict market movements, however, there is no surefire formula that determines exactly how the market will behave.

The change in general market interest rates can affect the value of an investment. This is called **interest rate risk.** When interest rates rise, the value of existing bonds usually falls: a bond that had been issued at 6.5% will be worth less than a bond that now must be issued at 8% to meet prevailing interest rates. The higher the interest rate climbs, the less the older bond will be worth. Conversely, if interest rates fall, bonds that carry a higher rate of interest will increase in value. The gain or loss in value will not be realized unless the bond is sold, so a bondholder whose investment has theoretically fallen in value will not suffer a capital loss if the bond is held to maturity. There is a lost opportunity to have earned more on the investment. Interest rate risk affects stock prices as well. As interest rates rise, the company's cost of borrowing increases, leaving less profit for owners/shareholders and causing stock prices to fall. If interest rates fall, the price of stock tends to increase. Changes in interest rates also affect the value of fixed assets such as land and buildings. If interest rates rise, the business owner might be more reluctant to invest in new property as the total cost of the acquisition (land and interest charges) increases. In order to keep monthly expenses within a targeted range, the price of the property needs to decrease in order to absorb the effect of rising interest rates.

Inflation risk is commonly referred to as purchasing power risk. When market prices increase faster than the revenue that a firm receives or the interest that an investor earns, the real value of the investment has decreased. A bank that issues a fixed rate mortgage is subject to inflation risk if interest rates rise and it is required to pay more to depositors than it receives from mortgage income. This situation occurred in the 1980s and contributed to the savings and loan failures. A retired worker may calculate living expenses and invest in order to provide that level of income. If the cost of goods and services increases, the fixed income from investments will not keep pace with living expenses, and the retiree will have suffered from inflation risk.

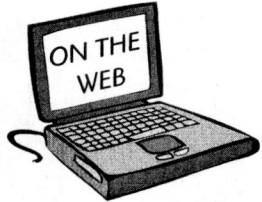
ON THE WEB

Between 1966 and 1979 interest rates fluctuated dramatically in part as a response to high levels of inflation. Because savings and loan associations were limited in the amount of interest they could pay on deposits and were also restricted from investing in anything other than home mortgage loans, the stage was set for a financial disaster.

The Federal Deposit Insurance Corporation (FDIC) provides an outline of the factors that led to the savings and loan crisis, including the effects of interest rate and inflation risks.

For more information go to www.fdic.gov/ and look at the tab called Bank Data. You'll find a section entitled Banking Industry, which provides analysis, statistics, and history.

Inflation risk is also tied to interest rate risk. During inflationary periods, the Federal Reserve often pushes interest rates higher as we will see in Chapter 4. Inflation causes the price of goods and services to rise, interest rates to rise, and stock prices (and profits) to fall. The rate of inflation has a strong enough effect on the economy that we often separate it from interest rate calculations and talk about interest rates, the inflation rate, and the real rate of interest, which is the market interest rate less the rate of inflation.

Governments and municipalities create regulations and impose taxes in order to provide for the public good. **Political and regulatory risk** describes the costs that result from those decisions. If the government wishes to stimulate the economy and lowers taxes in order to do so, the cost of operating a firm may decrease. If the government imposes a tariff on imported goods, the cost of goods sold increases, which could adversely affect the firm. Changes in capital gains taxes have been debated for many years in Congress as well as during presidential elections. A change in this law might affect investors' willingness to hold or sell certain types of securities and could increase the risk for issuers. A change in pollution control laws affects corporate expenses, which in turn affect the rate of return for shareholders.

Any firm that engages in international trade or any investor who invests in global securities incurs **exchange rate risk.** Currency values fluctuate in relationship to one another and converting income between currencies can result in a gain or loss. Procter & Gamble Corporation manufactures and sells consumer goods around the world. The revenue earned in Great Britain could be combined with revenue from Mexico to fund the expansion of a plant in Cincinnati, Ohio. A contractor in Ohio wants to be paid in dollars, so Procter & Gamble must convert its earnings into the currency desired by that specific vendor. In some cases it will be dollars, in others it may be the yen, the peso, or the euro. Each time the conversion is made, however, the company may receive a different ratio of dollars to yen or pesos to euros. The difference in exchange rates can have a significant impact on a multinational corporation such as Procter & Gamble. It can also affect a small company whose largest client is an

---

In the News

Pension funds that offer a defined monthly benefit often contain a clause that raises the monthly allowance in step with the increase in the consumer price index (CPI). Cost of living adjustments (COLAs) are meant to increase monetary payments in order to maintain purchasing power. For senior citizens, the CPI might not be an accurate gauge.

An article in *Business Week* explains that expenses for elderly have risen 3.5% since December 1982, compared with 3.3% for all consumers. The difference is largely due to the cost of health care, which has increased at a faster rate than other components of the CPI. For senior citizens, the general inflation rate may understate the increase in their cost of living.

Source: der Hovanesian, Mara. "Seniors, Beware of a Thief called Inflation." *Business Week*, July 30, 2001, p. 96.

Toolbox

Measuring risk is important, however, the calculations can be complex. What portion of investment risk is attributable to financial risk assumed by a firm and what part to interest rate risk? How much of a factor is inflation? Tax policy? How will all of these factors affect an investment in a specific stock or bond issue?

There are a few published tools that can assist an investor. No formula or designation can guarantee the level of risk that is being assumed, but there are some guides.

As we will see in Chapter 13, the coupon rate (or interest) that a bond carries is determined in part by the level of financial or business risk of the issuer. The higher the bond rating, the less risky the bond is. An investor who wishes to minimize business and financial risk can choose a bond with a rating of AAA through A, leaving the more risky bonds to other investors.

Although it is difficult to predict how the stock market will perform, it is possible to describe how a particular stock will do relative to the market. A beta coefficient is an index of risk that measures the stock's return relative to the market. If the stock has a beta of 1.0, it moves exactly with the market as a whole. If the market is down 10%, the stock will decline by 10%. A beta coefficient of less than 1.0 means that the stock is less susceptible to market fluctuations, whether the market goes up or down. A coefficient of 0.7, for example, means that if the market increases in value by 10%, the stock will increase by only 7%. That may not be desirable in an expanding market but in the case of a recession, the stock will lose less value relative to the market as a whole. A coefficient of 1.2 means that the stock will increase 12% when the market gains 10% and will lose 12% if the market decreases by 10%. Beta coefficients are published by Value Line, a company that sells investment reports. Firms that are interested in obtaining a report can subscribe to the Value Line service or contact the firm for specific reports. Many libraries have a copy of Value Line in their reference section.

overseas buyer. In both cases, exchange rate risk describes the fluctuations in earnings that can occur simply because of the variability of exchange rates.

TERMS TO KNOW

Time value of money	Sinking funds	Call risk
Consumer price index (CPI)	Annuities	Market risk
Future value	Discounted cash flow	Interest rate risk
Maturity value	Risk	Inflation risk
Simple interest	Return	Political and regulatory risk
Compound interest	Liquidity risk	Exchange rate risk
Present value	Business risk	
	Financial risk	

TERM PAPERS AND PROJECTS

1. If you currently receive a stream of payments such as an annuity or military retirement income, contact some of the companies that purchase cash flows and see if you can figure out the discount rates they are using when they make the cash offer for your annuity.
2. Interview a business broker who buys notes from owners who have financed the sale of their house. Ask what criteria are used to value the note.
3. How does a financial manager for an insurance company, pension fund, or lottery commission determine what investments need to be made in order to make sure that organization can fund its liabilities?
4. Bethlehem Steel announced that it would file for bankruptcy protection in November 2001. It stated that one of the reasons for its financial difficulties was that the number of pensioners was five times the size of its current workforce and that funding future retirement benefits had become an unwieldy expense. What has happened to the company since then? Did it emerge from bankruptcy? If so, how did it handle its long-term pension obligations?
5. Can you afford to retire? See Supplement A.

REVIEW QUESTIONS

1. What do we mean by the future value of money?
2. Describe simple and compound interest. Give a short example of each.
3. What is maturity value?
4. What is present value?
5. Describe a sinking fund. What is its purpose? Give an example.
6. What is an annuity? Give an example of an annuity and why it might be preferable to a lump sum payment.
7. Name and describe the types of risk associated with investments.
8. Discuss how the finance manager can moderate the level of risk assumed by the firm.

PROBLEMS

1. Rebecca got an income tax refund of $650. If she invests the money in an account that pays 8% interest, compounded quarterly, how much will she have at the end of 10 years?
2. Ralph invests $1,500 in his credit union account, which pays 6.5% interest, compounded daily. What will be the value of Ralph's account in 5 years?
3. Nancy wants to go to Europe the summer after she graduates from college. She expects to graduate in 2 years and would like to have $7,500 for her trip. How much does she have to invest today in an account that yields 6% interest, compounded monthly, in order to have the amount she wants?
4. Brian and Kristin want to begin saving for a house. They estimate that they will need $35,000 for a down payment and plan to buy the house in

4 years. How much should they put away each month in an account that yields 6% interest per year?

5. Georgia has received a lump sum settlement as a result of an accident. She would like to invest a portion of the settlement so that it provides $25,000 of income for the next 25 years. If the investment company is willing to offer 5% interest, compounded annually, how much will Georgia pay for the annuity?

6. Ted's grandmother has been adding $500 per quarter to a college savings account. She began saving 15 years ago and the account has earned 4% interest per year, compounded quarterly. How much is the account worth today?

Supplement A:

CAN YOU AFFORD TO RETIRE?

Although retirement seems to be very far away, we will see that saving small amounts regularly is the key to having a good amount of money at retirement. But how much do you need to save? That is the point of this exercise.

Where to start:

1. Estimate the number of years you believe you have until retirement.
2. Estimate how many years you will live after you retire.

Now for the figuring:

Identify each investment account you have by type. Is it one that has a balance now but will not be added to on a regular basis? Then you will need to look at it as a "lump sum." Do you have a pension or an IRA that you add to on a regular basis with a predictable amount of money? That is two accounts: the lump sum value that is in the account now and the annuity that you will be adding in the future.

Think about this, though: Those items that will be investments in the future are only those items that you might sell and use the proceeds in order to support yourself. Thus, if you plan to pay off the mortgage and continue to live in the exact same house, the house is not an investment. If you have property that would be sold at some point and the proceeds disbursed over time, that *is* an investment. If you plan to stay in your current house until you retire, sell it at that point and move to a less expensive place, the difference between the current value of your larger house and the current value of a house that would meet your retirement needs can be considered an investment since a certain portion of the equity in the house would be freed up.

The same logic applies to checking accounts. Most of us keep a certain amount of money in our checking account to cover the monthly bills:

(continued)

(continued)

utilities, mortgage, and food. If you are using your checking account as a money management tool, the value for investment purposes is zero. A savings account can be either an investment or a cash management tool as well. For example, if you keep only a small amount in your savings account to meet unexpected bills, it would have no future investment value since it is assumed that you will always want that stable and secure backup. If, however, you are using your savings account as a long-term investment, include it in your calculations.

The most efficient way to define your assets is to list each one in a worksheet such as the following:

RETIREMENT WORKSHEET

Asset	Definition	Current Value	Estimated Growth	Future Value
House	Current and future residence			None
Land held for investment	Lump sum	$15,000		
Savings account	Current working funds or investment?			It depends on its definition
Checking account	Current working funds			None
Pension:				
Current value	Lump sum	$43,250		
Contributions	Annuity	$3,600/year		

You will need to calculate:

3. The lump sum future value of your current investments.

Calculate the future value at some interest rate that reflects the amount you believe you will earn on your investments. You can choose differing discount rates for each type of investment, such as a pension fund invested in stock or the piece of property in a rapidly growing area. Each asset needs to be valued.

You will also need to adjust for inflation. Rather than come up with an astronomical number that we cannot equate to current spending patterns, subtract what you believe will be the growth in the economy over the long-term horizon that you envision. For example, if I believe that stock market investments will grow at their historical rate of 10% per year, and I believe that inflation can be held to 3% per year, I will use an

(continued)

(continued)

adjusted rate of 7%. If I have invested in a certificate of deposit that earns 4.5%, the inflation-adjusted earnings are only 1.5%. Use the column labeled "Estimated Growth" to define the rate of increase you expect by asset.

Using the tables found in Appendix A, determine the future value for each asset. For example, the land held for investment may be appreciating at a rate of 12% per year because it is located in an area where demand for housing has increased. If inflation is assumed to be 3% per year, the after inflation rate of growth is 9%. Using the number of years until your retirement and the future value of a lump sum table, calculate the inflation-adjusted value of the property. This value should appear in your worksheet under the heading "Future Value." Note that the assets that are assumed to remain in use, such as your residence, have been assigned no value.

When you have valued each item separately, combine them to determine the estimated future value of your current investments.

Next:

4. Using an inflation-adjusted rate of return and the number of years you estimated that you will live *after* retirement, calculate the value of the annuity you would receive from that lump sum. Compare the value with your estimate, in today's dollars, of the income that would provide the lifestyle that you desire during retirement. Remember that if you have calculated no value for your house but have assumed that it will provide shelter, your future housing costs will be different from your current costs.

There may be a shortfall at this point. Now you will have to work backward:

5. How much more would you like to have when you retire (in current dollars)?
6. What is the present value of that investment at the end of your working life? Remember, you are working backward now.
7. That "present value" becomes a future value for this next question. How much do you need to start saving now to have that future value/present value on the day you retire, given the earning assumptions you have chosen?

One final thinking question: In your own words, explain what effect it would have on your decision making if you inherited money from Great-Aunt Matilda. What effect would an unanticipated lump sum bequest have on your financial planning?

CHAPTER

3

MONEY

LEARNING OBJECTIVES

1. Define money and describe its four functions.

2. Describe the four characteristics of money.

3. Discuss money's role in facilitating trade.

4. Discuss the cultural implications of the designs printed on money.

5. Examine the benefits of the euro and recognize the concerns surrounding its introduction.

6. Describe virtual money and discuss the possibility of a cashless society.

Finance is all about **money:** investments, expenditures, profits, and wealth are described using the medium of money. Yet money, in and of itself, has a fascinating history and future. It also has some deeply symbolic aspects that we would do well to consider.

WHAT IS MONEY?

Although we tend to think of money in the form of currency and coins, money is actually anything that is generally accepted as a unit of exchange. There are two very important components to the definition: *anything* and *unit of exchange*.

In simple economic systems, barter was (and still is) the method of exchange. Goods were traded for other goods or services, with each participant attempting to determine the relative worth of the items in the transaction. There were inefficiencies to this system, of course. Sometimes more than one trade would need to take place in order to get the desired goods to the appropriate buyer.

Money was developed to serve four basic functions:

1. a medium of exchange;
2. a unit of account;
3. a store of wealth; and
4. a standard of deferred payment.

Money comes in all shapes and sizes. (Getty Images, Inc.)

Medium of Exchange

As trade developed, a more uniform **medium of exchange** was needed. Evolving economic systems developed money, some sort of token that was accepted within that community as the unit of exchange. Early money was created from natural resources. Many societies used precious metal minted into coins. In the Pacific Northwest, certain types of shells were used. Each of these items facilitated the exchange of unlike goods and services within the economic community. More transactions could take place because there was less need to seek out a direct transfer of goods or services. Economies grew and foreign trade prospered, when money replaced barter systems.

Unit of Account

Notice that whatever the objects were that became "money," they represented the worth, or value, of other objects. In that way, money serves as a **unit of account.** It describes the relative value of one item compared with another. This had profound effects on an economic community and, in the present, on

ON THE WEB

If you were able to follow the dollar bill you just got in change, where would it take you? You can find out at www.wheresgeorge.com. The Web site lets people register the serial number of their currency and then visit again to see how far the money has traveled.

If you get a bill that has been stamped with the Web address, click onto the site and see where it has traveled.

the decision making of a company. Having a common unit of account allows people to decide how to allocate scarce resources with some certainty of the relative exchange value of each alternative.

For example, a firm may have the choice of buying a new machine to replace a malfunctioning one versus fixing the machine. The money used to buy the new machine can be directly calculated. The value of the decision can be further quantified by determining how much production could be improved with the new machine, hence how much additional revenue would be produced. The other alternative would be for the firm to use part of that same sum of money to fix the machine and invest the balance in another asset or a savings account for later use. The cost of repairing the existing machine could be quantified. There might be no added revenue as a result of productivity improvements, however, the remainder of the cash would also be expected to produce some sort of revenue, whether it was invested in a different productive asset or earned interest. The proceeds from each decision would differ but could be expressed in a single format: the monetary value that they consumed or produced, expressed in terms of the currency used by that firm.

Store of Wealth

By choosing the latter alternative, the firm has, in effect, utilized another component of money—its ability to **store wealth.** Money not needed now can be saved until it can be put to use more efficiently. In the book *Silas Marner,* the title character, a weaver, hid all of his earnings under a stone in his floor. A thief stole the money, which was not recovered for 16 years. However, because the money was gold it had retained its store of commercial value, even if its psychological value to the former miser had changed.

Money left idle does not earn income. Money, unless it is put to use, keeps the stated value that it had on the day it was earned. Its **purchasing power,** the amount of goods or services for which it can be exchanged, does not increase. In fact, during times of high interest rates or inflation, money actually loses a portion of its value over time. Although it is still a unit of exchange, the number of units needed to complete a specific transaction will have increased. When inflation subsides, prices may return to lower levels or they may not. That is why most organizations do not bury their idle cash under the floorboards but find income-producing investments that are meant to offset the effects of inflation.

What happens when a country's currency steadily loses value over time? Does it cease to be money? We'll come back to these questions at the end of the chapter.

Standard of Deferred Payment

The last major function of money is its use as a **standard of deferred payment.** If money is a unit of account accepted within the economic community, it represents an accumulation of wealth and also serves as a standard of deferred payment. If the company had repaired the machine rather than buy a new one and put the idle cash into a 6-month certificate of deposit at the local bank, the bank would return the principal along with the agreed-upon interest at the maturity date. The bank deferred the payment of interest until the end

Have you ever traveled to a foreign country and been left with just a bit of pocket change? It's not enough to bother converting back to U. S. currency and there isn't anything you really need to buy, so you stuff the change into your purse or pocket. When you get home, you dump the change into a pile.

For years I've kept the Canadian currency separate, because it's likely that I will return to Canada and the currency will still be valuable to me as a medium of exchange. However, the other coins have been deposited into a change bowl where they are mixed together.

Unless the name of the country is written in my native language, English, or the Spanish that I took in high school, I can no longer tell which coins belong to which country. It is further complicated by the fact that much of the money came from countries that members of my family have visited but I have not. I can't "remember" the coins since I never used them.

Some have Arabic writing, but there are many countries that use Arabic so that's not much of a clue. Other coins have characters that to my unknowledgeable eye, could belong to any one of the Asian countries. Even if I were to travel to countries that I know my family members have visited in the past, the coins would do me no good. I cannot puzzle out which coins belong to which countries.

For any token to be useful as money, it needs to serve all four functions of money: a medium of exchange, a unit of account, a store of wealth, and a method of deferred payment. Although the coins continue to store value and could be used as a unit of account for some sort of deferred payment, they have ceased to be money for me because I cannot use them as a medium of exchange. I do not know where or with whom they could be exchanged!

In a sense, by "saving" them in my little coin box, I have turned them from money into mere bits of nicely decorated metal.

of the loan and both parties agreed that this was acceptable. Without the belief that the currency will retain its value as a unit of exchange, the firm would not accept deferred payments.

The idea of money as a standard of deferred payment is important if the economy expects to grow in the future. In order to fund long-term projects, lenders need to be assured that the currency used in the transaction will retain its value. As we saw in Chapter 2, **interest** rates are adjusted to take into account the risk of future inflation, but the fundamental faith in the future value of currency is what turns paper into money.

CHARACTERISTICS OF MONEY

Money has taken many forms over time. There are four characteristics that help determine whether an item would serve well as money.

Portable

Money has to be **portable.** If money is used as a unit of exchange to facilitate trade across borders, whether internationally or just from one community to the next, the item needs to be easily carried. For that reason, most early money was in the form of coins, small disks of precious metal that could be tucked into a purse or pocket. Some coins were designed with center holes so that they could be strung and perhaps worn under a shirt, safe from view. Shells, used by Native Americans, were also strung together, making them easier to carry. Some Japanese coins still have a hole in the center.

Durable

Money needs to be **durable.** Because it will be exchanged often, it must be able to endure the wear and tear of many handlings. Money is not only exchanged from hand to hand (between the grocery store shopper and the cashier), but is also used in vending machines, ATMs, and other automated payment systems. Coin and currency must be sturdy enough to withstand repeated use. In today's world, it must also be safe from its owner's neglect. If you leave a dollar bill in one pocket and a facial tissue in the other, which one will survive a trip through the washing machine?

Divisible

As we said earlier, money serves as a unit of exchange, so the units must be of small enough denomination that even relatively inconsequential exchanges can take place. In a sense, the smallest unit of currency determines how finely we can measure the value of goods and services produced by an economy. For example, if the smallest coin we had was a quarter, each change in the price of an item would have to move by 25 cents. Apples could either be 25 cents per pound, 50 cents per pound, or 75 cents per pound. There would be far less price sensitivity because the currency could not adapt within a tight enough range. Thus, the amount of **divisibility** within a monetary system has profound impact on pricing decisions and purchase behavior.

The problem is in deciding how small that monetary unit should be. In the United States, we have kept pennies in circulation even though many people argue that pennies are worthless. How many of you actually stop to pick up a penny from the sidewalk?

There is a fascinating pricing strategy that deals in a unit of exchange that we do not possess and yet we all accept. Most gas stations price gasoline to include a third decimal place, for example, $1.299. If I buy only 1 gallon of gasoline, I cannot pay the stated price because I do not have a tenth of a penny and, in fact, the pump rounds the purchase price up to $1.30.

In the same way, the New York Stock Exchange used to price all stock transactions in dollars and fractions. At first, the fractional unit was eighths, which would translate into 12.5 cents. Since we have no half-cent pieces, a single unit of stock would, in theory, have to be rounded up to the next penny but could only increase or decrease in increments of 12.5 cents. Traders wished to trade in a narrower range, so stock prices began to move in 16ths of a dollar, 32nds, and even 64ths. In practice, purchasers rarely purchase one share of stock at a time, and transaction costs are added to the final purchase price, so the fractional unit of currency disappeared from the final settlement statement. However, expressing stock prices in units other than those into which our currency could be divided was awkward.

Eventually the stock exchange decided to align stock prices with the existing currency and decimalized stock prices. Looking at stock prices in the newspaper is much more comfortable now that they are expressed as $12.50 per share instead of $12-½!

Difficult to Counterfeit

The last characteristic of money is that it must be **difficult to counterfeit.** Remember that money represents value but does not have intrinsic value of its own. Therefore, the authority to produce money is given to a centralized organization, usually the government of a country, which also has the responsibility for making economic decisions. If currency is easy to counterfeit, there is no assurance that any of the units have value and, in time, all units will become worthless. Accepting money in exchange for tangible goods or services performed is a measure of belief in the integrity of that currency, both at the time of exchange and in the future. In situations where counterfeiting of the local currency is rampant, people tend to revert to a barter system or use a currency other than their own.

Countries are taking increasing precautions to safeguard their currencies. Some of the measures they use are to add watermarks that are only seen when the bill is held up to the light. Others feature almost dizzyingly geometric patterns that would blur when copied by scanners or high-resolution printers. The Korean 10,000 won note has a stripe of silver metallic thread running through it that is only visible on one side. The newly redesigned American dollar features color-shifting ink that changes from green to black when the bill is moved. All of these strategies are meant to make it more difficult to counterfeit official currency.

MONEY AND CULTURE

By this point, you can see that money has taken on symbolic attributes. It is a token of value, but it also represents some of the most basic values of the country that issues it. Often those values are expressed in the decorations that adorn currency.

When you are traveling, your first thought is probably how much each of the strange coins and bills would be worth if they were dollars and cents. But if you look more closely, money tells a story. Many countries feature prominent citizens, not all of whom are or were political leaders. French francs featured artist Paul Cezanne and composer Claude Debussy. The Australian 10-dollar note features A. B. "Banjo" Paterson who wrote the lyrics to "Waltzing Matilda." These men represent aspects of their countries' artistic culture.[1]

Some countries do not use portraits at all but represent other aspects of their culture. The 1-pound note from Egypt has a mosque on one side and the

[1]David Standish, The Art of Money, *Smithsonian*, August 1998.

immense statues of Abu Simbel on the reverse. The two images represent both modern-day Islamic tradition and the ancient Pharoahs. The watermark embedded in the note is the golden funeral mask of King Tutankhamen. King Tut was one of the lesser Pharoahs, however, his image is familiar to people around the world because his tomb, although relatively inconsequential, remained unplundered for centuries. When it was finally excavated, the magnificence of the burial items hinted at the richness that the Ancient Kingdoms possessed. King Tut, or rather his artifacts, traveled the modern world and brought new attention to an ancient civilization. Egypt's currency reflects the melding of ancient and modern worlds.

Our young nation is no different in its wish to memorialize elder statesmen. In 1929, a committee decided that portraits of past U. S. Presidents would be featured on bills, since they were assumed to be among the most familiar Americans. The $1 bill, the most circulated piece of currency, features the portrait of our first President, George Washington, and the $5 bill features Abraham Lincoln. These two men are arguably our most famous presidents, and their images are also found on coins (the quarter and penny, respectively). But the committee also honored other Americans who may not be as well known even to our own citizens. The $20 bill, which is frequently used in ATMs, features Andrew Jackson, a lesser-known President, and the $10 bill features Alexander Hamilton, the first Secretary of the Treasury. The backs of our bills, except for the $1 bill, showcase buildings such as the White House and the Lincoln Memorial. Our coins, too, feature Americans of distinction on the face with a symbol of our country on the back. Thomas Jefferson's face appears on the nickel, with his home, Monticello, on the reverse.

We are taking the idea of culture, history, and coinage even further with the issue of the 50 State Quarters™ Program. Between 1999 and 2008, quarters will be issued that feature George Washington on the front along with a picture representing one of the states of the Union on the reverse. The North Carolina quarter, issued in 2001, shows a rendition of the Wright brothers' first flight at Kitty Hawk, a major historic and technological event of the 20th century. The quarter honoring Georgia, another southern state, features the peach, the

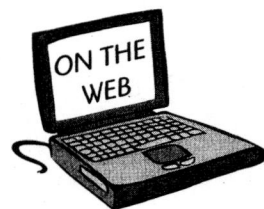

The Bureau of Engraving and Printing produces Federal Reserve notes (dollar bills in various denominations), postage stamps, and other security documents such as naturalization papers and Treasury bills and notes. The bureau also researches methods to prevent or reduce counterfeiting of bills. The Bureau of Engraving and Printing Web site (www.bep.treas.gov) has facts about currency, both existing and historic.

The U. S. Mint (www.usmint.gov) was created by Congress in 1792. The Mint is responsible for manufacturing all of the coins used as currency as well as uncirculated coins designed for collectors. The Mint produces national medals as well as American Eagle Gold and Silver Bullion Coins, which are held as investments. The Mint also safeguards and controls the movement of the country's stock of gold, located at the West Point Gold Depository in New York and the Fort Knox Bullion Depository in Kentucky.

official state tree (the live oak), and the state motto Wisdom, Justice, Moderation. The commemorative coinage even comes with lesson plans for teachers, which can be found at the U. S. Mint Web site!

These few simple examples show how powerfully currency is linked to a country's sense of identity as well as its national economy. Is it any wonder then that the euro has engendered debate, concern, and outright hostility among citizens of the European Union?

THE EURO

On January 1, 2002, twelve countries in Europe exchanged their national currencies for a single new currency called the **euro.** The nations of Austria, Belgium, Finland, France, Germany, Greece, Ireland, Italy, Luxembourg, the Netherlands, Portugal, and Spain agreed to fix their exchange rates to the euro, which did not exist in physical form until January 2002.

By setting the exchange rate, gains and losses from trading the various European currencies were erased. In 1998, the cost of currency exchange was estimated at $65 billion annually, all of which could be poured into new investments if it weren't funding currency exchanges.[2] For businesses, the euro makes it easier to see price differences across borders that are a result of worker efficiency rather than currency exchange rates. In theory, the euro was

The color of money: One euro currency with myriad faces

The common face of euro coins is shown at left. At right you can see both sides of the euro bank notes. Notice that the bank notes decrease in size as they decrease in value. (Travel Weekly)

---

[2]Joan Warner, The Great Money Bazaar. *Business Week*, April 27, 1998, p. 96.

> ### Looking Back/Looking Forward
>
> An independent Irish currency is a relatively recent historic event. Coins were first issued by Ireland in December 1928. The poet W. B. Yeats chaired the design committee, which decided that each coin would have a representation of a harp on the obverse side of the coin, along with the date of coinage and the name of the country, Eire.
>
> The first design group stipulated that the reverse side of each coin show animals or birds that were important in Irish life. When decimal currency was introduced in 1971, some of the designs were altered. Ornamental bird details from an illustration in the *Book of Kells* appears on the reverse of the two-pence piece, while the one-pence piece has a bird design from the Second Bible of Charles-the-Bald. The rest of the coins in use before the introduction of the euro continued to have depictions of animals: a salmon, horse, bull, and woodcock.
>
> Modern Irish currency has been in existence for less than 75 years. The coins featured carefully planned representation of Irish symbols. In anticipation of the introduction of the euro in January 2002, J. C. Walsh and Sons of Dublin offered sets of circulated Irish coins with a brief history of the coinage.
>
> Unlike the change in the little coin box, I do know where these coins originated. However, since January 2002 they have ceased to be money and will merely serve to decorate my office wall.
>
> *Source*: Irish coin collection, J. C. Walsh & Sons, Ltd., Rathfarnham Village, Dublin 14, Ireland.

supposed to create a borderless financial world where capital would be moved to the most efficient supplier, regardless of national boundaries. A common economic policy is set by the European Central Bank, which is discussed in Chapter 4.

In actual practice, the euro experience has been a bit rocky. An additional goal of the euro was to promote European harmony. A single currency for Europe was proposed after World War II in order to link Europe so closely that another continental war would be nearly impossible. It is this political linking and feared loss of national sovereignty that have caused Britain, Denmark, and Sweden to remain outside the currency union. In September 2000, Danes voted against joining the currency union in part due to fears of being absorbed into a large European entity in which their small nation would have a limited voice.

Another grave difficulty for the euro is that it was, at first, an entirely virtual currency. For a 3-year transition period, shopkeepers posted prices in a medium that could not be exchanged physically. Credit card transactions were denominated in euros and paychecks issued into euro-denominated checking accounts, but a "euro" could not be touched or seen. For people used to exchanging francs or marks or lira, the intangibility of the money was a drawback.

```
┌─────────────────────< In the News >─────────────────────┐
```

Beginning January 1, 2002, liras, deutschemarks, pesos, and Irish pence were replaced by a new European currency, the euro, which is meant to unify Europe, easing business transactions and making it easier to travel from one country to another.

While the goal of the euro is to create a seamless currency zone, special euro coins are being minted for each participating country. Eight denominations of coins have been issued. A common side shows the denomination of the coin, while the opposite side, the "national side," differs from country to country. Dutch coins, for example, feature a portrait of Queen Beatrix. Euros will be accepted in any of the 12 participating nations, regardless of the nation of origin.

The seven euro banknote denominations will be easily distinguished by size and color. The smallest bill in value is also the smallest in size.

_____

Source: www.euro.ecb.int

A SYMBOL OF ECONOMIC STRENGTH

Money grew out of the need to facilitate trade, including exchanges that occurred across international borders. Throughout time, traders have had to exchange one currency for another. An **exchange rate** establishes the relative value between different currencies at that point in time.

For several years, the American Express Company promoted its travelers checks with the slogans "Don't Leave Home Without It" and "Everywhere You Want to Be." Travelers were urged to buy American Express products both to ensure against loss as well as to assure that the store of value travelers carried in U. S. currency could be converted easily to the unit of account in the country they were visiting.

Before there was a sophisticated network for currency exchanges, whether through the use of travelers checks, charges to a credit card whose issuer performs the currency exchange, or the simple exchange of money at a currency window in any international airport, traders preferred to receive payment in monetary units that they knew had value across borders. During certain periods, some currencies have been preferred to others. Usually preference was due to the political power and economic stability of the issuing country. Roman coins made their way to the far reaches of the Roman Empire, even as far away as Britain, which was one of the most isolated outposts of the empire. During the 1500s when Spain ruled the seas, her currency was accepted along all of the trade routes that her ships traversed. The concept of an internationally accepted unit of exchange existed long before the euro was created.

Although merchants and traders have long gravitated to the most useful or influential currency of the time, until the advent of the euro, each country has maintained its own currency and implemented its own monetary and

> ## Looking Back
>
> What happens when a country's money loses value over time? Does it cease to be money?
>
> One evening, during the early 1980s, my husband and I were visiting with friends of my grandparents in their apartment in Chicago. My husband was lamenting the high inflation that was then gripping our nation. Interest rates were at unbelievable levels and, as a young couple just starting out in life, he couldn't see how we would ever be able to afford to buy a house—our little part of the American dream.
>
> Our host excused himself and returned with a banknote. "You do not know inflation," he said gently, handing the note to me. It was a Reichsbanknote, issued in Berlin with the date 15 December 1922.
>
> What is remarkable is that the eintaufend mark (1000) note, printed with black ink on tan paper, is overstamped with red ink. Both front and back had been stamped to read "Eine Milliarde Mark."
>
> "When I was a boy," my grandmother's friend continued, "my mother used to take fists full of these notes to the market and beg the baker to give us a loaf of bread for our dinner. The government kept printing them and stamping them and bread became dearer and dearer."
> "Keep it," he told me. "It's not worth anything now."

fiscal policies. Because of this, money has also been a symbol of economic strength.

In order to stabilize European economies after World War II and prevent the sort of economic chaos that had led, in part, to the war, exchange rates were pegged to one another in what came to be known as the Bretton Woods Accord. The goal of the accord was to provide economic stability by describing the relative value of varying units of account (currency). By the 1970s, inflation had weakened the fixed rate exchange system and industrialized countries moved to a floating exchange rate.

Floating exchange rates allow currency traders to assess the relative strength of international economies and determine which currencies they wish to hold. The United States is the world's largest single economy, producing more goods and services than any other nation. Because of its economic strength and political stability, the U.S. dollar has become a unit of exchange accepted in many business transactions around the world. The value of other currencies is often measured against the dollar.

When the U. S. dollar is "strong," that is, it has a higher value in relation to other currencies, consumption shifts away from American goods. The higher exchange rate has made our products more expensive abroad. Rising prices tend to lower demand and a strong dollar reduces exports which, in turn can slow the growth of our domestic economy. As the economy weakens, the value of the dollar often falls, reducing the price of exported goods and stimulating trade. Fortunately, although the exchange rate fluctuates, the dollar has remained relatively steady over time.

```
┌─────────────────────────────────────────────────────────┐
│                    ⟨ In the News ⟩                       │
│                                                           │
```

In order to stabilize their own economies, some Latin American countries, including Argentina, have pegged their currency to the dollar. The idea was that pegging their currency to the dollar would create incentives for the governments to adopt disciplined spending policies that would keep the relative value of the currencies in line. Argentina allowed its pesos to circulate alongside dollars. Prices were expressed in both pesos and dollars. Bank accounts could be established in either currency. Long-term contracts and consumer debt were often expressed in terms of dollars. However, the Argentine government continued to print and distribute pesos and paid government workers in pesos, not dollars.

In November 2001, after 4 years of recession, Argentina asked its lenders for debt relief, saying that it could not pay its national debt. In order to stimulate its economy and make its products more competitive on the world market, the value of Argentinian pesos should decline relative to stronger currencies. However, since the government pledged that there would be a 1-for-1 convertibility between the peso and dollar, that decision was unpopular at best. The country eventually uncoupled the two currencies, which led to economic as well as political upheaval.

HEDGING

Currency **hedging** can be a form of speculation or an attempt to protect the value of exchange. Some traders buy or sell bundles of currency, hoping to benefit from the temporary pricing differences between currencies. Think of it as a circle: the trader buys euros with dollars, then converts the euros to yen, and sells the yen for dollars. He is hoping that the final transaction nets more dollars than he originally had.

A different sort of hedging takes place when an international or multinational company locks in the exchange rate immediately after signing a sales contract. If a Korean company sells a piece of equipment to a British firm, the contract might be written in British pounds sterling. In order to fix the sales price, in terms of won, between the date of contract and the payment date, the Korean firm could hedge the pounds. They could agree to sell the pounds to a currency trader at an agreed-upon date for a specified quantity of won. The Korean firm has eliminated the risk that the value of the pounds they will receive in the future will have declined in value relative to the Korean won. If the value of the pound increases, the Korean firm will have lost the opportunity to benefit from the increased value of the pounds sterling. However, by hedging the transaction they know the value of the sale in terms of their own currency.

 **Book Report**

Money Makes the World Go Around: One Investor Tracks Her Cash Through the Global Economy, from Brooklyn to Bangkok and Back
By Barbara Garson, New York: Viking, 2001.

If money is meant to facilitate trade, then it is logical to assume that money travels around the world. Barbara Garson decided to follow her money around the world and investigate where it went and how it was used.

Garson invested part of the cash advance for the book and then attempted to follow its path. One portion of the money was invested in a local bank. The next day, the bank sent a sizeable deposit to Chase Manhattan, a major market bank, to satisfy its reserve requirements. Although there was no certainty that the deposit Ms. Garson made was forwarded on to Chase, she chose to follow the money that was sent from her small-town bank into the larger world. In the course of her research, she flew to Thailand, Singapore, and Malaysia and describes the flow of funds to an oil refinery and small businesses that might have been financed by Chase's international letters of credit.

Her second investment was in a mutual fund. Among its holdings was Sunbeam Corporation, a maker of small appliances, which was struggling. Ms. Garson went to two towns: Portland, Tennessee, and Biddeford, Maine, sites of Sunbeam factories, to interview workers and see the human side of the company in which her money had been invested.

Garson's journey did not trace the actual physical transactions of specific units of currency for goods or services. It is a more abstract view of the role of money in facilitating trade and international economic development.

Source: Harris, Marilyn. "How One Woman Followed the Money." *Business Week*, March 5, 2001.

EXAMPLES OF ITEMS USED AS MONEY

When economists talk about money, they include more than just coins and bills. One of the most commonly used definitions of money is **M1,** which measures only the most liquid forms of money, those that are closest to cash. The traditional definition of M1 includes currency and demand deposits (checking accounts).

It is easy to see why a checking account would be a form of money. A check is merely a piece of paper that authorizes the bank to pay the recipient a specified sum of money on demand, hence the name demand deposit. Banks may have a policy that limits cash withdrawals in order to protect against overdrafts, however, in theory, a check is as good as cash. A debit card is not an addition to the definition of M1; it is merely another tool, like the check or a bank withdrawal slip, for gaining access to the money in your checking account.

Travelers checks are another form of money. They are a prepaid store of future value, readily accepted in many countries. Travelers checks can be purchased in several denominations and be exchanged for a variety of goods, services, and even local currency around the world. Travelers checks have their own security feature—the requirement that the person using the check countersign the check in the presence of the vendor. For that reason, issuing companies tout travelers checks as safer than carrying currency. The additional cost of obtaining travelers checks, beyond their face value, is a fee for the service of providing portability and security rather than a reflection of the underlying worth of the check.

A relatively new development is the creation of **smart cards** that allow the holder to fill the card with a specified amount of money that is transferred from a savings, checking, investment account, or a credit card account. Visa says that its smart card, Visa Buxx™, can be used anywhere that the Visa card is accepted and can be replenished. Because the card carries with it value that is expressed as dollars, it is a form of money. If the card is widely accepted by merchants, it would meet the test as money. We have, however, taken a step away from what we might traditionally consider money: bills and coins.

This plastic card is actually money. Unlike credit cards, a smart card contains a specific monetary value and does not incur a loan. (Dorling Kindersley Media Library)

───〈 **Just For Fun** 〉───

Why Isn't a Cow a Good Form of Money?
Jack and the Beanstalk

Once upon a time, there was a boy named Jack who lived with his mother in a little cottage. Jack and his mother were very poor; all they had was one cow. Each day, Jack's mother would send him to the market with the milk to get some food for their dinner.

When Mom sends Jack to the market, she is probably expecting him to barter the milk for bread, cheese, fruit, and maybe a bit of meat. These are simple transactions and could very easily be accomplished through trade. No money need ever change hands.

One day the cow gave no milk. She didn't give any the next day or the next. Finally, Jack's mother told him that he would have to take the cow to market. "Get the best price you can for her. She's all we have left."

Now, neither the cow nor the milk are a form of money for many reasons. As long as there was milk, the cow was a productive asset (and could have been listed as such on their balance sheet) that would add to their income into the future. Using the cow as collateral, Jack and his mother might have been able to enter into a long-term contract that allowed them to purchase an item with payment expressed in terms of gallons of milk to be delivered at regular intervals. That would be utilizing the milk as a form of deferred payment, which is one of the functions of money. However, the milk could not be used as a store of wealth. If it were not sold and consumed in a relatively short period of time, it would lose all value. As for the cow, it could not be divided into smaller units of account and still be productive.

Jack was very sad but he took the cow to market. On his way, he met an old woman who offered to trade some magic beans for the cow. She assured him that their magic was very powerful so Jack took the beans and gave her the cow.

Jack's Mom is not very happy when he comes home with beans rather than the coins that she was obviously expecting. In her own mind, Mom had put some sort of value on the cow and it was expressed in terms of money, not magic beans. Although several transactions have taken place we still have no money, a fact that Jack's Mom is acutely aware of.

When Jack got home, he excitedly told his mother about the magic beans. "Fool!" she said, "exchanging our only cow for a handful of worthless beans! What will become of us now?" She flung the beans out the window and both she and Jack went to bed hungry.

(continued)

(continued)

When Jack awoke the next morning, he was amazed to see a giant beanstalk growing taller than his eye could see. Remembering the old woman's words, he decided to climb the beanstalk.

This is the point in the story where money is finally introduced, along with some ethical dilemmas (fairy tales are not always tidy). Jack discovers a giant's castle at the top of the beanstalk. On his first visit, he steals a bag of gold coins from the giant's table. He takes it back to his mother who is overjoyed. They use the money until it runs out. Then Jack returns to the castle and brings back the hen that lays the golden egg. Once again he has a productive asset because the hen produces a commodity that can be converted into currency. The golden egg would have to be assayed before its true worth could be determined; therefore, although the bag of gold was money, the golden egg is not. On the third trip, Jack steals the singing harp, which calls out and awakens the sleeping giant who chases the thief down the beanstalk.

The singing harp is a curiosity, perhaps even a collectible, but I'm not sure what value we would assign to it; perhaps it is a liability!

NON-MONEY

There are other mechanisms that facilitate trade or indicate financial well-being that may appear to be money but aren't.

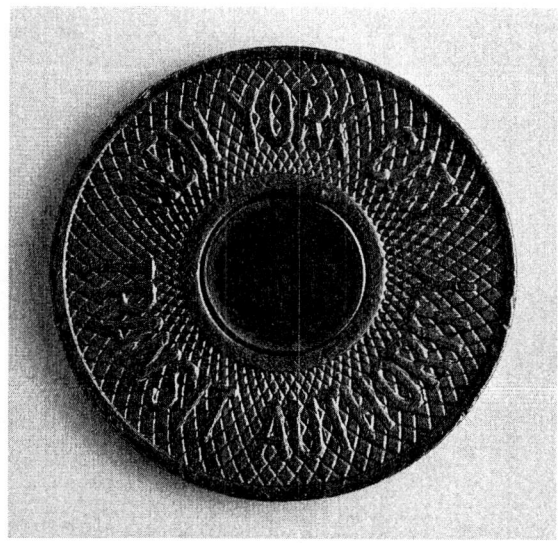

Subway tokens facilitate exchange—you can use them to catch a ride home. However they are not generally accepted as units of exchange for other goods or services so they are not money. (Dorling Kindersley Media Library)

Credit Cards

A debit card is a form of money but credit cards are not. The use of a credit card facilitates exchange in a marketplace but, far from being a source of stored value, the use of credit cards creates a source of stored debt. Until cash is paid or a check written, money has not been used. Think of it in an accounting sense. When you purchase a new pair of shoes using a check (or debit card), the money is immediately deducted from your checking account. There has been a transfer of value from one asset (cash) to another (clothing). When you pay with a credit card, you take the shoes home with you but you have incurred an account payable. The transaction has increased the assets (clothing) and the liabilities (that bill which will show up all too soon). Money does not change hands until you pay the bill, therefore, this has been a moneyless transaction.

Lines of Credit

Like a credit card, a line of credit allows a business to purchase goods that they otherwise would not have been able to afford. The line of credit carries interest and is clearly a loan that must be repaid with money.

Previously, we said that smart cards were a new form of money. But this does not mean that all of the dollar-denominated plastic cards floating around are money. Gift cards are portable, durable, and divisible. They carry value that is expressed in terms of dollars (and cents), and the value can be stored until the recipient wants to use it. But that use is confined to the store, or company, that issued the card. A card from Home Depot cannot be used at Barnes and Noble or Kroger. Because they are not accepted as units of exchange anywhere but the issuing company, this type of card should not be considered money, although it is a marvelous tool for facilitating exchange.

Stocks, Bonds, and Mutual Funds

In the 1990s, many people saw the value of their stock portfolios increase dramatically. Unquestionably their wealth increased, but wealth is not money. The stocks and bonds and mutual funds were not a medium of exchange. The assets had to be sold and converted into cash. As we have seen, the 2001 stock market wiped out many of the paper gains that had been amassed during the 1990s. For an investor who was planning to liquidate portions of the stock portfolio to provide retirement income, the loss of value had a direct effect. For younger investors, years away from retirement, the losses were psychological more than financial. The value of stock holdings is not money until the investments are cashed out.

Gold

Precious metals, especially gold and silver, have often been used as money. Coins were made from gold and were often redeemed by weight rather than face value, since it was possible to shave some of the soft ore from the coin. During the California gold rush of 1849, gold dust became a unit of exchange. Miners brought the ore to assayers who measured its weight. Most stores had scales on the counter that were used to weigh gold dust in exchange for food and sundries. Although paper money had existed for a long time, gold was a popular form of money during that time period.

As recently as 1933, the value of American money was tied to the value of gold and silver. Banks were required to hold gold or silver reserves for every dollar of currency they issued, and dollar bills were called silver certificates. As we will see in Chapter 5, a healthy and expanding banking system allows a country's economy to grow. As long as banks were required to hold gold for every dollar issued, their ability to issue currency was constrained by the amount of gold they had on reserve. In addition, currency was directly redeemable for gold or silver. This tie of gold to currency caused turmoil in the late 1920s and early 1930s. Fearing that their paper currency could become worthless, customers flocked to banks and traded in dollars for gold coins, which they then hoarded. The amount of currency in the economy quickly diminished, which even further slowed the pace of economic recovery.[3]

Today we have the golden dollar coin featuring Sacajawea. It is gold-plated for color but does not contain substantial gold. Gold, in the form of coins or ingots, has become an investment like stocks and bonds, and must be converted into cash before it can be spent.

Many investors choose to buy solid coins, believing that they hold value regardless of the economic condition of the country or any political instability. Many investors believe that gold is desirable because it can be readily exchanged for any currency that the investor desires. Although gold coins are held as investments, they are no longer a form of money.

 **Book Report**

The Power of Gold: The History of an Obsession
    By Peter L. Bernstein, New York: John Wiley and Sons, Inc., 2000.

What explains our fascination with gold? It is pretty and shiny and valued by many. It can be fashioned into jewelry and coins and used to decorate ceremonial objects. It quite simply glows and throughout history, people have desired it.

Peter Bernstein has written an engaging book about the lengths to which individuals, rulers, and countries have gone to extract gold from the earth and put it to their own use. He takes us from the story of King Midas to the controversy over the gold standard. In between he weaves a fascinating account of the effects of this shiny metal, which has very little practical use but incredible value.

[3]T. J. Stiles, As Good as Gold?, *Smithsonian*, September 2000.

THE FUTURE OF MONEY

E-money: Digitally Encoded Units of Account

Because a debit card is tied to a demand deposit, debit cards are a tool for accessing money from an existing account. From that standpoint, they are like checks. But in a very real sense, debit cards have forced us to make a leap from a physical representation of money (either cash or paper checks) to the idea that money can be pieces of data, accessed with a little plastic card. Money, or the concept of money, has become very abstract and much of our money is "virtual"—it exists as bits and bytes of computer information rather than cold, hard cash.

Think of the transactions you make on a regular basis: many of us have our paychecks deposited into our checking account by electronic funds transfer. In this process, our employer sends information to our bank informing it that money has been transferred from our employer's account to ours. The transfer is performed by computer links, often in the middle of the night, long after most of the employees of both institutions have gone home. We may get a "check" in our morning mail delivery but it is, in truth, a receipt. The perforated part of the check, which records taxes paid and deductions taken, looks the same but the portion where one would expect to see "Pay to the Order of . . ." contains a message that this is *not* a negotiable instrument.

However, regardless of how it arrived, there is money in your account. Well actually, money may have been sent to several accounts. Go back to those deductions for a minute. More than one monetary transfer has taken place. If you have a pension fund to which you contribute, your portion has been deducted from the paycheck and sent to the pension fund's custodian, who is most likely not your local bank. The charitable contributions you make through an annual giving campaign can be deducted from your paycheck and sent directly to the charity. Your mortgage payment can be sent to the out of state bank that offered the lowest interest rate. Your auto loan has been sent to your credit union, a different institution from the one that holds your checking account, and your auto insurance premium can be sent on to the insurance company. All of these transactions have been done in the blink of an eye and are based on the single fact that you got paid.

The electronic transfer of money continues. On your way home from work you stop at the grocery store where you pay with your debit card. Since it is payday, you settle in front of the computer and pay bills on-line, authorizing the utility company to deduct the cost of electricity from your checking account.

More money transfer services are available. Money orders can be purchased from the U.S. Post Office and other designated outlets during regular business hours. Now money can be sent by e-mail by a variety of services, regardless of the time of day. Many of these services have developed as a response to consumers' desire to purchase using Internet technology. Paypal is one such service that allows bidders on the eBay auction site to authorize transfer of funds to the seller of the item. The buyer could write a check and mail it to the sender but that would slow down the transaction time.

Virtual money has important ramifications for the finance manager. If bills can be paid online with almost instantaneous transfer, the company can

┌─ **Just For Fun** ─┐

Could you go for a whole week without using currency and still do everything you normally would?

Think about the transactions you make daily or weekly: bills are paid using checks or electronic funds transfers. Few vendors like receiving cash in payment for a large bill. Rent is usually paid by check. Grocery stores, gas stations, and retailers accept checks, debit cards, and credit cards—no need for cash there. Many of us are paid by check, although if you are working in a restaurant or similar setting, part of your compensation is in the form of tips, which are often cash.

Many exchanges can take place using substitutes for coins and bills, however, some smaller transactions still require that we use cash—many fast-food restaurants will not accept anything but cash. Garage sale ads often state that sales are for "cash only." Most vending machines accept coins even though some also accept debit or credit cards. If I treat myself to a cup of coffee and pastry in the morning, I don't pull out a debit card. Instead, I use the few rumpled dollar bills I've stuffed in my coat pocket, and the change is tossed in the tips jar. Coin-operated laundry machines are exactly that, coin operated. And don't forget the parking meter. My town installed new parking meters a few years ago that have a slot into which you can insert a card. The plan was to sell prepaid parking cards, but time has passed and I still need quarters if I am going to shop downtown for longer than my first 16 minutes of free parking.

Although we are increasingly substituting paper, plastic, and electronic forms of money for coin and currency, tangible forms of money still play a large role in our daily transactions.

lengthen the number of days that it holds cash before paying bills without incurring finance charges. Losses on accounts receivable might be lowered if the company sets up automatic deduction from its clients' accounts. Paperless money also means that companies involved in international trade can more easily transfer assets using whatever currency is appropriate. We'll look at more of these options when we develop working capital strategies in Chapter 9.

TERMS TO KNOW

Money	Interest	Exchange rate
Medium of exchange	Portable	Hedging
Unit of account	Durable	M1
Store of wealth	Divisible	Smart cards
Purchasing power	Difficult to	Virtual money
Standard of deferred	counterfeit	
payment	Euro	

TERM PAPERS AND PROJECTS

1. Explain how Russia created a new currency system after the collapse of the Soviet Union. How did the country restructure the monetary system? What images are depicted on the new currency?
2. What happens to the exchange rate of currency when a country is at war? Examine the U. S. dollar during the period of the Persian Gulf Conflict or the War on Terrorism.
3. How did Germany integrate two currencies during reunification?
4. What does the Euro mean for trade? National sovereignty? Political and economic interrelationships? The ability of individual governments to set monetary and fiscal policy?
5. Argentina "dollarized" their economy. What happens when a country has pegged currency to dollars and its own economy is not in balance? How is Argentina doing now?
6. Discuss the decorations on money and how they tie to a country's culture and history.

REVIEW QUESTIONS

1. What are the functions of money? Give a brief example of each.
2. What are the four characteristics of money? Give a brief description of each.
3. Give three examples of items that have been used as money.
4. What is the difference between a debit card and a credit card? Which is considered money, and why?
5. What is a line of credit? Is it a form of money?
6. What is e-money? How does it work? What is it presently used for?
7. Discuss the role of e-money transactions in the economy. Can you envision a cashless society within the next 10 years?

4

THE FEDERAL RESERVE AND OTHER CENTRAL BANKING SYSTEMS

LEARNING OBJECTIVES

1. Describe the difference between fiscal and monetary policy.

2. Explain the four functions of the Federal Reserve System.

3. Describe the structure of the Federal Reserve System.

4. Describe the two types of inflation.

5. Explain the tools available to the Federal Reserve to counteract inflationary or recessionary trends in the economy.

6. Explain the role of the twelve Federal Reserve Banks.

7. Discuss the role of the Chairman of the Board of the Federal Reserve System.

8. Understand the relationship between the Federal Reserve System and other central banks.

There are two basic ways for a country to manage its economy: fiscal policy and monetary policy. **Fiscal policy** involves raising revenue through taxes or returning money to citizens by lowering tax rates or authorizing one-time tax rebates. Changes in tax policy might be suggested by the president, who is a member of the executive branch of government, but can only be enacted by Congress, the legislative branch. It is usually a time-consuming task and not well suited to quick actions to change the course of the economy.

Monetary policy affects the supply of money in the economy. When more money is released into the economy, people tend to spend it, thus increasing the consumption of goods and services. Companies that are producing desirable products will see their revenue increase, and it is expected that they will choose to reinvest those profits through the purchase of capital equipment or by hiring more employees—both of which continue the expansion of the economy. On the other hand, when the money supply is reduced, competition for loans

> ⟨ **In the News** ⟩
>
> Most adjustments to fiscal policy are met with partisan wrangling in the U.S. Congress. Proponents of tax cuts often state that putting money back into people's pockets will induce them to spend, thus stimulating the economy. Opponents of tax cuts counter with the argument that the federal government requires a certain level of revenue in order to fund social programs, infrastructure construction and repair, and investments in defense, all of which create jobs and stimulate the economy. There is agreement that the economy must grow at a steady pace and stimulus should be applied when growth slows or the country enters a recession. Disagreement stems from differing opinions on how that stimulus should be applied.
>
> It is now agreed that the U.S. economy ended its 10-year growth cycle in March 2001 and entered a recession. The Congress passed a tax relief bill in spring 2001, which was meant to encourage consumer spending as a means to pull the nation out of recession. As we will see later in this chapter, fiscal measures were not enough in light of the September 11, 2001, terrorist attacks, which further eroded economic growth.

increases, raising the market interest rate. As money becomes more expensive, consumers are less inclined to spend, companies reduce their capital expenditures, and the economy contracts. Monetary policy is set by the members of the Board of Governors of the Federal Reserve System in consultation with the board of directors of the 12 regional Federal Reserve Banks.

THE PURPOSE OF THE FEDERAL RESERVE SYSTEM

The **Federal Reserve System** (the Fed) was created by Congress in 1913 to provide the country with a safe, flexible, and stable monetary and financial system. The Federal Reserve acts as the central bank of the United States and is largely independent of the three main branches of government. The board's Web page (*www.federalreserve.gov*) describes the four main duties of the Federal Reserve:

1. conduct the nation's monetary policy;
2. supervise and regulate banking institutions and protect the credit rights of consumers;
3. maintain the stability of the financial system; and
4. provide certain types of financial services to the U.S. government, the public, domestic financial institutions, and foreign governments.

Board of the Governors of the Federal Reserve System

20th Street and Constitution Avenue, NW, Washington, DC 20551

About the Fed
Press Releases
Monetary Policy
**Banking Information
and Regulation**
Payment Systems
**Economic Research
and Data**
Consumer Information
Community Development
Reporting Forms
**Publications and
Education Resources**
Career Opportunities

Contact Us
FOIA

FAQs
Search
Site Map
Subject Index
What's New
What's Next

Accessibility
Disclaimer
Privacy Policy

The Federal Reserve, the central bank of the United States, was founded by Congress in 1913 to provide the nation with a safer, more flexible, and more stable monetary and financial system.

Today the Federal Reserve's duties fall into four general areas: (1) conducting the nation's monetary policy; (2) supervising and regulating banking institutions and protecting the credit rights of consumers; (3) maintaining the stability of the financial system; and (4) providing certain financial services to the U.S. government, the public, financial institutions, and foreign official institutions.

The duties of the Federal Reserve System. *(http://www.federalreserve.gov)*

THE STRUCTURE OF THE FEDERAL RESERVE SYSTEM

The Federal Reserve System consists of 12 regional banks, each headed by a president and supervised by the Board of Governors. **The Board of Governors** is analogous to a Board of Directors in a corporation or a Board of Trustees at a college. They set strategic goals and coordinate the activities of the member banks.

There are seven positions on the Board of Governors. Each member of the Board of Governors is nominated by the president and confirmed by the Senate. A full term lasts 14 years and begins on February 1 of even-numbered years. If the person appointed to a full term does not serve for the entire length of time the unexpired portion is filled by a new board member. The term expires on its statutory date regardless of the length of time that the current governor has held the seat. Board members cannot be reappointed after serving a full term, however, members who have filled an unexpired term may be appointed to a full term.

The term structure is important because once a member is confirmed by the Senate, he or she becomes quite independent of political influence. Presidents are limited to two consecutive terms in office, for a total of eight years. Assuming that the appointee serves a full term, a member of the board who is seated at the beginning of a president's term will still be influencing monetary

⟨ **Looking Back** ⟩

In October 1907, speculation in copper caused F. Augustus Heinze to lose $50 million in less than 24 hours. His attempts to corner the copper market cost him his fortune and brought down the stockbrokerage firm, Otto Heinze and Company, owned by his brother. The spectacular financial collapse created headlines.

Unfortunately, the damage was not limited to the fortunes of the two brothers.

F. Augustus Heinze was president of Mercantile National Bank and, as such, had formed close business relationships with several banking institutions. In 1907, there was no central bank, so local banks formed a clearinghouse—an association owned by member banks that facilitated the transfer of funds written on accounts held at the member banks. Mercantile National Bank was part of the New York Clearing House Committee. As his financial woes deepened, Heinze was pressured by the Clearing House Committee to resign from the presidency of Mercantile National Bank. It was announced that the Clearing House would contribute funds to cover withdrawals by Mercantile National's customers.

The reassuring words were not enough to stop a bank panic that spread to other financial institutions and threatened to undermine the stability of New York's banks. New York was then, as it is now, the major financial capital of the country, and a run on the banks would be devastating to the economy.

By the turn of the century, J. Pierpont Morgan was the wealthiest man in America and controlled a business empire with more resources than the U. S. government. When the financial conditions in New York continued to deteriorate a week after Heinze's collapse, J. P. Morgan decided to intervene. He had no official mandate to fix the problem, however, he had enough wealth, power, and influence to affect the course of events.

Through a variety of efforts, J. P. Morgan helped contain the panic of 1907. Morgan encouraged the U.S. Treasury to deposit $25 million in New York banks to provide liquidity. John D. Rockefeller, an oil tycoon, deposited $10 million of his money in New York financial institutions. Morgan convinced bankers to pool their assets and provide a $25 million fund that would shore up the brokers and the stock exchanges, which were also threatened with collapse. When European investors became leery of the security of New York City bonds, Morgan worked with the mayor of New York on measures that would restore investor confidence in the bonds.

Although the financial crisis subsided by mid-November, it had become clear that centralized leadership would be necessary in the event of another banking calamity. In 1910, Senator Nelson Aldrich of Rhode Island introduced legislation for a central United States bank that would increase oversight of financial institutions. The bill did not pass until 1913, six years after the crisis in New York.

Source: *Panic of 1907*, a publication of the Federal Reserve Bank of Boston.

policy after that president has left office. In the same way, every president inherits policy makers appointed by previous administrations. Because they cannot be reappointed to a second full term, the members of the Board of Governors are freed from the necessity of trying to create policy that will please the people who would, in effect, fire or rehire them. Monetary policy thus becomes removed from direct political influence.

This is not to say that there is no communication between the Federal Reserve Governors and elected officials; quite the contrary is true. The chairman of the Federal Reserve is required to testify twice a year before the Senate. During that testimony, the chairman describes the state of the economy and signals the economic direction that the Board of Governors believes would best serve the country.

Members of the Board of Governors are often economists and many have had experience in the area of public policy. Some have been academics, others have worked for the federal government, and still others have worked in finance, banking, or consulting in the private sector.

Although it is an integral component of the U. S. financial and economic system, the Federal Reserve is not a member of one of the three main branches of government—executive, legislative, or judicial—nor does it receive funding from the Congress. The Federal Reserve pays for its operation by investing in treasury notes and from income earned on services provided by regional Federal Reserve Banks to the member banks.

THE MISSION OF THE FEDERAL RESERVE SYSTEM

In this section, we will examine the four main areas of responsibility for the Federal Reserve System.

Conduct the Nation's Monetary Policy

The primary duty of the Federal Reserve System and its Board of Governors is to conduct the nation's monetary policy. The seven-member Board of Governors and five representatives from the Federal Reserve Banks form the **Federal Open Market Committee (FOMC)**. The president of the New York District Bank is a permanent member of the FOMC. The four other chairs rotate on a 1-year basis, ensuring that every region of the country will be represented.

The FOMC must meet at least four times a year and is responsible for setting policy that will promote economic growth, maintain full employment, encourage stable prices, and sustain international trade and payments. In a perfect world, our economy would grow at a steady pace. There would be enough money available at reasonable interest rates so that corporations could invest in new technology to expand and improve their businesses. Increased production would require hiring more employees, and the profits from successful decision making could be used to pay good wages. Workers would have enough disposable income to buy the products that were being produced, which, in turn, would allow companies to further invest. The problem arises when there is a supply or demand imbalance. Inflation and recession are both forms of economic imbalance.

Inflation is a period of rapidly rising prices. There are two main causes of inflation: cost-push and demand-pull. Cost-push inflation occurs when the price of raw materials or labor forces the company to increase the price it charges for goods or services. When the price of oil rises precipitously, airfares usually increase soon afterward. Because the cost of fuel is such a major component of their expenses, airline companies attempt to pass along the increase to the customer. As prices for goods in the consumer marketplace rise, employees demand higher wages to maintain their standard of living. The increased wages push the cost of goods up further. This often leads to an inflationary spiral.

Another form of inflation is demand-pull inflation. When consumers feel economically comfortable, they spend more. Their demand for products and services pulls prices up. Think about an auction: as soon as more than one person bids on an item, the price rises. An auction becomes exciting when multiple bidders desire the same item and the price rises quickly—sometimes reaching unbelievable levels. That is demand-pull inflation. If bidders are feeling less sure of their finances, bidding will progress slowly, if at all.

However, not all items are bought at face-to-face auctions. We can see the effect of demand-pull inflation even when the "bidders" are not simultaneously on-site. An auto dealer will be far less likely to negotiate the price of a new car, either by reducing the sticker price, offering favorable financing rates, or increasing the trade-in allowance when business is good. If you choose not to buy the car at the dealer's "best" offer, he or she knows more customers are coming along later that day or the next and they may be more inclined to purchase at the dealer's preferred price.

Consumer spending on high-priced items is often financed by debt. Houses are typically financed with 15- or 30-year mortgages. Automobiles, large home appliances, computers, and other durables are often financed for 1 to 5 years. Whether consumers are willing to take on additional debt is determined by the interest rate they are being charged as well as their perception of their current and near-future financial condition. If the economy is booming, jobs are being created, and companies are experiencing growth and profit then consumers are more likely to spend, including buying with debt financing. Perception and psychology have a marked effect on consumer spending choices.

Recession is a period of declining economic growth. Unemployment is usually high and consumer confidence is shaken. Rather than spend freely, consumers look for bargains, clip coupons, and defer expensive purchases. Companies feel the pinch of lower sales. They may cut capital spending or lay off employees. As more layoffs occur and unemployment rises, the country can enter a recessionary spiral.

The goal of the Federal Reserve System is to smooth these cycles. At the meetings of the Federal Open Market Committee, staff economists from the district banks report on consumer spending, new construction, prices and wages, interest rates, manufacturing productivity and investment, and other indicators of the state of the economy. Due to the differences in economic bases, one district may be experiencing difficulty while another may be flourishing. Agricultural regions may be hard hit by severe weather conditions at the same time that inflation is creeping into manufacturing regions unable to find enough skilled workers. It is the goal of the Federal Reserve System to balance the overall economic health of the nation.

When a consensus emerges about the direction of the economy and whether intervention is needed, the FOMC has several interrelated tools that they can use to adjust the money supply. In so doing, they attempt to move the market in the desired direction.

Open market operations   As the central bank for the United States, the Federal Reserve holds currency and acts as the sales agent for government debt, called treasury notes or bonds. The Fed buys and sells these securities in order to adjust the supply of money in the economy. These transactions are called open market operations. The Fed buys and sells to private investors, banks, mutual fund managers, and others who are interested in holding treasury securities. If the economy is expanding too rapidly and the Fed is concerned about inflation it will sell treasury bonds. By selling bonds, it is taking cash out of the system. When a bank buys bonds it has transferred money to the Federal Reserve, which means that it does not have the cash available to lend. By soaking up excess cash in the economy, the Fed is attempting to decrease the amount of lending that takes place, thus cutting consumption and bringing demand-pull inflation under control.

If the economy is in a recession, the Fed buys treasury bonds. The Fed has added money or liquidity to the economy by exchanging an income-producing bond for cash, which must be invested in order for the bank to earn revenue. Investment, in this case, means that the bank will originate loans, which will spur consumption, hopefully creating more jobs and growth in the economy.

Changing the reserve requirement   Banks are required to keep a certain percentage of their deposits on reserve, that is, in their account at the Federal Reserve Bank. **Reserve requirements** vary depending on the nature of loans that the bank is making. As the risk level of the bank's loan portfolio increases, the level of reserves that the bank is required to keep also increases. The Federal Reserve has the authority to adjust the percentage of each type of reserves that the bank must hold. Therefore, if the Federal Reserve felt that banks were making too many home mortgages with low or no down payment, the Fed could increase the reserves required for each dollar of home mortgage lending the bank held. When the reserve requirement is raised, money is taken out of the economy

---

The Tools of the Federal Reserve System

- Open market operations
    Buy or sell treasury bills, notes, or bonds
- Change the reserve requirement
    Lower or raise the amount of money financial institutions need to keep on deposit at their Federal Reserve Bank
- Change the discount rate
    Raise or lower the cost of borrowing for financial institutions

---

The tools of the Federal Reserve System. *(http:www.federalreserve.gov/otherfrb.ht)*

In the News

Although the Federal Reserve Banks do buy and sell treasury bonds, they are not the only bond traders. Many bond-trading firms buy and sell corporate and government bonds on behalf of corporations, mutual fund companies, pension funds, and institutional and private investors. Bond-trading firms typically settle their trades using banks to transfer funds between buyer and seller.

After the September 11, 2001, attack on the World Trade Center, some of the funds transfers were interrupted due to damage to the communication infrastructure. In order to maintain an orderly flow of capital and to maintain the stability of an already shaken financial community, the Fed stepped in to purchase all government securities offered for sale on the Thursday and Friday immediately following the attack. During those two days, $151.45 billion of bonds were purchased by the Federal Reserve.

The Federal Reserve provided immediate liquidity to the financial markets and averted widespread panic. In so doing, it maintained the stability of the country's financial system.

Source: Wall Street Journal, October 18, 2001.

---

and held on account at the Federal Reserve. It is no longer available to the bank for use in originating new loans. If reserve requirements were lowered, the opposite would happen—more money would become available for loans.

In practical terms, adjusting the reserve requirements is an awkward way of managing the money supply. There are many types of deposits, each with its own set of reserve requirements, and many thousands of depository institutions. It is far more elegant to modify reserves through open market transactions. Imagine, the amount of money on deposit in the form of reserves can stay constant (as a percentage of deposits) and the Fed can add to those reserves by selling treasury bonds. Each additional unit of treasury debt that a bank buys goes into the bank's account at the Federal Reserve, just as a higher level of reserves would be deposited. Buying bonds reduces the amount held on account at the Fed, in essence reducing the "reserved" assets of the banking community. The decision to buy or sell bonds can be made more quickly than an across-the-board change in the reserve requirement, giving the Fed a more potent tool to adjust the money supply.

Changing the discount rate   Although banks are required to keep a specified amount on reserve, sometimes they fall short. When they do, the Federal Reserve Bank will cover their shortfall, something like the overdraft protection you have on your checking account. A bank may fall short for several reasons. Its inflow of money may not equal the outflow for that day. If the dominant employer in town pays employees on Thursday evening, a disproportionate amount of cash may be drawn out of the bank on Friday—bills are being paid, groceries purchased, and cash withdrawn in anticipation of weekend activities. The amount of money in the bank's reserves may slip below the required amount by close of business Friday. This is not to say that the bank is unstable. Loan payments will be received at the beginning of the next week and bills paid by employees on Friday will be deposited back into the bank on Monday or Tuesday by local vendors. Friday night's shortfall is a cash flow issue. Rather than keep too much idle cash on hand, banks may choose to borrow from the Federal Reserve overnight, knowing that their reserves will be back in balance by Monday.

A bank may also make a strategic decision that causes it to dip into its reserves. The bank may choose to issue a loan to one of its long-standing clients. The amount of the loan may exceed the amount that the bank truly has available to lend on the day that the funds are disbursed. However, the banker knows that the bank can cover the shortfall in a short period of time, even days, through the normal course of its operations. In addition, the banker knows that the customer has excellent credit and has borrowed money in the past with no repayment difficulties. The new loan will be repaid in specific increments, with an attractive rate of interest. If the value of the loan is important, both in terms of the interest earned and the continuation of a business relationship, the bank may choose to go ahead and make the loan even if it causes the reserve account to be temporarily out of balance.

Whether or not the loan makes good business sense, Federal Reserve rules require that each financial institution has its reserves fully funded. If the amount in the bank's Federal Reserve account has fallen below the required level of reserves, the bank will have to take out a loan. These short-term loans can come from one of two places: another bank or the Federal Reserve itself. If another bank has excess in its reserves, it can lend its excess and earn what is called the **federal funds rate**. Lending is between the two banks, with the Federal Reserve facilitating the automatic transfer from one account to the other and the subsequent collection of interest from the borrower bank. The other way to cover the shortfall is for the bank to borrow from the Federal Reserve. In that case, the interest paid by the bank to the Federal Reserve is called the **discount rate**.

The Federal Reserve's Open Market Committee sets targets for the discount rate and the federal funds rate. The discount rate is usually slightly lower than the federal funds rate, but both can be understood as the interest rate that banks pay for loans. With that as a benchmark, banks will adjust their commercial and consumer lending rates accordingly. Soon after a change in the discount rate, banks will adjust the **prime rate**, the interest rate that is charged to the most creditworthy borrowers. The prime rate is an indicator of the direction of corporate and consumer lending rates. Variable interest rate loans are often quoted as "prime plus" some percent.

When the Federal Reserve is worried about inflation, it raises the discount rate. A higher discount rate causes banks to increase their lending rates and increases the cost of any goods that are financed. It may also make it difficult for consumers or companies with poor financial resources to get credit at all. Spending will slow, thus easing upward pressure on prices.

During a recession, the Federal Reserve wants to encourage an increase in spending, so they reduce the discount rate. Banks usually follow the Fed's lead and reduce their prime lending rate. Although the purchase price of goods remains the same, the actual cost decreases due to lower interest costs. The lower interest rates spur spending, which pulls the economy out of recession.

< **In the News** >

As we saw earlier in the chapter, fiscal policy was not enough to pull the economy out of recession during 2001. Many consumers used their tax rebate to pay down debt or add to savings, which was not the economic stimulus that Congress had intended. After the September 11 attacks, consumer confidence fell further and the economy actually contracted in the third quarter of 2001.

The Federal Reserve used the discount rate to attempt to stimulate the economy, cutting the rate a total of 11 times during 2001, and pushing the real rate of interest below zero.

The real rate of interest is the difference between the market interest rate and inflation or the rate of increase in the economy. By the end of 2001, the economy was expected to grow at an annual rate of 2%, with the Fed Funds rate set at 1.75% and the discount rate set at 1.25%, which resulted in a slightly negative real rate of interest.

Although the mission of the Federal Reserve System is to provide the country with a safe, stable, and flexible monetary and financial system, managing the money supply is not the end of the Fed's responsibilities.

Supervise and Regulate Banking Institutions and Protect the Credit Rights of Consumers

The Federal Reserve sets standards for the safe operation of financial institutions. These standards can be expressed in the form of regulations, rules, or guidelines. Some of the regulations are specific provisions under laws passed by Congress. Many of the laws are a result of the turmoil associated with the savings and loan crisis in the 1980s when many banking institutions suffered serious losses. Other regulations are a result of policy guidelines and interpretations of the laws. Both types of regulation are administered by the Federal Reserve.

Banks do not make money unless they lend their deposits. There will always be some risk of default when money is loaned, but you cannot predict which loans will default. If you could do that, you wouldn't transact the loan. A certain level of loss is unavoidable, but if a bank demonstrates a pattern of poor loans or a deteriorating financial condition, the Federal Reserve will help develop a plan to correct the problems. If problems persist, the Federal Reserve has enforcement powers that include the right to remove directors or officers of the bank and assess fines.

The Federal Reserve also monitors the level of reserves a bank keeps and whether it is consistently violating the reserve requirement. We discussed earlier that banks are allowed to borrow to cover short-term reduction in reserves and may even choose to dip below the required level. The occasional use of Fed Funds is acceptable. If the bank cannot seem to keep its reserves funded, the Federal Reserve may intervene.

In addition to its role in protecting the integrity of the financial system, the Fed has been given the responsibility to protect the banking and credit rights of the public. In Chapter 5, we will look at the effect of bank mergers and acquisitions that have resulted in "megabanks." Before a bank merger can be completed, the Federal Reserve examines the effects of the merger. They assess the financial and personnel resources of the proposed combination along with its effect on the communities it serves. If the merger would result in reduced banking competition or reduced levels of access to banking services, the Federal Reserve can block the merger or require that certain assets be sold to another bank.

Banks provide many services to their clients. The Federal Reserve protects the credit rights of consumers and provides information on vehicle leasing, credit cards, home mortgages, home equity loans, and other types of credit. It writes and interprets regulations that carry out many of the consumer protection laws such as the Fair Housing Act of 1968 and the Equal Credit Opportunity Act (1974). These acts, and others, prohibit discrimination in lending. The Federal Reserve Banks monitor and investigate consumer complaints and concerns about lending practices or banking policies in their region.

Each Federal Reserve Bank has a community affairs officer whose role is to facilitate communication between banking institutions, government agencies, and community groups. The Federal Reserve Banks promote investment in community development by both private and public organizations.

Maintain the Stability of the Financial System

Banking institutions are only a small part of the overall financial system in this country. Corporations such as General Motors have finance subsidiaries that provide loans to new-car buyers at the dealership. Department store charge cards extend credit (loans) to customers and can be used to finance major purchases. Savings and retirement funds are flowing into the stock market. Each of these is a part of the financial system over which the Federal Reserve has no direct control. How, then, can the Fed maintain financial stability?

The Fed influences these transactions by ensuring that there is liquidity in the market. When the Fed tightens the money supply, General Motors will have to make an internal allocation decision: Do we use the cash flow we have to invest in new equipment or to provide more loans to our consumers? Because there is now a more scarce resource, General Motors will have to determine where it can earn the most return on its available cash.

The stock market did not seem entirely rational during the 1990s, but even it is sensitive to the decisions made by the FOMC. When the cost of money increases (the discount rate is raised), stock prices tend to level out or fall. Investors are concerned about the effects of increased interest costs and perhaps reduced revenues (due to decreased consumer spending) on the profits of the companies whose stock trades on the exchanges. When the stock market weakened in early 2001, the Fed began a series of interest rate cuts. The rate cuts were intended to lower the cost of borrowing, which was designed to stimulate the economy and increase consumption, which in turn would allow companies to sell goods, keep workers employed, further increase consumer confidence, and help push stock prices up. Whew!

Provide Certain Types of Financial Services to the U.S. Government, the Public, Domestic Financial Institutions, and Foreign Governments

The Federal Reserve System functions on two levels: it sets major monetary policy objectives and implements them through open market activities and adjustment of the discount rate. It also provides a wide range of services that facilitate the day-to-day functioning of our banking and economic systems.

In the next section, we will look more closely at some of the financial services that the 12 individual Federal Reserve Banks provide to member banks such as supplying bills and coins to member banks, facilitating electronic funds transfers, and providing check processing. All of the services are similar to the services that you require of your local banker. And, like your local bank, the Federal Reserve also offers a sort of safe deposit box.

The Federal Reserve Bank of New York has a vault that contains the largest concentration of monetary gold in the world. Gold ingots are stacked in locked cages, each numbered to represent its owner. Heavy gold bars can be transferred from one cage to another when payments are made between countries. Many of the gold bars were brought to the Federal Reserve for safekeeping during any one of the many wars that have torn countries apart. They are kept closely guarded and not even the attendants know which cage belongs to which country.

The Federal Reserve Bank of New York, on behalf of the Federal Reserve System, provides a number of banking services to foreign governments and international institutions.

Checks drawn on U. S. banks and denominated in U.S. dollars are sent by foreign banks to the New York Fed for collection. The funds are transferred to the foreign banks' accounts at the New York Fed. Foreign banks can also deposit U. S. currency into these accounts. When the bank needs currency, the Federal Reserve will either ship the notes or make arrangements for the currency to be picked up at the New York Fed Bank.

The New York Federal Reserve Bank buys and sells treasury and other securities on behalf of foreign central banks and international institutions. The Federal Reserve does not provide investment advice but will facilitate the sale or purchase on behalf of foreign banks.

Finally, the New York Federal Reserve, acting on the instructions of the FOMC and the U. S. Treasury, buys and sells international currency.

The primary focus of the Federal Reserve System is to maintain the stability of the U. S. economy. However, since financial markets have become increasingly interconnected, the Federal Reserve does act in response to international financial events as well. For example, if European interest rates are significantly higher than American rates, investors would sell U.S. treasury notes in favor of investing at a higher rate of return in Europe. If too much investment capital is left, it would cause a reduction in the funds available to American businesses, pushing up the cost of the increasingly scarce funds. The increase in interest rate costs would begin to fuel inflation, leading the Federal Reserve to push the discount rate higher. The higher rate would be more attractive to international borrowers, thus encouraging them to reenter the American market and providing increased borrowing capacity. Therefore, although the Federal Reserve was not directly reacting to the level of European interest rates, those rates would have triggered a chain of economic reactions that could cause the Fed to act.

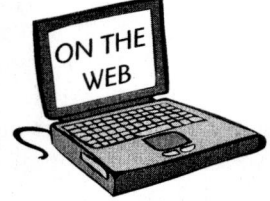

The Federal Reserve System provides a wealth of information on its main Web site (*www.federalreserve.gov*) along with links to the individual district banks. On the main Web site you will find general information on the purposes and functions of the Federal Reserve System, biographies of the members of the Board of Governors, press releases, and testimony and speeches by members of the Federal Reserve Board. You can also access economic research and papers written by economists at the various district banks.

Consumer credit information is available at the main Web site along with information about community affairs programs sponsored by the Federal Reserve.

The district banks maintain their own Web sites, which offer a wealth of economic information and educational resources.

THE ROLE OF THE 12 FEDERAL RESERVE BANKS

The 12 **Federal Reserve Banks** are the operating units of the Federal Reserve system. Several of the district banks have branches that provide services within a smaller geographic area.

The Federal Reserve Banks act as the bank for bankers. A major bank such as Bank of America or Citibank has depositors in many states and around

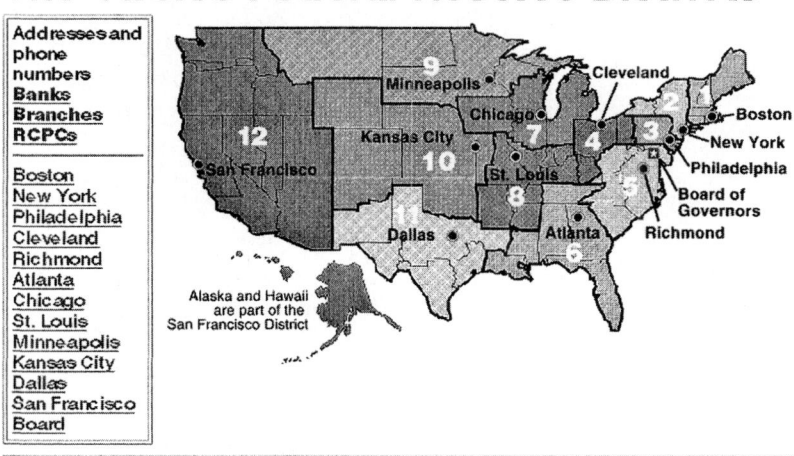

The 12 District Federal Reserve Banks. *(http://www.federalreserve.gov/otherfrb.htms)*

the world, and a system of branches to accommodate those depositors. They need to maintain enough currency on hand to stock ATMs, cash payroll checks, and sell rolls of quarters for lemonade stands. Although these ordinary tasks are critical to the smooth functioning of our economy, many banking transactions are not only these local ones but also involve transfers of money between towns, states, and countries. Individual banks need a banker to facilitate those transactions. Their "banker" is one of the 12 Federal Reserve Banks.

As the banks' banker, the regional Federal Reserve Banks offer the following important services:

1. provide currency services;
2. process checks;
3. facilitate electronic funds transfers;
4. transfer reserves between banks;
5. perform regional economic analysis;
6. regulate member banks within the region;
7. oversee and enforce consumer credit protection laws; and
8. act as the nation's banker.

Currency Services

Banks deposit their unneeded cash into their Federal Reserve account and withdraw it when demand for cash increases. The need for cash on hand at bank branches varies by season and even by the day of the month. More cash is needed on paydays and during the Christmas holidays as people withdraw money from their own accounts. Logically more cash would be required on Friday than, let's say, a Wednesday. Since most banks are not open on Saturdays and Sundays, an increased quantity of cash is required in order to stock the automatic teller machine in advance of weekend withdrawals.

The Federal Reserve Banks and their branches sort and count the money they receive. Worn or damaged currency is separated and destroyed. One-dollar bills, which see the most handling, usually wear out within 12 to 18 months. As the bills are counted, they are also checked to make sure that no counterfeit currency is put into circulation. Bills are bundled into stacks of 100 and stored in secure vaults until needed. The Federal Reserve Banks also distribute new coins and bills prepared by the U.S. Mint and Bureau of Engraving and Printing.

Each Federal Reserve Bank receives newly printed currency directly from the Bureau of Engraving and Printing. A letter and a number appearing on the left side of the portrait, below the serial number, indicate which Federal Reserve Bank authorized the initial distribution of the currency. The number designates the Federal Reserve district, with the corresponding letter of the alphabet preceding it, as shown in the table.

Boston	A1	Chicago	G7
New York	B2	St. Louis	H8
Philadelphia	C3	Minneapolis	I9
Cleveland	D4	Kansas City	J10
Richmond	E5	Dallas	K11
Atlanta	F6	San Francisco	L12

⟨ **Just For Fun** ⟩

Where did your money originate?

Each piece of paper currency bears a mark that indicates where the bill originated. On the older bills, the letter appears inside a seal on the left side of the face of the bill. The letter indicates the district bank that issued the note and the circular seal contains the name of the bank that issued the Federal Reserve Note. On the newer bills, the letter and number designation appears on the left side of the bill, immediately below the serial number.

I live in the region served by the San Francisco Federal Reserve Bank. Any currency issued from "my" bank would have an L12 on the face of the bill. However, as I type this, the bills in my wallet come from New York (B2), Cleveland (D4), Richmond (E5), St. Louis (H8), Kansas City (J10), and Dallas (K11), as well as San Francisco.

Process Checks

Not all transactions are made with cash. Many of the exchanges we make are paid for with checks that we give to local merchants or send thousands of miles away. Most of the time the bank on which the check is drawn is not the same in which it is deposited. The Federal Reserve Banks are responsible for processing billions of checks per year and settling accounts between banks.

Here's how the system works. I have a checking account at a bank in Olympia, Washington. During the Christmas shopping season, I order from a company that is headquartered in Miami, Florida, and send a check in payment. Miami is about as far from Olympia as you can get, but they will still take my check in payment for the merchandise. The company deposits my check into their bank account. Their bank sends my check to the Federal Reserve Bank in Atlanta, Georgia, or one of its branches (in this case, probably the branch in Miami) where it is sorted along with the other checks received. The code on the bottom of my check is read by the sorter and payment is transferred from my bank's account at the Federal Reserve Bank of San Francisco to the Miami bank's account at the Federal Reserve Bank of Atlanta. The transfer between the two banks is done electronically even though I issued the piece of paper that authorized the transfer. The Federal Reserve Bank in Atlanta sends the check back to my bank, which deducts the amount from my account.

The Federal Reserve Banks are performing the same service for my bank that it does for me—facilitating the transfer of assets so that I do not have to go in person, cash in hand, to make every purchase transaction.

Facilitate Electronic Funds Transfers

The Federal Reserve Banks also operate Fedwire, which allows the electronic transfer of payments between participating financial institutions. This system is used for batch transactions such as direct deposit of payroll checks and automatic payment of mortgages. The electronic transfers take the place of checks and allow customers from one region of the country to make transfer payments to banks in other regions without issuing checks.

Money moves from my account in Olympia to Miami by mail however settlement is handled electronically by the Federal Reserve Bank of Atlanta and the Federal Reserve Bank of San Francisco.

Transfer Reserves Between Banks

As we discussed earlier, banks and other depository institutions are required to keep reserves on account in specified proportions depending on the types of deposits they hold. The reserves are held in an account at the Federal Reserve Bank and cannot be loaned out. If the bank exceeds its lending capacity and reduces its reserves below the minimum level, the Federal Reserve Bank will transfer reserves from another member bank's account to cover the shortfall. The Federal Reserve Bank charges interest to the borrowing institution and credits the lending institution.

Perform Regional Economic Analysis

Another important task that the local Federal Reserve Banks perform is to analyze the economic conditions within their region. Although the U. S. economy is well integrated, each region of the country reacts differently to economic influences. For example, banks in the Dallas Federal Reserve district were significantly affected by the drop in oil prices in the 1980s. As oil prices fell and oil workers were laid off, lending institutions were unable to collect on mortgages and other loans. Newspapers in Dallas wrote stories about people who left their house keys in the mailbox or under the doormat and simply walked away from their homes. Bank reserves were depleted by nonperforming loans and the inability of lending institutions to sell abandoned properties for the amount of the remaining loan. On the other hand, lower petroleum prices benefited some manufacturers, therefore, the Cleveland and Chicago districts, which include several traditional industrial regions, were not as severely affected.

Each Federal Reserve Bank prepares an economic analysis that is presented to the Board of Governors and the Federal Open Market Committee at their meetings. Using data collected by the district banks, the FOMC comes to a conclusion about the direction of the economy and whether there is a need for shifts in monetary policy.

Regulate Member Banks Within the Region

The Federal Reserve Banks employ bank examiners who audit the operations of member banks to ensure that they are in compliance with federal banking laws and regulations. The bank examiners also check the level of risk in the bank's loan portfolio. If the bank is out of compliance or is carrying greater risk than the Federal Reserve Bank believes is wise, the Fed can call for corrective action to be taken. In the event that the Federal Reserve Bank believes that the member bank's operations could cause financial instability, the Fed has the power to remove the officers of the bank and seek reorganization.

Oversee and Enforce Consumer Credit Protection Laws

Congress has passed several consumer protection laws that cover fair lending practices. The Federal Reserve Banks are responsible for monitoring compliance with this legislation. Bank examiners can ask to see mortgage lending records to ensure that banks are not practicing redlining—refusing to make loans based on the neighborhood rather than the creditworthiness of the prospective borrower. They review interest rates for evidence of predatory pricing or other discriminatory practices. The Federal Reserve also investigates complaints registered against member banks for violations of consumer protection laws.

Act as the Nation's Banker

The Federal Reserve Bank handles banking tasks for the government. The U.S. Treasury maintains accounts with the Federal Reserve, which it uses to deposit payments such as the quarterly transfer of payroll taxes withheld, corporate income taxes, and unemployment premiums. In addition, local Federal Reserve Banks process millions of dollars worth of checks issued by the federal government such as income tax refund checks and payments to vendors. The Federal Reserve Banks redeem food stamps, issue and redeem U.S. savings bonds, and sell treasury bills and notes directly to the public.

Although the Federal Reserve System is not a profit-making entity, it does charge fees to member banks for its services. The fees cover the Fed's operating costs and any excess is returned to the United States Treasury as income.

THE TRUE POWER OF THE FEDERAL RESERVE

By buying or selling bonds, the Fed signals that there is too much or too little money in the economy. By raising and lowering the discount rate, the Federal Reserve signals that the existing level of lending is not supporting stable growth. Most of the success of the Federal Reserve hinges upon the signals it gives rather than its actual ability to soak up money or provide all the liquidity the country requires.

Although it is required to meet four times per year, since 1980 the Federal Open Market Committee has been meeting eight times per year. Before each

Stop and Think

If the Fed is the nation's banker, what does the U. S. Department of Treasury do?

The Treasury Department (www.ustreas.gov) is a Cabinet office, part of the executive branch of the government. The Secretary of the Treasury assists the President in developing and implementing domestic and international financial, economic, and tax policy. Like the members of the Federal Reserve Board of Governors, the Treasury Secretary is appointed by the President and confirmed by the Senate, however, as a member of the executive branch, he or she continues to serve at the pleasure of the President. The cabinet departments do not have the same continuity over time that the Board of Governors does. The Secretary of the Treasury is actively involved with setting international and domestic policy and represents the United States at international economic meetings. Past Secretaries of Treasury have negotiated loan packages and restructured international debt for countries who faced economic turmoil, as well as worked with representatives of other nations to stabilize and expand the world's economy.

However, most of the responsibility of the Treasury Department is to manage the day-to-day transactions involved in running the government. Operating bureaus carry out the specific tasks of the department. For example, the Internal Revenue Service is responsible for collecting internally generated funds such as personal and corporate income taxes and Social Security payments. The U. S. Customs Service, another bureau, was originally established to collect duties and taxes on imported merchandise. That task has been expanded to include checking for drug trafficking at U. S. ports of entry. Some of the bureaus that currently report to the Secretary of the Treasury may be reassigned if a cabinet-level Department of Homeland Security is established.

The Treasury Department is responsible for creating, but not issuing, money. The Bureau of Engraving and Printing (*www.bep.treas.gov*) designs and manufactures currency (bills). They also design and manufacture postage stamps, revenue stamps, and customs stamps, all of which produce revenue for the government. The U. S. Mint, a different bureau, produces coins. From 1999 through 2008, the U.S. Mint (*www.usmint.gov*) will issue five new quarters a year honoring each of the states of the Union. These quarters are legal currency but they also create an interesting revenue source for the government: the minting and selling of uncirculated quarters as collectibles.

meeting, staff representatives from the district banks send economic reports and analysis to the members of the committee. Many of the Federal Reserve Banks publish economic reports and research in journals or make their findings accessible through their Web sites. Given the Fed's goal of maintaining a stable economy, these reports can give an indication of what the Board of Governors might do to direct the economy.

Members of the Board of Governors routinely meet with Treasury Department officials and the President's Council of Economic Advisors to assess the direction of the economy. They also meet with representatives of banking industry groups, members of Congress, academicians, and representatives from foreign banks and other central banks.

Federal Reserve officials give direction to the economy through speeches to industry groups or testimony before Congress. If a member of the Board of Governors addresses a meeting of bankers and chides the industry for lax lending rules that have led to high rates of default, you can bet that the Fed will be scrutinizing bank loans more closely and perhaps selectively increasing reserve requirements for banks whose loan portfolios indicate higher levels of risk. If a member of Congress asks the Chairman of the Federal Reserve what he thinks about a tax cut, the Chairman's opinions will carry weight. Remember that tax cuts are fiscal policy and tend to move through the economy slowly. The Chairman's words, reported that night on the evening news, will immediately provide a signal or an indication of the direction the Fed believes the economy should go.

THE ROLE OF THE CHAIRMAN OF THE BOARD

As the Chairman of the Federal Reserve System, Alan Greenspan's words are closely analyzed. Much to the dismay of headline writers, Greenspan has a reputation for speaking in convoluted sentences full of multisyllabic words. Greenspan's speech in early summer 1995 prompted a flurry of contradictory headlines. Some newspapers reported that Greenspan would support an interest rate cut, others, after reading or hearing the same speech, said that rates would remain unchanged. The February 7, 2000, edition of *Business Week* published an article entitled "Greenspan for Greenhorns: How to Decode the Moves of the Fed and its Chairman." Why so much interest in the words of one man?

If the main power of the Federal Reserve lies in its ability to signal the direction that the economy should take, Greenspan, as head of the Federal Reserve System, articulates the signals. Unlike his predecessors, Greenspan is willing to talk publicly about the economy before the Federal Reserve makes its monetary policy decisions. Through testimony to Congress and speeches to industry groups, Greenspan is able to voice concerns about the economy, as he did in December 1996 when he lamented the "irrational exuberance" that was leading to dramatic increases in stock prices. After that speech the stock market retreated, at least temporarily. In 2001, Greenspan attempted to calm stock markets by pointing out that productivity gains, which had led to the 10-year economic expansion, had not all been realized. He stated that profits, which had slipped, would rebound as corporations found even more efficiencies through the use of technology.

Alan Greenspan has been on the Board of Governors of the Federal Reserve since 1987. He presided over the longest economic expansion in recent memory and was in charge of the Fed when it acted decisively to mitigate instability in the financial system after the terrorist attacks. His power derives not only from his economic expertise but from the relationships he has been able to forge with bankers, policy makers, politicians, and the American public during his years on the Board of Governors. It will be interesting to see how the role of the chairman changes when Greenspan's term on the board ends.

Book Report

Alan Greenspan has been the subject of several books. In *The Greenspan Effect: Words That Move the World's Markets* (McGraw-Hill, New York, 1999), David B. Scilia and Jeffrey L. Cruikshank analyze Greenspan's writings and speeches and claim to help investors separate rhetoric from signals as to the direction the economy will take.

Two recent biographies attempt to illuminate Greenspan's influence on monetary policy and the American economy during the last two decades. *Maestro: Greenspan's Fed and the American Boom* (Simon and Schuster, New York, 2000) was written by Bob Woodward who knows Washington (D.C.) politics and describes Greenspan's career from the October 1987 stock market crash until the late 1990s.

Greenspan: The Man Behind Money (by Justin Martin, Perseus, New York, 2000) is a biography of Greenspan that begins before his emergence as an influential policy maker.

Few central bankers have had as profound an effect on the American economy as Greenspan has had, which is reflected by the fact that these are only three of the many books that attempt to profile the man. Although Greenspan does not possess the individual wealth and power that J. P. Morgan had, the fascination is still as intense.

Sources: Business Week, October 25, 1999, p. 162; and *Business Week*, December 4, 2000, pp. 23–24.

OTHER CENTRAL BANK SYSTEMS

In Chapter 3, we talked about the euro, the currency that was created to reduce trade and financial barriers between the independent countries in Europe. Monetary policy in the euro zone is determined by the **European Central Bank** and the national central banks of the countries that have adopted the euro. The European Central Bank (ECB) and the national central banks (NCBs) are collectively referred to as the "Eurosystem." Members of the European Union (an economic and trade organization) who have not adopted the euro as their currency conduct their domestic monetary policies independent of the decisions of the Eurosystem.

The primary objective of the Eurosystem is to maintain price stability within the euro's region. The basic tasks enumerated by the European Central Bank are

1. to define and implement the monetary policy of the euro area;
2. to conduct foreign exchange operations;

3. to hold and manage the official reserves of the Member States; and
4. to promote the smooth operation of payment systems.

The tasks are virtually identical to the goals of the Federal Reserve System.

As we saw with the 12 Federal Reserve districts, individual regions of Europe will respond differently to international economic stimuli based on the composition of their economies. In addition to common external influences, each member country has its own political environment, historic business customs and practices, and existing labor laws. The rate of potential productivity improvement is greater in Spain than it is in Germany where labor unions have significant political and legal power. Labor shortages are exacerbated in countries whose domestic policies limit immigration or restrict the ability of foreigners to obtain work visas. A country within the euro zone whose economy is lagging has lost its ability to apply monetary policy unilaterally.

Since the end of World War II, the German central bank, the Bundesbank, has emerged as a powerful financial institution in Europe. Along with the Bank of London, the Bundesbank has provided economic stability and an example of prudent money management. Germany has accepted the euro and, as a result, has ceded some of its decision-making authority to the ECB. The Bundesbank remains the banker's bank for credit institutions in Germany and acts on behalf of the federal government, just as the Federal Reserve System does. Until January 1, 2002, when euro banknotes and coins were issued, the Bundesbank also issued currency. That responsibility passed to the ECB when euro currency became available. The Bundesbank, like other national central banks, will become analogous to the district Federal Reserve Banks, which provide input to the Governing Board but do not act independently in setting monetary policy.

One of the factors that impedes a country's economic growth and development is the absence of a strong, disciplined central banking system. Without the ability to set stable monetary policy and provide transaction services to local banks, countries cannot develop economies that are fully integrated into the international market.

Without a strong, independent central banking system, a country's economy is more subject to political cronyism, severe economic swings, and limited ability to borrow on the international market. Private sector banks—free from central bank oversight—can open for business, accept deposits, and make preferential loans to bank directors. Without required reserves to back their loans, banks are more susceptible to failure. The lack of check processing facilities and electronic funds transfer procedures reduces the flow of money within the country and limits the ability to transact business internationally.

Governments without an independent central bank have the ability to print and then issue money to cover government expenditures; however, simply printing and issuing new money without corresponding growth in production leads to hyperinflation, soaring interest rates, and a decrease in the exchange rate of the currency. Unless currency trades within a predictable range, it will not be attractive to investors. Without a strong internal banking system, international lenders will require borrowers to repay loans in hard currency (such as the English pound, the euro, the Japanese yen, or American dollars).

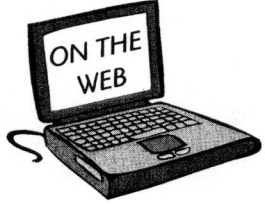

You can visit the European Central Bank (www.ecb.int), the German Central Bank (*www.bundesbank.de/en/*), and the Bank of Russia (*www.cbr.ru/eng/*) on-line. It is interesting to compare the purposes and functions of each bank. The ECB and Bundesbank appear to be very similar to the Federal Reserve, both in structure and in mission.

The Bank of Russia provides a brief history of the Central Bank of the Russian Federation (its official name), which was created in November 1991 along with the Commonwealth of Independent States, the successor to the Union of Soviet Socialist Republics (USSR). The State Bank of the USSR was disbanded in December 1991 and its assets transferred to the new Bank of Russia. The bank is comprised of 25 structural units, among them Research and Information, Payment Systems and Settlements Department, and the Open Market Operations Department.

Financial data available from the Bank of Russia include the bank's balance sheet by month. The bank also posts its annual reports, however, these are less current.

TERMS TO KNOW

Fiscal policy	Federal Open Market	Federal funds rate
Monetary policy	Committee (FOMC)	Discount rate
Federal Reserve	Open market	Prime lending rate
System	operations	Federal Reserve Bank
Board of Governors	Reserve requirement	European Central Bank

TERM PAPERS AND PROJECTS

1. What was the role of the Federal Reserve System during the Great Depression? How did it attempt to restore stability to the financial systems?

2. Alan Greenspan, the Chairman of the Federal Reserve System, has been called one of the most influential men in America, if not the world. Why? Greenspan's comments are analyzed for clues to the direction that the economy may go. Follow the public statements of Greenspan and other Fed officials. What are they saying about the economy? What actions does the Federal Open Market Committee take? How do bank interest rates and stock prices react to these actions?

3. Read one of the several excellent books about J. P. Morgan and compare the effect that he had as an individual with that of the Federal Reserve System which was created in response to the Panic of 1907 that Morgan was instrumental in resolving.

4. What actions did the Federal Reserve System take to stabilize the American economy after September 11, 2001? How did they work with other financial institutions and government agencies?

5. What is the governance structure of the European Central Bank? Who holds key positions and what are their educational backgrounds and nationalities? Does nationality matter?
6. Describe the functioning of the European Central Bank. How does the ECB set policy when there are differences in economic strength between its members?

REVIEW QUESTIONS

1. When and why was the Federal Reserve System created? How is it structured?
2. What are the four main duties of the Federal Reserve System? Briefly describe each one.
3. What tools can the Federal Reserve System use to adjust monetary policy?
4. Explain why selling treasury securities slows the economy.
5. What is meant by a cash reserve on account?
6. What is meant by the term *discount rate*?
7. What are the operational duties of the district Federal Reserve Banks?
8. What services do the Federal Reserve Banks provide to member banks?
9. What are the duties of the Treasury Department and how do they differ from the Federal Reserve System?
10. Explain what the European Central Bank does and how it differs from the Bank of England or the Bundesbank of Germany.

CHAPTER

5 | FINANCIAL INSTITUTIONS

LEARNING OBJECTIVES

1. Describe the difference between depository and nondepository financial institutions.

2. Give examples of each type of financial institution.

3. Describe the difference between asset-based lending and cash-flow lending.

4. Describe how banks create money.

5. Differentiate between the two types of pension funds.

6. Discuss the role of international financial institutions.

7. Identify ethical issues in banking and describe their effect on banking institutions.

As we discussed in Chapter 3, idle cash does not earn income. Financial institutions exist to transfer wealth from savers to borrowers. When businesses or consumers have excess cash, they can deposit it in a financial institution such as a bank or credit union, which then makes direct loans to borrowers. Nondepository financial institutions such as insurance companies do not take deposits, however, through their operations they generate sufficient cash to invest in long-term projects. In this chapter we will look at the different types of financial institutions and their function within an economy.

DEPOSITORY FINANCIAL INSTITUTIONS

The simplest way to understand depository financial institutions is to ask whether there is a specific account with your name on it that you can add to or withdraw from as you so choose. If the answer to this question is "yes," then you are working with a **depository financial institution.** Lines between banks, savings institutions, and credit unions are blurring as each begins to offer similar products and services. However, there are some differences between them in business purpose and ownership. Some of the differences are

Banks like this one transfer money from savers to borrowers. By pooling the assets of many small depositors, a local bank is able to provide financing to businesses in turn. Loans stimulate the economy, create profits, and improve the standard of living in a community. (Pearson Education/PH College)

related to the important role that each plays in facilitating the transfer of money from savers to borrowers.

Banks

When we think of depository institutions, we first think of banks. In fact, in Chapter 4 on the Federal Reserve, I used the word *bank* to denote any depository financial institution. Technically, a **bank** is a for-profit corporation owned by private investors. The investors can be local businesspeople and community members who buy shares in a local banking corporation or the shares can be traded on one of the large stock exchanges. Bank policies are approved by a Board of Directors, just like any other corporation. The senior managers of the bank can be inside members of the Board of Directors along with outside directors elected by the shareholders.

Commercial banks accept deposits from individual and business customers. They use those deposits to make loans. The interest on the loans provides the banks' revenue, which covers operating costs and profit. Traditionally, banks have offered checking accounts, savings accounts, and special short-term savings accounts such as Christmas Club accounts.

Banks make all sorts of loans—loans that are secured by some form of collateral, as well as unsecured loans such as lines of credit or signature loans. Many banks prefer to tie a large loan to the underlying value of some sort of collateral, whether it is inventory, accounts receivable, or a piece of property or equipment. That banking philosophy is called **asset-based lending.** In the event that the borrower defaults, the bank takes possession of the pledged asset and sells it to recover the balance due on the loan. The difficulty with asset-based

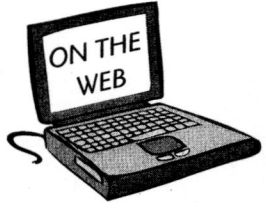

lending is that the loan is dependent on the value of the asset at the time that the loan is made. If for some reason the value of the underlying asset decreases over time, the loan may not be fully collateralized. In addition, bankers are not in the business of selling inventory, collecting accounts receivable, or selling property and equipment. They really do not want to repossess the assets; they want to make performing loans.

Cash-flow lending emphasizes receipts that are generated by the company rather than hard assets that could be seized. In order to become successful using a cash-flow lending strategy, the banker needs to get close to the customer's business and understand the nature of the business, the pattern of cash flows, and intangibles such as the experience and knowledge of the business owner. In many cases, the banker becomes an integral member of the business's financial team, providing advice based on experience gleaned from other organizations to whom the bank has loaned money. In a sense, it is simpler to justify a loan if there is tangible property backing it. However, many long-term banking relationships develop because the banker has been able to see a business's profit potential before the company has many hard assets.

The interest rate charged by banks varies according to the creditworthiness of the borrower. The best borrowers qualify for the prime rate. This rate is often quoted by news media when they discuss the cost of borrowing. When the Federal Reserve adjusts the discount rate, the prime rate tends to move in the same direction by a similar amount. Because not all borrowers qualify for the prime rate, the interest on their loans may be set at prime plus some percent.

All banks must be chartered and deposits insured. Banks can be chartered by the state in which they do business or can be federally chartered. Most banks, regardless of where they are chartered, belong to the Federal Deposit Insurance Corporation (FDIC), which insures accounts up to $100,000 in case the bank fails.

The New "Megabanks"

Banks, like many other businesses, have begun to differentiate their services and try to set themselves apart from their competition. Some banks have decided to increase their size, which allows them access to larger deposits they can lend. The increase in size is also supposed to reduce their overhead costs, leading to efficiencies of scale and the ability to offer a wide range of services to both

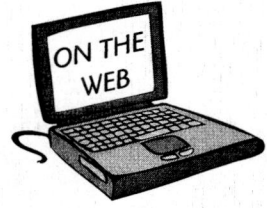

Banking has become very competitive and consumers have turned to the Internet to compare rates around town and across the country.

There are several Web sites that will search for competitive rates, given the borrower's parameters. Business borrowers can turn to www.ibank.com to look for commercial loans in varying amounts. iBank offers access to 160 lenders who are interested in various loans ranging from equipment leasing to lending to marinas or golf courses. According to the Web site, an average of 10 lenders view each loan request and there are an average of 2.7 bids on each request. Note the use of the term *bid*. In a sense, borrowers have put their loans out for auction and will have the opportunity to review various loan offers.

Bankrate, Inc., owns a group of companies that provide an Internet-based source of financial information. Its main site (www.bankrate.com) gives consumers easy access to information about bank services and fees by type of service and location. The site also offers general banking information such as programs that calculate loan payments or help set savings targets based on investment goals. The site also has feature articles on subjects ranging from taxes to personal finance to small business.

Most banks have Web sites, whether they are large interstate banks such as Wells Fargo (www.wellsfargo.com) or Bank of America (www.bankofamerica.com) or smaller local banks such as First Community Bank of Olympia, Washington (www.fcbonline.com) or First National Bank serving West Evanston, Kemmerer, Afton, Mountain View, and Pinedale, Wyoming (www.fnbwest.com). A quick glance at my local phone book showed that all of the banks, even the banks with one or two locations, listed not only the branch phone numbers but an Internet address as well.

Depending on the type of service they have requested, depositors can use the Web site to check balances, make transfers between savings and checking accounts, and pay bills on-line.

Sources: iBank (www.ibank.com); Bankrate, Inc. (www.bankrate.com); Qwest phone directory for Olympia/Lacey/Tumwater, Washington.

business and individual customers. Many of these large banks are headquartered in large cities and are the result of the merger of regional banks. The scale of these new "mega banks" is huge. On September 30, 2001, Bank of America had $339 billion of loans on its balance sheet and deposits of $459.9 billion! Chase, another megabank, claims 30 million individual and small-business customers. Bank One offers retail banking in 14 states and has operations in an additional 19 states and the District of Columbia.

Because of the nature of their services, banks traditionally served businesses and wealthier individuals. Large multistate banking operations are still geared toward that marketplace. One of the criticisms that has emerged from the consolidation of banking is that lending decisions are often made by a faceless banker from out of town who follows policies and procedures rather than getting to know the borrower.

Although the number of independent banks has declined through mergers and acquisitions, there is a market niche for small local banks. First National

> ⟨ **In the News** ⟩
>
> In November 2001, the Native American National Bank opened its first branch office in Browning, Montana. The goal of the bank is to provide lending to tribal governments and personal banking services on Indian reservations. In addition, the bank intends to offer commercial loans in order to stimulate economic growth. The founders of the bank say that Native American tribes are underserved by commercial banks, in part because the banks do not understand the political aspects of tribal government. They believe that the Native American National Bank, by pooling assets from many tribes, will have sufficient capital along with the knowledge of tribal political structure to be able to meet the financial needs of its intended clients.
>
> _Sources:_ The Associated Press, *The Olympian*, Sunday, November 11, 2001; The Associated Press, Great Falls Tribune, Sunday, November 5, 2001.

Bank serves southwest Wyoming with five branches. Their Web page promotes a commitment to the community: "First National Bank is locally owned which means your friends and neighbors sit on our Board of Directors." First Community Bank in Olympia, Washington, uses the slogan "We Belong Together" to emphasize their connection to the local community.

Smaller banks can effectively compete for business by tailoring their loan practices to the local community. The payment structure of an agricultural loan would be far different from the payment structure for the local fast-food franchisee. In addition, local bankers who know their community can make loans based on their knowledge of the past business practices of the potential borrower. If the financial projections meet only the minimum standards that the bank has set for granting a loan, local decision making allows the banker to make a loan based on the applicant's past history of honoring business commitments.

Savings and Loans (Thrifts)

Savings and loan associations, also called thrifts, had a very different mission from banks. They offered savings accounts but not checking accounts, and the loans they issued were primarily home mortgages or other forms of real estate financing. Savings institutions were either corporations or mutual organizations, which meant that by depositing funds in the bank, the depositors owned shares in the institution. Both forms of ownership required that there be an elected Board of Directors.

For many years, savings and loans were restricted in the types of investments they could make and they were insured under their own plan, the Federal Savings and Loan Insurance Corporation (FSLIC). The interest rates paid on passbook savings accounts were tied to the income derived from mortgages and stayed more constant than those of banks. In the 1980s, a period of high interest rates, savings and loans found it difficult to compete for deposits because the rates they could pay were well below the prevailing market rates. Depositors withdrew savings, causing a liquidity problem. Regulations were eased and savings and loans began looking for higher returns by investing a portion of their assets in higher-risk instruments such as junk bonds. Remember that the "return" offered for risk can be either positive (profit) or negative (loss). From 1983 to 1987, many savings and loans failed due to speculative investments and there was not sufficient money in the FSLIC pool to pay all of the depositors. In 1989, Congress passed the Financial Institutions Reform Recovery and Enforcement Act (FIRREA), which oversaw the creation of the Office of Thrift Supervision (OTC), the dismantling of the FSLIC, the transfer of insurance to the FDIC, and restructuring of many failed savings and loan associations.

Read More About It

During the late 1970s and early 1980s, interest rates increased dramatically. Savings and loans earned income by offering mortgages, most of which carried fixed rates over long periods of time. As interest rates climbed, savings and loans lost depositors who could invest their money in safe investments that earned more attractive interest rates.

In order to allow savings and loans or thrifts, to become more competitive, Congress passed a series of bills that loosened reserve requirements and allowed thrifts to pay higher interest rates. That did not change the underlying asset structure—long-term income-producing loans that paid significantly less than thrifts needed to earn in order to offer competitive yields.

With the loosening of reserve requirements, the Congress also allowed savings and loans the opportunity to invest in assets other than long-term real estate loans. Many thrift institutions began to invest in higher-yield but also higher-risk products.

The failure of some of the savings and loan associations was due to the imbalance between low interest mortgages and the need to pay higher deposit interest. However, some thrifts failed due to overly aggressive investment practices, carelessness, lack of internal controls, or simple greed. Many books have been written about that period of banking history including:

Big Money Crime: Fraud and Politics in the Savings and Loan Crisis, by Kitty Calavita, University of California Press, Berkeley, 1997.

Full Faith and Credit: The Great S&L Debacle and Other Washington Sagas, by Lewis William Seidman, Times Books, 1993.

The Big Fix: Inside the S&L Scandal, by James Ring Adams, Wiley, 1990.

Also of interest is the Federal Deposit Insurance Corporation Web site: (www.fdic.gov).

At this point, many of the former savings and loans have kept the name "savings" but become banks that are regulated by the Federal Reserve and state banking commissions and fully insured by the FDIC.

Credit Unions

Unlike banks, which are for-profit institutions with shareholder owners, **credit unions** are owned by their depositors and are not-for-profit institutions. Credit unions are governed by a Board of Directors elected by and drawn from the members of the credit union. Many credit unions were formed by employees of a large organization such as the Washington State Employees Credit Union or the Boeing Employees Credit Union. Originally, credit unions took small deposits and made loans for smaller amounts and shorter maturity periods. Credit union members were often less affluent customers whose financial needs were not met by banks or savings institutions.

Until recently, credit unions were restricted in the length of term they could offer for a loan, which precluded them from granting home mortgages. Now, however, credit unions are allowed to make longer-term loans and the lines between credit unions and banks are blurring. Larger credit unions offer savings accounts, loans, credit and debit cards, foreign currency exchange, and financial advice. An employee can have his paycheck deposited into a credit union account and authorize the credit union to direct a portion of the check toward a home mortgage payment, car payment, and savings account, all held within the credit union.

The main difference that remains between banks and credit unions is that the credit union is owned by its members in direct proportion to the value of their deposits. Each dollar invested in the credit union represents a "share." Because of this structure, some of the terminology for accounts is different. Rather than a checking account, the credit union member has a share draft account. Another word for check is a *draft*, so if you are a credit union member you are writing a draft against the shares you own in the credit union. If you invest in a certificate of deposit, you will earn a set amount of interest. However

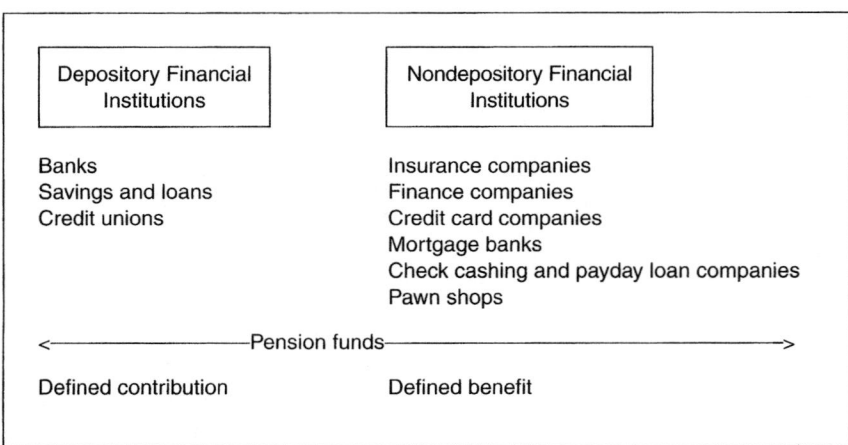

There are two types of financial institutions: depository and nondepository. Pension funds can be either.

Nondepository Financial Institutions **97**

your savings account earns dividends, not interest. The dividends are payments to you, the shareholder, that represent the difference between interest earned on loans and the amount needed to cover operating expenses.

In order to increase their asset base, many smaller credit unions have attempted to expand their membership beyond the original employee group. One method is to offer membership to residents of specific geographic areas where the credit union already operates. This has led to conflicts with local banks that see the not-for-profit status of credit unions as an unfair competitive advantage.

NONDEPOSITORY FINANCIAL INSTITUTIONS

There are a variety of other types of organizations that provide funds to borrowers. These **nondepository financial institutions** do not offer accounts that are owned by or can be withdrawn by a specific account holder.

Insurance Companies

Insurance companies collect a steady stream of cash from policyholders. Although your name is on the policy, you probably do not want to collect from the insurance company. If you receive payment on an auto insurance policy, chances are you've had an accident. If you are the owner of a life insurance policy, it is your beneficiaries who will receive the proceeds. You are not depositing money into a personal account; you are paying a fee in case you need the service that the insurance company provides.

Insurance companies calculate the price of a premium based on their expectation of the amount of cash they will have to pay in claims to all members of the group to which you belong, such as homeowner. For example, for each home that is insured, a certain percentage will suffer some sort of weather-related damage during the year, whether from hail storms, tornadoes, hurricanes, or lightning strikes. The insurance company attempts to calculate the likelihood of damage, although they cannot predict whose home will be affected.

Until the claim is filed, the insurance company receives a steady stream of cash inflows. The cash, like any other cash asset, could earn income if it were put to work. For that reason, insurance companies use the cash they receive from policy payments to invest in other assets. If you are walking near a construction site in a major city, check the list of funding sources. Chances are there is an insurance company listed.

Finance Companies

There are several types of **finance companies.** One of the most familiar is Household Finance along with other consumer debt consolidation companies. Investor owned and capitalized, these consumer credit providers issue a single loan that is used to pay many individual debts. Because individuals often turn to consumer finance companies when they are already burdened by debt and have few, if any, assets to pledge, they are more risky than a traditional bank customer and the finance companies charge higher interest in order to compensate for the increased risk of default.

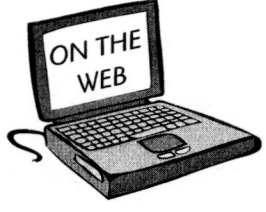

ON THE WEB

> When you think of GE (General Electric), you might think of lightbulbs or refrigerators or even jet engines. But one of the largest and most profitable units of the company is GE Capital.
>
> Check the company's Web site (www.gecfo.com) and you will see the wide variety of financial services that are provided. GE provides real estate financing, equipment financing, factoring of accounts receivable, and even loans to companies that are attempting to reorganize under Chapter 11 bankruptcy rules.

Many automakers have in-house finance companies. Ford Motor Credit and GMAC (General Motors Acceptance Corporation) provide financing that is available through the companies' dealer network. By offering loans at the place of purchase, automakers can encourage buyers who might be sitting on the fence. The interest rates charged by the automakers are not necessarily the same as market interest rates. In order to stimulate sales in the fourth quarter of 2001, automakers offered "0.0%" financing on certain models of cars and trucks. In order to make a profit, the automakers need to balance the income from vehicle sales with the cost of providing free or low-cost financing. When the automaker is able to offer competitive interest rates, providing a convenient financing opportunity allows the company to create profit from the initial sale and from the finance subsidiary.

There are also commercial finance companies that provide business loans. Boeing offers financing to customers who purchase aircraft. GE Capital a finance subsidiary, provides loans to a wide variety of businesses.

Credit Card Companies

In Chapter 3, we said that credit cards are not cash, however, they do facilitate exchange. Companies that issue credit cards are financial institutions. They provide unsecured loans with interest rates ranging from low introductory rates to over 20% as allowed by state law. Credit card companies such as VISA MasterCard, and American Express are funded by the initial capital provided by shareholders and earn income from fees charged to participating merchants and interest owed by consumers.

Some retailers like Sears or Macy's offer their own credit cards. Some retailers choose to collect the accounts receivable. Others have chosen to brand the credit card with their store name but sell the accounts receivable to a separate finance organization that will bill customers and collect the receipts. We will look at the ramifications of offering credit when we discuss working capital management in Chapter 9.

Mortgage Banks

Many of us think of going to a bank or savings and loan for a mortgage, however there are other avenues. Mortgage banks are corporations funded by investor capital, which take no deposits but grant mortgages. Some of the mortgage banks provide financing to customers who otherwise would not qualify for a home loan. In those cases, the interest rate is higher, reflecting the higher risk of missed payments or default.

Pawnshops such as this one offer goods for sale but also promote cash loans. (CORBIS)

Check Cashing Outlets and Payday Loans

Check cashing outlets cash paychecks for people who do not have a traditional savings or checking account. For a fee, the check cashing service will convert a check into cash. Let's say you've come up short of cash and you won't get paid for 3 or 4 days. What do you do now? For many people, taking a loan against their paycheck is the answer. Payday loans are legal in many states and allow the borrower to get a modest sum of cash immediately in return for writing a check to the loan company, dated for the next payday. The loan is not given free of charge, of course. Interest is deducted from the face value of the check at the time of the loan. The customer's check is deposited on the date shown on the face of the check unless the customer returns to the company and refinances the loan. If the loan is rolled over, another fee is charged.

Critics of the payday loan industry claim that fees are excessive and the companies prey on people who should be encouraged to save rather than given the opportunity to take on additional debt at significantly higher than market rates.

PENSION FUNDS

Pension funds can be in either depository or nondepository financial institutions, depending on the structure of the pension. Remember that a depository financial institution is defined as one that ties a certain pool of assets to a specific account holder.

For years, pension funds offered a **defined benefit.** For example, for every year you worked at the Questar Quarry, you would be credited with 2% of your final year's pay. If you started work when you were 18 and retired at 58, the 40 years of service would equate to 80% of your final year's pay as a retirement income. Defined benefit plans could be structured with any type of payment formula that the company and its workers agreed upon. The benefit

Book Report

Fringe Banking: Check-Cashing Outlets, Pawnshops, and the Poor
By John P. Caskey, New York: Russell Sage Foundation, 1994.

This book does not have the outrageous personalities, glamorous wheeling and dealing, and titillating scandals that we have run across in other books about finance. However, Mr. Caskey has done an excellent job of explaining how and why check cashing outlets and pawnshops have become the financial institutions of choice for many poor consumers.

It's easy to see that check cashing outlets provide financial services, however, it is less apparent that a pawnshop is also a financial institution. There is a retail element to pawnshops, to be sure. Items left in pawn that have not been reclaimed within the specified period of time are made available for sale. In addition, some pawnbrokers buy used items outright; the seller has no intention of reclaiming the item but merely wants quick cash.

However, much of a pawnshop's business comes from repeat customers who use the pawnshop as a method of obtaining a short-term loan, using the pawned item as collateral.

In Washington State, interest rates and fees are set by the state. Pawnshops compete on the basis of how much they will lend against pawned items and how courteously they treat their customers, both the borrowers and the retail clientele.

---

would be paid for however many years the retiree lived. If that was 40 more years, then the company would continue the pension, often with cost of living adjustments (COLAs) at regularly scheduled intervals. Once the recipient died, the pension ended.

Most plans allowed the retiree to elect a slightly lower retirement benefit in return for insuring the retiree and his or her surviving spouse for a period equal to the longer of the two lives. However, even with this adjustment, the benefit was defined and the pension was not something that the heirs would inherit.

Defined benefit pension plans are nondepository because the company offering a defined benefit plan is obligated to pay for the entire remaining lifetime, regardless of the value of the contributions made by the employee. There is no direct link between contributions and retirement receipts. Under a defined benefit program, the company is responsible for investing the pension fund assets in such a way to ensure that money will be available to provide benefits to the insured retirees.

Companies have a difficult time controlling the cost of these pension funds. They have incurred a fixed, long-term obligation and there is no certainty of the income that pension investments will earn. In the case of industries that are contracting, there may be fewer workers actively employed than there are retirees. The level of income and productivity that the present workforce has to maintain in order to fund existing pension obligations can be burdensome.

An example of a defined benefit system that is feeling the stresses of a shrinking worker base is Social Security. The Baby Boom generation, which began in 1946, will soon be entering retirement years. The number of Baby Boomers dwarfs the next generation and when added to the increase in life expectancy it will strain the system's financial resources. Some legislators have suggested changing at least part of the Social Security system to a defined contribution plan.

In a **defined contribution** plan, the employee's contribution is defined, not the benefit. The employee and employer each contribute a fixed dollar amount or percent of income into the employee's personal pension account. Once the employer has made its contribution, its responsibilities are nearly at an end. Because the funds now belong to the employee, he or she is responsible for the financial management of the account. In practice, most companies contract with an investment manager or mutual fund company to provide a variety of investment options for its employees. The company can restrict employees to the few funds that its manager has selected or it can allow employees wider latitude. Some plans include financial planning services or access to investment planning seminars or advice from the fund manager.

Regardless of the level of service tied to the pension funds, defined contribution funds are a form of depository financial institution. The amount of income available to the retiree is determined not by years of service but by the amount of contribution, the investment decisions that the employee made, and the life expectancy of the employee.

Unlike a defined benefit plan, there are no guarantees that the defined contribution pension fund will last as long as the contributor lives. However, any residual amount will become part of the contributor's estate upon his or her death and will pass to the heirs.

FINANCIAL INSTITUTIONS AND THE CREATION OF MONEY

It can be argued that the presence of a strong banking system is what allows an economy to grow and develop because banks are the mechanism by which money is created. We have talked about coins and currency and the effect of the Federal Reserve on economic stability, but it is really your local banker (along with other financial institutions) who creates money.

Money can be used as a store of value, and banks offer a convenient place to keep those savings as well as offering interest to depositors. By pooling the assets of small accounts, banks can provide loans to businesses that wish to expand. We can watch the creation of money by setting up

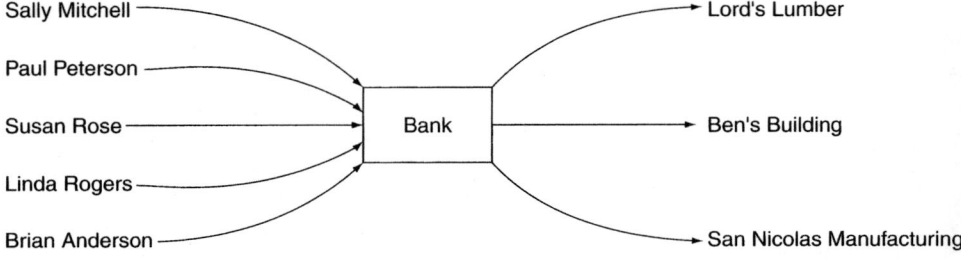

The creation of money. Savers deposit excess funds in the bank, which lends them to businesses and individuals who can use the funds to generate earnings and profits in the economic community.

a very simple economic system with one bank, two merchants, and a single individual saver. We'll set up T-accounts to illustrate the flow of money between the parties.

Hometowne Bank is the only bank in town. It began business with $1,400 invested by shareholders. It has added $400 in the form of deposits to savings accounts, $200 each from Ben's Building Company and Lord's Lumber Company. The total cash on hand is now $600 in currency, and the bank currently has $1,200 in outstanding loans. The cash that the bank holds is offset by the obligation to return that money on demand. Therefore, the savings accounts are a liability to the bank and are listed on the right-hand side of this simple ledger.

HOMETOWNE BANK—1

Cash	$ 600	Ben's Building	$ 200
Loans	$ 850	Lord's Lumber	$ 200
Ben's loan	$ 350	Susan	$ –
		Shareholders' equity	$ 1,400
Total assets	$ 1,800	Total liabilities	$ 1,800

Lord's Lumber Company is a modest-size business. They keep $200 cash on hand to meet their normal operating needs, have $600 in lumber on hand (inventory) and the balance, $200, in a savings account with Hometowne Bank. They finance a portion of their lumber purchases through the use of trade credit. The current balance of their accounts payable is $300 and owner's equity is $700.

LORD'S LUMBER COMPANY—1

Cash	$ 200	Accounts Payable	$ 300
Savings	$ 200	Equity	$ 700
Lumber	$ 600		
Total assets	$ 1,000	Total liabilities	$ 1,000

Ben's Building Company is a small start-up company. Ben currently has $100 in cash and a $200 savings account with Hometowne Bank. He has a truck with an approximate market value of $500 and has $350 left on the truck loan. Until recently, Ben worked for a major homebuilder in the area, but he wants to try his hand at running his own business. He's just signed his first contract but will need a short-term loan of $600 in order to obtain the materials necessary to begin the job.

If Ben were to go to Hometowne Bank right now, there would not be enough cash on hand at the bank to lend to him. Without the loan, Ben will not be able to buy the materials from Lord's Lumber Company. Lord's only makes a profit if they sell lumber, so Ben's lack of financing has affected more than just his own business.

Fortunately, Susan has recently moved to town and wants to open a checking account with $400 cash that she has brought from her previous bank. The cash that Susan adds allows Hometowne to make the loan to Ben's Building Company. Watch the ripple effect of this single transaction:

Susan's deposit shows up as a liability for the bank. Temporarily, Hometowne has $1,000 in cash.

HOMETOWNE BANK—2

Cash	$ 1,000	Ben's Building	$ 200
Loans	$ 850	Lord's Lumber	$ 200
Ben's loan	$ 350	Susan	$ 400
		Shareholders' equity	$ 1,400
Total assets	$ 2,200	Total liabilities	$ 2,200

The Hometowne banker remembers that Ben wants to borrow money, so he quickly calls Ben and arranges the loan. Ben signs the loan papers and is given a check for $600. As long as Ben holds the check, the bank still has $1,000 in cash. But the point of the loan was not for Ben to walk around town with a check in his pocket—he is going to cash it. Once Ben cashes the loan check, the bank's cash position falls back to $400, however, the total value of the bank's loans has increased to $1,800. In this example, we assume that Ben has chosen to withdraw the loan in cash so his savings account is not affected.

HOMETOWNE BANK—3

Cash	$ 400	Ben's Building	$ 200
Loans	$ 850	Lord's Lumber	$ 200
Ben's loans	$ 950	Susan	$ 400
		Shareholders' equity	$ 1,400
Total assets	$ 2,200	Total liabilities	$ 2,200

Ben's balance sheet has also changed. The cash balance has increased along with the loan liability.

BEN'S BUILDING COMPANY—3

Cash	$ 700	Loans	$ 950
Savings	$ 200	Equity	$ 450
Truck	$ 500		
Total assets	$ 1,400	Total liabilities	$ 1,400

At this point, money has not been created, simply moved from a saver, Susan, to a borrower, Ben. It is when Ben buys $600 worth of lumber from Lord's Lumber Company that money is, in essence, created. The transaction reduces Ben's cash to its previous level of $100 and increases his assets in the form of lumber. On Ben's balance sheet, there is merely a transfer of value from one asset to another. However, for Lord's Lumber Company, the sale results in a profit of $150. The lumber that Ben bought for $600 had been purchased by Lord's for $450. Compare the first balance sheet for Lord's with their new statement:

LORD'S LUMBER COMPANY—4

Cash	$ 800	Accounts Payable	$ 300
Savings	$ 200	Equity	$ 850
Lumber	$ 150		
Total assets	$ 1,150	Total liabilities	$ 1,150

Cash has been increased by the full $600 that Ben paid for the lumber, but the lumber account has only been decreased by $450. An additional $150 of value has been created as a result of the transaction. If that value were made tangible, an additional $150 of currency would need to be printed in order to represent the economic growth that took place as a result of the sale.

Since Lord's is in the lumber business, they will reinvest the cash earned from the sale. If they wish to maintain a stable inventory of lumber, they will use $450 to replenish inventory. The desired cash on hand is still $200, so the extra $150 will be deposited into the savings account at Hometowne Bank. Both the bank and the lumber company have experienced an increase in assets.

LORD'S LUMBER COMPANY—5

Cash	$ 200	Accounts Payable	$ 300
Savings	$ 350	Equity	$ 850
Lumber	$ 600		
Total assets	$ 1,150	Total liabilities	$ 1,150

HOMETOWNE BANK—5

Cash	$ 550	Ben's Building	$ 200
Loans	$ 850	Lord's Lumber	$ 350
Ben's loans	$ 950	Susan	$ 400
		Shareholders' equity	$ 1,400
Total assets	$ 2,350	Total liabilities	$ 2,350

We say that Hometowne Bank is responsible for the creation of money because its ability to lend to Ben allowed him to purchase the goods that Lord's Lumber had available for sale. Without access to funds not currently needed by savers, business and personal consumption will take place at a far slower pace.

Chapter 3 posed the following question: If money loses value can it cease to exist? In the case of currency that loses value, the answer is yes. In this chapter, we are now about to see money simply evaporate.

Ben has purchased lumber for use in a building project and has stored it in an outbuilding on his property that also houses his truck. During a particularly fierce thunderstorm, the building is hit by lightning and burns to the ground, destroying most of the contents. My story allows us to destroy this poor businessman's assets in one fell swoop. Look at the effect of the disaster on his balance sheet. The first balance sheet shows Ben's assets before the fire:

BEN'S BUILDING COMPANY—6

Cash	$ 100	Loans	$ 950
Savings	$ 200	Equity	$ 450
Lumber	$ 600		
Truck	$ 500		
Total assets	$ 1,400	Total liabilities	$ 1,400

Ben has $100 cash in his wallet, $200 on account at the bank, and the rest of his assets in the outbuilding. The loans are tied to the truck and lumber, and his personal equity reflects the difference between the asset value and the value of the loans he has assumed.

Now the fire:

BEN'S BUILDING COMPANY—AFTER THE FIRE

Cash	$ 100	Loans	$ 950
Savings	$ 200	Equity	$ 450
Lumber	$ 150		
Truck	$ –		
Total assets	$ 450	Total liabilities	$ 1,400

The first thing you will see is that the balance sheet is no longer in balance. The cash and savings account are unaffected by the fire. Ben was able to salvage some of the lumber, which he believes can be sold for $150, but the truck is a total loss. Those two asset categories have been written down to take into account the loss of value.

Without his truck, Ben cannot complete the project nor does he have enough lumber left. He sees only one choice: he declares bankruptcy and liquidates the remainder of his assets to pay as much of his debt as possible. After selling the lumber and stripping his savings and cash accounts, Ben is left with only $450 to put toward $950 in debt.

Let's look at the individual transactions that would be made and then we will simply erase money from this microeconomy.

The first transaction would be Ben's withdrawal of the $200 in his savings account, which reduces the bank's cash holdings to $350 and eliminates the liability of Ben's savings account. The second transaction is Ben's partial payment of the loan. The cash drawn from his savings account is used to pay down the loan and would be added back to the bank's cash position. The $200 is subtracted from the outstanding loan balance.

HOMETOWNE BANK—FIRST PAYMENT ON THE LOAN

Cash	$ 550	Ben's Building	$ –
Loans	$ 850	Lord's Lumber	$ 350
Ben's loans	$ 750	Susan	$ 400
		Shareholders' equity	$ 1,400
Total assets	$ 2,150	Total liabilities	$ 2,150

The second installment on the loan would come from the $100 cash that Ben had on hand and $150 that he was able to get for what was left of the lumber. The bank's cash account increases by $250 to $800 and the loan balance decreases to $500. However, there are no more assets that Ben can use to repay the loan.

HOMETOWNE BANK—SECOND PAYMENT ON THE LOAN

Cash	$ 800	Ben's Building	$ –
Loans	$ 850	Lord's Lumber	$ 350
Ben's loans	$ 500	Susan	$ 400
		Shareholders' equity	$ 1,400
Total assets	$ 2,150	Total liabilities	$ 2,150

Because there are no assets left, the loan will have to be written off or taken to a zero balance. When that happens, the bank's assets decline by $500. In order to rebalance the balance sheet, some entry on the liability and equity side needs to be made. Clearly, Susan and Lord's Lumber do not expect the value of their savings accounts to be affected by Ben's bankruptcy. The bank's equity account will be reduced by the $500 of lost asset value.

HOMETOWNE BANK—THE LOAN IS WRITTEN OFF			
Cash	$ 800	Ben's Building	$ –
Loans	$ 850	Lord's Lumber	$ 350
Ben's loans	$ –	Susan	$ 400
		Shareholders' equity	$ 900
Total assets	$ 1,650	Total liabilities	$ 1,650

Where did the money go? Theoretically, it has simply vanished from the economy. When banks make loans that perform, that is, loans that are repaid with interest, the interest earned and the profits that they allow vendors to earn create new money in an economy. When a bank suffers from a nonperforming loan or a loan that has defaulted, money is eliminated from the economic system.

In practice, Ben and his bank may work out a payment plan that allows Hometowne Bank to recoup more of the outstanding funds. In making the loan, the bank might have secured the loan with property as well as a personal guarantee. In the event that the assets did not satisfy the outstanding loan balance, Ben would have been responsible for payment of the loan. When Ben goes back to his job with the local homebuilder, the bank will have recourse to a portion of his pay for as long as it takes Ben to repay the loan.

Several major corporations have entered Chapter 11 bankruptcy in order to reorganize their finances. In many cases, one of the requests that they make is that lenders reduce the interest rate on outstanding loans or write down a portion of the loan balance. Although lenders are reluctant to do either, they often decide that it is better to accept a lesser amount of money in the future than to push the company into liquidation where the proceeds may be even lower. In either case, the money that is written off or subtracted from outstanding debt ceases to exist.

INTERNATIONAL FINANCIAL INSTITUTIONS

The need to transfer money from savers to borrowers does not stop at the borders of one nation. Two major international financial institutions were created in order to fund the growth of developing economies. Because these organizations facilitate loans between countries, there are bound to be political issues that arise from lending practices and loan covenants. In this section we will describe financial goals, not the political ones.

The International Monetary Fund

The **International Monetary Fund (IMF)** makes headlines when countries with severe financial problems request loans. Even bigger headlines ensue when the IMF stops payment of promised loans, as they have done with Russia and Venezuela. But lending money is only one of the many functions of the IMF.

The International Monetary Fund was created in 1946 to promote international monetary cooperation and exchange, to promote monetary stability, to encourage economic growth and high employment, and to provide temporary financial assistance to countries that find themselves in financial difficulties.

The depression in the 1930s was not limited to the U.S. economy. As the economy worsened worldwide, people lost faith in the value of paper money. Since many countries still tied the value of their paper currency to the value of gold, people began to demand that their paper notes be exchanged for gold. Some countries abandoned the gold standard, and faith in paper currency declined still further. The countries who kept the tie to gold were loathe to exchange currency with those who had abandoned the gold standard. Currency exchange became increasingly difficult and international trade was further eroded.

Even during World War II, countries recognized that some sort of international clearinghouse was desired. Final negotiations were concluded in 1944 at Bretton Woods, New Hampshire, and resulted in the creation of the International Monetary Fund.

Any country that conducts its own foreign policy and is willing to live up to the IMF charter is eligible to join. Each country deposits funds with the IMF based on the size of their economy. The pooled deposits are meant to provide the assets that the IMF might need in case a member country requires a loan. In a very real sense, the IMF was set up as an international credit union.

One of the key responsibilities of the IMF is to ensure that currency trades fairly and freely between member countries and that member countries do not impose any restrictions on the free exchange of currency.

The IMF is probably better known for its lending programs. If a country spends more than it takes in, it will have a balance of payments deficit. If the problem persists, the country may ask the IMF for a loan. The IMF grants loans if the country can demonstrate that the money will be used responsibly. In order to prove that it has become more fiscally responsible, the borrower usually promises to reduce government spending as a means of reducing the imbalance of payments.

Recall that the goal of the IMF is to promote economic growth, high employment, and monetary stability. Unfortunately, when financial controls have gotten out of hand these goals conflict. In order to reestablish monetary stability, the government needs to stop spending money that is not backed by actual growth in the economy. If the country does not have a number of large companies that can pick up the slack in the economy, reducing government spending will cause unemployment and hardship for its citizens. There are no easy answers.

The World Bank

The **World Bank** has a different mission. Its stated goal is to fight poverty by investing in infrastructure, protecting the environment, promoting health and education initiatives, and encouraging private business development.

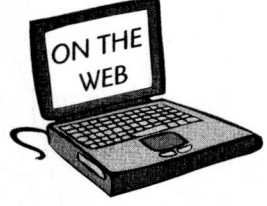

The International Monetary Fund Web site (www.imf.org) provides information about the history of the fund, its mission and goals, and its current activities. In addition, there are economic reports, articles about current economic issues, statistical reports, and research papers.

The World Bank Group, five closely allied institutions, can be found at www.worldbank.org. There are pages for each of the lending and development divisions, reports on the programs and activities of the bank, a history of its operations, and a discussion of issues that are important to the bank. Among the issues listed in July 2001 were AIDS and TB, corruption, globalization, and policy issues affecting middle-income countries.

The World Bank provides loans as well as advising client countries on policies and procedures. The World Bank has assisted countries that have emerged from civil conflict and funded reconstruction projects. Its consultants advised the former Soviet republics on how to establish central banking systems, pension funds, business law frameworks, and efficient financial markets, which they did not have once they became independent nations.

Unlike the IMF, the World Bank is not a mutual association or credit union–type organization. The World Bank has two main agencies, each with its own funding source. The International Bank for Reconstruction and Development, which accounts for approximately 75% of the World Bank's lending, obtains most of its capital by selling bonds and other securities to pension funds, insurance companies, and other institutional investors. The International Development Agency, which provides interest-free loans to the poorest countries, gets its funding from donor nations including not only developed nations such as the United States, France, Germany, and Japan but also countries that have been borrowers from the fund in the past.

ETHICAL ISSUES

Banks and other financial institutions transfer money from savers to borrowers. There are many ethical issues involved in banking. One issue that has received attention in recent years is the desire for banks to control the movement of money, including money used for criminal or terrorist purposes. Another issue concerns **subprime lending** practices: Should banks market loans to low-income or high-risk customers and at what rate of interest?

Bank Fraud and Money Laundering

It is relatively easy to move money around the world and to do it quickly. The technology that allows us to pay bills on-line could also allow us to invest money in many different places and keep it moving so quickly that it is difficult to keep track of where it all is. In fact, several best-selling novels have been written about people who use wire transfers to embezzle money and then move it to protected sites.

The issue of money laundering, or moving money from place to place in order to cover its origin, is not limited to drug traffickers. In late 1999, the Bank of New York was used as a conduit for money leaving Russia, including allegations that some of the money being moved was from the IMF loans intended to help rebuild Russia's economy. The United States and its allies are investigating ways to restrict the flow of funds used by suspected terrorist organizations. The ease and speed with which money can be transferred across borders adds to the difficulty in tracking the movement of both legitimate and questionable transfers.[1]

Subprime Lending

In July 2001, the FDIC took over the failed Superior Bank in Oakbrook Terrace, Illinois. The bank specialized in making subprime loans—loans to patrons with poor credit scores. Superior was not the first subprime lender to fail. Banks are increasingly lending to customers with poor credit and underestimating the risk of default or delinquency.

Many subprime loans are made to customers with a history of missed payments, bounced checks, or already heavy debt burdens. The reason the borrowers do not qualify for a standard loan is because they are already at the edge of their financial capacity. As the economy softens and unemployment increases, their chance of default increases. Banks can manage subprime portfolios by keeping careful tabs on payment patterns and working with customers who fall behind in their payments.

Banks have traditionally compensated for the riskiness of a subprime loan portfolio by charging higher interest rates on the loans. Interest on subprime loans can be as much as 4% to 7% higher than market rates, which prompts accusations of predatory pricing. Some legislators are urging that caps be put on the interest rate that banks can charge. If this happens, banks will either have to curtail their higher-risk lending practices or accept lower profits on the loans.

TERMS TO KNOW

Depository financial institution	Credit union	Defined benefit
Bank	Nondepository financial institution	Defined contribution
Asset-based lending	Finance company	International Monetary Fund (IMF)
Cash-flow lending	Pension fund	World Bank
Savings and loan association		Subprime lending

---

[1]"Dirty Money Goes Digital By Gary Silverman in New York, with Margaret Coker in Moscow, Joseph Weber in Toronto, Laura Cohn in Washington, and Carol Mattock in Paris," *Business Week*, September 20, 1999; "The Russian Money Chase," by Mark Hosenball and Bill Powell, *Newsweek*, February 28, 2000.

TERM PAPERS AND PROJECTS

1. What is microlending? Investigate banks that make small loans in developing countries. Explain how these loans expand economic growth and have a multiplier effect.
2. Interview a local banker. Ask him or her about their lending philosophy. Is the bank an asset-based lender or cash-flow lender? What criteria does the bank use when assessing the creditworthiness of the borrower?
3. Investigate the trend toward social investing, not just in stock but the practice of making loans to socially responsible programs or borrowers. Is it good business?
4. Examine the fringe banking services in your community: check cashing services, money order outlets, and pawnshops. Compare interest rates and fees. Determine whether a low-income customer could be served less expensively by a traditional financial institution.
5. Investigate what banking services are available to small businesses in your community. Look at the availability of locally funded loans and the cost of service.
6. How can megabanks with their impersonal image compete with friendly local banks? Or, in contrast, how can small local banks compete with well-funded national financial institutions?
7. What are the mission and goals of the International Monetary Fund? What projects, other than acting as a lender of last resort, does the IMF pursue?
8. Research a country that has received a loan (or loans) from the IMF. What were the economic conditions that prompted the country to call upon the IMF? What changes had to be made in order to qualify for IMF assistance? What is the current condition of the country's economy?
9. Discuss projects undertaken by the World Bank. Focus on a large-scale project or a set of interrelated programs such as helping a country with reconstruction after civil war or investing in health and education initiatives in developing regions.
10. Several novels have been written about money laundering. How easy is it to move money quickly, quietly, and invisibly? Could you or I do it? What steps have the various regulatory agencies taken to reduce money laundering?

REVIEW QUESTIONS

1. What is the main characteristic that describes a depository financial institution?
2. Describe what types of loans would be made by a bank whose lending philosophy was asset based.
3. In cash-flow lending, why would the banker want to be more involved in the business of the borrower?
4. List three factors that may influence the interest rate of a loan.
5. What is the main difference between a bank and a credit union?

6. What are savings and loan associations? What was the main, important difference in the type of assets and liabilities that they held?
7. What are nondepository financial institutions? How do they differ from depository financial institutions?
8. How do check cashing and payday loan services provide financial services? Who do they primarily serve?
9. Describe the two different types of pension funds and discuss the benefits and drawbacks of each.
10. How is money created? Give a specific example and demonstrate the process.
11. What is the International Monetary Fund and how does it function? What is its purpose?
12. What is the World Bank? How does it differ from the IMF?
13. Why are ethics important in business and finance?

CHAPTER

6

ACCOUNTING OVERVIEW

LEARNING OBJECTIVES

1. Understand the types of accounting and their function within the firm.

2. Describe the relationship between accounting and finance.

3. Describe the four main financial statements.

4. Distinguish which financial statement is most useful for a specific purpose.

5. Perform ratio analysis and describe how ratios are used.

6. Analyze the health of a company using ratio analysis.

7. Explain the limitations of ratio analysis.

8. Define the concept of pro forma accounting statements and discuss when their use is appropriate.

9. Be able to obtain financial information for publicly traded corporations.

MANAGERIAL AND FINANCIAL ACCOUNTING

Accounting is the process of collecting, reporting, and analyzing the costs associated with operating a business. There are both external and internal users of accounting data. External users include the Internal Revenue Service, which uses accounting data to assess the firm's tax liability, banks that are considering extending credit to the company, and individuals who might be interested in investing in the corporation or donating to a charity. All publicly traded companies are required by the Securities and Exchange Commission to file accounting statements with the agency on a quarterly basis and to produce an annual report, which is distributed to shareholders of record at the end of the fiscal year. This type of accounting is called **financial accounting.**

Internal users of accounting require different types of information and the reports that are generated by the organization's accounting staff vary depending on the need of the user. For example, before a construction company bids on a major project, they would want to analyze the costs of any recently completed work that shared similar characteristics with the proposed project in order to come up with the most appropriate bid. A not-for-profit organization might want its accountants to track the pattern of donations throughout the year and contrast that with its expenditures. This type of accounting is called **managerial accounting**. Without the information provided by accounting reports, businesses, whether they are profit-making corporations, not-for-profit organizations, or governmental agencies, would lack a major financial management tool that they can use to make future decisions.

Because financial accounting is used by outsiders to assess the financial health of the firm, published financial statements must conform to a set of **generally accepted accounting principles (GAAP),** which are basic accounting standards and practices that have been agreed upon by the accounting profession and overseen by the Financial Accounting Standards Board (FASB). As businesses change, so too do accounting practices. FASB issues clarifications and interpretations of accounting rules to ensure that published statements are accurate, objective, consistent from year to year, timely, and comparable across companies and industries.

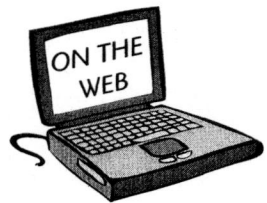

The Financial Accounting Standards Board (FASB) has a Web site at www.fasb.org. The Web site contains news releases pertaining to new FASB rulings, minutes of FASB meetings, and articles that discuss current accounting issues. The site is kept current. As an example, on October 1, 2001, FASB issued EITF Issue No. 01-10, *Accounting for the Impact of the Terrorist Attacks of September 11, 2001*, which was meant to determine the accounting principles used in the wake of an unexpected occurrence.

Another site that provides a professional opinion on accounting issues is www.aicpa.org, the professional association of certified public accountants (CPAs). The Web site offers news and analysis of accounting issues and links to professional seminars and publications.

Company executives who would like quick links to a variety of financial information should go to www.cfoexpress.com. Listed under the Business Research heading are many links to financial data, including a subsection for the Securities and Exchange Commission, the body that regulates publicly traded corporations. CEO Express provides quick access to the SEC databases along with other useful financial analysis links.

If you want to go directly to the SEC homepage, go to www.sec.gov. In addition to corporate filings, the SEC page provides a great deal of information about policies and procedures. Another way to access quarterly filings is to go to www.freeedgar.com, which provides basic financial information for public companies.

Remember that privately held companies are not required by law to divulge financial data. Hoovers (www.hoovers.com) estimates some financial data such as sales revenue, but information is scanty.

Managerial accounting is not subject to FASB rules because its purpose is to enable managers to make informed decisions. For example, the income statement records the actual revenues and expenses for the firm for a previous period of time. However, when the production manager is drawing up the budget for the next fiscal year, he or she will take the past data and adjust for any changes that are predicted to occur during the coming year. By using past numbers from the accounting department, the production manager's budget will become a projection into the future. In fact, he or she may derive several budgets using various sales and cost assumptions before settling on the one that makes the most sense given customer demand, investment in new technology, raw material costs, and anticipated changes in labor rates. The production manager is using accounting data to make strategic decisions.

Accounting is a system that communicates important information about the firm's operations. There are four main accounting statements: the balance sheet, income statement, cash flow statement, and statement of changes in ownership. Some statements reflect a single moment in time (the balance sheet) whereas some report the activities over a set period of time (quarterly income statements, for example). When raw data are converted into ratios, the data can yield an excellent comparison of the operation at several points in time.

Finance is the process of obtaining and employing assets that allow the firm to continue and expand operations. The finance manager is responsible for maintaining the steady supply of cash needed to sustain operations while minimizing the cost of keeping those funds. Accounting data are critical to financial decision making.

FINANCIAL STATEMENTS

Financial statements should be prepared for every business, regardless of its size or profitability. In this section we will focus on the statements provided by publicly traded corporations. Before we start, there are several assumptions that need to be stated. First, most companies use **accrual accounting;** expenses used in creating revenue are deducted from the revenue during that same period. For example, although property insurance premiums may only be paid semiannually, a retailer is using his store all 12 months of the year. The cash payment is periodic, however, the use of the insurance is continual. For that reason, the insurance expense is deducted from revenues on each month's income statement rather than only in the months it is paid. Accrual accounting focuses on the actual costs of the business rather than the flow of cash in a given month.

Some companies use a **cash basis of accounting,** recognizing expenses only when the cash leaves the firm. There are several weaknesses to this method, among them the fact that the firm could defer expenses and distort its actual financial health simply by timing the payment of bills.

The second assumption we need to reiterate is that every transaction is recorded twice. **Double-entry bookkeeping** records the changes that occur in assets, liabilities, and owner's equity as a result of the firm's activities. For example, if a company buys inventory on credit, the inventory account (an

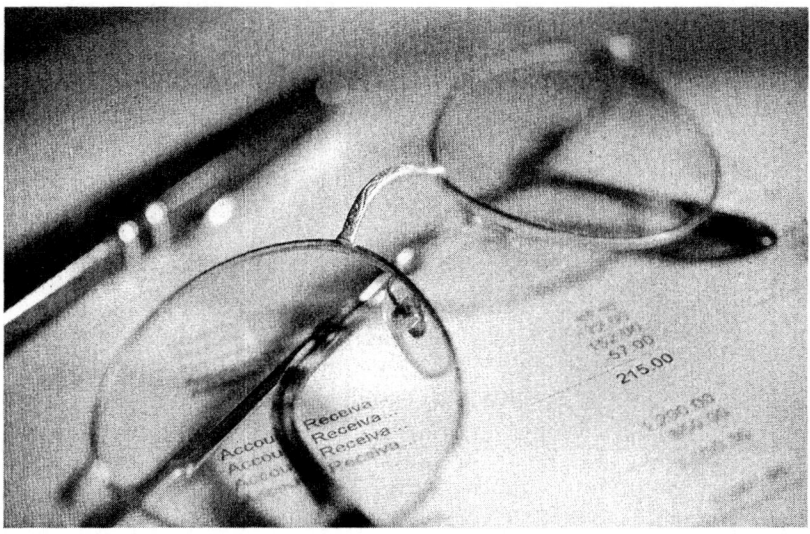

Accounting statements provide a good look at the company's financial situation. (Getty Images/EyeWire, Inc.)

asset) is increased along with the accounts payable (liability) account. The transaction has not only increased the amount of goods available for sale but has also increased the firm's indebtedness. If the purchase had been made with cash, the firm would have more inventory to sell but less cash on hand. Double-entry bookkeeping shows the effect of each financial transaction.

Balance Sheet

A **balance sheet** is a picture of a company at a single instant in time. The concept of the balance sheet is simple: the assets of the organization must balance the liabilities and equity.

$$\text{Assets} = \text{Liabilities} + \text{owner's equity}$$

Graphically, we have often presented balance sheets in a two-columned format, with assets on the left and liabilities and equity on the right. This allows us to see the balancing that occurs in the double-entry bookkeeping system.

Traditionally, we have described **assets** as what is *owned* by the organization and **liabilities** and **owner's equity** as what is *owed*, either to debtholders or to stockholders and owners. In the case of equity, however, that sense of owing money often gets confused with the ownership component. How can one be *owed* what one *owns*?

A better way of looking at the relationship between the two sides of a balance sheet is to think of the assets as owned but the liabilities and equity as a description of how those assets were financed. For example, the corporation buys a new piece of equipment for $250,000. If 20% of the purchase price is cash, there is a transfer of $50,000 from the cash account to the equipment account. Both transactions affect the left-hand side of the balance sheet because one asset (cash) is being reduced so that another (equipment) can be

On the left-hand side of the balance sheet are the items that the firm owns. The right-hand side describes how the acquisition of those items was funded. By thinking in terms of items and financing, it is easier to see that the liabilities and equity are alternative methods of funding the growth of the business.

increased. If the company takes out a loan for the balance, the $200,000 difference shows up on the left-hand side of the balance sheet in the equipment column and the loan is reflected as a liability on the right-hand side.

Suppose, however, that the company did not want to incur a loan. If the corporation issued stock instead of borrowing the capital needed, the asset entry would still be a $250,000 increase in equipment but the $200,000 difference would be credited to the owner's equity account on the right-hand side of the balance sheet, reflecting the additional ownership (in the form of stock) that now existed. In either case, the asset is owned but the structure of the financing is different, and that is what the balance sheet tells us.

Income Statement

$$\text{Income} = \text{Revenue} - \text{expenses}$$

The **income statement** measures the profit (or loss) that an organization has made over a set period of time, usually a quarter or a year. For a profit-making entity, **revenue** is most often derived from sales, and **expenses** are the costs directly involved in acquiring or manufacturing those items along with the general costs associated with running a business such as the acquisition and maintenance of facilities, executive compensation, and selling costs. Profits occur when the revenues exceed expenses. The last entry on an income statement is the net income (or loss) of an organization, often called the "bottom line." Most organizations would like to see a positive number on that line!

When we look at financial ratios later in the chapter, we will see that the nature of the organization determines where in the income statement we will

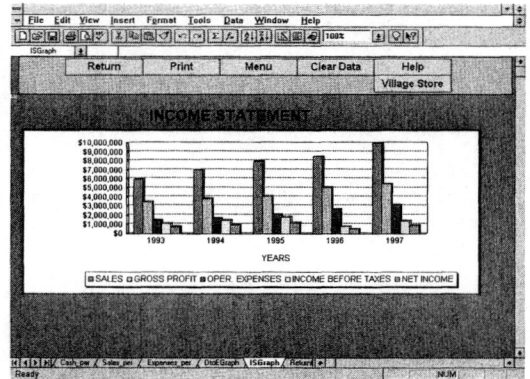

Spreadsheets can take data from an income statement and portray the changes in the company's operations and profitability. Financial managers can use this information to plan for the future. (Village Software)

find the bulk of the expense items and which ones are most strategically sensitive. For a pharmaceutical company involved in creating newly patented drugs, expenses such as research and development are considered general expenses and do not show up in the cost of goods sold. For a company that mass-produces the generic equivalent of medicine no longer covered by patent, a much higher proportion of costs will be associated with manufacturing since basic research is not a mission of the organization. For this reason, the detail in an income statement should be viewed in the context of the strategic mission of the organization.

In a not-for-profit organization such as the American Red Cross, revenue is more often a result of donations. For a public college or university, revenue may include direct receipt of tuition, but a greater proportion is a result of transfer payments such as government allocations or grants from private industry. In both cases, an income statement demonstrates the source of income and how it is spent.

Statement of Cash Flow

Although the balance sheet provides a picture of assets and their financing structure and the income statement describes the profitability of an organization, the two statements do not provide a complete picture of the financial activities of the company.

The **cash flow statement** combines aspects from both the balance sheet and the income statement to provide a view of the company's financial health. The cash flow statement begins with a section that describes cash provided by (or used in) operating activities. Ideally, this section should show that the company is generating cash through its continuing operations. The statement begins with net income, a figure from the income statement. An allowance is made for cash consumed by discontinued operations and charges that are related to accounting changes. Because it describes the sources and uses of cash, the cash flow statement can become very revealing.

Among the adjustments listed might be a provision for uncollectibles. Many companies have some degree of loss due to uncollectible accounts, but if this number rises dramatically it could signal that the company is obtaining sales at the expense of good credit practices.

If the cash flow statement shows an increase in receivables it should be measured against any increase in revenue. When revenue and receivables grow at the same rate and the rate of uncollectible debt does not rise alarmingly, the increase in receivables reflects a growing business. If, however, the increase in receivables outpaces the growth in sales revenue, the company is not collecting cash as quickly as it should.

Another adjustment is a change in the level of accounts payable. Again, during a growth phase when the company is increasing its inventory levels, accounts payable will show an increase that corresponds to the sales increase. However, another cause for increasing accounts payable could be that the company is delaying payment to vendors in order to conserve its cash. If this is the case, it could indicate financial weakness.

A significant adjustment to the cash flow statement adds depreciation expense to the net income (or loss). Depreciation is a noncash expense; even though it is deducted from the income statement, it does not represent cash that has left the organization. When a piece of property or equipment is purchased, the reduction in cash is reflected on the balance sheet as a transfer from one asset item (cash) to another (property and equipment) and listed in the second section of the cash flow statement under investing activities. The income statement is charged for depreciation expense over the useful life of the investment, which continues for several years past the time that the money actually moves through the firm. Depreciation is meant to offset the revenues produced by the investment by apportioning its cost over time. Therefore, depreciation (a noncash expense) is added back to the net income to more accurately reflect the cash position of an organization.

The last line in the operating activities section shows whether the company is generating positive cash flow from operations. Because of the method of assessing depreciation expense, it is possible for an organization to show a net loss at the same time that it has positive cash flow from its operations.

The second section of the cash flow statement details the cash provided by (or used in) investing activities. Investments can be either internal such as capital expenditures or they can result from the sale or purchase of stocks, bonds, commercial paper, or other businesses. Investments in property, plant, or equipment necessary for the continuation or expansion of the business have to be funded in some manner. If the operating section shows a positive cash flow, the company can choose to fund acquisitions from internally generated cash rather than being forced to seek financing. If the company is consuming cash merely to stay afloat, capital expenditures will either need to be cut or financed through additional debt or equity.

The third section details those financing activities. Repayment of long-term debt reduces cash whereas issuance of debt would increase cash. The shares of common stock that are issued or bought back are recorded in this section as are the cash dividend payments made.

The last three lines of a cash flow statement tie the income statement more closely to the balance sheet. The first records the net increase (or decrease) in cash and cash equivalents during the period. That sum is added to (or subtracted from) the cash and cash equivalents at the beginning of the period. The final entry gives the cash position at the close of the statement. This figure matches the cash entry on the balance sheet.

Let's first look at a cash flow statement for Artemis Enterprises. Artemis has net earnings of $209,100 and after depreciation has been added back, a total cash flow from operations of $338,300.

The second section of the cash flow statement describes Artemis's investment expenditures. During the year, Artemis acquired property and the assets of a small company. The purchase price of the property was offset by the sale of some equipment that Artemis no longer needed. The investment in property and equipment, which hopefully will result in increased profits in future years, reduced Artemis's cash position by $156,900.

The financing decisions are seen in the third section. In order to provide more liquidity, Artemis issued approximately $10,000 of long-term debt. They retired some short-term debt and paid the portion of long-term debt that came due this year. Normal dividend payments were made, which reduced the firm's cash, and the company also elected to buy back shares of its own stock. Of the $338,300 cash provided by operations, Artemis added $91,900 to its cash account for a total balance of $142,700.

Artemis Enterprises Cash Flow Statement
(All numbers in thousands)
Operating Activities

Net earnings	$209.1
Depreciation	$129.2
Net cash provided by operations	$338.3

Investing Activities

Purchases of property and equipment	$(161.2)
Payment for acquisitions	$(12.1)
Proceeds from sale of property and equipment	$16.4
Net cash used for investing activities	$(156.9)

Financing Activities

Proceeds from issuance of long-term debt	$10.1
Net borrowings (payments)—bank lines of credit	$0.4
Payment of short-term debt	$(5.0)
Payment of long-term debt	$(0.1)
Purchases of common stock	$(43.1)
Payment of dividends	$(51.8)
Net cash provided by (used for) financing activities	$(89.5)
Net increase (decrease) in cash	$91.9
Cash at beginning of year	$50.8
Cash at end of year	$142.7

Indigo Research also added cash to its balance sheet this year but did it in a decidedly different manner. Indigo is a young biotechnology firm that has operated for only 3 years. The company has yet to produce a marketable product, which is not unusual for the industry. Start-up costs are high because the investment in equipment, laboratory space, and salaries for highly educated professionals results in large outflows of cash during the first several years of operation. However, Indigo actually ended the year with more cash. Examining the cash flow statement shows how this is possible.

Indigo has a net loss of $107,500, which is only partially offset by $6,000 of depreciation. There was a net cash loss of $101,500 from operations. Add to that the purchase of $10,700 in additional scientific equipment and the firm has a cash outflow of $112,200.

The third section shows how Indigo has managed to fund its yearly expenses and add to its cash position. During the year, the firm issued $205,600 in common and preferred stock. The equity section of the balance sheet should show at least part of this infusion (reduced in the retained earnings section by the operating loss). The firm retired $16,300 in bank lines of credit, for a total infusion of cash from financing of $189,300. The new equity investment was sufficient to cover the operating losses and equipment purchases as well as to add $77,100 to the firm's cash position. How long will Indigo be able to raise cash through stock offerings if it does not have a marketable product? That is anyone's guess, but at least for next year they have enough cash on hand to sustain the same level of operating losses that they had this year. In order to continue as a going concern, they will have to produce revenue or they will face bankruptcy. We will look at short-term losses and bankruptcy in Chapter 7.

Indigo Research Company Cash Flow Statement
(All numbers in thousands)
Operating Activities

Net earnings	($107.5)
Depreciation	$6.0
Net cash provided by operations	($101.5)

Investing Activities

Purchases of property	($10.7)
Net cash used for investing activities	($10.7)

Financing Activities

Proceeds from issuance of ordinary and preferred stock	$205.6
Net borrowings (payments)—bank lines of credit	($16.3)
Net cash provided by (used for) financing activities	$189.3
Net increase (decrease) in cash	$77.1
Cash at beginning of year	$72.4
Cash at end of year	$149.5

Another simple example shows how the balance sheet and income statement may both look positive even as the company is suffering. Again, the cash flow statement would show the problem. Before beginning his office furniture store, Sam lined up investors who provided enough start-up capital for Sam to acquire the assets he needed—the store lease and equipment along with the inventory. His balance sheet showed that the financing came from shareholders' equity and the assets were neatly accounted for. After only a few months, Sam's business was successful and his income statement showed that he had a net income after all of his expenses had been paid. What's not good about that? Suppose that Sam had given his customers 90 days to pay. The income statement recognized the revenue when it was received and his balance sheet would show the corresponding value being transferred from the inventory account to the accounts receivable category. Sam needs to keep a constant supply of inventory or he will not have a continuing business. If his vendors require him to pay within 30 days of receipt of goods, and he is not collecting from his customers for 90 days, Sam will quickly face a cash crunch. The balance sheet and income statements, while technically correct, do not demonstrate the illiquidity, which will be seen in the cash flow statement.

Changes in Financial Condition

The statement of **changes in financial condition** is also referred to as the statement of owner's equity or statement of stockholders' equity. The statement of cash flows describes the effect of operations on the cash position of the firm. The statement of changes in financial condition describes the change in owner's equity as a result of both operations and financing decisions.

The statement opens with the equity balance as of the previous statement. The period of time covered by the statement of changes in financial condition must be reconciled with an income statement from the same period. Any amounts of capital added to the firm during the period are added to the beginning equity balance. The net income for the period is added (or net loss subtracted). If dividends have been paid or equity withdrawn by the owners that amount will be subtracted, leaving an ending equity balance. The statement acts as a bridge between the income statement and the equity portion of the balance sheet.

ANALYSIS OF FINANCIAL STATEMENTS

Vertical Analysis

Vertical analysis is the process of analyzing the entries on a financial statement as they relate to some benchmark. For example, a vertical analysis of a balance sheet would describe each asset as a percent of total assets. Each section of the liabilities and owner's equity section would also be computed, using the same base value of total assets (since total assets equal total liabilities and equity).

Let's look at the balance sheet for Artemis Enterprises. You can see that 8.9% of the assets are in cash and 13.8% are in accounts receivable. Cash and accounts receivable are significantly higher than inventory, but property, plant, and equipment is the asset with the greatest value. On the liability side we can see that the firm has far more equity than debt.

Artemis Enterprises 2001 Balance Sheet
(All numbers in thousands)

Assets	$	%	Liabilities	$	%
Cash	$ 128.6	8.9%	Current liabilities	$ 207.7	14.3%
Accounts receivable	$ 199.8	13.8%	Long-term obligations	$ 81.9	5.7%
Inventory	$ 132.4	9.1%	Other non-current liabilities	$ 168.1	11.6%
Other current assets	$ 26.3	1.8%	Total liabilities	$ 457.7	31.6%
Total current assets	$ 487.1	33.6%			
Investments and long-term receivables	$ 63.5	4.4%	*Shareholders' Equity*	$ 991.5	68.4%
Property, plant, and equipment, net	$ 808.4	55.8%			
Other assets	$ 90.2	6.2%			
Total	$1,449.2	100.0%	Total	$1,449.2	100.0%

On the income statement, the net sales figure is set to 100% and all of the expenses are calculated from that point. The income statement for Artemis Enterprises shows that cost of goods sold is 71.5% of the total sales dollars generated (less returns and allowances). After administrative expenses and interest and taxes are subtracted, Artemis's profit margin is 12.5%. Vertical analysis allows the reader to quickly see the relationships of expenses within an income statement, but it does not describe changes over time nor does it give any indication whether the firm's profits are comparable to other firms in its industry.

Artemis Enterprises 2001 Income Statement
(All numbers in thousands)

Net sales	$1,678.6	100.0%
Cost of goods sold	$1,199.5	71.5%
Gross profit on sales	$ 479.1	28.5%
Selling, general, and administrative costs	$ 174.8	10.4%
Earnings before interest and taxes	$ 304.3	18.1%
Interest income	$ 3.2	0.2%
Interest expense	$ 6.9	0.4%
Earnings before income taxes	$ 300.6	17.9%
Provision for income taxes	$ 91.5	5.5%
Net earnings	$ 209.1	12.5%

Horizontal Analysis

Horizontal analysis allows us to analyze changes over time but in order to do so we need at least two periods of data. Since we are comparing the most current financials to previous data, the formula for a horizontal analysis is

$$\frac{\text{Value in new time period} - \text{value in old time period}}{\text{Value in old time period}} \times 100 = \text{percent change}$$

Horizontal analysis compares the change in each line item on a statement with the same item in a previous statement. Unlike vertical analysis, the percentages do not illustrate the relative importance of any given line item. For example, if inventory grows by 20% from 2002 to 2003 and long-term debt grows by only 10% during the same period, it does not mean that the inventory has grown by a larger absolute value than long-term debt. Inventory has increased from $100,000 to $120,000 (a 20% increase) while debt has increased from $250,000 to $275,000 (a 10% increase). The comparison is between the same line item in one period to the next.

Let's look at the income statements for Artemis Enterprises in 2001 and 2002. Sales for the company have grown by 5.8% during the past year, while the cost of goods sold has only increased by 2.3%. Because the percentage growth in sales was larger than the firm's increase in cost of goods sold, the gross income increased by 14.7%. At the same time, Artemis was able to reduce selling, general, and administrative costs as well as interest expense. The increase in interest income added to the lower levels of expenses allowed Artemis to increase the earnings before taxes by almost 25%. By the time you get to the bottom line, you will see that Artemis increased net income by 22.4% on a sales increase of only 5.8%.

Artemis Enterprises Income Statement
(All numbers in thousands)

	2001	2002	% Change
Net sales	$1,678.6	$1,776.4	5.8%
Cost of goods sold	$1,199.5	$1,226.8	2.3%
Gross profit on sales	$ 479.1	$ 549.6	14.7%
Selling, general, and administrative costs	$ 174.8	$ 174.7	−0.1%
Earnings before interest and taxes	$ 304.3	$ 374.9	23.2%
Interest income	$3.2	$ 6.7	109.4%
Interest expense	$6.9	$ 6.8	−1.4%
Earnings before income taxes	$ 300.6	$ 374.8	24.7%
Provision for income taxes	$ 91.5	$ 118.9	29.9%
Net earnings	$ 209.1	$ 255.9	22.4%

Ratio Analysis

In accounting courses, students commonly perform vertical and horizontal analyses and calculate dozens of ratios. The computation may be all that the student is required to know. In finance, we want to look behind those ratios and ask what they tell us about the health of our company, both in comparison to the previous years and to other firms in our industry. What strengths does the analysis indicate? Where are we weaker than our competitors and how much should that concern us? **Ratio analysis** is descriptive; it describes the situation that exists. It is not prescriptive; it does not tell the manager what to do. However, if the manager has the ability to look past the simple calculation of numbers and begin to see trends, decision making becomes easier.

Accounting ratios are also important to people outside the firm. A vendor should look at some form of liquidity ratio before extending payment terms. A banker may want to know how much debt the company has already incurred before authorizing more. Stockholders will want to know about profitability as will the Internal Revenue Service.

In the next section we will review the method for calculating some of the more common ratios. We will also discuss how financial ratios can be used to diagnose strengths or weaknesses within the firm.

COMMONLY CALCULATED RATIOS

Liquidity Ratios

Liquidity is the ability of assets to be converted quickly into cash. Ideally, a firm wishes to maintain enough liquidity to service current debts. Remember that the balance sheet lists as current liabilities all short-term debts (less than 1 year to maturity) and the portion of long-term debt that comes due within the year. It is assumed that the firm's inventory will be converted to cash during the course of a year so that the receipts from the inventory can be used to service the current debt. With that in mind, there are two commonly used ratios that measure a firm's liquidity: the current ratio and the quick (or acid test) ratio.

Current ratio   The current ratio is the ratio of current assets to current liabilities.

$$\text{Current ratio} = \frac{\text{Current assets}}{\text{Current liabilities}}$$

If the firm has used long-term debt to finance capital acquisitions, we would hope to see a current ratio larger than 1.0. If the ratio is less than 1.0, the firm cannot meet the debts that will come due during that year by converting current assets (at their full book value) into cash. The firm is in tenuous condition.

Quick ratio The quick ratio is the ratio of current assets, excluding inventory, divided by current liabilities.

$$\text{Quick ratio} = \frac{\text{Current assets} - \text{inventory}}{\text{Current liabilities}}$$

The current ratio makes the assumption that the company's inventory is being sold at a steady rate and, as a result, being converted to cash. However, for some companies inventory is sold on a seasonal basis or is more susceptible to economic downturns. If inventory turnover is not steady, the manager may want to see how easily the firm can pay its current liabilities using its cash and cash equivalents and accounts receivable. If the quick ratio is less than 1.0, the firm must plan on selling inventory in order to cover current liabilities. If the quick ratio is larger than 1.0, the firm can weather a more serious slow-down in sales.

Activity Ratios

Activity ratios are related to operations and operating efficiency because they measure how quickly the firm is converting assets into cash. The goal of the firm is to maximize revenues and minimize costs, and since there is a cost to carrying inventory and accounts receivable, the efficient firm will want to minimize the time that they hold noncash assets. The more quickly the firm is able to move through the cycle from inventory to accounts receivable to cash, the more profit they are likely to receive per dollar of assets.

Inventory turnover Inventory turnover measures how many times per period (usually a year) the firm sells through its inventory. To be more accurate, the firm should use an average inventory rather than the year-ending inventory.

$$\text{Inventory turnover} = \frac{\text{Sales}}{\text{Average inventory}}$$

Some firms prefer to calculate inventory turnover by using cost of goods sold instead of sales and dividing by average inventory at cost. The answer will probably be slightly different because the method shown above includes profit in the numerator (since sales are assumed to be at more than the cost of goods sold). As long as the person calculating the ratios is consistent throughout the analysis, either formula can be used.

Another way of looking at inventory turnover is to calculate how many days of sales are tied up in inventory.

$$\text{Days of sales in inventory} = \frac{\text{Inventory}}{\text{Sales per day}}$$

In the fast-food industry it makes sense that inventory turns over quickly since there are relatively few days of sales in stock at any given time. On the other hand, a jeweler might have items that stay in stock for months before selling. Comparing ratios among firms operating in the same industry is appropriate. Comparing across industries is not valid.

Accounts receivable turnover   Accounts receivable turnover is the annual credit sales of the firm divided by the accounts receivable.

$$\text{Accounts receivable turnover} = \frac{\text{Annual credit sales}}{\text{Accounts receivable}}$$

While it is possible for the firm to calculate this ratio, it may be more difficult for an outsider to do so. Although firms are required to report sales (on the income statement) and accounts receivable (on the balance sheet), there is no requirement that they report the percentage of sales that are financed. For an outside analyst it may be necessary to approximate this ratio by using total sales instead of credit sales. This substitute is calculated as

$$\text{Accounts receivable turnover} = \frac{\text{Annual sales}}{\text{Accounts receivable}}$$

Again, as long as the analysis is consistent across time periods and the use of total annual sales is clearly noted, the ratios can be compared.

As we will discuss more fully in Chapter 9 (working capital), accounts receivable are a form of financing provided by the vendor to the buyer. If the buyer pays within the allowable time period, no interest charges are incurred. For many purchasing agents the payment terms offered by a vendor become a key negotiating tool. When the buyer defers payment, it allows the buyer the use of the money. On the other hand, during that allowable period the vendor has lost the use of that money. For that reason, most firms try to balance the benefits of selling goods on account with the very real costs of doing so. Keeping track of the accounts receivable turnover ratio is critical, especially during recessions.

Average collection period   Average collection period is a different way of looking at accounts receivable turnover. Also called "days of sales outstanding," the average collection period describes the average time it takes to collect accounts.

$$\text{Average collection period} = \frac{\text{Receivables}}{\text{Sales per day}}$$

A 365-day year (exact time) is usually used, however, a 360-day year (ordinary time) can be used as long as the analyst is consistent and notes the assumptions.

The firm should take note when the receivables turnover time begins to exceed the firm's customary credit terms. This may be an indication that credit is being extended to buyers who are not as creditworthy or that existing customers are having difficulty meeting their obligations. It could also mean that the vendor is not aggressively working to collect accounts in a timely manner and customers have learned that payment terms can be stretched with no penalty to them. All of these should be of concern.

Inventory conversion cycle   The inventory conversion cycle combines the days of sales in inventory and days of sales in accounts receivable. It gives the firm an idea how long it takes to convert inventory to accounts receivable and, subsequently, into cash.

$$\text{Inventory conversion cycle} = \text{Days of inventory} + \text{days of sales outstanding}$$

Again, the inventory conversion cycle will vary depending on the industry. Fast-food restaurants do not offer accounts receivable. Most of their sales are for cash, so the inventory conversion cycle would be virtually identical to the number of days of inventory on hand. By contrast, a manufacturer that offers its customers the opportunity to finance their purchases would have an inventory conversion cycle that reflected both the number of days of inventory in stock and the length of time its customers were taking to pay their bills. During a recession, demand often falls and customers are slower to pay their outstanding balances. The firm must be careful to match production to sales, thus minimizing unsold inventory on hand, and must keep close track of outstanding accounts so that the inventory conversion cycle does not lengthen unnecessarily.

Asset turnover   The first set of activity ratios looked at how quickly inventory could be converted into cash. The second set of activity ratios are concerned with the efficient use of fixed assets. The goal is not to sell through the fixed assets but to maximize the efficiency of those assets. A barber shop maintains minimal inventory. The true test of its efficiency is not inventory turnover but how many sales (haircuts) can be generated in the space available. The shop is a fixed asset, and the revenue is derived from the efficient utilization of the space. For service industries, fixed asset turnover ratios are a better indicator of success.

Fixed asset turnover   Fixed asset turnover looks at sales in comparison to the long-term assets of the firm (i.e., property, plant, equipment, land).

$$\text{Fixed asset turnover} = \frac{\text{Sales}}{\text{Fixed assets}}$$

A firm that provides warehouse and transportation services can also be evaluated by its utilization of fixed assets. In order to be more profitable, the firm should maximize the amount of warehouse space that is being charged to customers and minimize empty truck miles. Calculating the revenue produced as it relates to the value of the trucks and warehouse space and comparing ratios over time allows the firm to evaluate whether it is improving its operating efficiency.

Total asset turnover

$$\text{Total asset turnover} = \frac{\text{Sales}}{\text{Total assets}}$$

Total asset turnover combines the effects of current asset management (the conversion of inventory and accounts receivable into cash) and fixed asset management. It allows the firm to compare how well it is managing each type of asset. If total assets are turning over more slowly than fixed assets, the firm is not aggressively managing the current assets of cash, accounts receivable, and inventory. As we will see in Chapter 9, poor working capital management can lead to liquidity problems in the future.

Leverage

One of the primary responsibilities of a financial manager is determining what level of debt is appropriate for a firm. Debt has a fixed value; that is, if the firm is making regular payments, the principal value of the loan decreases over time. If the firm is growing, any increase in value goes to the shareholders, either in the form of dividends or reinvested capital. If the firm can earn more than the cost of interest attached to the debt, it may be worth incurring additional debt or leveraging the firm.

Debt-to-equity ratio   The debt-to-equity ratio allows you to see the relationship between debt and equity.

$$\text{Debt-to-equity ratio} = \frac{\text{Debt}}{\text{Equity}}$$

The more debt a firm has in relationship to equity, the more **leveraged** it is and the more risk it has assumed.

Another way of looking at the financing choices of the firm is to compare the debt burden to the value of the total assets.

$$\text{Debt ratio} = \frac{\text{Debt}}{\text{Total assets}}$$

The optimal capital structure will depend on the industry and will change over time. For manufacturing firms where investment in long-term assets is high, firms may be more highly leveraged than service industries that throw off large amounts of cash with little capital investment. The level of debt will also be affected by whether the business is in a cyclical industry. Automobile manufacturers incur high fixed costs and sales are cyclical— they are very much affected by the state of the economy. It would stand to reason that an automaker would want to conserve cash during growth periods, thus increasing the level of total assets and adding to shareholder equity. During a recession, total assets would fall even if debt remained constant because automakers would be forced to spend the cash they had saved in more prosperous periods. Although debt had remained constant, it would increase as a proportion of total assets due to the cyclical nature of the industry.

Times-interest-earned ratio   Debt obliges the firm to make specified payments of both principal and interest at regular intervals. In a recession firms may find it difficult to service the debt they have. In some cases, the lender will allow a firm in distress to suspend principal payments, in effect deferring the maturity date of the loan, if they continue to make interest payments. At the very least, a lender would like to know if the firm is capable of servicing the interest they already have.

$$\text{Times-interest-earned ratio} = \frac{\text{Operating income} \atop (\text{earnings before interest and taxes})}{\text{Interest}}$$

The times-interest-earned ratio enables a lender to evaluate the firm's ability to service existing interest obligations and gives an idea of whether additional interest expense could be added.

Profitability

The preceding ratios described the ability of the firm to pay its current debts (liquidity), the efficiency of its operations (activity), and its financing structure (leverage). Since the goal of most corporations is to earn a profit, these next five ratios are the most important for many managers.

Gross profit margin The gross profit margin is the broadest measure of **profitability.**

$$\text{Gross profit margin} = \frac{\text{Revenues} - \text{cost of goods sold}}{\text{Sales}}$$

Gross margin measures profit before operating expenses, interest, and taxes are subtracted. Arguably, a firm that cannot manage a positive gross profit margin should not be in business, and probably won't be for long, since the cost of goods sold exceeds revenue.

Earlier in the chapter, we looked at the cash flow statement for Indigo Research Company. You will recall that they had a net loss of $107,500 but were able to increase their cash balance through the sale of stock. Here is the income statement for Indigo:

Indigo Research Company Income Statement
(All numbers in thousands)

Revenue	$ 2.0
Cost of revenue: Research and development	$ 94.2
Gross profit (loss)	($ 92.2)
Sales, general, and administrative expenses	$ 14.7
Gain (loss) from operations	($106.9)
Interest income	$ 2.6
Interest expense	$ 3.2
Net profit (loss)	($107.5)

You can see that the yearly revenue is $2,000, while research and development costs were $94,200, resulting in a loss from operations. There is no gross profit margin that can be computed for Indigo since there is no gross profit.

Operating profit margin   Operating profit margin examines the income of the company before taking into account the interest and taxes. We saw the operating profit margin for Artemis Enterprises when we performed the vertical analysis.

$$\text{Operating profit margin} \ = \ \frac{\text{Earnings before interest and taxes}}{\text{Sales}}$$

The key difference between gross margin and operating margin is that the latter takes into account overhead costs, not just the direct cost of goods sold. As we saw in the horizontal analysis of Artemis's income statements, the firm was able to increase its operating profit margin by a greater percentage than the gross profit margin by reducing its selling, general, and administrative costs.

For a company that is highly leveraged and whose net income is adversely affected by interest payments, the operating profit margin allows the firm to demonstrate that absent the interest burden, it would be profitable.

Net profit margin   Realistically, because a company does owe interest and taxes, the net profit margin offers a better look at their profitability.

$$\text{Net profit margin} \ = \ \frac{\text{Net profit (earnings after interest and taxes)}}{\text{Sales}}$$

The net profit is also called the bottom line, and the net profit margin is the most often used measure of a firm's profitability.

Return on assets   Profitability is not just the relationship between sales and the current costs to obtain those sales, it is also a matter of employing assets wisely.

$$\text{Return on assets} \ = \ \frac{\text{Net profit (earnings after interest and taxes)}}{\text{Total assets}}$$

Return on assets (ROA) is a tool that many companies use to evaluate the performance of line managers. How well does the manager employ the tools that he or she has in comparison to another manager? In many organizations, a benchmark ROA is set for divisions or departments and consistent failure to meet that target can result in divestiture of the division.

Return on equity   Before investing in a savings account, you would want to compare the earnings of that account with other investments of similar risk. Shareholders look at a company's use of its assets to determine whether they are earning a proper rate of return.

$$\text{Return on equity} = \frac{\text{Net profit}}{\text{Owner's equity (total assets} - \text{total liabilities)}}$$

Whether the profit is returned to the owners in the form of dividends or reinvested in the company, management needs to be aware of the fact that return on equity should compensate shareholders for the level of risk they are undertaking when they buy shares of stock. In theory, a firm whose return on equity (ROE) does not match the return of similarly risky investments should see the value of its stock decline until the shareholders feel that the stock value reflects the earnings rate of the company. Taking the argument one step further, if the firm is consistently unable to meet a risk appropriate rate of return on equity, shareholders should demand that the firm be restructured, reorganized, or liquidated so that their holdings can be invested in holdings that provide a suitable return.

This leads us to the idea of market values.

Market Values

A marketer would declare that the value of a company is simply what someone is willing to pay for its stock. If demand for the stock increases, so will the price. Ideally, an increase in share price is tied to expectations of increased future earnings. However, if one were to look at the "dotcom" frenzy in the late 1990s, one would have to wonder about the concept of market values. Stock prices began to resemble a roller coaster, with steep climbs and precipitous falls.

Many financial managers and investment professionals believe that the **market value** of a firm should in some way reflect its underlying value. Some of the benchmarks that determine share prices are book value and earnings per share. These values can be calculated from the accounting statements.

Book value

$$\text{Book value} = \frac{\text{Total assets}}{\text{Number of shares outstanding}}$$

If the assets are valued fairly and then liquidated, each shareholder would receive his portion of the book value of the firm. There are, of course, several fundamental assumptions that belie the usefulness of this method. First, book value assumes that the assets are valued at current market rates. It also assumes that the assets could be sold for their stated value in the event of dissolution. Neither of these assumptions may be true. It also does not take into account the revenue that is produced as a result of employing the assets. Assets that are not being efficiently utilized are less valuable than assets that are producing a higher rate of return for shareholders.

Earnings per share

$$\text{Earnings per share} = \frac{\text{Net income} - \text{preferred dividends}}{\text{Number of shares outstanding}}$$

Like so many of the other ratios, this one cannot be viewed in isolation. In order to determine what is a valid earnings per share value, you would need to look at trends over time or the earnings of other companies in the same industry.

Unfortunately, earnings per share (specifically quarterly earnings) have been given far more importance recently and, as we discussed in Chapter 1, the emphasis on meeting set targets has led some companies into questionable ethics.

Price-earnings ratio

$$\text{Price-earnings ratio} = \frac{\text{Market price of the stock}}{\text{Earnings per share}}$$

In the News

The quarterly earnings dilemma

Stock prices rise and fall depending on analysts' perceptions of the future value of the corporation. In recent years, firms have attempted to smooth the fluctuations that accompany quarterly earnings reports by giving hints of performance before the numbers were released. Stock market analysts, especially those who work for brokerage firms, reach a consensus of what earnings per share will be. If a company is profitable but misses the earnings target, its stock usually falls by a significant margin. Interestingly, if the company has a loss but the loss is less than analysts predicted, the stock price usually rises.

With such an emphasis on quarterly income numbers, there has been some concern that companies are timing their reporting of accounting data to mitigate the stock swings. For example, a company that knows it will miss the analysts' projections may choose to load a poor quarter with extraordinary charges rather than wait until the next quarter when more appropriate charges might appear. Since the stock will already be adversely affected by lowered earnings, some companies would rather take all of the bad news at once, allowing them to improve earnings in future quarters.

It's not just earnings disappointments that cause the company to adjust accounting assumptions. Statistically, a company that narrowly exceeds quarterly earnings estimates will gain less in percentage terms than it would lose if it narrowly missed targets. In order to smooth the stock prices, some companies will defer sales from one quarter to the next in order to avoid suffering the penalty of missing targets in the future quarter.

The short-term focus on quarterly earning statements distracts the firm from making sound, long-term strategic decisions in favor of short-term stock price considerations. It also favors behavior that can lead to fraud.

The price-earnings ratio compares the market price of the stock with its earnings. Again, it is subject to the industry as well as the expectation of future growth in earnings for that company.

The DuPont Model

What we must remember is that accounting data and the ratios that are derived from the data are merely descriptive; they report what has happened. If ratios fall short of expectations, attempting to fix a single number will not solve the problem. In fact, since many of the ratios recycle the same numbers such as some component of assets, the degree of debt, and a measure of profit, it is interesting to look at the DuPont model.

We said that shareholders want to see a good return on their equity. Those returns (the profits) are a function of using assets wisely to produce the most sales. The DuPont Corporation developed the model in order to better describe what components lead to the profitability of a company and allow management to adjust their decisions to better utilize scarce resources.

The DuPont model breaks return on equity into its activity component, the degree of leverage, and profitability.

The basic return on equity equation is

$$\text{ROE} = \frac{\text{Net income}}{\text{Total equity}}$$

If we multiply by total assets / total assets (which is the same as multiplying by 1), we do not change the value, however, we have described ROE as the product of two different ratios.

$$\text{ROE} = \frac{\text{Net income}}{\text{Total equity}} \times \frac{\text{Total assets}}{\text{Total assets}} = \frac{\text{Net income}}{\text{Assets}} \times \frac{\text{Assets}}{\text{Total equity}}$$

Note that the result

$$\frac{\text{Net income}}{\text{Assets}}$$

is return on assets (ROA) or what we described before as a tool to evaluate whether the firm (or manager) is using assets effectively to produce a profit.

The second component that we have is

$$\frac{\text{Assets}}{\text{Equity}}$$

which is called an equity multiplier. It is $1+$ debt-to-equity ratio.[1] Note that the equity multiplier will become larger as debt becomes a greater percentage of the financing of the company, whether it is because the firm borrows additional money or reduces the amount of equity. In either case, the multiplier shows the degree of leverage that the firm has incurred.

Perhaps a more intuitive view of the equity multiplier is to see it as a description of the dollar value of assets owned by every dollar of equity. Thus, if the equity multiplier (assets / equity) is 2.75, it means that $2.75 of assets are owned for every dollar of shareholders' equity.

The DuPont model goes one step further and breaks the return on assets into two components: an activity ratio and a profitability ratio. This time, we will multiply the ROA component by sales / sales. Since we are once again merely multiplying by a factor of 1, we do not change the value, however, we do change the appearance of the return on equity formula.

$$
\begin{aligned}
\text{ROE} &= \frac{\text{Net Income}}{\text{Assets}} \times \frac{\text{Sales}}{\text{Sales}} \times \frac{\text{Assets}}{\text{Equity}} \\
&= \frac{\text{Net Income}}{\text{Sales}} \times \frac{\text{Sales}}{\text{Assets}} \times \frac{\text{Assets}}{\text{Equity}} \\
&= \text{profit margin} \times \text{asset turnover} \times \text{equity multiplier}
\end{aligned}
$$

[1]The math: $\dfrac{\text{Total assets}}{\text{Total equity}}$ is the same as $\dfrac{\text{Debt} + \text{equity}}{\text{Equity}} = \dfrac{\text{Debt}}{\text{Equity}} + \dfrac{\text{Equity}}{\text{Equity}}$.

Thus, return on equity is actually composed of a profitability measure, an activity ratio, and the degree of leverage. Return on equity is the result of three distinct types of decision making within the firm, each of which must be addressed if the firm is to maximize shareholder value. Graphically, the DuPont model can be arranged in the following manner, which will better demonstrate its usefulness:

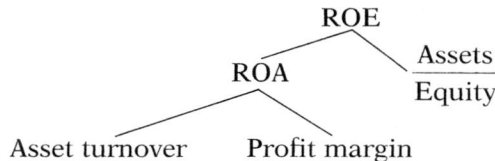

Asset turnover can be further divided into current asset turnover (such as inventory turnover or accounts receivable turnover) and fixed asset turnover. The DuPont model allows a firm to assess the types of relationships that exist and attempt to manage them. For example, pricing of services within the warehouse and transportation services industry may be very competitive and profit margins may be slim. If the firm is unable to raise prices in order to provide increasing returns to shareholders, it must wring the most dollars out of the investment it has in fixed assets by ensuring that the warehouse stays full and trucks are fully utilized.

The effect of the equity multiplier is to allow the firm to evaluate the effect of debt on shareholder returns. If the firm is highly leveraged, the effect of an increase in profit margin will be magnified for shareholders. Debt payments are fixed so the increase in profit flows directly to shareholders, positively impacting the return on their investment.

USING FINANCIAL RATIOS

By now you are scratching your head, wondering how you could possibly use half of the ratios we have just described. The point is that you have to choose the ratios that describe those aspects of your company that you believe are most important or that have significant strategic impact.

Assume that you are in the building supply industry in the Midwest and your main customers are residential construction companies. You know that it is both a seasonal and cyclical industry. In Minnesota, January is not a good month to begin framing a house. Contractors are less likely to be buying lumber packages in January, so your sales will be lower than they would be in spring. Knowing this, the firm can adjust its inventory levels in advance of the slower season so that the inventory turnover does not take as steep a dive. If the inventory turnover plummeted compared with the same period in the previous year, it might indicate that inventory controls had become lax. Note that the comparison was made to the same period. Suppose that the spring season arrives, but home mortgage rates and unemployment figures are rising. If you have stocked up in anticipation of normal conditions, inventory turnover will be slow. At the same time, the firm should be keeping a close

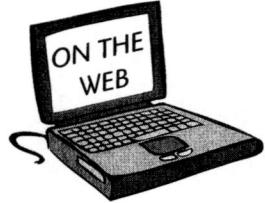

There are several sources for accounting information on the Internet. The *CPA Journal* posts its articles on-line at www.cpaj.com. Articles cover a wide range of subject areas including taxation, financial planning, computers and accounting, and the effect of FASB and SEC rulings. Articles are written for the practitioner and are timely and easy to apply to small and large businesses.

All of the major public accounting firms maintain Web sites. The primary goal of their sites is to communicate with clients and prospective clients, however, they also provide some research and survey information for general users. Often the sites will provide opinion pieces and text of addresses that senior managers have made to industry groups. Some of the sites also provide a link to EDGAR data at the SEC.

www.dttus.com
www.ey.com
www.kmpg.com
www.pwcglobal.com

eye on the accounts receivable turnover rate and the days of sales outstanding. As economic conditions worsen, even your best customers may be slow in paying their bills. Both the inventory and accounts receivable components of the operating cycle have lengthened. Unless you are aware of the slippage, your company could find itself with a cash drain. Because accounts receivable and inventory are both current assets, the current ratio may not show the weakening condition of your business. By keeping track of the key indicators for your business, you will be able to adjust more rapidly to changing conditions.

Unlike the building supply company, a law firm does not carry inventory. In the case of a privately owned service business, the appropriate ratios would be those related to operating efficiency. How much revenue was generated per employee? How profitable was the firm? What was the relationship between the increase in revenue and operating expenses? Financial ratios must be adapted to the needs of each firm.

ACCOUNTING RATIOS FOR NOT-FOR-PROFIT ORGANIZATIONS

Most of this book will focus on financial decision making in a for-profit organization. Revenues derive from marketing a product or service at a price higher than the expenses, so profitability ratios become very important. For a not-for-profit organization, the "price" of the service to the consumer may be free or highly subsidized. There is no revenue for a bag of groceries distributed by the local food bank. However, there are costs involved: the cost of renting a building and operating expenses such as electricity and phone service. If there are paid employees there are salaries and income tax obligations. Donors, whether individual or corporate, provide the revenue for not-for-profit organizations. They want to know the costs of producing the goods or services and how they are defrayed. At the very least, simple accounting statements are required. More sophisticated donors may calculate activity ratios to assess whether the organization is utilizing its assets efficiently.

PLAYING WITH THE BOOKS

"Figures don't lie but liars figure."

Accounting data are true. They have to be, right? There are generally accepted accounting principles (GAAP) that set the guidelines for how transactions should be recorded. A company involved in the retail trade knows what it paid for the merchandise it sells. Manufacturers know how much their raw materials cost along with the cost of labor to produce goods. Tax bills are sent from municipal agencies and paid by check or electronic funds transfer from real bank accounts. All of these are documented twice, thanks to that double-entry method. So, how can I "play with" the books? For the creative accountant there are lots of ways, and it doesn't have to be a multinational company to make not so "minor" adjustments.

Start with the balance sheet. Remember that the balance sheet is a snapshot in time. The time period that the balance sheet was created can have a profound impact on the picture that it provides. Cash and accounts receivable are the major components of the quick ratio. We assume that accounts receivable are turning over at a steady rate and, if the quick ratio is greater than 1, we can cover our short-term debts. However, the day-to-day fluctuations may not be as steady as that. Consider the timing issues of payroll and income taxes. In a new company or one that is facing tenuous circumstances, cash on hand may be severely depleted to pay those obligations. Without a steady inflow of cash from accounts receivable, the quick ratio could begin to look bleak. If I were an entrepreneur in need of a short-term loan, would I rather take my banker a balance sheet the day before I made payroll (when the cash looked pretty healthy) or the day after when my cash position didn't look as flush? Both balance sheets would be accurate, but because of the nature of the timing, each would provide a different picture.

For a seasonal business, inventory may build up before being sent through the distribution channel. A balance sheet produced just before the sales are registered would show a far different relationship between current ratio and the quick ratio than a balance sheet that was drawn up after the inventory started flowing to buyers.

And just how is that inventory being valued? In an industry where the cost of goods is not stable, the inventory valuation method that the company chooses may understate or overstate the value of inventory, potentially inflating the total asset value (and owner's equity) of the firm.

In recent years we have seen both a boom and a bust among e-commerce businesses. Many entrepreneurs started out with good ideas but entered bankruptcy when they could not turn their ideas into a steady revenue stream that included profits. Shareholders who bought stock in dotcom companies with the expectation of rapid future growth and high profits were further disappointed when the failed companies were forced to liquidate. In many cases, inventory was sold for pennies on the dollar. Other tangible corporate assets such as furniture and computers could not be sold for book value, even after being depreciated appropriately. There was simply too much supply and not enough demand—the normal laws of economics drove prices well below book value. Worse yet, proprietary software packages, which were listed as assets, had no value at all to other companies and therefore had no resale value. Were the assets overvalued? Not necessarily. The financial distress that would lead a company to declare bankruptcy does not allow it to hold out for the best price for its inventory and assets. Accounting standards include the assumption that the company will continue to be a going concern, not that it will enter liquidation relatively soon after its inception.

Look at accounts receivable. In the absence of an income statement, we do not know how many days the accounts receivable are staying on the books. Has the company parked bad debts on the balance sheet, long after they can logically be collected? Or, has the company used generous payment terms to "stuff" the distribution channel? Both practices have been used by companies that wish to improve the appearance of a balance sheet.

Retailers have to decide whether to buy or lease retail space. If they own the store, they have a fixed asset that is usually financed by long-term debt. Another choice would be to lease the store. The cost of the lease payments becomes an expense and only the current cost of a long-term lease shows up as a liability. With the same level of sales, the company that leases the storefront will have a better return on assets than the merchant who owns his space. Long-term lease arrangements must be disclosed in the notes to the financial statements, but unless you read the notes carefully and add in the cost of the lease, the balance sheet and income statement will give very different earnings ratios depending on whether the space is owned or leased.

PRO FORMA STATEMENTS

A common thread running through this chapter is the fact that ratios are only valid if they are used to evaluate comparable sets of data. But how can you compare data for a company that is in its infancy? A start-up firm needs to convince potential lenders and investors that it has a well-conceived business plan, along with prospects for growth and profit. Pro forma financial statements are prepared, giving estimates for revenue, costs, and profits as if the firm were a going concern. Pro forma statements are also drawn up when the company envisions a significant change in business such as might result from a merger, acquisition, or large-scale expansion. These pro forma statements must be viewed very carefully, with an eye to the assumptions

Consolidated Mineral Holdings Corporation
Pro Forma Consolidated Balance Sheet
December 31, 2000
(in thousands, unaudited)

	Jaspar Corporation	Agate Enterprises	Pro Forma Adjustments	Consolidated Mineral Holdings
Assets				
Current assets				
Cash	$2,655	$850		$3,505
Accounts receivable	$1,575	$2,300	$400	$3,475
Inventory	$6,580	$5,500		$12,080
Total current assets	$10,810	$8,650	$400	$19,060
Long-term assets				
Investments	$5,000	$1,200		$6,200
Property, plant and equipment, net	$12,450	$13,500	$3,000	$22,950
Total assets	$28,260	$23,350	$3,400	$48,210
Liabilities and shareholders' equity				
Liabilities				
Total current liabilities	$7,500	$8,500	$300	$15,700
Long-term debts and other obligation	$6,500	$12,765		$19,265
Total liabilities	$14,000	$21,265		$35,265
Shareholders' equity				
Common stock	$4,260	$600		$4,860
Retained earnings	$10,000	$1,485		$11,485
Total equity	$14,260	$2,085		$16,345
Total liabilities and equity	$28,260	$23,350		$51,610

Jaspar Corporation and Agate Enterprises have agreed to merge. The combined companies will shed duplicate assets and streamline their operations. The pro-forma balance sheet is meant to show shareholders the desired effects of the merger.

underlying the entries. They gain credibility when the issuer has had experience in the business and shows reasonable restraint in estimating revenues and expenses.

The use of pro forma statements has been proliferating, and some companies use them to cushion what would otherwise be bad news. Occasionally, a company will experience unusual business conditions that significantly affect the performance of the company. Under the circumstances, the company does not want to compare their bottom line, or net profit (or loss), to previous periods. If a severe hurricane along the Atlantic Coast caused the Northon Hardware stores in the region to close for a week, you would logically expect this year's profits to fall when compared with the previous year's. In addition, the damage sustained by the stores would cause expenses to increase. Although the company would report the expenses as extraordinary costs and describe the circumstances in its notes to the financial statements, many companies are afraid that casual readers will not read all of the fine print, settling only on the difference between this quarter's profit and the previous year's profit in the same quarter. For that reason, many companies are issuing pro forma earnings results to accompany the statements created under GAAP. If the mishap is truly extraordinary, one that is not likely to recur, pro forma statements serve a valid purpose.

Unfortunately, there has been an insidious temptation to redefine extraordinary costs and lump long-term capital expenditures into the category. What benefit does this technique provide? Let's assume that the Northon Company upgrades its hardware stores on a 5-year cycle. Under normal accounting rules, renovation costs would be an ongoing expense that would not affect gross income but would reduce net income. Let's assume that the stores that were damaged by the hurricane were already slated for renovation. If the company lumps the entire cost of renovation into the extraordinary costs category and then creates a pro forma earnings statement, it has, in effect, overstated income for the period. The "as-if" earnings have been padded by reducing normal operating expenses, moving them to the extraordinary expense line, and then subtracting all of the extraordinary costs from the pro forma statement. If the company can cause enough positive coverage of its adjusted pro forma results to mask the GAAP income figures, it can create a misleading impression of its financial condition.

TERMS TO KNOW

Financial accounting	Assets	Vertical analysis
Managerial accounting	Liabilities	Horizontal analysis
Generally accepted accounting principles (GAAP)	Owner's equity	Ratio analysis
	Income statement	Liquidity
	Revenue	Activity
Accrual accounting	Expense	Leverage
Cash accounting	Profit	Profitability
Double-entry bookkeeping	Statement of cash flows	Market value
Balance sheet	Changes in financial condition	

TERM PAPERS AND PROJECTS

1. Perform an industry analysis, using several companies in the same basic industry. Examine the financial statements to determine which is the healthiest company. Review the chairman's letter to the shareholders in the most current annual report to see if she or he addresses any weaknesses you have found in the company's financial statements.

2. Compare the financial condition of the major U.S. airlines in their fiscal year 2000, 2001, and 2002. Determine which weaknesses might have been a result of the existing market conditions, which might have been caused by the turmoil in the fourth quarter of 2001, and which airlines have successfully weathered the subsequent economic downturn.

3. Enron, an energy services company, created many "off balance sheet" transactions. Enron has already been the subject of many newspaper and tabloid articles describing the corporate culture and wild goings-on. Try to separate the gossip from the accounting issues. Examine Enron's financial collapse and attempt to determine what items were off balance sheet and which financial structures might have been acceptable under generally accepted accounting principles. Were there any innovative approaches to accounting or was it completely a house of cards?

REVIEW QUESTIONS

1. What is GAAP and why is it important?
2. What is the difference between financial accounting and managerial accounting? What is each used for? Give examples of each.
3. What are the four main accounting statements? Give a brief description of each.
4. What is accrual accounting? How does it differ from cash-based accounting?
5. Why is a statement of cash flows important in evaluating a business?
6. Differentiate between vertical analysis and horizontal analysis of a financial statement.
7. What is a liquidity ratio? Why would it be important?
8. In which of the following businesses would inventory turnover rate be the highest: a McDonald's franchise, the local auto dealer, or a yacht sales yard? Why?
9. When would it be prudent for a firm to acquire more debt?
10. Why is return on equity important for a firm that is seeking new financing?
11. What is a price-earnings ratio? How is it calculated?
12. How can a firm use the DuPont model to improve efficiency?
13. What is the difference between a seasonal industry and a cyclical one? What financing implications does that have?
14. What are the advantages and disadvantages of using ratio analysis?

REVIEW PROBLEMS

1. A firm with sales of $180,000 has $70,000 in inventory. The industry average for inventory turnover is 4.0. If the firm can achieve the industry average, what affect would it have on the inventory value assuming sales remain constant?

2. Using the following financial statements, calculate:
   a. Current ratio
   b. Quick ratio
   c. Inventory turnover
   d. Accounts receivable turnover
   e. Gross profit margin
   f. Operating profit
   g. Net profit
   h. Return on assets
   i. Return on equity

Ashline Industries
2000 Balance Sheet

Current assets		*Current liabilities*	
Cash	$125	Accounts payable	$180
Accounts Receivable	$500	Accrued liabilities	$700
Inventory	$800	Total current liabilities	$880
Total current assets	$1,425	Long-term debt	$115
Fixed assets	$1,400	Shareholders' equity	$1,830
Total assets	$2,825	Total liabilities and equity	$2,825

Ashline Industries
2000 Income Statement

Net sales revenue	$1,900
Cost of goods sold	$1,250
Gross profit	$650
Total operating expenses	$445
Operating profit	$205
Other income and expenses	$125
Earnings before taxes	$80
Taxes	$65
Net income	$15

CHAPTER

7 BREAK-EVEN ANALYSIS AND PROFIT

LEARNING OBJECTIVES

1. Describe the difference between efficiency and effectiveness.

2. Perform break-even analysis in terms of units and revenue.

3. Understand the difference between fixed costs and variable costs.

4. Describe why fixed costs might vary at differing production levels.

5. Discuss the trade-offs involved in substituting fixed costs for variable costs.

6. Describe the relationship between breakeven and profit.

7. Discuss pricing and break-even analysis within context of the product life cycle.

8. Understand the difference between short-term loss and the consequences of sustained operating losses.

9. Compare and contrast Chapter 11 bankruptcy with Chapter 7 bankruptcy.

In order for a firm to be profitable, managers from all areas of the business must cooperate. Break-even analysis is a tool that enables finance, purchasing, and marketing managers to make sound decisions regarding the products the firm offers for sale, the price charged, and the financial structure of production. Although the subject of this book is finance, it is important to see how decision making must be interrelated for a company to flourish.

EFFICIENCY AND EFFECTIVENESS

Efficiency refers to matching the available inputs with outputs to provide a service that consumers value. For most firms, the amount of inputs (i.e., equipment, investment funds, personnel hours, and technological knowledge) is limited. An efficient organization produces the best possible product while minimizing resource costs. Finance helps clarify which investment decisions will help the organization meet its goals of efficiency.

Effectiveness refers to the firm's ability to produce goods and services and can also be used as a description of the quality of those goods. For example, an Internet service provider might contemplate providing instant Internet access with the highest technologically attainable speed to every possible subscriber worldwide. In order to do that they must invest in expensive equipment and continually monitor quality levels so that as they add customers, the capacity does not become overtaxed and speed does not diminish. However, this commitment to speed comes at a literal cost to the company, which they must be able to pass along to their customers if they are to be successful (and profitable).

BREAK-EVEN ANALYSIS

While the goal of most businesses is to make a profit, at the very least they need to break even. Breakeven is the point at which all of the costs of running the business are covered by revenue earned. There is no profit, so the first way of looking at breakeven is

$$\text{Total revenue} = \text{Total costs}$$

Each side of the equation can be divided into two components. **Total revenue** is simply the income produced from selling the firm's product, therefore

$$\text{Total revenue} = \text{Price per unit sold} \times \text{quantity of units sold}$$
$$\text{TR} = \text{P} \times \text{Q}$$

Total revenue will be affected by the price charged and the number of units sold. As the price rises, the number of units that the firm must sell to break even decreases. For a product with a normal demand curve, fewer goods are likely to be sold as the price rises. In addition, sales of the product can be affected by the economic climate. During recessions, sales of higher-priced items tend to fall as consumers shift their spending to lower-priced goods or substitute products. For example, shoppers may choose to buy boxed macaroni and cheese and hot dogs rather than more expensive take-out food from the grocery store's deli. Total revenue for the macaroni and cheese maker will rise since the quantity sold has increased, even though the price has remained the same. This component of **break-even analysis**— estimating demand for a product under differing economic assumptions—is usually the responsibility of the marketing department. However, since the total revenue of the firm does affect its ability to service its debts and buy new capital equipment, the finance manager is acutely interested in revenue projections.

The second component of break-even analysis is **total costs.** Costs of production can be broken into two components: costs that vary with production, such as materials, and costs that do not vary, such as interest on the company's debt. Costs that vary are called **variable costs** (VC) and costs that do not vary are called **fixed costs** (FC). The equation for total costs is

---

Fixed costs could include

- Cost of the corporate headquarters
- Cost of the factories, warehouses, and distribution centers
- Wages for salaried workers
- Property taxes
- Insurance
- Advertising
- Research and development costs

Fixed costs.

$$\text{Total costs} = \text{Fixed costs} + \text{variable costs}$$
$$TC = FC + VC$$

Fixed costs are constant regardless of the level of production. Let's use a tomato canning factory as our example. Tomatoes are a seasonal crop and the factory will only be in full operation for a portion of the year. Fixed costs are most easily seen during the facility's downtime when it will still require funding for the monthly mortgage, annual property taxes, a base level of electricity even though the plant is not operating, and the salaries of the plant manager and the full-time maintenance crew. The plant itself has costs associated with it, but it is also part of a larger organization that includes the firm's executives and staff, such as members of the accounting and legal departments. Fixed costs also include any employee benefits that do not vary with production such as the cost of maintaining a day care or fitness center. A portion of these corporate costs will be allocated to each factory as overhead.

We often talk about fixed costs as though they will never change. In the short term, that is true. Over time, as the company expands or contracts production, fixed costs *will* change. The increase will be like stairsteps rather than the smooth line that we see with variable costs. The increases often come in the form of new capital investment or increased staff (as opposed to line workers whose wages are variable costs). For the rest of this chapter, we will assume that most of the fixed costs do remain constant. In Chapter 8 we will examine what happens when the firm experiences significantly different levels of production or sales, and how the changes affect the finances of the firm. But for now, we will make only minor adjustments.

Variable costs are those that change according to the level of production. At the tomato canning plant, the costs of the tomatoes, the cans, and the labels are direct material costs. The wages paid to the line workers and their benefits are direct labor costs. The increase in utilities during the canning season is also directly attributable to the manufacturing process.

Here is where the purchasing department becomes a key component of the equation. The more efficient a company is in obtaining the lowest cost for raw materials, the lower its variable costs will be and, at the same level of sales, the higher its profits. But even variable costs can become somewhat fixed. Long before the tomatoes turn red, the purchasing agent should have

---

Variable costs include

Inputs required to produce a product

- raw materials costs
- direct labor
- electricity to power the production machinery
- taxes related to direct labor or the cost of new materials

Variable costs.

negotiated a favorable price for the cans and labels. Contracts can be signed with local growers to supply their crops at a set price per pound. The variable price per unit will stay constant; what will vary is the quantity of cans that can be produced that season. Variable costs can therefore be expressed as

$$\text{Total variable costs} = \text{Cost per unit} \times \text{quantity of units produced}$$

BREAKEVEN AND PROFIT

Even when the firm is producing no products, it incurs fixed costs. Since the costs exceed revenues (no products would equal no revenue), the firm is losing money. While that may seem to be an obvious statement, it has significant financial ramifications. One of the strategic decisions a firm must make is to decide the level of fixed costs at which they feel comfortable. The tomato canning company would most likely want its own factory, but does it need to own its warehouses? If it owns warehouses, the costs associated with them are fixed. Is there a minimum level of warehouse space that must be maintained year-round? Could the rest be leased on a seasonal basis, dependent solely on the level of anticipated production? Empty warehouses are an unproductive asset and the goal of the firm is to utilize assets as fully as possible.

The first step for the firm is to determine the quantity of goods it must sell in order to cover all of its costs. We can obtain that quantity by rearranging the components of the break-even equation.

$$\text{Total revenue} = \text{Total costs}$$

is the same as

$$\text{Sale price per unit} \times \text{\# units} = \text{Fixed costs} + \text{variable costs}$$
$$\text{Price} \times \text{quantity} = \text{Fixed costs} + (\text{cost/unit} \times \text{\# units})$$
$$PQ = \text{Fixed costs} + (CQ)$$

We want to simplify this in order to separate out the quantity that will allow the firm to break even, therefore

$$PQ - CQ = \text{Fixed costs} + (CQ) - (CQ)$$
$$PQ - CQ = \text{Fixed costs}$$
$$Q(P - C) = \text{Fixed costs}$$
$$Q(\text{Quantity to break even}) = \frac{\text{Fixed costs}}{\text{CM}}$$

The difference between the sales price of each unit of product (P) and the variable cost to produce it (C) is called the **contribution margin** (CM). It is the amount of revenue that each sale contributes to offsetting fixed costs and, eventually, to creating a profit for the firm. Contribution margin is a very useful tool to have because it allows you to calculate very quickly the break-even point for any change in sale price or variable cost.

Let's say that the tomato canning plant can produce a 1-pound can of tomatoes for $.16 and can sell it for $.32 per can. The monthly fixed costs are $64,000. How many cans of tomatoes would need to be sold per month in order for the company to simply break even?

Going to the original formula gives us a variable, Q, on both sides of the equation:

$$TR = TC$$
$$\$.32 \times Q = \$64,000 + (\$.16 \times Q)$$
$$\$.32Q - \$.16Q = \$64,000$$
$$Q = \frac{\$64,000}{(\$.32 - \$.16)}$$
$$Q = 400,000 \text{ cans of tomatoes per month}$$

Whew! That's a lot of tomatoes. It's also more work than we needed to do. For any combination of price and variable costs, we could have obtained a contribution margin. If we presume that fixed costs will stay constant, it is the price and variable costs that will be more subject to market or economic fluctuations. An increase in the raw materials costs due to unseasonably cool weather or the wage increases for direct labor will force us to make a decision: Do we raise the price to keep the break-even point fixed or do we accept a lower contribution margin and increase production to cover fixed costs?

CHANGING THE LEVEL OF FIXED COSTS

Break-even analysis also allows us to tinker with the idea of changing the level of fixed costs. Suppose, in the example given above, the plant manager could buy a new piece of equipment for $6,000. The machine will automate a portion of the assembly line, requiring fewer personnel hours and reducing direct costs by $.04 per can. What effect would that have on the break-even quantity? In this example, we are making a simple substitution of fixed costs for variable costs; we are not making a significant change in our operations. We'll leave that for the next chapter.

The price per can is still $.32 and the new variable cost is now $.12, while fixed costs have increased to $70,000. Breakeven is

$$Q = \frac{\$70,000}{\$.32 - \$.12}$$
$$= 350,000 \text{ per month}$$

At any level of sales over 4,200,000 cans per year, the investment appears to be a wise one.

We have been dealing with pennies in this example and four cents may not seem like a huge savings in direct costs, but when you compare it in percentage terms, the difference is 25% of the original variable cost (.04/.16). Can the company truly save that much with the purchase of this machine? What if the savings is only $.015 (a penny and a half) per can? At that rate, the investment decision becomes more complicated.

$$Q = \frac{\$70,000}{\$.32 - \$.145}$$
$$= 400,000 \text{ per month}$$

If the investment in new machinery produces only a $.015 reduction in costs, the break-even quantity remains the same as it did before the new machine was factored into the equation. What then? The answer is not found in the break-even formula.

By simplifying the break-even equation and looking specifically at the contribution margin, we can quickly see the effect of changes in price and costs in a spreadsheet.

BREAK-EVEN QUANTITY

Sales price per item	Variable cost per item	Contribution margin per item	Fixed costs	Break-even quantity
0.32	0.16	0.16	$64,000	$400,000
0.32	0.12	0.2	$70,000	$350,000
0.32	0.145	0.175	$70,000	$400,000

This tool allows all of the managers involved in decision-making to ask "what-if" when adjusting for changing business conditions. For example, if direct labor costs are escalating and we do not feel that we can raise the price we charge for our product, can we substitute fixed costs (in the form of new machinery) for the rising variable costs? We would be attempting to meet the goal of efficiency—knowing that rising labor costs will increase our break-even point. Can we minimize the impact on our firm by investing in technological inputs rather than personnel hours? Break-even analysis also allows managers to make explicit statements about what levels of production are likely to trigger changes in fixed and/or variable costs.

As long as there is unused capacity in the plant, fixed costs should not rise. If the plant has been running two 8-hour shifts but more tomatoes come in, the plant can add a third shift and not increase the fixed costs. When the plant reaches

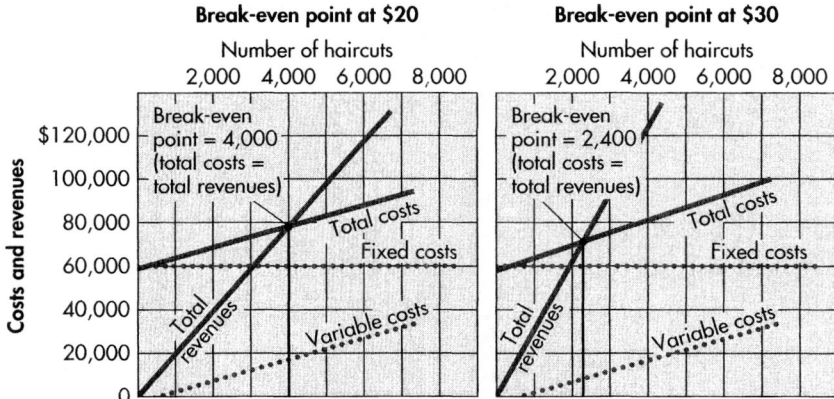

These charts reflect the change in break-even quantity as a result of a change in price from $20 to $30. (C. Bovée & J. Thill. *Business in Action.* Upper Saddle River, NJ: Prentice Hall, 2001.)

the point that adding workers is no longer possible, the firm will be faced with a decision: Is it more advantageous to obtain added capacity or would it be better to forgo producing the additional product? At a specified level of production, the fixed cost component will need to be adjusted to reflect this decision point.

CHANGING THE LEVEL OF VARIABLE COSTS

Variable costs will also change, depending on the volume of business. Although we stated earlier that variable costs can be predicted using long-term contracts, those contracts may include volume discounts, which would reduce the variable cost per unit when certain quantities were met. Raw material costs are only one piece of variable costs. Labor is often a large portion of the direct cost of a product. Overall, variable costs could rise if increased production required the use of overtime or shift differential wages in staffing a 24-hour factory. Accurate record keeping and good historic data can provide the firm with some indication of where these cost junctures occur. We will look at this again in Chapter 8.

THE IMPORTANCE OF DEMAND

Although break-even analysis is a very powerful tool, we have left one major question unanswered: Can we sell the quantity that we need to make in order to break even? Is it realistic to assume that we will be able to sell an average of 400,000 cans of tomatoes per month? Can we even sell the lower amount necessary to justify the investment in new machinery? Again, we must rely on the marketing and economic forecasting departments to provide us with realistic projections of **demand** for our product at specified price points.

We can use a variation of break-even analysis to determine the break-even point in dollars. At the break-even point, the price of the item first covers the direct costs associated with production. The remaining portion (which is the contribution margin) can be expressed as the percentage of the price that is allocated toward reducing fixed costs and, eventually, contribute to profit.

$$\text{Break-even revenue} \times \text{CM (expressed as a percent)} = \text{fixed costs}$$

In the example above, the contribution margin changes each time a new assumption is made, which means that the break-even point in sales revenue changes.

BREAK-EVEN ANALYSIS: SALES REVENUE NEEDED TO BREAK EVEN

Sales price per item	Variable cost per item	Contribution margin per item	Contribution margin as a percent of sales price	Fixed costs	Sales revenue required to break even
0.32	0.16	0.16	50.0000%	$64,000	$128,000
0.32	0.12	0.2	62.5000%	$70,000	$112,000
0.32	0.145	0.175	54.6875%	$70,000	$128,000

Another way to determine breakeven in dollars is to multiply the break-even quantity times the price per unit, but that assumes that you have already calculated the break-even point in units.

PROFIT

Until now, we have only been interested in covering our costs, but most businesses prefer to show a profit. In the simplest definition, profit is any amount left after total expenses are subtracted from total revenue.

$$\text{Profit} = \text{TR} - \text{TC}$$

You will recall that in Chapter 6 we talked about several different types of profit: gross profit, profit from operations, and net profit. Each of these types of profit demonstrates different things about an organization, but the one that most people focus on is net profit, or the bottom line (what is left after all of the expenses are paid). We can use the break-even formula to create a spreadsheet that will demonstrate profits (or losses) at each level of production.

The managers of the tomato canning company could produce a spreadsheet that illustrates the effect of varying sales quantities on the profit of the company. In the following table, we show the first assumptions that we made. The table can be changed to reflect the purchase of a new machine or the increase in labor costs. It illustrates the profit sensitivity of various pricing and cost structures and can be expanded as needed. For example, if the company wants to know the operating profit of a given business unit before assigning corporate overhead, the fixed cost column could be split out. Interest costs could likewise be separated from the profitability analysis. The choice of which charges to itemize will depend, in part, on where the company or product is in its life cycle.

BREAK-EVEN ANALYSIS: PROFIT PROJECTION

Quantity sold per month	Sales price per item	Revenue	Variable cost per item	Total variable costs	Contribution margin	Fixed costs	Profit/ (Loss)
100000	0.32	32000	0.16	$16,000	$16,000	$64,000	−480,00
150000	0.32	48000	0.16	$24,000	$24,000	$64,000	−40,000
200000	0.32	64000	0.16	$32,000	$32,000	$64,000	−32,000
250000	0.32	80000	0.16	$40,000	$40,000	$64,000	−24,000
300000	0.32	96000	0.16	$48,000	$48,000	$64,000	−16,000
350000	0.32	112000	0.16	$56,000	$56,000	$64,000	−8,000
400000	0.32	128000	0.16	$64,000	$64,000	$64,000	0
450000	0.32	144000	0.16	$72,000	$72,000	$64,000	8,000
500000	0.32	160000	0.16	$80,000	$80,000	$64,000	16,000
550000	0.32	176000	0.16	$88,000	$88,000	$64,000	24,000
600000	0.32	192000	0.16	$96,000	$96,000	$64,000	32,000

PRICING CONSIDERATIONS AND THE PRODUCT LIFE CYCLE

Pricing decisions and a discussion of the product life cycle may seem more appropriate for a marketing text rather than a finance text. In fact, they are an expression of one of the fundamental strategic goals of an organization. As a result, they are (or should be) intimately tied to the financial structure of the organization. We will look at a couple of examples to show the financing implications.

A significant marketing concept for financing decisions is the **product life cycle.** Briefly, products can go through several stages during their life cycle. First is the **introductory stage.** The company has just begun to market a new product that they hope will be successful, although there are no guarantees. Before the product ever hits the shelves it has incurred costs—investment in research and development costs, the initial production run including variable costs once the product is successful, and initial marketing costs. These are sunk costs; if no products are sold, the costs will not be recovered and the company will show a loss. Once sales have begun, the product must cover its variable costs and ongoing fixed costs, and repay its sunk costs before it can contribute to profit. Most companies set earnings expectations for new products based on the amount of money that goes into development and the expected future cash flows of the product. Adding an additional flavor to a line of cake mixes requires much less investment, more chance of consumer acceptance, and more predictable long-term sales than creating a freezer-to-microwave-to-table frosted cake mix. The company will analyze the level of risk and require higher initial reward (in the form of profit margin) from the less certain investment. In this case, it is far more certain that consumers will understand and accept the idea of a new cake flavor than it is that they will try the new-fangled technological marvel. Although new products are considered the lifeblood of a growing organization, initial financing costs can restrict the

Stop and Think

Some products are not designed to last for a long time. Think about Teenage Mutant Ninja Turtles or Transformers. They are fad products designed to move in and out of the distribution channel, earning as much profit as possible before their popularity wanes.

Toys tied to popular movies are a classic case. For more than four decades, little girls have played with Barbie. But how many of you have Jasmine (from *Aladdin*) or the Little Mermaid in your toy chest? Try buying them at Wal-Mart or Target. They aren't there.

Fad items are profitable if they can be sold when the movie is playing and excitement is high. Fast-food restaurants offer toys in their children's meals that are to tied in to the latest, greatest children's movie. Toymakers have been equally anxious to capitalize on a branded opportunity.

However, some of these promotions have fallen flat. Although *Star Wars: Episode 1—The Phantom Menace* produced $1 billion in merchandise sales, many retailers were left with unsold inventory long after the movie had moved to second-run theaters. As a result, toymakers and retailers reduced their inventory of movie tie-ins for *Harry Potter*, *Lord of the Rings*, and *Monsters, Inc.*, all of which appeared at the end of 2001.

As a result, *Business Week* reported that by November 17, just one day after the opening of *Harry Potter and the Sorcerer's Stone*, some customers were finding it difficult to buy movie-themed toys. For the shopper, the lower levels of inventory were a disappointment. For the manufacturer and retailer, it meant that the product was sold at its estimated price, no markdowns were taken, and profits should have been maintained, all of which have financial implications.

Source: "Boffo at the Box Office, Scarce on the Shelves," *Business Week*, December 3, 2001, by Christopher Palmeri in Los Angeles and Diane Brady and Nanette Byrnes in New York.

number of products a firm has in development. Only the most likely to succeed are funded.

During the second life cycle stage, or **growth stage,** consumers have clearly accepted the new product and competitors are starting to emerge. If the company has been outsourcing production, it should consider investing in plants or equipment that would require additional financing. Whether the investment comes as purchase or a capital lease, the company will make a long-term commitment that comes with exit costs should the product not succeed. In addition, during the growth stage sales volume increases but profit per unit decreases as firms compete for sales by lowering their prices. For the finance manager, all parts of the profit picture are moving—price per unit is falling, but total revenue should be increasing because of the increased sales volume. Variable costs may also fall as more production is brought on line and volume discounts on materials are realized. Direct labor costs may decline as workers become more skilled at producing the product or increased automation is added to the mix. Fixed costs may increase when production hits certain levels. This may be one of the more demanding times for the finance manager because the product has not attained a steady sales volume or price point.

Although the introduction and growth stages offer the greatest potential for high profit margins, it is the **maturity stage** that provides the most predictable cash flow for the organization. Products in the maturity phase such as detergent, soap, spaghetti sauce, and canned pears have predicable costs (both variable and fixed) and stable revenue. Profit per unit falls because competition has increased; thus the finance manager's job is to carefully manage the trade-off between fixed costs and variable costs.

Manufacturers such as Procter & Gamble, Anheuser Busch, Ford Motor Company, General Mills, and others operate in highly competitive, mature markets where product differentiation is difficult. The goal of the organization is to convince the consumer that there is some added value for their brand. In reality, the difference between brands is minimal. For example, there are many brands of toothpaste: one has blue sparkles, another might have a streak of color running through it, yet a third comes in child-pleasing flavors. The technology for producing these products is fairly standard—you need an automated production line that can put paste or gel into tubes or bottles. The ingredients are predictable from one batch to the next and should be procured using long-term contracts. Thus, variable production costs are probably fairly low. But what about advertising? In a highly competitive market, advertising may be necessary and prompts a strategic decision: Is advertising a fixed cost or variable cost? If we allocate our advertising expenditures as a percent of sales, the link between product and advertising is direct, therefore it would increase the variable cost per unit. Using this philosophy, income generated by sales could be used in the following month to fund advertising. The advertising budget (and cash budget) would vary by month. If, however, we assume that there is a fixed amount of advertising that we will run every year, regardless of sales volume, we have created a new fixed cost and advertising is seen as an investment just as a new piece of equipment would be. It would have to be figured into the list of fixed expenses that would need to be financed during the year.

While it initially appears to be a marketing decision, the corporate philosophy toward advertising or marketing expenses does have serious financial implications. For example, not all products allow for flexibility in funding. Capital equipment sales often take months or years to develop. The price of the equipment is high and it is purchased infrequently. For companies who sell this type of specialized product, advertising is less important than maintaining a professional salesforce and a technical support staff who work closely with potential clients, often over the course of years. The monthly sales volume for capital equipment companies is not as predictable as that of toothpaste and is far more subject to cyclical downturns in the economy. We have seen an example of this recently in the computer hardware industry. Reductions in capital spending on the part of major corporations have severely impacted the sales of computer companies. Financing decisions need to take into account the high level of fixed costs, including production costs and personnel costs, and recognize the need for large cash reserves to weather periods of slower sales.

In a stable economic environment, the cash thrown off by mature products such as toothpaste, laundry detergent, and packaged food can be used to

> ### In the News
>
> When a product enters the maturity phase of the life cycle, it becomes more difficult to make a decent profit margin. This is especially true if the product is a commodity that is relatively easy to produce.
>
> In the mid-1990s, Archer Daniels Midland thought they had the answer. If they could find a way to convince their competitors to hold the line on prices, everyone would make money. ADM was certainly not the first to figure this out. Several companies have introduced some variation of "every day low pricing" to try to avoid deeply discounted sales, which only lead to lower profit margins. However, ADM didn't just hold the line on prices, it engaged in an effort to fix prices for lysine, a livestock-feed additive.
>
> The corporation eventually pleaded guilty to **price fixing** and several of the senior executives received prison sentences. But before they did, what had been a rather dull case of corporate mischief had turned into a soap opera. The company was exposed by a manager who was then found guilty of embezzlement, seriously compromising the government's case against ADM.
>
> You can read more about this in two recent books:
>
> *Rats in the Grain: The Dirty Tricks and Trials of Archer Daniels Midland,* by James B. Lieber, Four Walls Eight Windows, 2000.
>
> *The Informant: A True Story,* by Kurt Eichenwald, Broadway Books, 2000.
>
> My advice? Every day low pricing is fine. Price fixing is not a good strategy!

fund incremental competitive changes in existing goods as well as investment in new, more innovative offerings. In the absence of cataclysmic market changes, finance managers can count on a stable source of internally generated cash. In fact, these mature products are often called cash cows. We could be clever and say that it is because they can provide a steady stream of liquid assets (cash).

Once a product is well-established, it would be nice if its maturity stage lasted forever. The predictability of cash flows and investment costs makes them easy on the budget. However, it can become necessary to kill a product or discontinue an entire line of business that has serious financial problems. It seems obvious to discontinue a product when it no longer breaks even and the prospect of future sales improvement is nil. However, the decision is not always that straightforward.

A product enters the decline stage when sales can no longer be maintained at a steady level and profits fall steadily. The product's sales do not respond to increased marketing efforts such as distributor incentives or increased advertising.

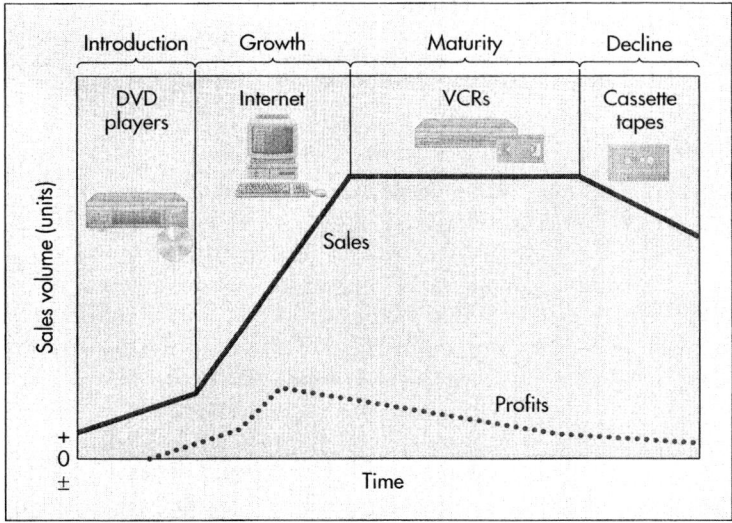

Products that are in different stages of the product life cycle. (C. Bovée & J. Thill. *Business in Action.* Upper Saddle River, NJ: Prentice Hall, 2001.)

Before discontinuing the product, both marketing and finance managers should consider several factors related to both revenues and costs. What if the product is unique and considered irreplaceable by its consumers? Rather than discontinue production, could the firm raise the price enough to cover costs? Is the market willing to absorb the increase in cost rather than try to find a substitute product? On the cost side of the equation, as the amount of product demand falls, can the fixed costs dedicated to this product be reallocated within the firm, thus lowering the fixed cost component? For example, is the production line generic enough to be switched between multiple products, allowing a lower volume of product to be produced and still maintain profitability?

The manner in which a company chooses to discontinue a product has an effect on its financial health. The company needs to determine how to dispose of the existing inventory of finished goods. If the company decides to liquidate, it might have to write down the value of its inventory, which would create an expense for that time period. Property or equipment that was solely dedicated to the product would have to be sold or converted to other uses, which might also create an expense. Although it is wise in the long run, the decision to discontinue a money-losing product creates additional short-term loss for the business.

Some firms choose to subsidize money-losing units. Although it would seem to violate the concept of efficiency, the firm may have decided that discontinuing certain products would have a negative impact on the corporation. Among the reasons for continuing such an operation might be the desire to keep trade secrets in-house. In that case, the value of guarding a proprietary formula might offset the higher production costs. There might also be some emotional attachment to a product, which makes it more difficult to make the financially wise decision to kill it.

LOSS AND BANKRUPTCY

Short-Term Loss

In Chapter 6, we talked about pro forma statements and how some companies use them to disguise poor earnings results. But pro forma statements are also appropriate when the company is just starting out and expects to have losses. Before beginning a company, or when significant changes in ownership or structure occur, the finance manager should construct a set of pro forma statements that covers several years. The statements should show projected start-up and continuing expenses, both on an income statement and a balance sheet. Understandably, the income statements for the first period of time will show losses as the company's start-up costs outpace revenue. Sales projections should be developed with both price and quantity estimates and forecasted several years into the future. Underlying assumptions of demand and price sensitivity should accompany the revenue estimates. Pro forma cash flow statements show the uses of cash, which tie in to the balance sheet and income statement figures, along with the expected cash source. Serious questions should be addressed before the company approaches potential investors, among them: How does the firm expect to finance the initial losses—through borrowing, investment by the owners, or sale of stock? How long do the owners expect losses to continue, and what steps would be taken if costs exceed estimates?

After the firm has been established, actual monthly, quarterly, and year-end financial statements can be compared with the pro forma statements to determine whether the company is on pace to become profitable. Deviations from the pro forma statements, whether positive or negative, can be used to revise the original estimates. A complete set of financial statements is created when the company is starting from scratch, but even a well-established company should create revenue and expense projections when it is launching a new product or discontinuing an operation. We will look at these types of estimates in Chapter 8 when we develop capital budgets.

Short-term losses can also occur at well-established businesses for many reasons including poor planning, economic or competitive changes, or changes in public policy. Industries that are highly dependent on petroleum products, such as airlines, may face short-term losses if the price of jet fuel increases dramatically. Makers of luxury goods are affected by lowering consumer confidence and recessions. Companies that do not keep pace with technological or competitive improvements can suffer from lower sales and reduced profits. In any case, losses are a signal to the company that fundamental decisions need to be reassessed and cost structures reexamined.

In some cases, short-term losses, whether in a particular operating unit or across the corporation, result from long-term strategic decisions. Let's assume that we have a manufacturing company that produces toys to sell to consumers via mass merchants like Target, Kmart, and Wal-Mart, as well as selling bulk quantities to fast-food merchants. The inputs would be similar: the toys are made with basic raw materials, perhaps on similar assembly lines, and shipped in standard-size cartons. However, the toy business is very competitive. Several major toy manufacturers have merged in recent years, creating fewer but larger companies. Toys are in the maturity phase of the product life cycle, and there is not a huge demand for increased toy making capacity. In order to compete effectively, our company may have to choose one type of customer over the other.

Go back to the discussion of inventory valuation from Chapter 6 and the decision to discontinue a failing product from earlier in this chapter. In a going concern, finished goods inventory would be valued the lower of cost or market, assuming that the current market price could be obtained. Fixed assets used in production would be valued at cost less accumulated depreciation. Recall from your accounting courses that depreciation is a charge against earnings and, depending on the method employed, may or may not reflect the actual current market value of the machinery. The same is true of a factory or commercial site. If the facility was designed for a specific purpose and is not easily transferable to another use, the value of the property may be worth less than its book value. Now think of our toy company. When we exit one of the businesses, will we be able to liquidate the remaining inventory at its book value or will we have to significantly discount it? In a highly competitive business will the machinery we no longer need have a resale value equal to the value we assigned to it? Will we need all of our factory space and warehouses or will some be left idle or sold for a discount? When all is said and done, the assets may be worth far less than we had valued them and their disposal will cause a one-time expense, often referred to as a restructuring charge. Should this cost, even if it is significant, deter us from making the decision to close that division? No, not if we have done our homework. The one-time charge may result in a net loss for the fiscal year but can enable the company to increase earnings by concentrating on the potentially more profitable or growing division of the company.

Cumulative Losses and Bankruptcy

Many investors will tolerate short-term losses with the expectation that the company will become profitable in a reasonable period of time. Investors buy shares of biotechnology companies and small pharmaceutical companies that have not produced a marketable drug, if the investors believe that the company is making scientific advances that will lead to exciting new medicines. Investors also take chances on start-up companies that have lots of ideas but no profits. Investors also buy shares of stock in companies that have lost money in previous quarters or years. What about a company that has persistent losses? At what point does it cease to be a going concern and enter bankruptcy?

A simple answer is that as long as the company has larger current assets than current liabilities, it is a going concern. Current assets are those balance sheet items that are expected to be converted into cash during the year, and current liabilities are those items that come due during the same year. Current assets include cash, accounts receivable, and inventory. As long as the company continues to convert accounts receivable and inventory into cash, it can service the current liabilities. It is when the cash flow dries up or current liabilities start to expand disproportionately that the company is in trouble. Since total assets have to match total liabilities and owner's equity, another place where you would see bankruptcy looming is in the equity section. A company that has negative equity has more total liabilities than assets, which is not a good financial situation.

There are several alternatives available to the distressed organization depending on its legal structure: sale of all or part of the organization, reorganization, or liquidation.

Before entering formal **bankruptcy** proceedings, a company may attempt to stem its losses by selling operating units or corporate assets. Which assets to sell becomes tricky. The most valuable assets may be the ones that are most likely to lead the company to future profitability. Although the sale of assets would provide a major infusion of cash and allow the business to pay down a portion of debt, the loss of revenue from the assets could compromise the future plans of the organization. On the other hand, the sale of underperforming divisions might not generate enough cash to significantly alter the debt burden of the company. Still, selling assets may buy enough time for the company to address its difficulties without incurring the stigma of bankruptcy.

Reorganization often occurs under the protection of Chapter 11 bankruptcy. The company voluntarily declares bankruptcy and seeks court protection while it develops a new business plan. The company continues operations under the supervision of a bankruptcy judge, but its debt obligations are suspended during that time. Without the requirement to pay interest or even the current portion of long-term debt, the company retains the cash it has generated from operations. Understandably, creditors do not want the company to enter Chapter 11 and simply languish there. The company must submit a reorganization plan within a reasonable time frame. A typical plan includes:

- Cost reductions: layoffs, restructuring lease payments, reducing the number of product lines, and altering labor contracts are often components of cost reduction.
- Debt relief: paying a portion of outstanding debt, lengthening loan terms, lowering the stated interest rate, refinancing mortgages, issuing equity in return for debt, and even obtaining new loans are some of the ways that companies can reduce their immediate debt burden.
- Sale of assets: companies may sell current assets such as accounts receivable or long-term assets such as stores, warehouses, or land held for future expansion.

Once the plan has been submitted to the court, the creditors must vote whether to accept the company's proposal. If accepted, the company begins operation under the plan and emerges from bankruptcy protection. Why would creditors agree to a restructuring plan if it means reducing interest payments or lengthening a loan to a struggling company? The theory of risk and return argues for increasing interest rates and shortening the lender's exposure. However, creditors may feel that restructuring the outstanding debt and allowing the company to continue operations provides a greater chance for recovering their investment than forcing the company to **liquidate.** If the company is liquidated, there will be no further opportunity for repayment. Because creditors have to be assured that the company is making a good-faith effort to remedy the problems that led to bankruptcy they may impose strict conditions on the renegotiated loans.

If the plan is not accepted, the company may be given a chance to devise a new plan or the creditors can force it into Chapter 7 bankruptcy. Chapter 7 bankruptcy requires liquidation of all corporate assets and the disbursement of funds to creditors in the following order:

- The cost of liquidation (court expenses)
- Unpaid labor expenses
- Taxes
- Secured debt
- Unsecured debt
- Preferred stock
- Common stock

Obviously, if the company has negative owner's equity, the sale of assets will not be sufficient to compensate common stockholders. Even when the balance sheet states that there is equity remaining, the liquidation value of assets may not be the same as the book value. If the business has been incorporated, the liabilities are paid until there is no more money. Those creditors who have subordinated claims, that is, claims lower in the payment order, will not be paid or may be paid pennies on the dollar. However, if the business is a partnership or sole proprietorship, creditors have the right to attach liens to the personal property of the owners of the company. A business's bankruptcy can also bankrupt the owners, even if their personal assets will not cover the remaining debt.

TERMS TO KNOW

Effectiveness	Fixed costs	Maturity stage
Efficiency	Contribution margin	Decline stage
Break-even analysis	Demand	Price fixing
Total revenue	Product life cycle	Bankruptcy
Total cost	Introduction stage	Reorganization
Variable costs	Growth stage	Liquidation

TERM PAPERS AND PROJECTS

1. In a previous chapter, it was suggested to examine the relationship between Bethlehem Steel's workforce and the obligations they face for future retirement benefits as a reason for their bankruptcy filing in November 2001. At this point, you might want to take a look at the financial statements for domestic steel companies. What type of profitability does the industry show? If there are losses, do they come from inventory problems, slow turnover of accounts receivable, low gross profit margins, or the result of interest payments on debt? Can you diagnose the problem with the industry? How have the tariffs imposed by President Bush helped the industry, or have they? Can you calculate their effect?

2. Develop a break-even analysis for a start-up company or new product for an existing organization. Consider different levels of production and assess

the effect of outsourcing production or leasing some of the equipment or space rather than purchasing fixed assets.

3. What pricing strategies could be employed by a firm if it offered varying levels of service to its customers? For example, what if a cleaning service offered "quick clean" or "spit and polish" services? Would there be enough of a cost savings to justify creating separate service categories? Conduct a break-even analysis for each level of service and justify the prices charged.

REVIEW QUESTIONS

1. What is meant by a break-even analysis? How is it computed and why could it be important?
2. Define fixed costs and give two examples.
3. What types of assets would be variable assets?
4. What are the stages in the product life cycle?
5. Give some examples of mature products and what financial considerations are involved in marketing them.
6. The cost of advertising can be considered either a fixed cost or a variable cost. Why? Give examples of situations where advertising would be one or the other.
7. What are some of the factors that management must evaluate when considering the discontinuation of a product.
8. Distinguish short-term loss from cumulative loss and bankruptcy.
9. What is meant when a company is called a going concern?
10. What are possible alternatives to bankruptcy? What use can a company make of its assets short of liquidating the firm?
11. Describe the difference between Chapter 11 bankruptcy and Chapter 7 bankruptcy.
12. Under what forms of business can an owner, or owners, be held personally liable for the business losses? What can be done to avoid personal liability?

CHAPTER

8

PLANNING, FORECASTING, AND BUDGETING

LEARNING OBJECTIVES

1. Differentiate between the methods for planning annual expenses.

2. Discuss issues to consider when setting baseline assets and liabilities.

3. Calculate pro forma financial statements based on change in financial situations.

4. Evaluate the validity of assumptions made in determining budgets.

5. Calculate a cash budget and plan for shortfall or excess of cash.

6. Discuss how cash budgets assist financial decision making.

FORECASTING FUTURE EXPENSES AND REVENUE

One of the most important aspects of managing a business is developing accurate predictions of **income** and **expenses.** Revenue does not always match the timing of expenses; in fact, it is the rare business where revenues and expenses coincide neatly. The goal of the finance manager is to have money available when expenses occur and invest excess capital when it is not needed. Budgets allow the manager to see the timing of borrowing and investing and reduce the number of unpleasant surprises.

For most companies, the annual budget is developed over a period of several months with the assistance of the managers who will be responsible for administering funds in the coming year. Ideally, the budgeting process involves both upward and downward communication. Senior managers establish the strategic direction of the company including any expansion or divestiture plans, while lower-level managers make sure that the expenses for the year accurately reflect their departmental costs.

161

METHODS FOR PLANNING ANNUAL EXPENSES

Historic Budgeting

Many businesses use historic data as the beginning point in establishing the next year's budget. Some companies, in fact, merely roll over the previous year's budget and add an inflation allowance. The benefit of the **historic budgeting** method is that seasonal sales patterns can be easily seen. Past data also suggest expense fluctuations such as an increase in utility costs during winter or summer, and they remind the manager of the timing of recurring cash outflows such as insurance premiums or quarterly tax payments.

The major weakness of this system is that it assumes that the business will continue to operate exactly as it has in the past. There is no allowance for increasing the size or scope of the operations nor is there recognition of significant technological changes that could impact the organization. Because managers have not been asked to scrutinize their current expenditures there may be less likelihood that savings can be made or efficiencies gained in the coming year.

For an organization that is experiencing difficulties, the historic method may lead to across-the-board budget cuts. The theory is that if the pain of budget cuts is shared equally, no department will have the right to complain. In fact, this is a foolish strategy that encourages managers to overstate their needs when times are good in hopes of having more if there is a downturn. Efficient operations are punished, and the true cost of producing goods is masked.

Competitive Budgeting

Another method is called **competitive budgeting.** This is often used when setting marketing or advertising budgets. The company compares its market share to that of its competitors and sets its budget proportionately. For example, the largest jewelry store in town sells approximately $2,000,000 of merchandise and has an estimated advertising budget of $15,000. My store has sales of $1,400,000, which is 70% of the competition, so I will set my advertising budget at $10,500. Setting budgets based on competitive spending assumes that the competition knows what they are doing and that they are spending their promotion dollars wisely. It also discounts the value of a clever or long-standing promotional campaign that instantly reminds consumers of your business. Nor does competitive spending make allowances for more or less desirable locations.

Competitive spending cannot be applied across the board when creating budgets. The county assessor calculates property tax based on the assessed value of the property, not as a percent of market sales. Personnel costs are influenced by supply and demand in the labor market and the value of specialized skills. In addition, it is difficult, if not impossible, to obtain detailed spending for your competitors. Even publicly traded companies that are required to file quarterly financial statements aggregate the data. Determining precisely how much is spent under each budget code would be more time consuming than creating a budget that reflects the current needs of your own organization, which leads us to zero-based budgeting.

Zero-Based Budgeting

In a perfect world, managers would begin each budget cycle with a blank pad of paper. Not a single number would appear until far into the process. The first step would be to determine how each department fits into the strategic plan of the organization. What products or services does each unit provide to the organization, will those products or services be needed in the coming year, and in what quantities? Are there changes in technology, personnel, or materials costs that will significantly affect the manner of doing business? Like Chapter 7 on break-even analysis, this discussion seems to be straying from finance toward management issues. However, finance is merely one contributor to the success of an organization. Without taking time to analyze the strategic direction of the company, scarce financial and other resources will be wasted. By starting at zero, managers build a department budget that more closely depicts the needs of the organization based on the strategic direction that it has chosen.

   Zero-based budgeting is especially valuable when the organization has a new or expanding unit. Although the actual dollar expenditures seem relatively small, investments in capital equipment may represent a significant increase in percentage terms. For example, the Sycamore Street Medical Clinic divides its operations by medical specialty. For the coming year, Sycamore expects an overall budget increase of 10%, however, the number of patients seen by the geriatric department is expected to increase by 19%. The manager of the department should develop a budget that reflects realistic expenditures for equipment, personnel costs, supplies, and overhead based on the estimated patient load. There is no guarantee that the organization will be able to fully fund all of the items on the manager's wish list; however, without an accurate picture of the department's needs, the company cannot make realistic decisions about scarce resources.

   The exercise of creating a new budget each year also requires the manager to examine current expenses and their relationship to the overall mission of the organization. It could be that this examination will reveal areas of duplication within the firm and provide opportunities for more efficient use of resources.

   There are several criticisms of zero-based budgeting. The first is the amount of time given to budgeting. For an organization used to taking last year's budget and simply increasing it by a factor, the exercise of starting from scratch seems wasteful. Where the previous budget could be completed by a simple click to a spreadsheet, zero-based budgeting requires many hours of thought and meetings between many different managers. There are inevitable conflicts when managers are forced to describe what they do and how it should be funded. An organization that is not used to this method may believe that the time would be better spent "doing what we do" rather than planning.

   A second criticism of zero-based budgeting is that budgets created from scratch are not realistic and invariably contain too many wish list items instead of recognizing the cold hard facts of business. In fact, zero-based budgeting done properly leads an organization to state explicitly its strategic objectives and quantify what it will take to achieve them. If there is more money budgeted than is available, the process of identifying the fit with corporate objectives should make it easier to trim expenses judiciously rather than based on political clout. It also provides the organization with a clear view of what financing will be needed in the future to reach the objectives it has set for itself.

In some cases, the exercise of starting from nothing may reveal that a company is overspending in an area. If the ideal size of a department appears to be seven employees and 10 are currently employed, the organization should reduce the department to bring it into line with expectations. Here we are back at a management issue: downsizing. There is a connection with finance, though. If the organization can utilize the employees in another department, it saves itself the cost of recruiting new employees and demonstrates to its current employees that change can be accomplished with minimal disruption. If employees do not possess transferable skills, the firm must recognize severance costs as an expense in the next budget cycle.

Whatever method is used, budgets are only as accurate as the data that are used to derive them. Sales forecasts can be obtained from reports by the salesforce, historical trends, primary research sponsored by the company, or secondary data from government or trade associations. Several budgets may be created based on possible changes in economic conditions such as inflation, unemployment, and interest rates. Long-term contracts for commodities used in production reduce the uncertainty of costs, as can negotiated labor agreements. It may be more difficult to predict the cost of such raw materials as oil, electricity, and natural gas. The goal of writing a budget is to describe the nature and timing of expenses and revenue so that the company maintains the proper level of borrowing and investment.

When developing the annual budget, it is tempting to lump together the spending by department for the year and hand the manager a list of budget codes with a single dollar value allocated to each code. In order to be useful, what we have been calling "the budget" should actually be pro forma accounting statements including a projected monthly cash flow statement, balance sheet, and income statement. Without these, it will be far more difficult to track the variations across the year and make the necessary adjustments.

ESTABLISHING BASELINE ASSETS AND LIABILITIES

Although zero-based budgeting is ideal and managers should start the process with a blank pad of paper, the truth of the matter is that ongoing concerns do have financial statements. There are assets such as bank accounts and equipment and liabilities in the form of mortgages, long-term leases, or simply accounts payable. However, as part of the exercise of analyzing the efficiency of our organization, we should begin each annual budget cycle by questioning the level and composition of those **baseline assets and liabilities.**

Cash

What is the comfort level for cash? Most organizations feel the need to maintain a certain level of cash on hand in excess of anticipated monthly outlays. We discuss the mechanics of cash management in Chapter 9, but the budget process needs to establish a base amount of cash that the organization considers its safety net. Cash outflows may exceed cash inflows during certain months, and borrowing should include an allowance not only for that difference but to replenish the cash on hand account.

Inventory

Inventory turnover is one of the ratios used to determine the efficiency of an organization, and minimizing the level of inventory can increase the company's return on assets. Because inventory management is affected by the nature of the product or service being sold, simply cutting back on inventory may not lead to higher profits. A retailer who is routinely out of stock of advertised items on the first day of a sale will discover that cutting inventory has cost him or her sales. If the shelves can be replenished within 24 hours, a better strategy would be to vary the inventory levels by day, based on historic purchasing patterns. The retailer may discover that 25% of the week's sales occur on the first day of the sale, 17% on the final day, and the remaining 58% is spread fairly evenly across the remaining 5 days. Keeping 1 day's inventory in stock at all times will not be efficient.

Seasonal and service businesses also need to closely monitor inventory levels and the types of inventory on hand. During the summer months, a landscaping company will need sufficient topsoil, brick, landscape timbers, fertilizer, and planting materials to complete its projects without interrupting the flow of work. The landscaper may choose to buy some of the inventory in bulk quantities rather than restock by day or week if the cost of the materials can be significantly reduced. By the first frost, most, if not all, of the inventory should have been depleted since that season's work is over. Inventory levels increase before the summer planting season in preparation for jobs that were contracted for in the winter months, but there should be a period of time when the landscaper shows virtually no inventory. In the budgeting process, these types of variations need to be addressed.

Liabilities and Debt

Inventory has to be funded, either through cash disbursements or by setting up accounts payable. Therefore, inventory management immediately affects the base levels of cash and accounts payable for the firm. As inventory levels increase, there will be a subsequent increase in that portion of accounts payable related to inventory. Some liabilities such as mortgages, bond payments, and leases are fixed by contract. As part of the annual budgeting process, managers can examine alternative ways to finance the company's operations. Using industry-appropriate financial ratios as guidelines and honest self-appraisal, the budgeting process can yield important insights.

Let's say that an analysis of your company's financial statements reveals that inventory turnover is becoming quicker. With the same volume of sales, a lower level of inventory needs to be kept on hand. This may allow the firm to reduce the amount of warehouse space needed to house its own inventory. If the warehouse is owned by the company, the excess capacity could be leased to another firm. If the warehouse is leased by the firm, it might be possible to renegotiate the lease or find a smaller space. If not, the firm may be able to sublet a portion of the warehouse, thus lowering its own fixed costs.

Another way to change the financial structure of the company is to sell fixed assets that are currently owned by the company, eliminate the debt associated with the assets, and lease what the firm needs. Many companies who have purchased their own buildings have found that the maintenance and debt service consume more time and funds than they desire. By selling an office or factory building to a property management corporation, the firm reduces its fixed costs and debt while focusing its investment on producing the product or service that creates revenue. The cost of leasing the building that it formerly owned is an expense that can be charged against revenues in the period.

PREDICTING CHANGES IN FINANCIAL CONDITION

We've talked about fluctuations due to the seasonality of a business. A firm may also have increased need for funds due to expansion. As the firm grows, some assets increase in proportion to the growth in sales. For example, at the same inventory turnover rate, actual inventory levels will expand as the firm increases sales. Cash and accounts receivable increase as revenue flows into the organization. Accounts payable, which are tied to inventory, increase. Other assets, especially long-term assets like property and equipment, will not spontaneously increase, but may if the growth is sustained.

Let's look at year-end financial statements for Bannock Building Supply, a home improvement center that sells to local contractors and do-it-your-selfers. Bannock's managers have just completed the Income and Balance sheets for fiscal year 2001 shown as follows and are preparing for next year.

BANNOCK BUILDING SUPPLY
Income Statement: Fiscal year 2002

	$	Percent
Revenue	$250,000	100.0%
Cost of Goods Sold	187,500	75.0%
Gross Profit	62,500	25.0%
SG&A Expenses	50,000	20.0%
Operating Income (EBIT)	12,500	5.0%
Interest Expense	2,550	1.0%
Income before Taxes	9,950	4.0%
Income Tax	2,550	1.0%
Net Income	$7,400	3.0%

Because of the growth in their community, Bannock's managers antici-pate a 20% increase in sales during the next year to $300,000. The current warehouse store can handle the increase in sales and Bannock's managers believe that the operating expenses will remain constant as a percentage. What they need to determine is which balance sheet accounts will increase as a direct result of the increase in sales. The percent of sales method allows a firm to tie balance sheet items to corresponding changes in income. Any difference between the growth in assets and the growth in liabilities must be financed by some other means. Rather than be caught by surprise, Bannock's managers want to begin to put in place the financing they will need in the coming year.

BANNOCK BUILDING SUPPLY
Balance Sheet: July 1, 2002

Assets			Liabilities		
Cash	$12,500		Accounts Payable	$25,000	
Net Receivables	20,000		Short-term Debt	16,500	
Inventories	30,000		Current Liabilities	41,500	
Total Current Assets	62,500		Long-term Debt	8,100	
Property and Equipment	8,600		Equity	21,500	
Total Assets	$71,100		Total Liabilities	$71,100	

Several assets will expand as Bannock increases sales. Because cash, inventory, and accounts receivable are directly tied to the daily operation of the business, they will vary in proportion to the increase in sales. Since Bannock is not planning to add an additional location, property and equipment are assumed to remain constant.

Accounts payable are tied to the purchase of inventory and they, too, will increase proportionate to sales. Bannock's long-term debt is mortgage and equipment financing and is not subject to change. Other liabilities, such as short-term debt, are initially assumed to be constant. If Bannock's business grows to the point that additional staff need to be hired or current staff add overtime hours, Bannock will have to adjust the accrued wages payable liability. To keep this illustration simple, we will ignore that possibility for now. We will also assume that Bannock's managers are comfortable with their current levels of inventory, debt, and cash.

Let's take a look at Bannock's balance sheet, given the assumptions we have just stated. We want to see what relationship exists between cash, accounts receivable, inventory, accounts payable, and the current sales revenue of $250,000.

BANNOCK BUILDING SUPPLY
Balance Sheet: July 1, 2002

Assets			Liabilities		
Cash	$12,500	5.0%	Accounts Payable	$25,000	10.0%
Net Receivables	20,000	8.0%	Short-term Debt	16,500	
Inventories	30,000	12.0%	Current Liabilities	41,500	
Total Current Assets	62,500	25.0%	Long-term Debt	8,100	
Property and Equipment	8,600		Equity	21,500	
Total Assets	$71,100		Total Liabilities	$71,100	

At the end of the year, cash was 5% of the total revenue ($12,500/$250,000). The other percentages were calculated using the $250,000 sales as base. Note that only the accounts that vary with sales are illustrated. Therefore, the asset side shows 25% of sales and the liabilities reflect 10% of sales.

Once the percentages have been determined, the new value for the assets can be calculated by multiplying next year's estimated sales by the established percentages. This will change only the four line items we have identified as being tied to an increase in sales. One thing you will notice is that our balance sheet no longer balances. Assets are greater than liabilities and we have created entries seemingly out of thin air, which does not conform to GAAP nor the double-entry system of bookkeeping. What we have actually done is set a budget for Bannock Building Supply to meet and now we have to figure out how they are going to do so.

BANNOCK BUILDING SUPPLY
Balance Sheet: July 1, 2003

Assets		*Liabilities*	
Cash	$15,000		
Net Receivables	24,000	Accounts Payable	$30,000
Inventories	36,000	Short-term Debt	16,500
Total Current Assets	75,000	Current Liabilities	46,500
		Long-term Debt	8,100
Property and Equipment	8,600	Equity	21,500
Total Assets	$83,600	Total Liabilities	$76,100

Remember that a balance sheet is a snapshot of the organization at one single point in time. The balance sheet that the Bannock management created at the conclusion of fiscal year 2002 has been adjusted to show what they hope to see at the conclusion of fiscal year 2003. In other words, they have 12 months to fund that increase in assets in a way that *does* conform to accounting principles.

The half-finished balance sheet tells us that during this expansionary year, Bannock's inventory will increase $6,000 from $30,000 to $36,000. That increase will be partially funded by the $5,000 increase in accounts payable ($30,000−$25,000) since a portion of the inventory is purchased on account. While there is a shortfall of $1,000, it is becoming clearer how those two entries will be made—as merchandise is purchased during the coming year, the inventory account will be increased as will the accounts payable. The $1,000 of inventory that is not financed by vendors will have to be paid for out of the cash account, which should reduce the cash account by a corresponding $1,000. However, our cash account is expected to increase, not decrease.

In our projected balance sheet, cash is expected to increase as a result of the cash transactions Bannock has added, and accounts receivable, the amount that is outstanding from local general contractors, has also grown in proportion to sales. What is the source of this money? Go back to the income statement. During the coming year, sales of $300,000 should yield $9,000 in net income if Bannock continues its current operating efficiencies. That income does not come as a lump sum on the closing day of business but will flow into the organization on a daily or weekly basis in the form of sales in cash and accounts receivable. Profit, or net income, is the premium that buyers are willing to pay for the value added by the seller. Remember from Chapter 5 on banking that the added value provided by the seller is one of the components that creates money. The portion of net income that is reinvested in the firm in the form of inventory, capital purchases, or simply cash (all asset accounts) is entered on the liability side of the balance sheet as retained earnings, an equity account. There you have the double entry and the mystery is solved.

In the case of Bannock Building Supply, their projected net income actually exceeds the amount that they needed to cover the expansion of their business. The projected excess can be allocated (or budgeted) into whichever category the managers choose or can be used to pay dividends to shareholders or increase the bonuses given to employees. In the following spreadsheet, note that the excess has been added to the cash account, which increases it from the $15,000 that was budgeted to $16,500. Understand, though, that these projections assume that Bannock will be able to maintain its current operating cost structure.

BANNOCK BUILDING SUPPLY
Balance Sheet: July 1, 2003

Assets		*Liabilities*	
Cash	$16,500	Accounts Payable	$30,000
Net Receivables	24,000	Short-term Debt	16,500
Inventories	36,000	Current Liabilities	46,500
Total Current Assets	76,500		
		Long-term Debt	8,100
Property and Equipment	8,600	Equity	21,500
		Retained Earnings	9,000
Total Assets	$85,100	Total Liabilities	$85,100

Let's make some different assumptions, any of which could affect Bannock. We have initially stated that all of the net income is available to be reinvested in the business, but Bannock has historically paid 30% of their net income into a profit-sharing plan for employees. Profit sharing is guaranteed to hourly workers through their union contract, and management has traditionally given salaried employees the same benefit. The effect of this agreement is to reduce the amount of retained earnings from $9,000 to $6,300.

BANNOCK BUILDING SUPPLY
Balance Sheet: July 1, 2003

Assets		*Liabilities*	
Cash	$15,000	Accounts Payable	$30,000
Net Receivables	24,000	Short-term Debt	16,500
Inventories	36,000	Current Liabilities	46,500
Total Current Assets	75,000		
		Long-term Debt	8,100
Property and Equipment	8,600	Equity	21,500
		Retained Earnings	6,300
Total Assets	$83,600	Total Liabilities	$82,400

We began by assuming that none of the operating expenses would increase as a result of the increase in sales, however, that may not be a logical assumption. A 20% increase in sales volume may very well require Bannock to increase store hours, add additional staff members, increase the amount of overtime for sales staff, or convert part-time employees to full-time employees, which would increase the cost of employee benefits. If selling and administrative expenses increased from 20% to 21%, net profit would be reduced by $3,000. The amount of retained earnings available to Bannock is $6,000 before the profit-sharing plan was funded. The balance sheet is even further out of balance. Bannock has not generated enough internal funding to finance the expansion in business. If they are convinced that this expansion will occur, Bannock managers will have to finance the shortfall by increasing short-term debt.

BANNOCK BUILDING SUPPLY
Balance Sheet: July 1, 2003

Assets		*Liabilities*	
Cash	$15,000	Accounts Payable	$30,000
Net Receivables	24,000	Short-term Debt	16,500
Inventories	36,000	Current Liabilities	46,500
Total Current Assets	75,000		
		Long-term Debt	8,100
Property and Equipment	8,600	Equity	21,500
		Retained Earnings	4,200
Total Assets	$83,600	Total Liabilities	$80,300

We can see that two simple changes have made the expansion a little more complicated. Imagine how much more difficult this transition would be if Bannock managers had not developed pro forma budgets and financial statements.

It is exciting to be able to build a balance sheet for an expanding company. However, sometimes the task is to decrease the size of an organization. Suzy's

Toolbox

The May 2001 edition of *Harvard Business Review* included an article titled "How Fast Can Your Company Afford to Grow?" by Neil C. Churchill and John W. Mullins. Churchill and Mullins provide a range of worksheets and clear-cut instructions that will help any business, large or small, calculate how much growth can come from internally generated funds. The article and the step-by-step worksheets are clearly explained and simple to use. The concepts apply equally to a multimillion-dollar business or a small company that is trying to decide how much more business it can support using internally generated funds.

Source: Neil C. Churchill and John W. Mullins, "How Fast Can Your Company Afford to Grow?", *Harvard Business Review*, May 2001, pp. 135–143.

Salon has been in business for many years and caters to a mature clientele. As her clients have aged, Suzy has been tempted to broaden her business by bringing in younger customers, but she does not want to upset her regulars. She has seen a decrease in business and anticipates that her sales revenue will decrease by about 11% this year to $800. Before deciding whether to begin to advertise to a younger market, Suzy wants to know what effect the reduction in sales would have on her business. In this case, we will have to build a balance sheet in which assets are reduced. Suzy's current income and balance sheet are shown as follows.

SUZY'S SALON INCOME STATEMENT

	$	Percent
Revenue	$900	100.0%
Cost of Goods Sold	603	67.0%
Gross Profit	297	33.0%
SG&A Expenses	216	24.0%
Operating Income (EBIT)	81	9.0%
Interest Expense	9	1.0%
Earnings before Taxes	72	8.0%
Taxes	27	3.0%
Net Income	$45	5.0%

SUZY'S SALON BALANCE SHEET

Assets		Liabilities	
Cash	$45	Accounts Payable	$45
Inventories	90	Other Current Liabilities	148
Prepaid Assets	119	Short-term Debt	15
Total Current Assets	254	Current Liabilities	208
Property and Equipment	458	Long-term Debt	225
Total Assets	$712	Total Liabilities	433
		Equity	279
		Total Liabilities	$712

Once again we will look at the accounts that vary with sales: cash, inventory, and accounts payable. Suzy accepts major credit cards but does not carry her own accounts, so there are no accounts receivable.

SUZY'S SALON BALANCE SHEET

Assets					
Cash	45	5.0%	Accounts Payable	45	5.0%
Inventories	90	10.0%			

In the new budget, cash will fall to $40, inventory will be $80, and accounts payable will be reduced to $40. Let's see what the reduced balance sheet will look like.

SUZY'S SALON BALANCE SHEET

Assets		Liabilities	
Cash	$40	Accounts Payable	$40
Inventories	80	Other Current Liabilities	148
Prepaid Assets	119	Short-term Debt	15
Total Current Assets	239	Current Liabilities	203
Property and Equipment	458	Long-term Debt	225
Total Assets	$697	Total Liabilities	428
		Equity	279
		Total Liabilities and Equity	$707

Suzy's assets have decreased by $15 while the liabilities have only been reduced by $5. In essence, Suzy's lower need for cash and inventory could be used toward paying down some of the other liabilities that she has. If Suzy anticipates that her income will continue at the lower level, she might be well advised to begin paying off some of her debt. Her loans most likely carry a fixed rate of interest and as her earnings fall, the interest she is required to pay will become a larger percentage of her earnings, in the process reducing her net income. At some point, the times-interest-earned ratio will become dangerously low, and the bank might decide to call in the loans. It would be better for Suzy to begin reducing her debt now before she is forced to do so.

In this section we have looked at only four balance sheet items: cash, inventories, accounts receivable, and accounts payable. However, at some point in either an expansion or reduction in sales, the firm might need to change its mix of property and equipment. Increased sales or production could call for investment in new equipment that would have an effect on breakeven (Chapter 7), profit, and budgeting. We will look at capital budgeting in Chapter 10.

We have also accepted that the four balance sheet items will expand or contract in direct proportion to sales. Is that a valid assumption? Do we necessarily have to increase our inventory holdings at exactly the same rate as sales or are there efficiencies that we can attain with the larger volume of sales? As we grow, is the mix of inventory we sell changing? If so, does that affect how much we keep on hand or even how we store it?

Accounts receivable is another area we should examine. In their rush to compete in the late 1990s, computer hardware companies offered generous payment terms to many start-up e-commerce and telecommunications companies. The proportion of sales funded by accounts receivable rather than cash increased. Since both are current assets, you could argue that the distinction between increasing cash and receivables is a moot point.

Unfortunately, as the e-commerce companies struggled to become profitable they stretched out payment of their accounts, causing the receivables to stay on manufacturer's books longer, in effect turning the manufacturer into a financier. Those e-commerce companies that eventually went bankrupt left manufacturers with worthless accounts receivable and in possession of machinery that could only be sold for pennies on the dollar. Just as profit can create money, these losses in effect erased money from the balance sheet of many computer hardware companies.

THE CASH BUDGET

The last document that we need in order to complete our budgeting process is a **cash budget.** The cash budget can be constructed on a monthly or quarterly basis, depending on the needs of the organization. Its primary function is to describe excess and shortages of cash during the business cycle, allowing the finance manager to have appropriate levels of cash available to finance the operations of the firm. Funds that are not immediately needed to operate the business can be invested in short-term interest-bearing accounts (such as a certificate of deposit) that can be timed to mature when the funds are required. Companies that utilize short-term loans or wish to establish a line of credit can negotiate more favorable terms if they go to their bank with a statement describing when they will need temporary financing and for what period of time.

The best place to begin is with historic data. By looking through past accounting records, the firm can see payment and revenue patterns. There

	January	February	March
Sales	$145,000	$100,000	$150,000
Cash sales	$36,250	$25,000	$37,500
Collections (30 days)	$45,000	$65,250	$45,000
Collections (60 days)	$30,625	$25,000	$36,250
Other income			
Total cash inflows	$111,875	$115,250	$118,750
Direct labor	$21,750	$15,000	$22,500
Salaries	$25,000	$25,000	$25,000
Income taxes payable	$9,350	$8,000	$9,500
Cost of goods sold	$65,250	$45,000	$67,500
Property taxes due			$10,000
Other disbursements			
Total cash outflows	$121,350	$93,000	$134,500
Change in cash	-$9,475	$22,250	-$15,750
Beginning cash	$15,000	$5,525	$27,775
Ending cash	$5,525	$27,775	$12,025
Desired level of cash	$5,000	$5,000	$5,000
Excess (shortage) of cash	$525	$22,775	$7,025

A sample cash budget.

may be some seasonality to the revenue stream—holiday and back-to-school shopping create increased revenue for clothing retailers, and summer construction work causes an increase in sales for lumberyards and home improvement centers. Disbursements, too, will vary by month. Property taxes are often collected twice a year, income tax transfers are made quarterly, and insurance premiums may be paid semiannually. Other expenses are paid monthly but vary with activity; direct labor along with its associated benefits is one example.

It is important to remember that a cash budget is not the same as an income statement. Revenue is only recognized when it is converted to cash. Accounts receivable will not appear on a cash budget, only the portion of receivables that has been collected. Nor will the firm recognize the accrued liabilities or the allowance for depreciation. Unlike an income statement that matches expenses to the period in which they occur, the cash budget tracks only the actual flows of cash. Since depreciation is a noncash expense, it will never be reflected in a cash budget.

Cash budgets can be as simple or complex as the organization needs. We will begin with a template for a simple cash budget.

Sample Cash Budget

	January	February	March
Cash Receipts			
Cash sales			
Accounts collected			
Other cash receipts			
Total cash receipts			
Cash Disbursements			
Variable cash disbursements			
Direct labor			
Inventory purchases			
Supplies purchases			
Fixed cash disbursements			
Staff salaries			
Rent			
Periodic payments			
Taxes paid			
Other disbursements			
Interest paid			
Total cash disbursements			

Change in Cash

Cash gain (loss) during the month
Cash position at beginning of month
Cash position at end of month

Excess or Shortage of Cash

Desired level of cash
Excess (shortage) of cash

It may seem obvious, but the first step in building the cash budget is to organize all of the knowledge and assumptions that the firm has. Knowledge comes from historic data: past revenue trends and accounts receivable collection history. The firm may know that accounts receivable turnover varies somewhat depending on the time of year. If so, cash receipts can be predicted accordingly. Assumptions about the estimated rate of increase in insurance premiums, property taxes, and even revenue should be included and a decision made about the range of cash on hand that the firm considers sufficient. The range should describe the lowest amount of cash that the firm feels it needs readily available, as well as the largest amount of cash it will keep on hand before investing. Decisions made before the cash budget is completed will allow the finance manager to assess different investment and borrowing opportunities.

The first section details the cash that will flow into the business during the month. Some portion of the month's sales is cash and that will be recorded as it is received. The second line describes cash that has been collected in payment for past months' credit sales. There is no allowance for bad debt—the uncollected portion of accounts receivable will simply never be converted to cash. Other cash receipts include the conversion of a certificate of deposit into cash. As long as funds are invested in some form of security such as stocks, bonds, or certificate of deposit and not immediately available for use, they are not considered cash. When the security is sold or the certificate of deposit matures, the investment becomes cash. The third line recognizes that conversion. Other cash receipts can be described as needed: receipt of cash as a result of the sale of stock, cash received as a result of settlement of a lawsuit or insurance claim, or interest earned on investments. Monthly receipts are then totaled.

The second section details cash that is spent during the month. On our spreadsheet the first subheading is variable payments, including direct labor expenses. Remember that this is only the portion that is paid during the current month, so the portion of the wages that are actually issued to the employees will be entered, but company-paid insurance premiums will only be recorded when the company pays the insurer for the coverage. Inventory purchases are recorded as they are paid, whether it is a direct cash payment to the vendor or payment on account. A second subheading is for fixed cash disbursements, which would include staff salaries and rent or mortgage payments. We can add as many lines as our firm needs to accurately describe the flow of funds. There is no requirement that variable costs be separated from fixed costs, however, the point of a cash budget is to describe cash outflows accurately and allow the firm to make financing decisions. The third subheading is for periodic payments.

Just as the firm receives lump sum payments at irregular intervals, so it makes payments. This is also the section where the firm enters cash that has been invested. Cash used to purchase stock or certificates of deposit is disbursed; the investment certainly has value to the firm, but the cash is not available for use. At the end of this section, the value of all cash disbursements is tallied.

The finance manager now uses the projections to estimate the amount of monthly increase or decrease in cash and how that will affect short-term financing. Change in cash is the difference between the cash receipts (a positive number) and the cash disbursements (a negative number). When receipts are greater than disbursements, the change will be positive. In months during which outflows exceed receipts the actual change will be negative. Whether or not one month's change is negative or positive does not necessarily determine whether the firm will need to borrow funds that month. The change in cash is added to the cash position at the beginning of the month and the sum of those two numbers is the cash position at the end of the month, if the firm did not borrow any money. The cash position at the end of one month becomes the cash position at the beginning of the next month.

Students begin to get nervous when the cash position at the end of the month enters negative numbers. They argue that the firm has to do something and do it quickly. The best strategy, however, is to proceed with the third section, carrying forward either the loss or the positive balance. The point of the cash budget is to describe the flow of cash as the firm conducts its normal business. If the firm is profitable, there should be more positive cumulative cash than negative.

The first line in the fourth section is the desired level of cash. At the beginning of this discussion, we suggested that the firm set a range of cash that it felt it needed to keep on hand to operate the business. The line item entry should be the low end of the range since that is the minimum desired cash that the firm wants on account at all times. The desired level of cash is subtracted from the end of month cash position to determine the excess or shortage of cash. The excess or shortage is the difference between what the firm would have from operations and what it would like to have on hand. It does not reflect any borrowing or investing.

Let's look at a 3-month cash budget for Thelma's Garden Design. Thelma has a small landscape and design company that she operates from her home. During the winter months, Thelma's business is quiet. In April she did a few design consultations for which she received payment in May. Some of Thelma's clients pay her by the week and others have accounts. Business typically starts to pick up in May, and the busy season is June, July, and August.

Thelma tries to purchase landscape timbers, soil, and fertilizer a month before she needs them, although her purchases are somewhat restricted by cash constraints. Thelma has one employee who is paid $10 per hour. His hours vary depending on how much work Thelma has. Thelma is the only salaried employee. She rents a large garage from a neighbor, where she stores yard equipment and supplies she will need to complete the contracted projects. Income taxes are due in July and her business license needs to be renewed in May. Thelma would like to keep $2,000 cash on hand. It seems that all of the bills come before her income starts!

The calculations are complete. Now the thinking begins. Thelma cannot meet her expected cash outflows with the cash she has on hand at the beginning of May. Even if she were willing to spend all of her $2,100 savings (which would not be wise), Thelma would still be $1,850 in the hole. It would be tempting to advise Thelma merely not to spend as much in May, however

THELMA'S GARDEN DESIGN

	May	June	July
Cash Receipts			
Cash sales	$2000	$8000	$12000
Accounts collected	250	3000	6000
Other cash receipts	0	0	0
Total cash receipts	$2250	$11000	$18000
Cash Disbursements			
Variable cash disbursements			
Direct labor	$800	$1600	$2000
Inventory purchases	2000	3000	3500
Supplies purchases	250	250	250
Fixed cash disbursements			
Staff salaries	2000	2000	2000
Rent	650	650	650
Periodic payments			
Taxes paid	0	0	3000
Other disbursements	500	0	0
Total cash disbursements	$6200	$7500	$11400
Change in Cash			
Cash gain (loss) during the month	−3950	3500	6600
Cash position at beginning of month	2100	−1850	1650
Cash position at end of month	−1850	1650	8250
Financing Needed			
Desired level of cash	2000	2000	2000
Excess (shortage) of cash	$−3850	$ −350	$6250

without the investment in supplies and inventory, she cannot effectively run her business. Thelma has been in business for several seasons and she knows that by July she should have a surplus of $6,650. Because she has drawn up a cash budget and has past years' data to support it, her banker will be able to see that she can easily repay the short-term loan she needs in a matter of months.

Another benefit of the cash budget is that it allows Thelma to analyze the expenses she expects to make and decide whether any of them can be deferred, thus reducing the amount of money she borrows. May's expenses are unavoidable, in Thelma's mind, however in June she would only have a shortfall of $350. She can either defer some of the expenses until July when she'll have more cash or she can live with a cash balance of $1,650. By July, the height of her income-producing season, she'll have enough money in the bank that she might think about investing some of it.

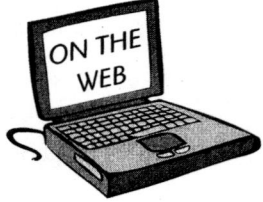

There are several resources on the Internet for business plan templates. Business Owner's Toolkit (www.toolkit.cch.com) provides basic Business Finance worksheets, as well as planning tools under the Starting Your Business heading. Under the latter you will find a Cash Flow Sensitivity Analysis that allows you to make "what-if" decisions.

Small businesses that want a quick check on operations can go to www.cfo.com and use the Small Business Checkup/Evaluation Tool. The calculator will provide an analysis of the business based on the type of business being evaluated, as well as simple balance sheet and income statement data.

These are just two of the sources for business planning advice and templates. Another good source of information is the Small Business Administration, which maintains offices throughout the country. Check the phone book for a listing or contact your local college. In many cases, there is a link between the college or university and a business resource center.

COMPARISON OF BUDGET WITH ACTUAL

Once budgets are written, the company needs to use them. A budget that is stuffed into a drawer is of no use to anyone. On a regular basis, either weekly, monthly, or quarterly, actual expenditures should be matched to the budget, and variances, the difference between planned and actual, should be reconciled. The budget provides an ongoing opportunity to monitor the performance of the firm compared with the plans it has made. Budgets that are developed in accordance with corporate strategies and objectives can help firms adjust to market conditions and attain strategic objectives.

Amber Property Management Budget Reconciliation			
	Budget	Actual	Variance
Rental income	$19,200.00	$16,800.00	−$2,400.00
Expenses:			
Mortgage cost	$6,788.40	$6,788.40	$0.00
Property taxes	$2,500.00	$2,436.00	−$64.00
Maintenance	$1,200.00	$1,526.00	$326.00
Property improvements	$5,000.00	$4,500.00	−$500.00
Utilities	$1,200.00	$1,155.00	−$45.00
Income before taxes	$2,511.60	$394.60	−$2,117.00
Income tax	$678.13	$106.54	−$571.59
Net Income	$1,833.47	$288.06	−$1,545.41

Amber Property Management uses budget analysis to compare the actual rental income and expenses with the budget that they set at the beginning of the year. Their year-end analysis revealed that rental income was less than budgeted. The result was anticipated because one of the rental units went unoccupied for several months. Expenses also varied from the original budget.

Some employees feel that budgets are used in a punitive manner to criticize performance that lags behind plan, whether the original budget was accurately derived or not. The best budget should be viewed as simply another tool to ensure that the firm is operating efficiently and effectively. Budget variances can give clues to business opportunities as well as shortcomings. As a matter of fact, a budget variance will occur when sales exceed expectations! If the firm is not comparing projected sales volume to actual receipts, it could be caught unprepared, experiencing either stock-outs or a lack of service personnel to handle the increased volume of sales. If the firm does not quickly adjust to increased demand it will lose not only the immediate sales but irritate new and potential customers.

Budget variances also occur for reasons over which the firm has no control. Several years ago there was a severe ice storm in our town that caused power outages that lasted for many days. The grocery store near our home used generators to provide what power they could, but there was no sense restocking freezer and dairy departments until electricity could be restored. Still, the store stayed open as best it could with the employees who could struggle in to work. Meat, dairy, and produce products were sold immediately or discarded, however, the store was able to provide the neighborhood with bread, canned goods, bottled water, and paper products for several difficult days. Although the comparative sales figures must have been dismal, rather than penalize the local manager for missing sales targets, the corporate managers should have commended him for keeping the store open at all, considering the logistical difficulties that he faced. In that example, budget variances represented the significant challenge that the store manager overcame in order to serve his longtime customers.

TERMS TO KNOW

Income	Competitive budgeting	Baseline assets and
Expense	Zero-based budgeting	liabilities
Historic budgeting		Cash budget

TERM PAPERS AND PROJECTS

1. Develop a budget for a start-up company, complete with projected cash flow statements.
2. Examine the revenue projections for a municipal golf course, swimming pool, or other public revenue-generating facility. Pay particular attention to the budgeting methods used.
3. Work with a not-for-profit organization to develop annual budgets, including cash flow projections.
4. Write a grant to fund a project or proposal. Include budgets along with rationale.

REVIEW QUESTIONS

1. Distinguish between the historic and zero-based budgeting methods of planning annual expenses.
2. What are the assets and liabilities that should be considered when adjusting a budget for expansion or contraction of a business?
3. Give examples of typical forms of liability and debt. How do these items affect the planning and budgeting process?
4. Why are past financial statements important in planning, forecasting, and budgeting? Which two are the most often used?
5. What is a cash budget and how does it operate?
6. Why doesn't accounts receivable show up in the cash budget?
7. Why would a company need a line of credit?

REVIEW PROBLEM

1. Genetics is a fast-growing pharmaceutical company. Last year they did not show a profit, however, with increased distribution and sales of their patented cure for the common cold, Genetics believes that they will become profitable. The following is their balance sheet and income statement for the just concluded fiscal year.

Genetics Company
2001 Balance Sheet

Assets		Liabilities	
Cash	$11,417	Accounts payable	$1,298
Accounts receivable	$1,580	Accrued liabilities	$3,255
Inventory	$1,603	Total current liabilities	$4,553
Total current assets	$14,600	Shareholders' equity	$10,511
Fixed assets	$464		
Total assets	$15,064	Total liabilities and equity	$15,064

Genetics Company
2001 Income Statement

Sales	$11,200
Cost of goods sold	$1,680
Gross profit	$9,520
Operating expense	$16,530
Operating profit	($7,010)
Interest expense	$790
Profit before taxes	($7,800)
Taxes	$0
Net profit	($7,800)

a. Genetics expects sales to double in the coming year.
b. Cost of goods sold as a percent of sales will remain constant, which means that the gross profit margin will also remain constant.
c. Operating expenses and interest will remain the same.
d. Profits before taxes will be taxed at 20%.
e. All profits will be reinvested in the company.

Calculate the balance sheet that Genetics would expect to see at the end of the current year. Will the company need to borrow to fund its growth?

CHAPTER

9

WORKING CAPITAL MANAGEMENT: THE MANAGEMENT OF SHORT-TERM ASSETS

LEARNING OBJECTIVES

1. Describe the principle of matching sources and uses of funds.

2. Define working capital.

3. Explain why working capital management is essential for a firm's success.

4. Describe the factors that contribute to working capital management policy.

5. Compare the types of cash management strategies available to the firm.

6. Describe how accounts receivable management contributes to working capital management.

7. Discuss the costs of credit.

8. Discuss inventory policy including inventory valuation, turnover rates, and safety stock considerations.

9. Determine economic order quantity.

10. Describe how current liabilities management affects working capital management.

A major principle of finance states that a financial manager should match the source of funds to their use. Most of our discussion in the last few chapters has focused on the operational aspects of a firm: analyzing past performance (Chapter 6), determining breakeven and profit (Chapter 7), creating budgets that will allow us to expand or contract our business in an orderly fashion and forecasting cash flows (Chapter 8). This chapter continues that theme by examining the proper management of current assets. Fixed assets such as buildings and capital equipment, which have a useful life measured in years, are usually financed by long-term debt. We will look at that type of financing in later chapters.

DEFINITION OF WORKING CAPITAL

One of the most important responsibilities of the finance manager is to provide the funds required so that the firm can engage in day-to-day operations. Although the firm may invest in new machinery or property, those decisions are made infrequently. Buying and selling inventory, paying the employees who provide service to the customers, and collecting the accounts due are a continual concern. Wise management of the daily tasks allows the firm to continue as a profitable enterprise.

In Chapter 6 we looked at dozens of financial ratios, each of which gives some indication of the financial health of our company. Here we focus on one of the simplest and most critical relationships: the difference between our current assets and current liabilities, commonly referred to as net working capital.

Think back to the balance sheets we have used. Assets are separated into current assets, those which are expected to be converted into cash during the normal yearly **operating cycle,** and fixed assets. Fixed assets have a long useful life; they are not expected to be converted into cash during the course of the next 12 months. Fixed assets may stay constant or may change due to the expansion or contraction of a business. The key is the expectation that they will last, or have lasted, longer than the current year.

In a figurative sense, the current assets work hard for us because they are constantly turning over—cash is cycling through as payments are received and bills paid, accounts receivable are incurred with sales and remitted by our customers on a regular cycle, and inventory is moving through the company. In fact, we have calculated the turns these assets take in the form of days: we have days of sales outstanding, inventory turnover, and an operating cycle, which is described as the number of days it takes to sell inventory and collect the corresponding account receivable. Because current assets move through the firm on a constant basis, they are referred to as **working capital** (or sometimes gross working capital). They are the assets that we can continually reallocate based on our current needs.

Current liabilities come due within the same yearly operating cycle. They, too, are continually changing based on the activity of the firm, and they provide the firm with some financing opportunities. For some of the liabilities, such as accrued income taxes, we have very little room for creativity—the Internal Revenue Service does not give discounts for prompt payment and imposes serious penalties for late payment. However, there are areas where attention to detail can reduce the firm's cost of financing. Net working capital is the difference between current assets and current liabilities. Working capital management is the way a firm manages that balance. Working capital management is crucial to a business's success because many business failures are due to mismanagement of current assets and their financing. As we will soon see, a careful analysis of our business and some thoughtful planning will go a long way toward avoiding that type of failure.

WORKING CAPITAL POLICY

Working capital policy varies depending on the nature of the business and the length of its operating cycle. The **operating cycle** is the time it takes for the firm to convert inputs into outputs and receive payment for that activity. Inputs can come in the form of raw materials that are converted into finished goods or the time it takes a service provider to complete a project. Outputs are the goods or services the firm provides.

For some firms, the operating cycle is very long. The operating cycle for a custom-built home begins when the builder draws up the initial contract with the customer. The operating cycle doesn't end until the builder receives payment for the completed home. In the interim, the builder has procured materials, paid for site improvements, and hired and paid workers. The operating cycle is measured in months. The builder's largest current asset is work in progress: a house that will not be sold until completed, and the inventory of lumber, pipes, flooring, and roofing material that is designated for that specific house. In contrast, the operating cycle for a restaurant is very short. Many transactions take place daily and they are paid for at the time of service. Inventory sells rapidly and can be replenished daily if needed. The working capital policies for these two businesses would be very different. The custom home builder will most likely rely on accounts payable and perhaps short-term debt to finance the construction of the house; whereas the restaurateur will have sizeable cash flow through the organization and inventory will be paid for within days of being ordered and delivered.

Working capital policy is also affected by the timing of sales (whether they are seasonal or subject to economic downturns), the firm's credit policy (whether it is willing to finance purchases), and management's risk tolerance. If sales are seasonal rather than steady, the firm may have to increase inventory levels before sales revenue is generated. If the firm then extends credit to its customers, there will be an additional lag before it receives payment. The firm will have to finance the initial inventory and calculate carrying costs, the costs it incurs to fund its operations.

A firm's **credit policy** also affects working capital management. If the standard payment terms for our industry are net 30 days, increasing our accounts receivable policy to net 60 days gives our firm a competitive advantage. It also lengthens the operating cycle by a whole month. If our cost of borrowing is 12% per year, we have effectively cut our profits by a full percentage point.

Management's risk tolerance factors into working capital policy decisions. What level of inventory is considered safe? Is management willing to have a stock-out or does the inventory level have to be high enough to prevent any chance of running short? The cost of a stock-out is both the lost revenue and the chance that a customer will seek other vendors. Those costs must be weighed against the cost of carrying inventory and the potential for obsolescence. In the case of our restaurant, a daily special that is written on the blackboard at the restaurant's entrance will simply be erased when inventory is depleted. The main menu offerings, however, should definitely be available.

The consequences of various policies will be discussed as we examine each component of working capital.

CURRENT ASSET MANAGEMENT

Current asset management consists of minimizing the cost of holding cash, marketable securities, accounts receivable, and inventory. If we can reduce our holding costs, we become less dependent on financing.

CASH MANAGEMENT

The goal of **cash management** is to maximize our return. We earn money by capturing the value added between the cost of inventory and the revenue we earn. Money facilitates those transactions, but money left idle does not create value. Cash on hand earns little interest. Some banks offer interest-bearing checking accounts, but the interest rate is so small that we should not leave too much money in our checking account.

Efficient cash management revolves around two basic strategies: (1) hastening collection of monies due us and carefully managing disbursements, and (2) investing excess cash in savings accounts or marketable securities that provide protection of principal with a higher rate of return than we earn in a checking account. Specific policies for managing the turn of receivables and payables will be discussed later. Here we focus on moving cash efficiently.

In order to maximize the time that money is in our possession, we need to manage the float. **Float** is the time that elapses between writing a check from our account and when the money is actually deducted from that account. In Chapter 4 we described the system by which the Federal Reserve Banks clear checks. When we pay bills, we write a check and put it in the mailbox. Although we have subtracted the amount of the check from the balance in our account, the money is still there. If the company we have paid is located at some distance from us, a number of days will pass before the check reaches its destination where it is then deposited in the vendor's account at the local bank. The bank transmits the check to its district Federal Reserve Bank, which processes payment. Only then is the amount of the check actually withdrawn from our

- Minimize cash on hand
- Pay bills on time but not too early
- Take advantage of early payment discounts
- Move idle cash to interest-bearing investments
- Use electronic funds transfer to minimize "float"
- Carefully assess credit practices

Keys to successful cash management.

account. During the time that the check is in transit, we are earning some interest. The longer it takes the check to clear, the longer we will collect interest on that money. It is perfectly legal for us to collect interest on money that is legitimately in our account. It is not legal to create sham accounts and quickly move money from place to place to take advantage of the float between each settlement. That is called check-kiting and it is definitely illegal.

Electronic funds transfer is another method of managing cash disbursements that almost entirely eliminates float. Under an EFT system, a company authorizes a direct transfer of funds from its checking account to another through the use of computerized transactions. Electronic funds transfer is most efficiently used for batch or routine payments such as payroll or payment to established vendors.

How we manage float depends on the policies we have established with our customers and our vendors. Some companies and government agencies accept a postmarked date as the date of payment on account. An example is the annual income tax payment that is due on April 15 of each year. Because the postmark is proof of payment, taxpayers who owe money should theoretically manage float by mailing their payment at midnight on April 15, and many do so. However, many companies do not accept the postmarked date as proof of payment for accounts receivable. One reason is that most companies are automating their check processing systems and the check is almost immediately separated from its envelope. There is no proof of postmark. Another reason is that allowing the postmark to serve as payment date lengthens the time that accounts receivable are outstanding by the number of days it takes for payment to reach the vendor. Most companies state that payment must be received by the due date, not mailed by that date.

Either policy has an impact on our cash management strategy. If the vendor allows postmarks to count as payment, our firm should mail each payment on exactly the date it is due, thus utilizing float, if the cost of using paper checks is less than the amount we can earn on the float. If the vendor requires payment by the due date, the firm should employ electronic funds transfer and make a direct payment on the due date. Cash stays in our account until the final possible day and the cost of issuing paper checks is eliminated, as is the chance that the check will be delayed in transit.

Electronic funds transfer has an important place in the internal management of funds. An organization that has multiple locations, especially those that are geographically separate, can use electronic funds transfer to move money between units quickly and cost-effectively. Remember that money has become far more abstract. A retailer needs a certain amount of currency on hand to make change for cash customers. Aside from that, most transactions can take place by transferring bits of information between computers, which is far less expensive than writing checks. Careful use of electronic funds transfer reduces the amount of cash that the company needs to keep on hand because it knows precisely when payments will clear the system. The firm does not have to keep a safety stock of cash just in case a check clears sooner than expected.

In addition to hastening the collection of funds and delaying disbursements, cash management also involves moving excess cash to short-term investments that will pay a higher rate of return while still preserving capital. For a large corporation, there are many types of investments available such as

Stop
and
Think

In an article in *CFO Magazine* (also available at www.cfo.com), Ronald Fink describes the difference between efficient working capital management and the use of negative working capital. If net working capital is the difference between current assets and current liabilities, negative working capital means that the firm has a larger amount in payables and liabilities than it does in current assets such as cash, receivables, and inventory. Having read Chapter 6, red flags should appear when you read that statement.

Fink argues that although minimizing receivables, inventory, and payables allows the firm to free up cash to be invested in the firm, the strategy requires the agreement of both customers and vendors. Customers who feel strong-armed to pay bills will choose other suppliers, while vendors who are strung out for too long will either increase the cost of goods sold to compensate for the slow payment or will refuse to sell altogether.

There is no question that liquidity is important. Fink goes on to illustrate his case using Amazon.com. Amazon's sales are converted to revenue within a few days since all transactions are handled by credit cards; however, payables come due later. If Amazon runs with virtually no cash, they will find themselves strapped when revenue falls off in the first quarter and bills for fourth quarter sales (holiday sales) come due. It is a case of timing payments and revenue streams.

Source: Ronald Fink, "Forget the Float?" *CFO Magazine*, July 1, 2001.

commercial paper. Commercial paper is a short-term unsecured promissory note issued by corporations for periods of between 1 day and 9 months. Commercial paper is an unsecured debt, not asset backed, so only firms with good credit will be able to find a market for their paper. Commercial paper is usually issued in denominations of $100,000 or more, so it is not an investment that a typical small business would use. It would be far more likely for an entrepreneur to invest in a short-term certificate of deposit or use a sweep account.

Certificates of deposit are savings accounts that require a specific minimum balance and have a fixed maturity date. The shortest maturity date is usually

In the News

Commercial paper has been available to the most creditworthy customers. In recent months, as markets become more nervous about the quality of reported financial data, the accessibility of commercial paper has decreased dramatically even for companies that had used it in the past. Many firms are finding that they are no longer able to issue short-term promissory notes and are increasingly turning to short-term bank loans or bonds as a source of funds.

3 months, although CDs are available for longer periods of time. The certificate carries a higher rate of interest than a traditional passbook, however, there is a penalty for early withdrawal of the funds. Since principal and interest are insured, they offer a safe, short-term alternative to a standard savings or checking account. Most certificates of deposit automatically roll over, or reinvest, unless the depositor gives instructions to the contrary. For that reason, the firm needs to pay careful attention to the term structure of its CDs.

Sweep accounts tie a checking account to any number of savings accounts and mutual funds managed by the bank. Excess cash can be immediately transferred into a mutual fund or money market fund that pays a higher rate of interest than the firm's checking account. The business owner is required to keep a specific minimum balance in the checking account. Each day the bank "sweeps" the excess cash into the investment fund. If the checking account balance drops below the minimum, funds are automatically swept back into the checking account.

Some firms combine their holdings of cash and cash equivalents as a single item on the balance sheets. Cash equivalents are short-term, highly liquid investments that can be readily converted into a known quantity of cash and are so near to their maturity date that they pose little risk of loss due to interest rate fluctuations. Cash equivalents must be securities that are issued with a maturity date of 3 months or less. 3-month treasury bills, commercial paper, and money market accounts can be considered cash equivalents. A 2-year treasury bill that

Toolbox

Sweep accounts are not free. The issuing bank usually requires a substantial balance in a checking account and may limit the number of transfers per month. Fees for sweep accounts vary from bank to bank, along with the level of services offered. Before choosing an account, the firm should answer the following questions:

How closely can the firm predict its own cash needs?

What fees are being charged by the various banks?

How do the fees compare with the interest rate earned on the investment portion of the account?

What is the minimum balance required in the checking account?

A company could create its own version of a sweep account by utilizing some of the on-line services offered by many banks. If the company's financial institution allows on-line transfers between accounts, the company could delegate cash management duties to one of its financial managers. At the end of each working day or week, the manager would assess the anticipated cash needs of the organization and make the transfers accordingly. As with the sweep account, the firm should ascertain whether its bank charges fees for "excess" transactions.

It would behoove the firm to comparison shop, for example, ask for quotes from several lending institutions and specify what services your firm requires. Then choose the bank that best suits your needs.

is purchased 3 months before its maturity date is considered an investment, not a cash equivalent.

In addition to cash equivalents, a firm could choose to invest in securities such as U.S. Treasury bills, corporate or municipal bonds, or stock. They are marketable items, that is, they can be sold. But the fact that they have to be sold means that they are not an immediate source of cash. There are transaction costs and a very real risk of loss of principal.

Here is an area where corporate strategy, the timing of cash flows, and management's risk tolerance come together. Automobile manufacturers operate in a cyclical industry that also requires a large degree of investment in fixed assets. When the economic climate is healthy, automakers can keep factories at high levels of production. Fixed assets are being efficiently utilized, and the company has a healthy revenue stream. If consumer confidence falls or the country enters a recession, consumers defer large purchases first. Sales of automobiles and other durable goods fall and factories run below capacity. Although production has fallen, the manufacturer continues to have high fixed costs to maintain factories and equipment for which there is no secondary use. Knowing that this cycle occurs with some regularity, automakers manage cash over a period of years, not months. Revenue received in good economic times is used to increase existing productivity levels but also invested in such a way that it is available in case of an economic slowdown. The amounts of money that can be stockpiled during flush times are too large to simply sweep into a certificate of deposit. Because the need for funds will not be immediate even as the economy begins to slow, automakers (and other manufacturers of durable goods) can use their excess capital to purchase the stocks and bonds of other companies in addition to Treasury bills and notes. The investments can be converted into cash as needed but do not have to be converted immediately, hence they are investments, not part of the firm's working capital.

We will discuss the specifics of stocks and bonds in later chapters, but it is important to note that investment in securities carries with it some risk. There is no guarantee of the underlying value of shares of stock. The reason companies invest excess cash in stock is because they expect a higher return

---

In the News

In March 2001, the American economy had started to slow. An article in *Business Week* described a change taking place among senior executives: they were attempting to conserve what cash they had and beginning to stockpile cash that they felt they would need during a possible recession. In addition to timing receivables and payables, firms were beginning to cut production levels, close plants, and lay off employees. Slowing production would reduce inventory levels and cut current operating costs, which could be seen in the current liabilities accounts.

Source: "In Today's Corporate America, Cash Is King," Business Week, March 12, 2001, p. 40–41. By David Henry, with Steve Rosenbush, in New York, Dean Foust in Atlanta, Joann Muller in Detroit, and bureau reports.

than they would be able to earn on a savings account, however that chance of return carries with it the very real risk that the company could lose what it invested. Investing in bonds carries somewhat less risk because bonds are a form of debt, but they, too, can lose value. If the firm expects to need access to cash in a relatively short period of time, it should exercise caution when buying securities. If excess cash is not needed as soon, and management is risk tolerant, investing in securities is an option.

ACCOUNTS RECEIVABLE MANAGEMENT

Because we are so familiar with accounts receivable, it is easy to overlook how important they are to the success or failure of an organization. Accounts receivable are both a marketing tool and a form of financing that companies provide to their customers. With proper oversight they can increase sales revenue and profit. Left unattended, they can drain valuable working capital from the firm. We distinguish accounts receivable from credit card sales, which are facilitated by an outside supplier such as VISA or MasterCard. Credit card companies provide collection service for retailers and other direct-to-consumer companies. For a fee, usually about 2% of the sales price, the credit card company will transfer cash to the merchant and collect from the purchaser. Credit card transactions that are facilitated by a third party are considered cash purchases that have been discounted. Accounts receivable, on the other hand, are credit that a business extends to its customers and carries on its books. Credit cards issued and managed by the merchant are considered accounts receivable.

Many consumers prefer to use credit rather than cash to purchase products or services. They base purchase decisions in part on the availability of deferred payment plans or whether the merchant accepts credit cards. If the business offers payment terms or a proprietary credit card, it is employing a finance tool to influence buying patterns, which is why the credit can be considered a marketing tool. Business customers purchase in such large volume that paying with cash would be unwieldy. The use of credit also allows the business customer to conserve cash reserves by extending the time between acquisition of goods and payment. To increase sales and effectively compete with other businesses that offer credit, a firm may decide to accept accounts receivable. Again, the use of accounts receivable is tied to marketing strategy. However, there are significant financial implications for the firm.

THE COSTS OF CREDIT

Offering credit involves costs. The first is the cost of setting up accounts and managing the collections. Often this involves hiring employees to supervise billing and receipt of payment. We assume that payment terms will be honored by our customers, but in some cases payment will be delayed and additional invoices need to be sent. Each additional invoice increases administrative costs.

A second cost is the opportunity cost of the cash on account. Opportunity cost describes the potential benefit that is given up when the firm chooses one course of action that precludes an alternative course of action. By choosing to extend credit to customers, we preclude using those funds to purchase additional inventory or expand our facilities. If we determine that the profits derived from credit sales are greater than the other uses of that cash, we should extend credit. If, however, substituting the use of third-party credit cards will provide the same sales at a lower cost, we should not finance accounts receivable.

A third cost of receivables is the potential for loss. Not all credit sales will be collected. Obviously, if we knew which ones would not be collected, we would not grant credit. One method of increasing the safety of accounts receivable is to require the borrower to pledge assets as collateral. In case of default, the seller repossesses merchandise that can then be resold. The debt may not be entirely discharged by the repossession of the property. If the seller does not realize the full value of the account receivable, any amount left on account remains the responsibility of the buyer. Unfortunately, if the merchandise needs to be reclaimed, the likelihood of recovering the additional amount owed is not great.

Before extending credit, the firm should analyze several components of its credit policy: a description of the level of risk it is willing to assume, the terms of credit, and collection policies. Federal and state laws regulate the granting of credit and allowable terms. Before establishing an accounts receivable policy, the company should research local and federal laws. In general, the company must establish explicit criteria for granting credit and offer the same terms to all creditworthy customers. Once the criteria are established, they apply to all applicants.

Establishing Credit Policies

The company should set credit policy based on its risk tolerance. Factors such as the borrower's ability to pay, whether the account will be secured with collateral, and the borrower's past payment history should be specified.

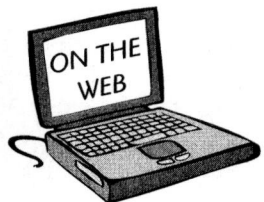

GE Capital is a division of the General Electric Company that provides a wide range of financial services for businesses. Among the services it offers, GE Capital can speed up the collection of cash from accounts receivable and inventory through several processes.

Another service offered by GE is a revolving loan that is collateralized by current assets such as accounts receivable or inventory. The "revolver" is nothing less than an asset-backed line of credit that the company can use to fund cash shortages. GE will also purchase accounts receivable, collect them, and report on the collections.

GE Capital is not the only firm that buys accounts receivable or provides current asset-backed financing, however, their Web site is interesting to read since it also offers stories about small- and medium-size companies that have used various GE products to increase their financial flexibility.

Source: www.gecfo.com.

Blue Rock Construction

238 North Street
Green Meadow, CA 94599
925-886-0208

Invoice No.

INVOICE ==

Customer

Name	White Rose LLP		Date	1/14/03
Address	3311 Mortimer Drive		Order No.	556
City	Green Meadow	State CA ZIP 94599	Rep	Sam Reed
Phone	925-412-5777		FOB	

Qty	Description	Unit Price	TOTAL
1	Replacement Window	$95.00	$95.00
3	Hours of Labor	$15.00	$45.00
		SubTotal	$140.00
		Shipping & Handling	
		Taxes State	$11.20
		TOTAL	$151.20

○ Cash
○ Check
○ Credit Card

Name _____
CC # _____
        Expires _____

Office Use Only

Thank you for your business!

A typical invoice lists the services provided and goods sold along with payment terms.

Whether the borrower is an individual or a corporation, the ability to pay is based largely on income and other sources of cash, such as bank accounts or investments. Even if the borrower has a high income, they could be refused credit if their current debt level would not support additional payments.

Not all accounts receivable are easily collateralized. A firm that provides cleaning services to major office buildings cannot use its services to collateralize receivables. By the time the account comes due, the service has already been provided and cannot be repossessed. In this case, the client's ability to pay and past payment history become more important. Even when the account can be collateralized, the lender does not want to take possession of the merchandise. Having sold it once, they do not want to have it back on their shelves. The effect of requiring collateral is partly psychological—an intangible balance sheet entry is tied to a very tangible item that the purchaser feels has value. The purpose of collateral is to tie payments to ownership.

Not the least important consideration is the past payment history of the borrower. Some companies make it a practice to use their accounts payable (your account receivable) as a financing tool and are willing to push the limit of payment dates if they can. Before extending credit to a new customer, a firm should obtain an independent credit report. In its policy statement, the firm can state that it will not extend credit to firms with poor payment history or a past bankruptcy. While past history is no guarantee against loss, it does provide a further level of safety. As long as the policy is enforced uniformly, it will be upheld.

After establishing the profile of an acceptable borrower, the firm must determine credit terms. These include the number of days between invoice date and payment date: Does the client have 30 days to pay or will we allow 45 or even 60? Lengthening the payment period increases our cost of offering credit. Payment terms also define whether payment must be received by a specified date or the envelope postmarked by that date. We looked at the ramifications of that distinction in the section on cash management.

Other possible terms could include a discount for early payment. Some invoices contain a series of payment instructions such as 2/10, n30, which translates into "2% discount if paid within 10 days, net due in 30 days." If the invoice for $1,500 is dated June 10 and the client pays in full on June 15, the amount remitted will be $1,470 ($1,500 less the 2% discount). A question arises: If the client is unable to pay the entire amount of the invoice but could make a partial payment of $800, will we allow a proportional amount of the cash discount? There is no single right answer. It is another issue that needs to be addressed within the credit policy.

At the end of the allowable payment period, the lender is allowed to charge interest up to the limits established by state usury laws. The rate that can be charged varies by state, so a firm doing business in many states could potentially have several rates of interest. The interest terms must be disclosed to the borrower when the account is established and updated when legislation or company policy causes a rate change. Rather than charge the highest allowable interest rate on unpaid balances, some firms choose to moderate the fee in order to compete for business. The firm must analyze the profit that is earned on incremental sales as a result of the lower rate of interest to determine the most beneficial combination of payment terms and sales.

We stated earlier that some accounts become uncollectible. The last major component of credit policy is how to handle delinquent accounts. At some point, the chance of collecting past due balances exceeds the cost of doing so. The business must decide whether it will write off the bad debt or sell it to a collection agency. The value of delinquent accounts will depend, to a degree, on how well the accounts were collateralized and whether the delinquency is due to short-term mismanagement by the borrower or an almost certain inability to pay.

Credit Strategies

We have said that the profile of an acceptable borrower will depend on the risk tolerance of the organization. Some businesses have specialized in granting credit to more risky consumers and advertise that they refuse no one. A higher proportion of these accounts receivable will default than ones that are granted to customers who are traditionally creditworthy. How, then, can companies afford to offer such seemingly generous terms?

There are several strategic decisions involved with this choice. Remember that credit is meant to stimulate sales that would otherwise not be made. A person or company with no credit, or extremely poor credit, will essentially be precluded from purchasing higher-cost goods and, unless a purchase is made, there is no profit potential. One of the definitions of money is that it can be used as a form of deferred payment: Five years from now, I will accept dollars in payment for the car I sold to you today. The act of extending credit is an expression of confidence that that form of money will still have value in the future and that the borrower will have access to that form of money for the duration of the loan. Some of the contributing factors to poor credit include low income or unstable work history, a past bankruptcy, or poor payment history. If the lender is careful, some of those factors can be mitigated. The firm could set as one of its criteria that the borrower have a stable source of income, whether it is earned income or a transfer payment (such as disability or retirement income). As the lender, I could require that an electronic funds transfer is set up from the purchaser's bank account to mine to be paid on the date that the purchaser receives income. That reduces the poor payment risk. A firm that utilizes this strategy has to accept that there will be a number of repossessed items. The loan would be completely collateralized, and the lender could shorten the time between the first missed payment and repossession. A higher interest rate could be justified based on the larger risk being assumed. And finally, the seller could charge a higher initial price for the item so that more of the profit was captured up front.

The preceding description seems to pertain primarily to personal consumers, but many small businesses fall into the category of those who have little or no credit due to low income and an unstable pattern of revenue. The payment terms just described could apply to the purchase of a copy machine as easily as they could to a personal-use item. As a small business builds its credit history and increases the dependability and size of its revenues, it will be offered more generous credit terms. In the beginning, however, credit may be expensive and hard to come by. We'll discuss more about payables later in the chapter.

One last accounts receivable strategy that we will consider is factoring. **Factoring** is the process of selling accounts receivable at a discount to another firm. A business may decide to sell all or part of its accounts receivable if it wants to convert them to cash. Factoring can be a standard operating policy or a response to pressing cash needs. A business might also use factoring as part of a marketing or inventory management program.

Here's an example. A local furniture store has decided to change their merchandise mix, increasing the amount of upholstered furniture and decreasing wood items like bookcases and entertainment centers. In order to stimulate excitement and, more importantly, immediate sales they are offering 90 days same as cash OAC (on approved credit—those are key words) for 4 days only! "Hurry in now and get the deals before they're gone!" You can see that we've strayed back to marketing, but, once again, marketing and financial decisions are inextricably linked. The furniture store accepts major credit cards and will continue to do so, but for this sale, they believe that the lure of 90 days' free financing will bring in enough customers to clear the inventory that they no longer wish to carry, both in the store and on the balance sheet. Their business, even after this weekend clearance extravaganza, is selling furniture, not lending money. Before they advertised the sale, they contacted a finance company that would buy all of the accounts at a specified discount from face value. Why bother? Because the profit that could be made in the span of this single weekend, and the savings in terms of carrying costs, will be greater than the discount the factor is charging. The store managers are making a wise financial decision.

⟨ **In the News** ⟩

Some of the excitement over Internet retailers has faded. Dotcom companies have been renamed "dot.bomb" or "dot.gone." For many consumers, the loss of an e-tailer causes little change in their shopping patterns. Patrons who had shopped at eToys can still buy toys on the Internet through a partnership between Amazon.com and Toys R Us. Investors who purchased stock in start-up e-tailers should have realized the speculative nature of the business model, but so should the vendors who sold to them.

When it declared bankruptcy in March 2001, eToys began selling inventory and equipment and attempted to sell its customized search engine, which would suggest toys based on the customer's demographics. The toys sold for approximately 25% of cost, and there were no takers for the warehouse system or search engine. Both Pets.com and Garden.com, two other e-tailers that declared bankruptcy, received approximately 30 cents on the dollar for their remaining inventory.

In addition to the retail goods, computer equipment purchased to support these companies entered the secondhand market. Much of it was relatively new and sold at bargain-basement prices.

The implications for the failed companies' vendors are significant. Not only do the original equipment vendors have to write off uncollectible accounts but the availability of so much "gently used" equipment also creates huge price pressures for the new equipment that the manufacturers have in inventory.

Source: *BusinessWeek*, e.biz, May 14, 2001.

ANALYZING AND MANAGING ACCOUNTS RECEIVABLE

Once the firm has determined that it will offer credit, it needs to continually monitor the accounts. We saw in Chapter 6 that total accounts receivable can be evaluated based on the average number of days it takes to turn credit sales into cash. The entire bundle of accounts can be analyzed in this way, but if we are managing our working capital astutely, we also want to look at specific accounts.

Most of the computerized accounting and bookkeeping software packages allow managers to specify payment terms when an account is set up and monitor the payment history of the account. The programs will produce reports detailing how many accounts are past due, by how many days, and in what dollar amounts. Customers whose accounts have fallen behind can be contacted before the next billing cycle and reminded that payment is due. Using software packages to provide routine information reduces the cost of managing accounts receivable and allows the manager to move quickly to collect late payments.

We have said that accounts receivable management includes setting policies for charging interest and collecting past due amounts. However, the truth is that when economic conditions deteriorate, accounts receivable will be one of the first areas affected and policies alone will not ensure timely payments. If economic activity is slowing, our sales revenue may very well be

> ### See for Yourself
>
> Several years ago, I wanted to buy one of the new energy-efficient washing machines, which would significantly reduce my water and electricity usage. My existing machine was still functional, so I needed an incentive to buy at that time rather than wait just a little bit longer. My local appliance store offered 90 days same as cash and I was sold.
>
> The credit agreement was set up through CitiFinancial (www. citifinancial.com) and my payments were sent to them. Once the paperwork was signed, the retailer could concentrate on delivering my washing machine, installing it, teaching me all about the neat new gizmos, and reminding me to return when I needed another appliance.
>
> If you visit the CitiFinancial Web site, you will see that their services are geared toward retailers of furniture, carpeting, electronics, and appliances. The type of merchandise they are financing has certain characteristics in common: it is infrequently purchased and may need to be financed over a moderate length of time. Accounts that are not paid in full by the end of the 90-day period will accrue interest from the beginning of the loan. CitiFinancial earns income from the interest charged on loans that are not settled within the 90-day time period. The retailer makes a sale that may otherwise have been deferred and has the ability to sell merchandise on credit without having to assume the risk of nonpayment.
>
> When the ice cream in my refrigerator's freezer started to melt a few years later, I returned to the same appliance store. This time I needed little incentive to replace the appliance. My account with CitiFinancial was still open, my credit was good, and a sleek, energy-efficient refrigerator was delivered the next day.
>
> I have the spiffy new washing machine, frozen ice cream, and, after calculating the time my check would be in the mail, was able to earn interest on my money for an extra 80 days each time I bought a new appliance. It's an example of efficient working capital management!

falling, and the timing could not be worse for accounts to be delayed. The finance manager needs to be diligent in following payment streams and closely monitor the financial condition of borrowers. If there is a significant change in creditworthiness, the firm can refuse additional credit.

Factoring allows a firm to borrow against accounts receivable and increase cash flow. Many firms provide factoring; some specialize in certain industries, others offer services to a wide variety of companies.

A simple search in Yahoo! Business and Economy (www.yahoo.com) yielded four single-spaced pages of factoring companies. In the thumbnail sketches provided on the listing page, firms offered both international and domestic factoring services. Some specialize in accounts receivable or

(continued)

inventory funding, while others offer advances on real estate commissions or medical insurance payments.

Once you have reached the Yahoo! homepage, the path to the factoring list is Home>Business and Economy>Business to Business>Financial Services>Finance and Receivables>Financing>Corporate Finance>Commercial Credit>Factoring. The richness of the path shows that there are many subheadings within Yahoo! alone under which a company could look for financing options.

Imagine how many I could have found if I had expanded my search to other search engines!

INVENTORY MANAGEMENT

The final portion of current assets that we will analyze is inventory. When you look at the balance sheet of many organizations, the largest current asset is inventory. The goal of **inventory management** is to ensure that the firm has enough inventory on hand to meet its sales or production goals while at the same time minimizing carrying costs. Here we will consider three main areas of concern: how often to order inventory, how to analyze whether inventory is moving efficiently through our system, and how to value what we are holding.

ECONOMIC ORDER QUANTITY

There are two contradictory costs associated with inventory management: the cost of keeping inventory on hand and the cost of not having inventory available for sale. Ideally, the firm would minimize its holdings. However, there are savings that accrue from ordering larger quantities. Quite often, there is a minimum handling fee per order. If the order is large, the handling fee is allocated across a greater number of inventory items, cutting the cost per item. Often a manufacturer will offer volume discounts once an order reaches a certain magnitude. The discount is not cumulative across the year's purchases but only valid on a single delivery. Again, the cost of goods is lowered as the volume increases.

When a firm purchases inventory, whether as goods available for sale or raw materials, it must finance it either through borrowing or the opportunity cost of the capital. Purchasing larger quantities may result in price savings per unit, however, interest costs need to be factored in. In addition, inventory must be stored. As inventory quantities increase, so do storage costs.

We also need to recognize the cost of not holding inventory, although that calculation may be more difficult and depends to some degree on the nature of the product. Not having inventory on hand for use or sale can mean the missed opportunity for a sale, and a potentially disgruntled customer who will seek out different suppliers. On the other hand, companies that sell custom-made items may publicize that each order is made to your exact specifications—the additional time involved in obtaining raw materials is worth the wait.

Inventory is checked in the warehouse. Most companies use barcodes, both on products and on the shipping containers, to accurately track inventory movement. The goal is to maintain sufficient inventory to meet customer needs while minimizing storage and carrying costs. (Getty Images, Inc.)

Using a formula called the **economic order quantity (EOQ),** most organizations can find the optimal order size for each type of inventory. The EOQ formula is

$$\sqrt{\frac{2CN}{K}}$$

where

C = cost of ordering
N = total annual demand for the item
K = carrying costs for the item, expressed as a dollar cost per inventory item

There is an immediate decision to be made. When we calculate EOQ, are we going to use past demand or our estimate of this year's total demand (N)? If the business is in a steady state in terms of its own growth, the nature of its industry, and the state of the economy, we can assume last year's annual demand. If the industry or company is rapidly changing, assumptions need to be documented and adjustments made to total demand.

Total ordering cost (C) for the item is an administrative cost. The simplest way to calculate ordering costs is to allocate purchasing department overhead evenly across the activity of the department, (i.e., number of orders). This calculation ignores the difference in complexity between types of orders—routine reorders that are highly automated would be far less expensive than negotiating terms with a new vendor. The firm could determine a charge rate based on hourly work involved with ordering. Reorders would carry a lower ordering cost than customized orders. However it is calculated, the cost per order will be expressed as a dollar value.

Carrying costs (K) are expressed as a per unit dollar value. The annual cost of carrying inventory includes the expenses associated with owning or leasing and maintaining warehouse space including the wages of warehouse workers, any property tax paid on inventory, insurance costs, and a calculation of any interest charges associated with financing inventory. The carrying costs are divided by the average inventory to obtain an estimate of carrying costs. There is a significant factor embedded in this formula: some of the costs of the warehouse are fixed, which means that at higher levels of inventory the cost per item is reduced. The formula may reward management for keeping higher levels of inventory if the fixed warehouse costs are larger than the variable costs of property tax and finance charges. The investment in existing warehouse space can skew the economic order quantity toward larger order sizes. Again, if we are comfortable with the status quo, this difficulty is minimized. But if we are experiencing rapid growth or contraction, the fixed cost component of carrying costs needs to be addressed separately.

Economic order quantity should be calculated for each type of inventory, based on its sales patterns. Let's say that a company sells 45,000 units per year, the cost of ordering is $36 and carrying costs are $1 per unit. Economic order quantity is calculated as

$$\sqrt{\frac{2(36)45,000}{1}}$$

Each order will consist of 1,800 units, and the firm will need to reorder 25 times per year.

As the cost of ordering increases, the frequency of orders should decrease because it becomes less economical to place orders. If there were no cost to placing orders, the firm should have continual deliveries and keep almost no inventory in stock.

Safety Stock

The minimum inventory level that we wish to maintain is called **safety stock.** Given predictable sales patterns, this is the amount that we will have on hand at all times. For some firms, safety stock is minimal and will vary by inventory type. The custom home builder may purchase nails and other fasteners in bulk but will special order tile and flooring products based on the design of each house. A hospital has higher levels of gauze pads than pacemakers.

Once the ideal order size has been calculated and payment terms negotiated, ordering costs can be reduced by automating the inventory supply system. Many retailers have set up direct reorder systems between individual stores, the company's warehouses, and even their suppliers. When a customer purchases a product, it is subtracted from the store's inventory. When store inventory reaches a specified level, the district warehouse is instructed to add that item to the next shipment. Inventory moves out of the warehouse to the stores as needed. When inventory levels at the warehouse reach a predetermined level, the system reorders from the supplier, who uses the purchase order to generate an invoice. If sales volume is steady, orders will be placed at a fairly consistent rate. For cyclical or seasonal businesses, the frequency of orders will coincide with the business cycle. Regardless of the nature of the business, automating the process significantly reduces ordering costs and provides detailed sales records for the company.

Toolbox

> For a firm with steady sales and reorder patterns, economic order quantity can provide another piece of the working capital management puzzle. Assume that sales at the local coffee bar are predictable from week to week, with only minor variations per day of the week. The company determines that paper goods such as coffee cups, napkins, and coasters can be ordered on a 2-week cycle, and the vendor will grant payment terms of 2/15, n/30. The coffee bar would have most of its daily sales in cash or checks, if not all, which means that there would not be a lag in collections. Since the consumption of paper goods is stable and deliveries come in a set pattern, the firm can adjust its cash management policies to take advantage of the discount offered by the vendor.

Automatic reordering systems do not guarantee that inventory is delivered from the manufacturer to the retailer's warehouse the next day. If delivery time is 3 days, a reorder should be placed when the inventory level equals the safety stock plus 3 days of sales on hand.

Just-in-Time Inventory Systems

Ideally, my firm would carry no inventory and yet sell millions of dollars per year of merchandise. Since there were no carrying costs, I could charge less for my product and my profits still would be much higher than a competitor who had to fund inventory. Is it a dream? No, it's **just-in-time inventory.** With careful coordination between a business and its vendors, inventory levels can be drastically reduced. Some manufacturers are encouraging suppliers to locate plants in close proximity to one another and are setting up daily delivery schedules tied to production plans. In order for this to work well, the buyer has to establish a close working relationship with its vendors and provide fairly detailed production plans. Buyers and vendors become working partners rather than the more traditional arm's-length relationship. As with every inventory management system, there are potential costs involved. Although just-in-time inventory systems can reduce carrying costs, both firms suffer if one has a production slowdown or labor dispute.

INVENTORY TURNOVER

Previously, we used factoring and an extravagant weekend sale to adjust the inventory levels at a local furniture store. How did management decide that it was time to change the product mix? A firm can look at activity and profitability ratios.

In Chapter 6 we calculated inventory turnover for the firm as a whole. We can also calculate inventory turnover for specific products or product lines. I inventory turnover for upholstered furniture was six times per year and wood furniture turned only three times per year, the volume of sales is weighted in favor of the upholstered furniture. The store manager could also look at the profit margin for wood versus upholstered furniture. If the profit margin or wood furniture was significantly higher than other types of furniture, it would provide a rationale for keeping a certain level of wood products. In fact, a combination of these two factors along with the manager's observations probably led to the decision to reduce the level of inventory.

Inventory turnover uses historic sales results, even if the benchmark is only last month's sales. It is important to watch not just the raw turnover number but also the trend that it indicates. If inventory turns slow, it indicates that sales are softening, which could be a result of economic conditions, consumer preference, or even a change in seasons. Just as the accounts receivable manager needs to set criteria for sending accounts to collection, the inventory manager needs to have policies that determine when a product line is discontinued or reassessed.

INVENTORY VALUATION

A firm purchases inventory at different times and often at fluctuating prices. When the firm sells inventory, what value do they ascribe to the sales and what value to the remaining inventory? This is not an insignificant question and it affects both the balance sheet and the income statement. The accounting calculations used to value inventory are straightforward, once the company determines which method best reflects its business.

The specific identification method of **inventory valuation** assigns a cost to individual inventory items. If the firm can trace a purchase order directly to the item available for sale, **specific identification** provides the most accurate cost data. Because automobiles carry a vehicle identification number (VIN) that can be matched to an invoice, specific identification is possible. However, in the parts department of that same dealership, specific identification of each oil filter and spark plug will be virtually impossible.

The second type of inventory valuation system assigns costs based on the timing of purchases. The **first in, first out (FIFO)** method assumes that the first items purchased are the first ones that were sold. The **last in, first out (LIFO)** method assumes that the most recently purchased (last in) items were the first ones sold. Both methods describe which items have been sold, not what is left in inventory. If the firm uses FIFO, it has assumed that the first ones have been sold (they are out). The inventory is the leftover quantity, that is, the last ones purchased. Be very careful of the distinction between what has been sold (out) and what is being valued.

If prices are stable there will be no difference between the two valuation methods. If prices are increasing dramatically, which method will produce the greatest inventory value? Think carefully about what is being valued. If prices are rising, the most expensive items are the last ones purchased. The highest inventory value will be reflected by the FIFO method. The lower-cost items, the first ones purchased, have been sold. Because we have chosen to use FIFO our inventory costs are rising.

Many firms use some form of averaging to smooth the effect of fluctuating prices. As each new purchase is made, the average cost of inventory is adjusted upward or downward. The precise calculations are not necessary here; it is more important to understand that inventory valuation, and by extension working capital management, is affected by the valuation choices that management makes.

If you read the notes to the financial statements, you will see that inventory is valued at the lower of cost or market. Ideally, the lower value is the company's cost of inventory, no matter which of the methods they used to value it. Sometimes conditions change drastically and the market value for products falls below their production cost. A company will not survive long term if it does not correct this imbalance. In the short term, the company will have to recognize an expense associated with the loss of value and write down the value of its inventory. Because net working capital is the difference between current assets and current liabilities, it will immediately decrease by the loss in inventory value.

In summary, managing current assets is a balancing act between the desire to minimize costs and maximize revenue. Without sufficient levels of cash, accounts receivable, and inventory the firm is in a less competitive position. If it overestimates the need for any of the three, the firm will be inefficient and less profitable than its competitors.

CURRENT LIABILITIES MANAGEMENT

Assets are things that the firm owns and liabilities are the way to finance those items. When we think of financing, we most often consider loans, whether they are long term or short term. We often overlook the fact that our short-term liabilities may be a very large source of funding for the firm.

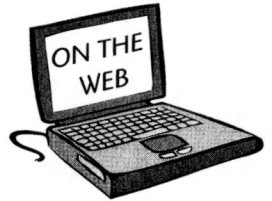

Occasionally a firm will miscalculate inventory, either because it has purchased items it cannot sell or because a new product does not perform as expected. Liquidation firms make a business out of buying inventory from distress situations and selling it at steeply discounted prices.

Big Lots! (www.biglots.com) states that it sells brand-name merchandise at prices from 20% to 40% below most discount merchants. In order to make a profit, the firm must have purchased the goods at less than the cost charged to retailers.

Tuesday Morning (www.tuesdaymorning.com) offers luxury products at 50% to 80% off regular retail prices. Tuesday Morning has higher-priced products but often single items rather than a full line of products. They advertise that they are a treasure hunt, and the Web site is distinctly upscale.

Both of these sites are geared more to the consumer than a firm that finds itself with excess inventory. In contrast, Liquidation World (www.liquidationworld.com) prominently features the services it can provide to companies in distress. Its range of customers includes banks, insurance companies, retailers, manufacturers, and distributors. Among other services, Liquidation World offers inventory appraisal, help with going out of business sales, auction of goods, and disposal of merchandise out of the market area, if needed.

A going-out-of-business sale means inventory is probably being sold at or below cost. Liquidators can assist businesses in disposing of excess inventory whether it is a result of overproduction or a business closure. (PhotoEdit)

Accounts Payable

Accounts receivable are a source of financing that we make available to our customers. By the same token, accounts payable are a source of financing for our company. Some of the accounts payable are tied to services our business consumes, but a large portion of payables are tied to the inventory and supplies that we purchase for the firm. If we are careful, we can use trade credit to further lower the cost of inventory.

Negotiating favorable payment terms is a key component in making our payables work for us. We will look at three types of discounts: quantity discounts, trade discounts, and cash or early payment discounts.

Quantity or volume discounts are perhaps the simplest to calculate. A manufacturer or wholesaler sets a sliding price scale depending on the physical quantity or dollar volume that its customers order. **Quantity discounts** reflect the efficiencies that are realized by larger orders. The cost to process and package an order for a single sweatshirt is essentially the same as shipping a dozen. The price per item falls when the overhead can be spread across more items and the seller passes along the savings. Quantity discounts can be structured so that each purchase qualifies individually or the seller can offer cumulative discounts. Cumulative discounts are usually applied at the end of the year based on total purchases during that year. The discount can be applied to the customer's outstanding account, sent as a refund check, or credited to the following year's purchases.

Trade discounts are allowances given to a customer who is willing to assume some of the tasks normally performed by the supplier. The discounts are expressed as a percent and subtracted from the list price of the item. There may be a single discount or multiple discounts available, but all of them must be given to any customer who qualifies.

Let's look at an example. Thelma, of Thelma's Garden Design, buys all of her supplies from Bannock Building Supply. Bannock provides delivery service but will discount purchases by 8% if Thelma provides her own transportation. In addition, Bannock will allow a 5% discount for any purchase over $1,500 and a 10% discount for purchases made on Monday, Tuesday, or Wednesday when the store is less busy. The transportation and day of the week discounts are trade discounts, while $1,500 is the level that triggers a quantity discount.

There will be occasions when Thelma needs only a few supplies and will not spend $1,500, in which case she would not qualify for that discount. However, if she can time her purchases to take advantage of the early week discount, she has reduced her inventory cost by a full 10% regardless of the dollar volume of the transaction. Understanding the available discounts and using them wisely can significantly reduce Thelma's cost of doing business.

The third type of discounts are tied to the timing of payments. Most accounts payable will specify a due date and some will allow a discount for **early payment.** Discounts are usually expressed in terms such as 2/10, n30, which means that 2% can be deducted from the net amount due if the bill is paid within 10 days. Payment terms are in addition to any trade discounts that have been allowed. If Thelma had an account at Bannock Building Supply, her statement would reflect a net amount after all of the applicable trade discounts had been subtracted. A Monday purchase would have been discounted 10% and could be further discounted 2% if she pays within 10 days.

As we saw in the cash flow statement, Thelma's business, like many other small businesses does not generate large sums of cash. She may not have cash on hand to take the 2% cash discount. Depending on her cost of borrowing, though, she may be better off borrowing the money she needs to earn the cash discount. How can this be?

Suppose that it is June 7 and Thelma's cash is tight. She has received an invoice from Bannock Building Supply for $2,500 dated June 5 with payment terms 2/10, n30. She has until June 15 to pay the invoice and deduct $50 (2% of $2,500). The discounted invoice would be $2,450, but Thelma only has $1,250 available and won't receive a large influx of cash until July 15.

In order to pay the invoice and take the discount, Thelma needs to borrow $1,200, which she can repay 30 days (one month) after payment is due. If her bank will lend the money at 12% interest per month, the interest cost would be

$$I = PRT$$
$$= 1200 \times .12/12$$
$$= \$ 12$$

It will cost $12 in interest to save $50 on the invoice. Borrowing the money will save Thelma $38. She can make the decision to borrow money based on the cash flow budget she developed and her ability to predict receipt of accounts receivable. If she keeps close watch on her receivables, she can reduce her purchasing costs by using payment terms.

Accrued Liabilities

Accrued liabilities represent obligations to pay money in the future. Under the accrual method of accounting, we assign a certain portion of expenses to each month, whether or not they have been disbursed. For example, payroll taxes are transferred to the Internal Revenue Service four times a year but reflect the weekly or monthly payroll. Unless we pay our employees at the conclusion of each day's work we will also have accrued payroll benefits. Because they are accounting entries and not directly cash payments, accrued liabilities can sneak up on a business.

Many small companies make the appropriate balance sheet entries for payroll taxes, insurance premiums, and property taxes that will come due but forget the timing of the cash disbursement. Even if a cash budget has been created, it does not always sit on the manager's desk. It is a rude surprise when the tax bill comes due and there are not sufficient funds in the firm's checking account.

Providing for payment of accrued liabilities is part of cash management. Many banks offer linked checking and savings accounts that can be used to separate and pool available funds. For example, a business could have a single account number with multiple suffixes. Each suffix could designate the intended use of the fund (i.e., payroll taxes, property taxes, sales taxes owed, or insurance premiums). Deposits would be credited to the suffix number and a balance would exist for that subheading. In practice, however, all of the cash would be in a single account under the control of the finance manager. Directing cash into accounts by final use would not restrict access or reduce the interest earned on the funds. If the accrual amount exceeded the eventual cash disbursement, funds could be redistributed to other subheadings. Having a segmented account provides the firm with a visual link between the liability and the funds available.

Short-Term Debt

Short-term debt has two components: the portion of long-term debt that will come due in the current year and debt that is structured to have a short life. These really should be separated, at least philosophically.

The current portion of long-term debt is tied, in a very real sense, to the long-term investments we have made in our firm. The current portion of the mortgage that is due this year is directly related to the acquisition of a piece of property whose use will continue for years. It is the cost of an already acquired long-term asset that has been deferred until this point and is being funded from the profits generated by its own productivity. When we look at capital budgeting in the next chapter, we will accept only those investments that create revenue in excess of their long-term cost.

What we need to examine in this section are the short-term financing options that add to working capital. We've touched on the idea of borrowing to take advantage of a cash payment discount and, in Chapter 8, simply stated that we would visit our banker with the cash budget in hand, assuming that we would walk away with financing.

There are several types of short-term debt instruments, and in a competitive banking environment new variations are created constantly. There are two basic types of short-term debt: short-term loans and lines of credit.

A short-term loan has a fixed principal value, a stated interest rate, and a maturity date. Payment terms may call for monthly principal and interest payments or a single payment on maturity date. Short-term loans are appropriate for a business that needs a set amount of cash at the beginning of a business cycle that will be repaid at the end of that cycle. Farmers often take out loans in order to buy seed and fertilizer during planting season and repay the loan after harvest. A manufacturer of seasonal merchandise like swimsuits might take out a large loan in order to buy material that will be repaid when retailers settle their accounts. In both cases, the operating cycle is very long and revenue does not come in a steady stream. The loan lasts for a season, which is shorter than a year, and is used for inventory and supplies. Short-term loans can also be called working capital loans.

A second form of short-term debt is a line of credit. **A line of credit** is an efficient way to cover the cash shortfalls that are occasionally experienced. After constructing a cash budget, the firm knows how much money it will be short and in which months. The shortfall may be sporadic and spread over the year. The firm does not want to pay interest for an entire year if funds are only needed intermittently. A line of credit is often obtained from our primary bank and can be part of a financial business banking package that would include a sweep account or automated payment transfer services.

A line of credit is the offer by our bank that they will lend money when we need it and we can repay the loan at any time, with the agreed-upon interest. A business applies for a line of credit in the same way that they apply for a standard loan, and creditworthiness is assessed using the same criteria: ability to pay and past payment history. The exact fee structure varies between banks and in some cases it can be negotiated. Generally speaking, the bank charges a loan application fee to set up the account, and interest is charged when the line of credit is used. Some banks charge a monthly fee to maintain a line of credit and charge interest when the credit is used. As with any loan, before establishing a line of credit the firm should compare fees and interest rates.

In the News

As we have seen, a firm should effectively manage its working capital. In July 2001, *CFO Magazine* published the results of its second working capital survey of companies clustered within 34 industry groups. The survey considered the Days of Working Capital (receivables + inventory + payables) ÷ (sales ÷ 365). If the payables exceed the sum of receivables and inventory, the Days of Working Capital would be negative. For each industry, the magazine also calculated an industry average.

We have already seen that the working capital requirements will vary within industries. The best comparison is between firms within the same industry type. Thus, if our company is involved in the grocery business, we would want to compare our working capital management policies to Kroger or Albertson's rather than Ford Motor Company, which is in an industry that has fewer inventory turns per year.

Indeed, we would see that Food Retailers and Wholesalers have an average of 15 days of working capital and inventory turns over 15 times per year. In contrast, the automobile industry (which includes original equipment manufacturers and parts suppliers) averages 58 days of working capital and only 10 turns per year.

Source: CFO Magazine, July 1, 2001, also available at www.cfo.com.

Effective use of working capital can minimize financing costs and improve the productivity of assets. Although we define current assets as those that will be turned into cash within a year, it is important to remember that the only asset that is completely liquid is cash. The success of a business often depends on how carefully the business manages its current assets and liabilities.

TERMS TO KNOW

Working capital	Sweep accounts	Specific identification
Operating cycle	Factoring	First in, first out (FIFO)
Credit policies	Inventory management	Last in, first out (LIFO)
Current asset management	Economic order quantity (EOQ)	Quantity discounts
Cash management	Safety stock	Trade discounts
Float	Just-in-time inventory management	Early payment discounts
Electronic funds transfer	Inventory valuation	Accrued liabilities
		Short-term debt
		Line of credit

TERM PAPERS AND PROJECTS

1. Examine the working capital management policies of a small business and suggest concrete improvements.
2. Assess the accounts receivable policies for a business and determine whether there are inefficiencies that could be corrected. Does the firm have a strategy for managing slow-paying customers?
3. Research the availability of sweep accounts at several financial institutions and compare their costs. Determine whether the same financial institutions offer on-line services that would substitute for a sweep account and whether that would be a more cost-effective strategy.
4. Determine the effect that a change in inventory valuation methods would have on a local business. How variable are inventory costs? Should that variability be reflected in the periodic financial statements or smoothed using one of the average cost methods?

REVIEW QUESTIONS

1. What is working capital and why is it critical to the functioning of a business?
2. What major factors should be considered when establishing a working capital policy? Why would policies differ from one business to another?
3. What are the four main components of working capital? Give a description of each component.
4. What are the two basic strategies of cash management?
5. Discuss three tools for managing cash.

6. What are marketable securities and why are they necessary in business operations?
7. List three factors that must be considered carefully when establishing credit policies.
8. What is a discount for early payment? What does 3/15, n30 mean? If an invoice for $2,000 is paid within the discount time, how much would be paid? What happens if the bill is paid after the due date?
9. Why would a business extend a 0.0% interest offer to consumers? Could this have an adverse effect on future sales and income?
10. Why is it necessary to analyze accounts receivable?
11. How does economic order quantity affect inventory management?
12. What is safety stock and what are the risks of setting it too low?
13. Discuss just-in-time inventory systems.
14. Describe the two most commonly used methods of inventory valuation.
15. Distinguish between accounts payable, accrued liabilities, and short-term debt. Why are these all considered forms of financing?
16. What is the difference between a short-term loan and a line of credit?

REVIEW PROBLEM

1. What is the economic order quantity for a firm that has annual demand of 40,500 units, carrying costs of $2 per item, and an order cost of $80? What is the estimated percent change in order quantity if the order cost rises to $100?

CHAPTER

10

CAPITAL BUDGETING

LEARNING OBJECTIVES

1. Describe capital budgeting and why it is important to the firm.

2. Identify the types of assets that are covered by capital budgeting.

3. Calculate costs and cash inflows associated with the purchase of a long-term asset.

4. Differentiate between start-up costs and ongoing expenses related to a new investment.

5. Discuss the effect of depreciation on the decision to purchase an asset.

6. Distinguish between an operating lease and a capital lease.

7. Calculate the payback period for an asset.

8. Explain why risk occurs in capital budgeting decisions.

9. Calculate the value of an investment using the net present value method.

10. Use the profitability index to evaluate investments with different levels of required funding.

11. Calculate the value of an investment using the internal rate of return.

LONG-TERM DECISION MAKING

The history of American business is full of stories of entrepreneurs who began what are now multimillion-dollar businesses by packing their wares into a canvas bag and selling them door-to-door or building the next best invention in the basement or garage. These visionaries started on a shoestring, but as their companies grew a structure emerged—office buildings, factories, and equipment all had to be procured. The items could be purchased or leased, but the acquisition of these long-term assets was necessary for the expansion and continued success of the organization.

And so it is for other businesses. In Chapters 8 and 9 we looked at relatively short time horizons such as annual budgets and even 10-day cash payment periods. In this chapter we address capital budgeting, or planning for the future of our organization when the future revenue stream is uncertain.

209

Capital budgeting can be a very complex subject, one to which we could devote several chapters or even books. The focus here will be on analyzing the strategic implications of various investment alternatives and examining three tools we can use to evaluate the alternatives: payback period, net present value and internal rate of return.

INVESTMENT IN THE FUTURE OF THE COMPANY

The crux of the long-term investment decision is that we are making choices in the present that will not realize their full return for several years. As a result, our analysis in this chapter will rely heavily on the time value of money concepts that were introduced in Chapter 2. In most cases, the cost of the equipment is known with some certainty but the returns will be best-guess estimates. This does not mean that companies should be paralyzed by uncertainty nor does it mean that they should leap into a new venture without doing any analysis whatsoever. It is simply a reminder that before the final decision is made, assumptions should be examined for decision biases, among them basing future sales growth only on recent trends, ignoring the effect of potential economic cycles, underestimating the effect of competition or government regulation, and continued consumer acceptance of our product.

Occasionally, the choice to make long-term investments are out of the firm's control. State and federal environmental regulations that call for companies to improve recovery of pollutants or clean up past waste sites may require that the firm invest in equipment specific to the task. Another example is replacement of an obsolete piece of machinery. At some point it becomes more expensive to repair or maintain equipment than to purchase new equipment. The decision is not whether to invest but which alternative is most efficient for the organization.

The types of assets we will consider will be primarily property such as land, buildings, and equipment, and either new technology or the replacement of existing machinery. For some companies, their most significant investment is the cost of research and development. The Pharmaceutical Research and Manufacturers of America, an industry trade group, estimates that it takes more than 14 years on average for a new medicine to go from lab to the marketplace and only 20% survive clinical trials and FDA scrutiny.[1] Once the drug makes it to the marketplace it has patent protection for 7 years, during which time the manufacturer hopes to recoup the investment in that drug as well as provide cash flow for further research and development. The length of the operating cycle and uncertainty of success make forecasting a challenge. The examples we will use are far more concrete.

All investments incur costs. The direct cost of a new truck can be calculated. Whether it is leased or purchased, there will be some form of payment (either monthly or in a lump sum) tied to the **acquisition** of the truck. However, we must not forget to factor in the change in **operating costs** that could accompany the acquisition such as increased insurance premiums or maintenance costs, the need for garage space, the additional license and property taxes

[1]"A Health Cost Time Bomb?" *Business Week*, August 7, 2000, p. 153.

and other recurring expenses attributable to the purchase. If they are significant, these cash flows could affect whether the investment is profitable.

In addition to estimating costs, the finance manager needs to predict cash inflows, a task that can be difficult. The most obvious place to look is in the gross revenue figure. The addition of a second retail outlet should increase sales volume. Adding a second production line will increase goods available for sale and, if we have correctly forecast demand, result in increased revenue. Other investments add value by reducing cash outflows. If the firm maintains the same level of sales revenue but by investing in improved production processes can reduce waste by 10%, raw materials usage (a component of inventory) should decrease, increasing the value of net working capital. The firm might also choose to invest based on its future expectation of costs. The decision to automate should include an analysis of current and projected labor wage rates. If wage rates are rising, the savings from technological investment may increase over time, thus justifying investment.

Estimating the Cost of the Investment

The first step is to calculate the cost of the investment, including any financing assumptions. Because the final purchase decision may depend on the availability and attractiveness of financing, all possible options should be examined. For example, if our firm is interested in buying a piece of commercial property, the seller may offer us several payment options: a lower price for payment in full or a higher price in three installments spaced 6 months apart.

The list that follows lays out some questions that the firm should ask before it analyzes the purchase of a fixed asset. Some of the questions pertain more to equipment than property and the list is by no means exhaustive, but it will help to frame the assumptions that the firm is making.

The first set of costs are one-time or start-up costs. When we set up the analysis, they will be allocated to the first year (with the obvious exception of the payment plan described above and the second entry in the following list).

- Determine the underlying cash cost of the equipment. What would the firm be charged to obtain this piece of equipment if payment were made in cash today? The buyer is not literally going to walk into negotiations with sacks of money. However, the point of the question is to determine the lowest possible price that could be negotiated now. Often a vendor will offer better terms if the customer is willing to pay in full because it increases the vendor's working capital and lessens the exposure to risk of default.
- Are there other purchase options with implied financing such as payment in three installments or an initial down payment, monthly interest charges, and final balloon payment?
- What is the **disposal value** of any existing machinery? If the company is replacing an existing asset, it may retain residual value that could either be applied to the purchase of the new asset or be realized through sale to another company. Conversely, there may be an expense associated with disposal of the old asset, which creates a liability for the firm.
- What installation or start-up costs are associated with purchase of the asset? Are there transfer costs such as title search for property transactions or fees for registering change in vehicle ownership? Does the asset

require significant shipping and assembly fees, either provided by the vendor or as additional work performed by hourly workers?

- Will the purchase of the asset require additional supporting fixed assets? If we buy two new trucks, do they fit within the existing garage or will we be required to expand? What would be the timing of the expansion?
- Are there training costs involved? The cost of training includes any enroll-ment (or service fees) involved as well as travel expenses, per diem food costs, and time away from regular duties.

In addition to the start-up costs, we may incur ongoing costs. Remember that we are looking only at costs now, not the benefits that will result from the purchase.

- Working capital adjustments. If the fixed asset is a retail location or production line, how will it affect inventory, cash, and accounts receivable needs?
- If we are financing a machine or a piece of real property, what will be the current portion of the long-term debt and how will that affect current liabilities, thus working capital?
- Does the acquisition require greater investment in personnel? Will the number of employees increase? Will we require employees with higher skill levels? Are there recruitment or severance costs associated with redistribution of the workforce?
- Do operating expenses increase such as utility costs, insurance, mainten-ance, or permits?
- Are there tax implications? Local and state property taxes, including inventory tax, may increase.

Profit From the Investment

Calculating the cost of the investment was easy compared with determining the profit that will result. Again, we will use a list to prompt the type of questions the firm should ask in determining where cost savings and profits will occur.

- Are we projecting increased sales revenue? If so, is sales quantity increas-ing? How will the increase in quantity sold affect the price per item? Are we projecting price per unit increases? How will that affect demand? How long will this investment allow us to have a proprietary advantage? How soon will our competitors be able to duplicate this technology and would that affect prices? Will the sales revenue gained from this product or ser-vice line decrease sales or profits in another area of the company? What is the net gain?
- Are we projecting cost savings based on current expenditures? If so, are the relevant costs increasing at the rate of inflation or at some other rate? Do we need to adjust our savings assumptions?
- Are cost savings tied to raw material use? Do cost savings come from a change in raw materials or inventory mix?

- How soon will savings begin to appear? What is the learning curve of this machine or technology?
- Will there be savings in personnel? If so, what proportion is direct labor and what is salaried overhead?

In a very real sense, the opportunity to purchase machinery or invest in technology has returned us to the assumptions we made in break-even analysis. The distinction is that the financial analysis we are about to perform will take place over an extended time period, as opposed to the single-period analysis that we performed for break-even analysis.

THE VALUE OF DEPRECIATION

The subject of **depreciation** has been conspicuously absent from this text. All of the preceding balance sheets have given a fixed asset value with no corresponding offset for accumulated depreciation; the asset value has been assumed to be a net value. Because depreciation is a non-cash expense, it was not included in the cash budget. However, depreciation does affect the purchase decision for long-term assets because the ability to deduct depreciation expense reduces the firm's income tax liability. As a result, some mention of it will be included here. For simplicity, we will use the Modified Accelerated Cost Recovery System (MACRS) method of depreciation that is accepted by the Internal Revenue Service. Within its financial statements a firm may choose to utilize one of the other depreciation methods (straight-line, units of production, sum-of-the-years, or declining balance method), however what we are interested in are the tax implications of investment decisions so we will use only MACRS. For more a detailed discussion of the benefits of various forms of depreciation, the firm should defer to its accountants.

The MACRS method of depreciation is used for any asset placed into service after 1986. It assumes no salvage (residual) value for any asset and puts assets into one of nine recovery classes. The chart is reprinted in Appendix B and is available from the Internal Revenue Service. Depreciation is expressed as a percent of the depreciable value (which will be the same as the original cost). Because depreciation expense reduces profit by the full amount of the depreciation deduction, thus reducing taxable income, depreciation causes a net cash inflow to the organization in a sum equal to the depreciation expense times the firm's tax rate.

For example, Ben is considering buying a truck to use in his construction business. The truck will cost $35,000 and Ben has a marginal income rate of 30%. Using the MACRS depreciation schedule, the first year's depreciation is 20% of the cost of the truck or $7,000. Depreciation is subtracted from operating income. The noncash charge of $7,000 saves Ben $2,100 in taxes ($7,000 less income taxed at a 30% rate). The savings is real money, although the depreciation charge is not. Since MACRS depreciation rates vary by year, the annual tax savings will also vary. Depreciation does not cost the firm cash out of pocket, but it can add to the attractiveness of an investment.

Just because a machine has been depreciated to zero, as it would be under the MACRS method, does not mean that it has no productive value to the firm. Capital budgeting plans need to take into account the actual productivity of the equipment rather than the "useful life" ascribed to it by the IRS and depreciation methods.

Remember, too, that while the useful life for depreciation purposes may be 5 years, it does not mean that the equipment will last that long. Depending on the rate of technological innovation, capital assets may become obsolete much sooner than current depreciation tables recognize.

LEASING EQUIPMENT

Before we begin to analyze whether the asset will add value to the firm, we need to consider the option of leasing rather than purchasing the asset. There are two types of leases: capital lease and operating lease. A **capital lease** meets at least one of the following criteria:

1. The lease culminates with a bargain purchase price.
2. The title transfers to the lessee at the end of the lease.
3. The term of the lease is longer than 75% of the economic useful life (as measured by the MACRS recovery chart).
4. The present value of the minimum lease payments cannot exceed 90% of the purchase price.

Under FASB rules, capital leases are accounted for in the same way as an asset purchased with financing from the vendor. For that reason, we will treat capital leases as a form of financed purchase.

An **operating lease** does not satisfy any of the conditions set out above. It does not show up as an asset on the lessor's balance sheet; it is simply an operating expense on the income statement and fully deductible from earnings.

A capital lease meets at least one of these criteria:

1. The lease culminates with a bargain purchase price.
2. The lessee owns the item outright at the end of the lease.
3. The term of the lease is longer than 75% of the MACRS useful life.
4. The present value of the minimum lease payments exceeds 90% of the purchase price.

The qualities that define a capital lease. If an item meets one of these four criteria, it must be shown as a capital lease in the financial statements.

QUANTIFYING COSTS AND BENEFITS

Numbers need to be assigned to each of the costs and benefits that the firm has identified since they occur over a set period of years. The template used can be as simple or detailed as the firm needs. If in answering the list of questions in the earlier section the firm determined that the investment decision would be subject to subtle shifts in cost or income projections, it might want to create pro forma income statements showing revenue patterns, cost structure, and the net income attributable to this specific investment during a several-year period. Creating a pro forma statement for each investment opportunity takes concerted effort, and a firm may decide that rougher estimates will suffice.

The simplest format would show a single number representing net cash inflow (after yearly operating costs) for each year of the asset's expected life. For example, Ben is thinking of buying a new truck for $35,000 to use in his construction business. He has estimated the added revenue attributable to the truck (minus yearly operating expenses) for each of the 6 years he intends to keep the truck:

BEN'S TRUCK

	Net cash inflow
Year 1	$15,000
Year 2	12,500
Year 3	11,000
Year 4	10,000
Year 5	7,500
Year 6	4,000

The total net cash inflow is $60,000. How Ben arrived at those calculations is anyone's guess. Without some sort of spreadsheet, we can't examine the underlying assumptions. Although we do not have that level of detail, we will accept Ben's projections and use them to demonstrate the three evaluation methods that follow.

PAYBACK PERIOD

The payback method considers how many years it takes for the cash inflows to equal the original cost of the item. If the cash inflows are constant over time, the **payback period** is

$$\text{Payback} = \frac{\text{Cost}}{\text{Net cash inflows}}$$

If Ben had assumed that the added value was $10,000 per year for all 6 years, his payback period would be 3.5 years ($35,000/$10,000). In Ben's case, the truck will add decreasing value as the years go by, perhaps because Ben is assuming that maintenance and repair costs will increase. Since the added revenue stream is uneven, Ben will estimate the payback period. After the firs year, it will have contributed $15,000 in increased revenue. The cumulative increase is $27,500 in year 2 and by the end of year 3, net inflow of $38,500 exceeds the purchase price. Sometime toward the end of year 3, the truck has paid for itself.

The payback method is simple to use, however, it does not take into account the time value of money. Using the payback method, the return on each of the following $10,000 investments would be equally valuable because the investment would have paid for itself at the end of the second year:

	A	B	C
Year 1	$5,000	$6,000	$2,000
Year 2	5,000	4,000	8,000
Year 3	5,000	2,000	2,000
Year 4	5,000		
Year 5	5,000		

Once the investment has paid for itself, the added value of later income i not considered. The payback method also does not allow us to adequately com pare mutually exclusive investments that have dissimilar patterns of return. I the preceding example, the firm would not logically forgo the income produced by investment A in favor of either B or C. Clearly, a more sophisticated method is needed.

RISK AND CAPITAL BUDGETING

As soon as we project savings or expenses into the future, we are introducing an element of **risk.** Ben's estimates of the incremental cash benefit of the truck were "best guesses" based, most likely, on a gut feeling of what would happen Every projection we make into the future includes the chance that we wil "guess" wrong: that inflation will rise, that consumers will not accept a highe price or new variety for our product, that wage rates will escalate beyond ou predictions, or that our cost of borrowing will change. The pharmaceutica industry knows that 80% of the products first created in the lab will not mak it into the consumer's medicine cabinet. If they knew which would fail, the wouldn't pursue them and risk would be reduced. Since it can't be eliminated the objective is to mitigate the risk and to set investment criteria that attemp to minimize loss while still encouraging innovation. Therefore, the cost o financing includes not just the cost of borrowing but an added risk premium

When analyzing the future benefits of today's investments, companie often develop risk profiles based on the type of change represented. Replacin obsolete machinery with more productive, lower maintenance equipmen carries a low risk. The chance for loss is minimized since we are not changin production techniques but in fact we are improving them. The change in ou end product may be so slight that the only way our consumer would notice an change at all is because we were able to reduce our price by a penny or two. Risk has been reduced to almost nothing.

Automating a production line may carry slightly higher risk—the investment in equipment is fixed where labor can be variable. A machine cannot be laid off during a recession, so our cost structure has become less flexible at lower production levels. The risk of making the "wrong" decision has increased somewhat. However, as wages rise, the risk due to lack of flexibility may be offset by the higher wage rate. Managers will have to decide what risk premium, if any, they want to add to the cost of financing.

Investing in production equipment dedicated to an entirely new product line adds yet another form of risk; the risk that consumers will not accept the product or its pricing in quantities sufficient to generate a profit. In order for the firm to invest in new capital equipment, it will have to meet a higher hurdle rate such as the financing cost and a more significant risk premium. These three simple examples of the varying levels of risk that a company might face illustrate the fact that capital budgeting decisions need to be analyzed in the context of the firm's current operations and future strategic goals.

NET PRESENT VALUE

In Chapter 2 we introduced the time value of money. We said that money we have now can be invested, either in a savings account or in a business, and earn income for us in the future. Money we will not receive until the future is earning interest for someone else and is worth less (or perhaps nothing depending on the level of risk) to us in the present. The **net present value** (NPV) calculation brings a stream of future payments into the present and subtracts the current cost of the investment. If the present value of the stream of future earnings is greater than the cost of the investment, we should proceed with the investment. If our calculation results in a negative net present value, we would be better off investing elsewhere.

The key to net present value is choosing the discount value. There are two factors involved: the cost of borrowing money and the risk inherent in the investment. Unless we can finance all investments from internally generated funds, we will have to borrow money to finance our operations. The income we could receive from this potential investment comes at the cost of borrowed funds. If we assume that the income is risk-free, that is, there is no possibility of loss from the investment, we would use our cost of borrowing (or cost of capital). If, however, there is significant risk involved with this decision, we will want to set a higher discount rate. We should estimate the return we would expect for a similarly risky investment and add it to our risk-free cost of capital.

Once we have established a **discount rate**, we need to move the future earnings back toward the present. If the earnings are a steady stream, we can use a present value of an annuity calculation. In the case of Ben's truck, the earnings are unsteady so each year's revenue needs to be moved back as a lump sum. The present value is totaled and the current cost of the investment is subtracted. If the result is a positive number, the investment should be made. A negative number shows that the cash derived from the investment does not equal the cost of financing the investment.

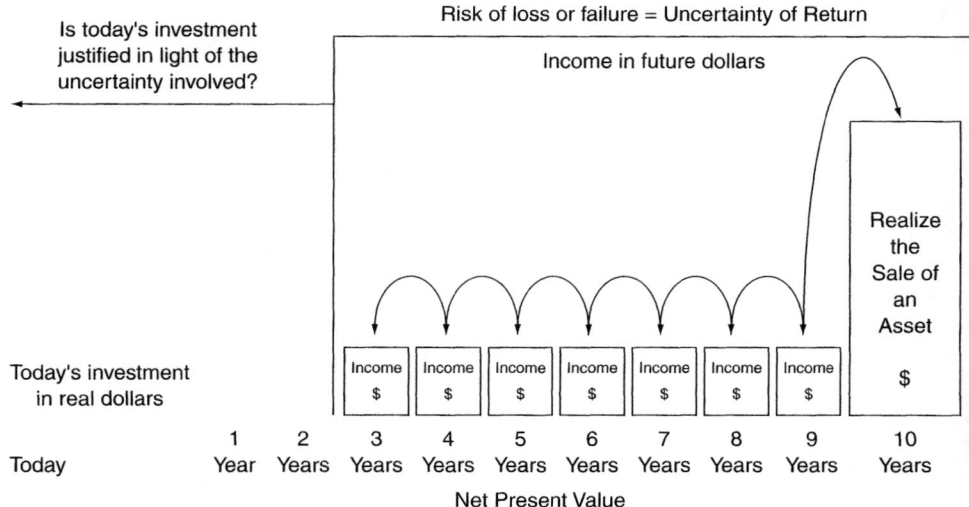

How do we assess the current value of an investment? The cost to us, in today's dollars should be less than the present value of the income stream and any residual value, discounted to reflect the level of risk inherent in the investment.

Let's return to Ben's purchase of the truck. We will assume that the discount rate is 9% since that is the cost of the loan that Ben's bank will provide. We also assume that the cash benefit comes at the end of the year, so the cash flow for each year is discounted to the end of that year.

Ben's truck: Net present value

	Cash inflow	Discount factor	Present value
Year 1	$15,000	0.917431	$13,761
Year 2	12,500	0.841680	10,521
Year 3	11,000	0.772183	8,494
Year 4	10,000	0.708425	7,084
Year 5	7,500	0.649931	4,875
Year 6	4,000	0.596267	2,835
Total present value:			$47,120
Cost of the truck:			35,000
Net present value			$12,120

Moving the cash inflows to the present and subtracting the current price of the truck leaves us with a positive benefit of $12,120. Ben should buy the truck.

Often there are multiple alternatives that are mutually exclusive. Let's recall the opportunities we looked at in the payback section. We have $10,000 to invest and three choices, each of which would appear equal under the payback method. Which, if any, should we invest in?

Our first task is to determine the discount rate. We begin by assuming that each of these options carries the same level of risk, which the firm decides requires a 2% premium, and each can be financed at the firm's current cost of borrowing, which is 8%. The total discount rate is 10%.

OPTIONS

	PV factor		Net cash inflow					
			A		B		C	
		$		PV	$	PV	$	PV
Year 1	0.909091	$5,000		$4,545	$6,000	$5,455	$2,000	$1,818
Year 2	0.826446	$5,000		$4,132	$4,000	$3,306	$8,000	$6,612
Year 3	0.751315	$5,000		$3,757	$2,000	$1,503	$2,000	$1,503
Year 4	0.683013	$5,000		$3,415				
Year 5	0.620921	$5,000		$3,105				
Present value				$18,954		$10,264		$ 9,933
Cost				$10,000		$10,000		$10,000
NPV				$8,954		$264		−$67

Given the risk assumptions the firm has made, alternative A is the preferred investment because it returns the greatest value over time. Examine alternatives B and C. Each of them seems to return $12,000 in cash inflows but given the timing of the inflows, only B would be a viable option. The difference is due to the time value of money.

Some investments are made in stages. A firm may not have the borrowing capacity to complete an investment at one time, or it may be able to negotiate purchase terms that include staggered payments. In that case, several alternatives and multiple time lines may have to be factored. If the firm can calculate cash inflows that are tied to the various investment alternatives, both the cash inflows and the timing of the cash outflows will need to be discounted back to the present, and the investment with the higher net present value should be chosen.

PROFITABILITY INDEX

Another way of looking at the capital budgeting decision is to compare the present value of the cash inflows with the present value of the cost. The ratio is called a **profitability index (PI)** and is calculated

$$PI = \frac{PV \text{ benefits}}{PV \text{ costs}}$$

For the three investments above, the PIs are

A: 1.895

B: 1.023

C: 0.993

This means that at the discount rate we chose, alternative A will yield $1.895 for every $1.00 invested. Both A and B return a profit, although B returns a much smaller one. Alternative C returns less than a dollar for every dollar invested, making it a poor choice. Note that the PI ratios will provide the same ranking that the NPV did.

One benefit to using a profitability index is to allow the firm to compare investments with different funding requirements. Look at the present value calculations for the following set of options, all discounted at 10%:

OPTIONS

	PV factor	$	PV	$	PV	$	PV
			P		Q		R
Year 1	0.909091	$5,000	$4,545.45	$7,000	$6,363.64	$6,000	$5,454.55
Year 2	0.826446	5,000	4132.23	5,500	4,545.45	4,500	3,719.01
Year 3	0.751315	3,000	2,253.95	4,500	3,380.92	3,000	2,253.94
Year 4	0.683013	3,000	2,049.04	3,000	2,049.04	2,500	1,707.53
Year 5	0.620921	2,000	1,241.84	1,500	931.38	1,000	620.92
Present value			$14,222.51		$17,270.43		$13,755.95
Cost			10,000.00		12,500.00		9,750.00
NPV			$4,222.511		$4,770.428		$ 4,005.95

Looking at the present value of the cash flows, it appears that option Q is the best choice. It returns a net present value of $4,770, which is the largest return. However, the cost of the investments varies. If we analyze the investments from the standpoint of profitability, our choice would be different. Option Q, which had the highest net present value, also requires the largest investment. When the alternatives are compared based on cost and benefits, option P provides the highest profit per dollar invested. Even option R, which returns the least in terms of real dollars, is a more profitable choice than option Q.

	P	Q	R
Present value	$14,222.51	$17,270.43	$13,755.95
Cost	10,000.00	12,500.00	9,750.00
NPV	$4,222.511	$4,770.428	$4,005.952
Profitability Index	1.422251	1.381634	1.410867

As with all of the other analytical tools we have seen, the profitability index is only as valid as the assumptions the firm has made. However, it does provide a straightforward way of comparing unlike investment choices.

PRESENT VALUE OF A NON-INCOME-PRODUCING ASSET

Not every investment can be credited with a discrete set of cash inflows. We said earlier that changes in government regulations may require a firm to invest in pollution control equipment. Although the firm has no choice, the purchase will not result in revenue. Fixed assets such as a maintenance shop or warehouse are part of the cost of doing business and do not add value directly. In evaluating those investments, the finance manager should look for the lowest negative present value. Let's look at an example.

San Nicolas Manufacturing is located in a light industrial park. Demand for their products is growing steadily, and they expect to increase sales by 20% in each of the next 2 years. After that the increase in demand will not be as dramatic, however they believe the company will continue to grow. Their current manufacturing facility has enough space to allow them to double production, but they have just about reached the capacity for their warehouse. Two adjoining parcels have come on the market and the company needs to evaluate which would be the better choice. Both pieces of property are the same acreage and have all of the required improvements: sewer, utilities, easements, and roads.

The north parcel is vacant land that would cost $250,000. San Nicolas does not need the warehouse space for 2 years, at which time it believes it could build an appropriate facility for $125,000. They estimate that the warehouse would last for 15 years with no substantial alterations.

The south parcel already has a warehouse on it. The cost of the second parcel is $300,000. The warehouse is adequate and could be used as soon as the firm needs it, however, it is several years old and San Nicolas estimates that it

222 CHAPTER 10   *Capital Budgeting*

would need to be refurbished in 7 years at a cost of $100,000. If San Nicolas uses an 8% discount factor, which alternative is the best? Since both of the alternatives require a cash outflow, they should choose the alternative that costs less in the present.

SAN NICOLAS WAREHOUSE

	North	PV Factor	PV
Today's cost	$250,000		$250,000
2 years	$125,000	0.857339	$107,167
			$357,167

	South		
Today's cost	$300,000		$300,000
7 years	$100,000	0.643506	$64,351
			$364,351

There is a very slight difference between the two alternatives. With the information we have been given, San Nicolas should buy the land and build the warehouse in 2 years because that decision represents the lower present cost. Of course, there are more questions San Nicolas could ask:

- If we buy the land, are we sure that we won't need a warehouse sooner than 2 years? Could we build before we ran out of space or would we have to lease elsewhere while we were building? What would that cost?
- If we buy the existing warehouse, can we rent it to another tenant, thus creating some cash inflow and reducing the current expense? How rapidly are construction costs escalating? Are we sure that years from now the warehouse can be refurbished for only $100,000?

The assets do not generate cash flows, so the uncertainty, or risk, of the investment centers around the costs inherent in the proposal. This type of investment is also one of the first that might be cut or scaled back in a recession.

INTERNAL RATE OF RETURN (IRR)

The **internal rate of return** describes the discount rate that will make the present value of the cash inflows exactly equal to the present value of the cash outflows. This particular rate of return is called an "internal" rate because it is specific to each investment and the cash it generates. In essence, the equation would be

$$\text{PV of cash outflows} = \text{Present value of cash inflows}$$

The present value of the cash outflows will be the present cost of the investment unless payments are being made in increments as we did in the San Nicolas warehouse. In that case, cash outflows need to be brought to the present.

In the net present value equation we chose the discount rate that we would use to bring the set of cash inflows to the present. In the internal rate of return, we assume that both present values are equal and solve for the discount rate that would make that true. If the cash inflows are a steady stream, we can solve the IRR with an annuity due table from Appendix A.

Let's assume that we have an investment that will cost $15,000 and yield $4,000 per year for 5 years.

$$PV \text{ cash outflows} = PV \text{ inflows}$$
$$\$15,000 = \$4,000 \ (PV \text{ of an annuity } X\%, 5\text{years})$$
$$3.75 = PV \text{ of an annuity } X\%, 5\text{years}$$

We need to look at the present value of an annuity table in Appendix A and find the interest rate closest to 3.75 in the 5-year column. Unfortunately, there is not an exact match. We estimate that the internal rate of return for this investment is somewhere between 10.0% (3.79079) and 10.5% (3.74286). Is that estimate good enough? If we want an idea of the investment's value, this method will suffice. It won't work if we have uneven cash inflows. For that, we need to use a spreadsheet program like Excel or a financial calculator.

The internal rate of return allows us to determine if an investment will yield more than our cost of borrowing or the hurdle rate we have set for projects with similar risk profiles. The internal rate of return and the net present value method are similar in that they use the cash inflows generated by an investment and adjust for the time value of money. Where they differ is in the discount rate. The net present value method allows managers to set the discount rate and analyze whether the investment meets that goal. The internal rate of return method seeks the rate that the project would generate and then allows the manager to decide if the rate is acceptable. Either method provides a valid decision tool, but many managers prefer the net present value method. It is easier to understand and allows the firm to set a discount rate that equals the cost of capital and a risk premium. If the investment meets its target, it is accepted. If it has a negative net present value, it is rejected. The analysis is relatively simple to calculate and explain.

THE EFFECT OF CORPORATE STRATEGY ON INVESTMENT DECISIONS

Corporate strategy has an enormous impact on long-term investment decisions. Pfizer and Apotex are pharmaceutical companies. Because they manufacture products that will be ingested, they must maintain factories that meet the highest standards of cleanliness and safety. Their products must be produced to exact specifications and require significant investment in plant and equipment. But although both produce medicines, Pfizer has chosen to develop new, patented, and branded drugs while Apotex produces generic equivalents. Pfizer's strategy calls for sizeable investments in research and

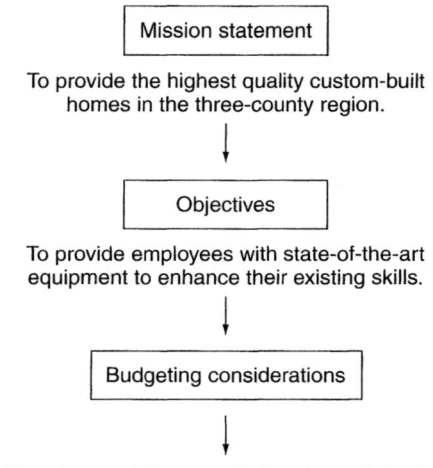

Mission statements often help define the types of investments that the firm will make.

development, which carries far greater risk than does Apotex's strategy. In both cases, equipment will be evaluated based on its ability to reduce manufacturing costs and increase productivity at a return that is greater than the cost of capital. However, given Pfizer's strategic direction a higher proportion of its investment dollars will be targeted to research. The cash inflows from its products have to support the risk that the company is taking.

There is no single framework that guarantees that the firm will always make a correct choice, however, the tools provided in this section will help take some of the guesswork out of long-term budgeting.

TERMS TO KNOW

Acquisition costs	Operating lease	Profitability index (PI)
Operating costs	Payback period	Internal rate of return
Disposal value	Risk	(IRR)
Depreciation	Net present value (NPV)	
Capital lease	Discount rate	

TERM PAPERS AND PROJECTS

1. Determine the cost of financing a long-term investment. Include all the costs associated with lease or purchase including loan origination fees, penalties for early repayment, and any sort of loan insurance. How does this affect the total cost, the payback period, net present value, and profitability index?

2. Compare the cost of leasing a long-term asset versus buying it outright. Be sure to include maintenance costs or the value of a vendor-supplied maintenance agreement, the value of depreciation to the owner, and any residual value that might be realized if the asset were purchased. In the case of the asset you evaluated, does lease or purchase make more sense?

3. Investment in capital goods including significant investments in computers, automated factory systems, and telecommunications improvements fueled a good portion of the economic growth in the late 1990s. When the economy contracted in 2001, capital spending fell. What has happened to corporate investment spending since then? How has capital spending affected the economy? Did the Federal Reserve rate cuts in 2001 spur the type of corporate investment that the Fed intended?

4. Investigate the types of warehouse space that are available for sale or lease in your community. What is the vacancy rate for warehouse space? Is it in demand or have occupancy rates declined? Look at the availability of unimproved land. What costs would a company incur if they needed warehouse space? The choices would include buying an existing facility, leasing space, or buying property and building a warehouse.

REVIEW QUESTIONS

1. Describe three situations where a company might find itself in need of long-term investments.
2. Distinguish between start-up costs and ongoing costs. Give examples of each.
3. Businesses intend to make money, therefore they must profit from their investments. Give examples of profit-related questions that a firm must ask when considering a long-term investment.
4. What is depreciation? How does it affect an investment? What are the advantages of depreciating equipment?
5. Describe the difference between a capital lease and an operating lease.
6. What is a payback period? How is it used in decision making?
7. Name two types of risk a company takes when making long-term investments.
8. Why is it important for a company to estimate present value and profitability index in evaluating long-term investments?
9. Discuss the factors that would influence the discount rate that a firm chose to use for a specific investment.
10. What can be determined from the internal rate of return?

REVIEW PROBLEMS

1. What is the payback period for an investment that costs $54,000 and is expected to generate the following cash inflows?

Year	Cash inflows
1	$17,500
2	$15,000
3	$12,000
4	$10,500
5	$ 6,500

2. A company is considering three projects. The company's cost of capital is 12%. The cash flow estimates for each project are given below. The first year's value represents the costs associated with the project.

Year	Project A	Project B	Project C
1	($5,000)	($4,000)	($5,000)
2	$3,000	$1,000	$ 0
3	$2,000	$2,500	$4,000
4	$1,000	$3,000	$6,000

a. Calculate the payback period for each project.
b. Calculate the NPV for each project.
c. Calculate the PI for each project.
d. Estimate the IRR for each project.
e. If the projects are mutually exclusive, which one should the firm accept?
f. If the firm can fund two of them, which two should it fund?

CHAPTER

11 MERGERS AND DIVESTITURES

LEARNING OBJECTIVES

1. Understand the difference between a merger and an acquisition.
2. Discuss the difference between a horizontal, vertical, and conglomerate merger.
3. Distinguish between acquisitions made for cash, stock, or debt.
4. Explain how purchase of an entire company is different from acquiring a single asset.
5. Describe the Justice Department's role in mergers and acquisitions.
6. Understand what a leveraged buyout is.
7. Discuss the difference between an acquisition and a hostile takeover.
8. Calculate the value of a business using present value assumptions.
9. Demonstrate the ability to value a business using capitalization rates.
10. Discuss the availability of valuation models on the Internet.

Firms change their financial structure either through internal growth or by external acquisition. In this chapter, we will discuss the types of business combinations, the strategy behind them, and some methods of determining the value of a business.

MERGERS AND ACQUISITIONS

A **merger** is a combination of partners and an **acquisition** is the purchase of one company by another. There is a difference between the two, both in financial arrangement and in perception.

> **In the News**
>
> On September 3, 2001, Hewlett-Packard and Compaq agreed to merge. The goal was to create a leader in information technology products. The new company would be called Hewlett-Packard and the Chairman and CEO of H-P, Carly Fiorina, would retain those titles in the new company. The CEO of Compaq, Michael Capellas, would become president.
>
> Both companies cited economies that would result from a merger as well as opportunities to sell packaged systems based on the products that each would contribute to the combined company. The Compaq Web page (www.compaq.com) provided a 12-page set of questions and answers to explain the benefits of the merger.
>
> Unfortunately, not everyone was pleased with the proposed merger. Both Walter Hewlett, eldest son of cofounder Bill Hewlett, and David Packard, the only son of cofounder Dave Packard, stated that they would oppose the merger on the grounds that Compaq was not the right partner for Hewlett-Packard. The two men did not control enough voting stock to derail the merger, however, their public disapproval did lead others to vote against the proposed merger.
>
> The merger was finalized in April 2002 by a margin of only 51.4% in favor of the merger.
>
> *Source:* "HP and Compaq: It's Official-Almost," *Business Week*, April 29, 2002, p. 48. Edited by Monica Roman.

TYPES OF MERGERS

Mergers and acquisitions are categorized as one of three types: horizontal, vertical, and conglomerate, based on their relationship within an industry. Mergers within the same industry, where the participants produce the same product and occupy the same position within the supply chain, are called **horizontal mergers.** The Exxon and Mobil merger was a horizontal merger. Both companies had refineries and retail locations across the country. We have also seen a number of horizontal mergers in the health insurance industry. The combination of two firms that serve a similar market segment can strengthen both companies through production efficiencies and the reduction of fixed cost overhead.

Vertical mergers are combinations of companies within the same industry but at different positions in the production process, especially when one company is a supplier to the other. For example, Anheuser Busch owns a subsidiary that produces cans. Since brewers buy cans, the can company is a supplier within that industry. The can company could also produce cans for soft drink companies which would make it part of that industry also. The partners do not have to belong exclusively to one industry for the merger to be considered a vertical merger. Many mergers are vertical since manufacturers or retailers want to assure themselves of a steady stream of the products critical to their organization.

Conglomerate mergers are the combination of companies in dissimilar industries. Conglomerate mergers were more popular in the 1970s and 1980s

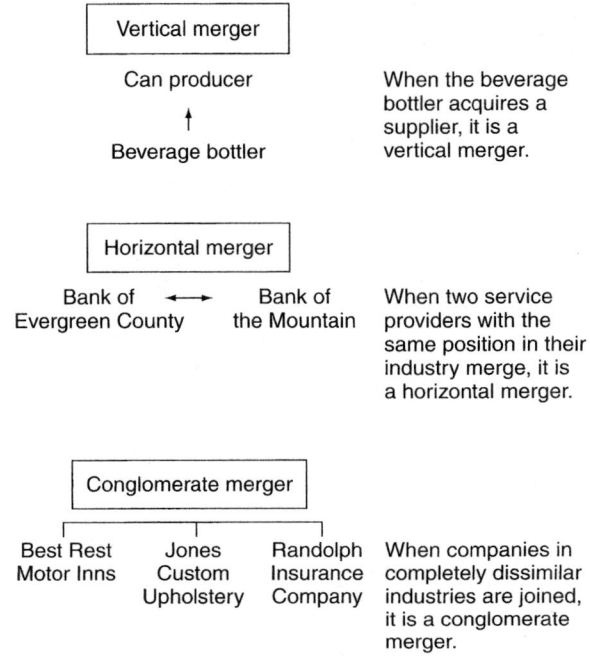

Vertical merger

Can producer
↑
Beverage bottler

When the beverage bottler acquires a supplier, it is a vertical merger.

Horizontal merger

Bank of ←→ Bank of
Evergreen County   the Mountain

When two service providers with the same position in their industry merge, it is a horizontal merger.

Conglomerate merger

Best Rest   Jones   Randolph
Motor Inns   Custom   Insurance
              Upholstery   Company

When companies in completely dissimilar industries are joined, it is a conglomerate merger.

There are three basic types of mergers that reflect the relationship of firms within the supply chain.

The prevailing management theory was that wise business practices could be applied across the board, regardless of industry. Many companies with diverse product lines grew through acquisition during that time period. Managers found that although conceptual skills are important, having to manage disparate production and distributions functions was not as cost efficient as focusing on a more limited product line or consumer market. By the 1990s, many conglomerates had begun to restructure, shedding businesses in which they did not have a commanding market share.

THE STRUCTURE OF A MERGER

In a joint proxy statement–prospectus dated May 19, 2000, the Chairmen and Chief Executive Officers of both Time Warner, Inc., and America Online, Inc., wrote to their shareholders informing them that the two companies had agreed to combine, subject to the approval of a majority of the shareholders of both corporations. The proxy statement–prospectus explained the terms that they had agreed upon and asked that the stockholders vote yes. The cover letter called it a merger of equals and stated the terms for exchanging shares of the individual companies for stock in a newly created company. Shareholders of America Online common stock were to receive one share of AOL Time Warner, the new corporate identity, while shareholders of Time Warner would receive 1.5 shares of the stock. When the calculations for preferred stock were included, former owners of America Online would hold approximately 55% of the new corporation and former owners of Time Warner would hold 45%. The unequal proportions were due to the relative economic value placed on each of the firms. Within the proxy statement–prospectus were financial statements for each company along with adjustments that the managers made to create pro forma financial statements for the combined entity.[1] The prospectus also stated the risks and challenges that the proposed corporation could face. We know that the shareholders agreed that the benefits of the merger outweighed the risks and voted to combine the companies into one. We also know that AOL Time Warner subsequently took one of the largest write-downs in business history, a recognition that the value of the combined entity did not live up to the expectations at the time of the merger.

Companies such as America Online and Time Warner agree to merge because they believe that synergy will occur. **Synergy** can be described as the idea that the whole is worth more than the parts. Two firms who are in similar or complementary businesses can achieve greater operating efficiency and profit through a combination of their efforts than either could achieve on its own or with internally generated growth. In the case of AOL Time Warner, management believed that the combination of a content provider (Time Warner) with an Internet provider (America Online) would create more growth opportunities for each company. America Online had technology that would connect consumers. However, what consumers wanted was not just connection but information. Time Warner provides information but needs a mechanism to deliver that information. Because it involved an Internet company, the merger was promoted as a transformation of business and society, but it was really as simple as bundling sets of services that together should reduce operating costs for the two partners and create increased opportunities for product creation. Unfortunately, the value originally ascribed to the business entity was not achievable.

A successful merger is negotiated carefully, not just in terms of the relative economic value that each partner brings to the combination but also in the roles that the managers of each individual firm will play in the new organization. One of the most important assets that many firms have is the knowledge and skill of its managers. Because a merger results in duplication along the chain of command, the largest potential cost is not the dollar value of the severance packages that may need to be offered but the loss of future value due to losing the "wrong" executive. The paper value created by the merger of two companies can be lost if the transition is not handled carefully.

The combinations of America Online with Time Warner and Hewlett Packard with Compaq were true mergers because each set of shareholders surrendered shares of the individual companies and were issued shares in an entirely new corporation. An acquisition differs slightly because one company purchases the assets of another and folds it into the existing corporation. Firms may choose to rename the combined organizations to take advantage of a strong corporate identity or the acquired company can be folded into the new parent.

PAYING FOR THE ACQUISITION

After the acquisition price has been established, the method of payment must be established. There are three basic ways a firm can acquire another: pay in cash, issue a certain amount of debt in trade for the firm's stock, or issue shares

[1]AOL Time Warner Merger, Joint Proxy Statement–Prospectus, dated May 19, 2000.

of its stock in trade for the acquired firm's stock. In some cases, a combination of these is offered to shareholders.

If the Plum Street Corporation pays cash for the assets of Henderson, Inc., it is trading one asset (its cash) for another (ownership of the other corporation). Plum Street has not incurred any additional debt and the equity of its existing shareholders is not diluted. The shareholders of Henderson have received cash that they can invest however they see fit. They do not automatically become shareholders in the new parent.

If Plum Street Corporation issues debt, Henderson's shareholders are not receiving an immediate payout. The price they are willing to accept may be higher than it would be had they been paid in cash, and their acceptance of bonds (or other debt financing) will be predicated on the financial strength and prospects of the acquiring company, in this case Plum Street Corporation. The issuing company adds a long-term liability to its balance sheet, and the interest paid becomes a yearly cash outflow. Henderson's former shareholders become creditors of the new parent and there is no dilution of equity for Plum Street's shareholders.

However, Plum Street may decide that it does not want to lower its cash reserves to the degree that it would need to nor does it want to obligate itself to a long-term debt and the interest that it carries. Plum Street could issue shares of its stock to Henderson's shareholders in order to acquire the company. Henderson's shareholders have become shareholders in Plum Street Corporation, but a new corporate entity has not been created. Depending on the number of shares issued and the earnings that Henderson, Inc., adds, the earnings per share may or may not decline after the acquisition.

The structure of payments for a company has tax implications for the acquiring company and the shareholders of the acquired company. For example, in an all cash transaction, the shareholders will be responsible for capital gains taxes. In a debt-financed transaction, the cost of interest can be deducted from the firm's income but is taxable to the former shareholders. Because the tax codes change and the structure of a purchase offer can become complex,

both parties should consult tax attorneys and accountants before the deal i
finalized.

Acquisitions are undertaken for many of the same reasons that com
panies merge: to take advantage of cost efficiencies in manufacturing and dis
tribution, the opportunity to expand or develop markets, and the financia
strength that a larger organization can provide. In October 2000 Kellog;
Company, the maker of many ready-to-eat cereal brands, announced that it hac
reached an agreement to acquire Keebler Foods Company, which makes cook
ies and crackers. Managers at Kellogg's lauded the managers of Keebler fo
having an extremely well-run company. They believed that the addition o
Keebler would add, among other things, diversity to Kellogg's existing produc
line and better utilize distribution channels and research and developmen
facilities.[2] The corporate name remained Kellogg's.

Another aspect of an acqustion that must not be forgotten is tha
Kellogg's was buying a company with its own balance sheet. The acquisitio
price was described as $42 for each of Keebler's shares as well as the assump
tion of Keebler's debt. Kellogg's cash offer eliminated the equity that Keebler'
shareholders held, but that still leaves current liabilities and long-term debt
Had Kellogg's only been interested in a manufacturing facility or a specifi
product line, it could have negotiated the purchase of that single item bu
in buying the entire operation, it became responsible for the existing capita
structure.

Many newspapers run advertisements for small businesses. Before
you make that "modest investment," you should thoroughly research
the business. (Getty Images, Inc.)

[2]Kellogg Company News at *www.kelloggs.com*, October 26, 2000.

PURCHASE OF EXISTING COMPANIES

When two local companies merge, the agreement can be negotiated between the entrepreneurs. However when two major corporations wish to join, whether through merger or acquisition, the combination is evaluated by the federal Department of Justice to determine whether the new firm would violate antitrust laws. In some cases, the Justice Department allows an acquisition under the condition that the firm sells specific assets, which would otherwise cause a concentration of power in the industry. When United Airlines made an offer for US Airways, the Justice Department ruled that the combined airline would result in reduced competition along certain routes. The company would have had to sell some of its gates at the affected airports to allow increased competition. In light of Justice Department rulings, the firms may decide that the assets they are required to sell make the proposed merger less attractive and they may not go forward. The Justice Department has the power to entirely disallow a proposed combination in order to maintain competition in an industry. Other government agencies also review mergers, for example, the Federal Reserve analyzes the impact of bank mergers on the availability and cost of consumer banking.

DIVESTITURES

On occasion a firm will decide that a business unit does not fit its long-term corporate strategy. It could be that the firm has added products that did not grow to the extent that the company had envisioned. Or the mix of products and services could be too wide to allow management to develop a competitive advantage in any one area. Perhaps a second retail location is taking too many sales from the original store without adding sufficient revenue to justify the expense. Whatever the reason, firms decide to divest operations by selling or spinning them off.

Divestitures can happen in several ways. If the company is selling a small business unit, it can approach another firm that operates in that industry and offer to sell the unit. Many years ago, General Electric sold their small appliance division to Black and Decker, which already made coffeemakers and toasters. The small appliances did not fit within GE's corporate strategic plan but added market share for Black and Decker, which they believed would increase their earning power. GE benefited by selling an unproductive asset.

If the unit is large enough to stand on its own but does not fit within corporate strategy, it can be spun off. The managers of the existing business unit become the chief executives of an independent corporation. Although there are several ways that the transaction can be financed, in many cases shareholders of the original corporation get a proportionate number of shares in the new company. They still "own" the business units that they did before but as separate business entities. It is up to individual shareholders to decide if they want to keep stock in both or either company.

<table><tr><td>

In the News

Polaroid Corporation filed for voluntary bankruptcy on Friday October 12, 2001. Burdened with more than $900 million in debt, Polaroid said it was seeking a sale of all or part of the company. In light of its financial difficulties, the company began an investigation into cost-cutting strategies. The cost cutting would include elimination of what it considered noncore products and businesses, the sale of assets, and closing facilities.

If assets such as machinery were sold, they could be valued using the tools we saw in Chapter 10. Facilities, too, could be valued as single items. However, if the company were to sell a "noncore business," the value of the business would have to take into account the long-term cash inflows that the acquirer could expect. A noncore business for Polaroid could very well prove to be the missing piece in another firm's strategic objectives.

Later in this chapter we will look at hostile takeovers. Interestingly, much of Polaroid's debt was as a result of "successfully" fending off a hostile takeover bid in 1989. If the debt has now crippled Polaroid, one has to wonder how successful their defensive strategy was?

Source: http://money.cnn.com/2001/10/12/companies/polaroid.

</td></tr></table>

Divestitures also occur if a corporation is strapped for cash. If the firm is losing money, it may be forced to sell assets including an entire division or operating unit. In this case, the sale is an attempt at streamlining the organization in hopes of improving its chance of survival.

Theoretically, a company should seek to maximize shareholder value. If that means acquiring additional manufacturing capacity or an entire company, the firm should do so. If a portion of the business is not adding sufficient value, it should be sold and the proceeds invested in areas of the business that will produce profits. That's the theory. In practice, it is difficult to quantify the long-term increase in shareholder value as a result of divestiture.

LEVERAGED BUYOUTS

During the 1980s several firms were sold, not to other companies, but to a management team, a relatively small group of individuals. Often the management team was comprised of the senior executives of the organization but in some cases, outside managers with an interest in the company bought it with the intent of running it. Some of these transactions occurred because the business unit was part of a conglomerate that was reorganizing. Some were a result of hostile takeover attempts (discussed in the next section) and still others were underperforming companies that chose to restructure rather than be acquired by another corporation. In essence, a small group of individuals bought the equity of the existing shareholders and turned the company into a private corporation.

The cost to acquire thousands, if not millions, of shares in a publicly traded firm is very high. In order to finance these transactions, management groups turned to investment banks for debt financing using the assets of the corporation itself to back the loans. These transactions were called **leveraged buyouts** (also known as LBOs) because they had an incredibly high degree of leverage (debt). The goal of the management team was to use the firm's existing cash flow to pay the current portion of debt and interest, restructure the organization to take advantage of any cost efficiencies it could, sell unproductive assets, and reduce overhead, often through the use of layoffs. There were no shareholders who had to vote on major restructuring changes so many management teams felt that an LBO would give them more flexibility to make the drastic changes that would quickly restore healthy profit levels.

Because the firms were so highly leveraged, the debt was riskier and carried a premium. Firms that were successful spent several years as private corporations and then took the companies public again, selling shares in the newly restructured organization and paying off the high interest rate debt. Not all LBOs were successful, however. If the organization's cash flow could not cover debt and interest payments, the firm went into default. Several large companies entered Chapter 11 bankruptcy as a result of taking on debt that they could not service. In many cases, the LBO debt was restructured into equity or paid at pennies on the dollar.

Pre LBO		
Assets	Liabilities	
100%	50%	A typical firm has accounts payable, notes payable, and some long-term debt.
	Equity	
	50%	A firm that has been in business for several years will have common stock, perhaps some preferred stock, and retained earnings.
Immediately After an LBO		
Assets	Liabilities	
100%	99%	After the LBO, the firm will have sizeable debt, which has been incurred by the managers in order to buy out the previous shareholders.
	Equity 1%	The goal is to streamline operations, reduce inefficiencies, retire the debt assumed during the buyout and, eventually, sell shares in a revitalized organization.

In a typical leveraged buyout (LBO), the managers use a great deal of debt to buy shares from the existing stockholders. They then restructure the firm, using its own current assets to pay down debt. The goal is to make the firm more efficient, with the intention of reissuing stock at a later date.

Book Report

Kohlberg Kravis Roberts & Co. (also known by their initials, KKR) is one of the most successful leveraged buyout firms. They were founded in 1976 and have participated in many large buyouts including Motel 6, Safeway, and RJR Nabisco. Some of their purchases were more lucrative than others, but KKR dominated leveraged buyouts throughout the 1980s—a period of intense activity.

Several books have been written about KKR or the deals in which they participated. Not all of the authors are laudatory, but they do a good job of describing the deal making that went on as companies took on exorbitant amounts of debt in order to, ironically, streamline companies.

Merchants of Debt: KKR and the Mortgaging of American Business, George Anders, New York, Basic Books, 1992.

The Money Machine: How KKR Manufactured Power and Profits, Sarah Bartlett, New York, Warner Books, 1992.

Barbarians at the Gate: The Fall of RJR Nabisco, Bryan Burrough, New York, Harper and Row, 1990.

HOSTILE TAKEOVERS

So far we have discussed combinations that are agreed to by two parties, each of whom sees benefit in the transaction. Not all acquisitions are friendly. In some cases, one firm wishes to acquire a firm that does not want to be acquired. The managers of the targeted company might not want to give up their independence or they may not feel that the offer price and terms are fair to the shareholders or their employees. If the first company persists, the stage is set for a **hostile takeover** attempt.

There were enough hostile takeover attempts in the 1980s that the participants were given names, like characters in a play, and there were several stories that were enacted. As we go through this example, think of the costs to the two companies both in actual dollars expended and the long-term effect that this drama might have on the companies' operations.

The acquiring company, the Suitor, had its sights set on a Target. This "Target" is not meant to be any specific company, the name is merely descriptive of the role in this typical hostile takeover. Members of Target's senior management team did not want to become part of the larger Suitor organization knowing that if they did, they would become redundant. The Target stated that the offer price was inadequate and they would have no further comment. But once the offer had been made, the Target company was "in play." Whether they liked it or not, Suitor's offer had drawn attention to the Target and interest in

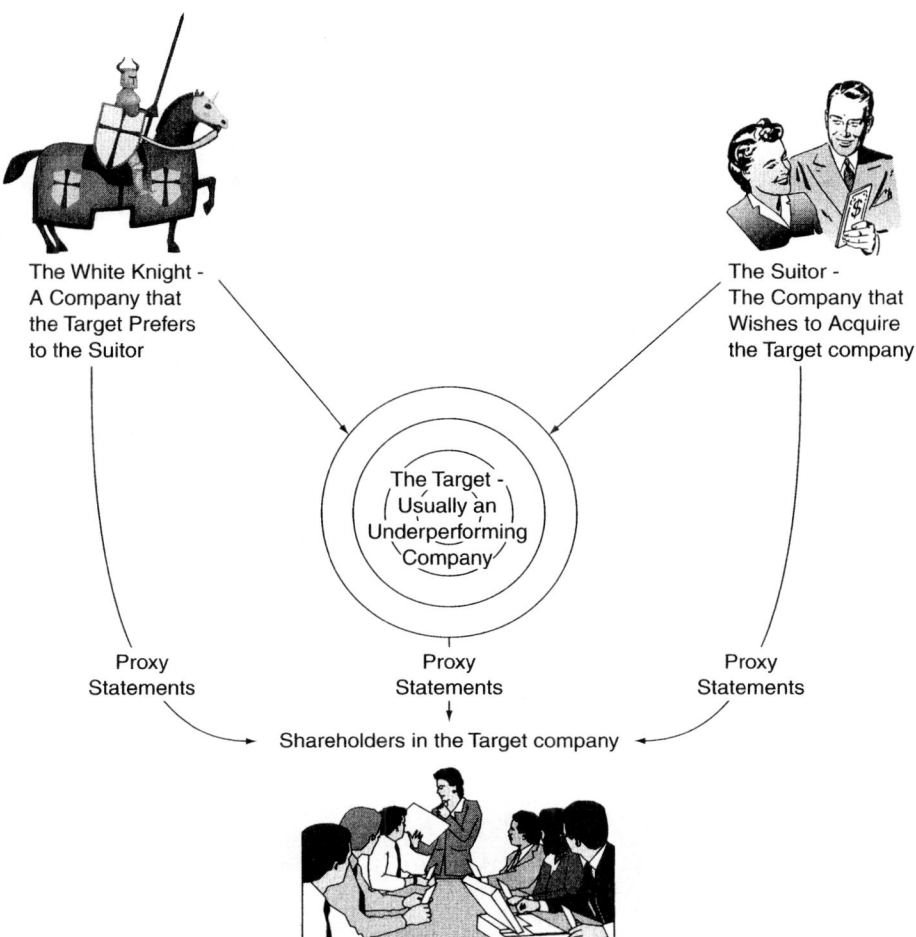

In a hostile takeover, the targeted company and its shareholders attract the attention of one or more interested parties. Shareholders are sent proxy statements by all bidders and the targeted company.

acquiring the Target would increase. At the very least, Suitor would increase its bid, which means for Suitor's shareholders the cost of acquiring this asset has increased. If Suitor is planning to finance the acquisition with additional debt funding, every increase in the offer price increases the debt-to-equity ratio and reduces the shareholders' claim on the assets of the corporation. There are very real costs to Suitor's shareholders. If Suitor becomes determined to win the Target at all costs, a bidding frenzy can erupt, causing Suitor to offer more than the Target is realistically worth. Emotion can overrule fiscal prudence and Suitor's shareholders will pay the price.

The Target can choose to fight and hope that Suitor gives up. Management might also consider a leveraged buyout if they can get financing to do so. If the Target's management succeeds in taking the firm private, its existing shareholders are paid in cash, and the Target's management now has to squeeze operational savings out to pay for the high debt levels. Operating costs just increased by the level of debt.

The Target can also choose to look for a purchaser of its choice, called a White Knight. The White Knight should offer a higher price or better combination of payment terms (i.e., a higher percentage of cash combined with some debt versus Suitor's all debt offer) or the Target's shareholders can sue management for failure to perform its fiduciary responsibilities.

The Target can attempt to sell so many parts of the business that it becomes unattractive to Suitor but, if it does so, it runs the risk of destroying its core business in order to fend off the acquisition. The cost is then born by the Target's shareholders who see the value of their assets decline.

Because they have a significant impact on the operation and future structure of the organizations, all of these strategies have to be approved by the Target's shareholders who will also be flooded with offers from Suitor and perhaps White Knight. One of the undefined costs of a hostile takeover is that it consumes so much of management's energy, both at the Target and at Suitor that the ongoing business suffers. There is also an emotional cost to employees at both firms, but especially the Target because of the uncertainty surrounding the company's future.

VALUING THE BUSINESS

Now that we've looked at the "whys" of mergers, acquisitions, and divestitures, we have to decide how much we're going to pay to acquire a business. Although we have just left the discussion of hostile takeovers, we will assume that this transaction has been agreed upon in principle between the buyer and the seller of a privately held corporation and all that remains is coming up with a price. Later we will talk about purchasing a company with publicly traded shares.

An ongoing concern has financial statements that describe the revenue stream (the income statement) and book value (balance sheet) of the company. The book value is the accounting value of an asset. It is calculated by subtracting accumulated depreciation from the cost of the asset. In Chapter 10 we discussed the tax value of depreciation when making a purchase decision. Depreciation reduces the book value of the equipment but does not necessarily reflect the cost to replace the asset. Book value, therefore, is only an accounting concept. When buying a business, the firm needs to determine its market value, the price at which the firm could be sold today.

The buyer's perception of the market value of a firm may not match that of the seller. The seller wants the highest price possible for the business and will use optimistic assumptions in order to support the price. The buyer wants the best price possible and may use a steeper discount or make different operating assumptions.

Before proceeding with the valuation techniques, it is useful to look at the planning that the acquirer should do even before attempting to determine an offer price. Unless the buyer had some interest in acquiring the seller's business, there would be no need for valuation analysis. However, the buyer might not have need for all parts of the seller's business or might make significant operational changes that would affect the cost the buyer was willing to pay.

The first step in analyzing the purchase is to document planning assumptions. Following are a list of questions that the acquiring firm might ask:

- How efficient is the current operation? What are the accounting ratios and how do they compare to ours? If the firm is being run less efficiently than the acquiring firm, there is room for improved performance, however, the inefficiencies have to be corrected first and that could take an investment in either finances or time.
- How competent is current management? If the current management and operations team is well trained, the costs to integrate personnel will be lower. If the firm is for sale because it is being poorly managed, there will be higher integration costs. Another way to look at this issue is to ask why the current owners are selling the business. If you are buying a small business and the owners have grown tired of managing the day-to-day business, have they let it slip in the last few months or years? Have they kept up with the necessary changes, or is the business itself in semiretirement?
- How compatible are the two firms' operations? Will significant amounts of training or new capital investment be required? Are there labor union issues that could change the cost structure of the combined firm?
- What type of market share does the firm enjoy? How do the existing products or services complement what our firm offers? Are there areas of overlap or products that would add no value? Would there be a cost to discontinuing certain products?
- Does the firm have assets that cannot be acquired elsewhere such as patents, licensing agreements, copyrights, high-quality research and development, or creativity?
- How critical do we believe this firm is to the attainment of our strategic objectives?

The last question is probably the most important one. If we believe that either a merger with this firm or the acquisition of this firm is critical to our future success, we will be willing to pay more for it than if it is merely a comfortable fit. Having stated their assumptions, the buyer is in a better position to set an opening price and assess subsequent counteroffers.

We will look at two valuation perspectives: one based on underlying asset values and the other based on cash flow analysis. In either method, the starting point in determining value is the firm's financial statements.

If you are buying a company with significant tangible assets such as a store with fixtures and inventory, you can build an offer price based on the value of each of the assets you will be acquiring minus any obligations that are outstanding. In essence you will be creating a pro forma balance sheet and income statement, adjusting the historic costs reflected in the firm's existing statements. The adjustments will be affected by the assumptions the buyer makes about the future operation of the business.

The Balance Sheet

Assets that are going to be used by the buyer in the business can be valued at their book value or adjusted to reflect replacement cost. Replacement cost is the cost of acquiring an asset today that performs the same function as the existing capital asset. Calculating replacement costs can be difficult if the asset is unique or technology has changed significantly since the asset was purchased. For example, a small business might have an older computerized accounting system that is perfectly adequate for their internal needs. If the computer has been depreciated to nothing, how should we calculate its value? In buying the business, are we going to want to use that system, does it have some sort of value to us, or is it so antiquated that we will be forced to buy a new computer? Those judgments must be made as we value the assets.

The value of accounts receivable as stated on the company's balance sheet needs to be weighed against the quality and collection history of the accounts. Rather than assume the accounts receivable, a buyer might want to sell them to a factoring service for collection and be assured of a specific amount of cash.

Another asset to consider is the value of inventory. What inventory is on hand, what is its age and quality, and how does it fit into our production plans? If the inventory does not meet our needs, we would have to value it differently. We might want to establish a liquidation value. The liquidation value is the worth of an asset if it is sold under duress. In clearing out unwanted inventory, the firm's goal is speed. The sooner the inventory is sold, the sooner the firm can reposition itself. Liquidation value is often significantly less than replacement cost or market value.

Real estate and buildings often carry an assessed value. Assessed values are set by municipalities in order to compute the applicable taxes and do not necessarily reflect the market value of the property. It would not be wise to use the property's assessed value as its asset value.

When buying a business, the firm will also be buying its history. One of the assets of a business could be the name recognition that it has established through the years. Is the acquiring firm planning to keep the previous name and if so, what is that worth? If the acquiring firm is replacing the old name with its own, the buyer may decide that the existing name has no value. The seller will argue that the positive association that has been established for many years will transfer to the new owner. Intangible assets such as the value of names or brands and the value added to the organization because of good management are very difficult to value. Goodwill is the asset that appears on a balance sheet when a business is sold for more than the value of the tangible assets. Goodwill represents the value of the reputation, faithful customers, and good management of the acquired company. Although the rules for amortizing goodwill are changing, goodwill is stated as an asset on the balance sheet and reevaluated over time.

The balance sheet also contains liabilities. The acquiring firm will need to decide which it will assume and which will remain the responsibility of the seller. If the buyer assumes liabilities, the cash purchase price will be reduced accordingly. For example, if the buyer is taking possession of a retail location and assuming the mortgage on the building, the building will be valued at market rate less the outstanding balance on the mortgage.

The difference between current assets and current liabilities is the firm's working capital. The acquirer wants to ascertain whether there is sufficient working capital cash flow to expand this operation. Current liabilities, along with the number of days they remain unpaid, should be examined along with the structure of short- and long-term debt. Increasing the level of debt or restructuring could add costs to the transaction.

Are there any potential liabilities that could become important? Pollution standards have increased over the last decades. Dry-cleaning businesses that have operated at the same location for generations may have tainted soil as

```
╭─────────────⟨ In the News ⟩─────────────╮
```

The article is titled: "The Enron Debacle: Byzantine Deals Have Shattered the Energy Outfit's Credibility."

By the time that Dynergy walked away from its proposed acquisition of Enron, Enron's liabilities were not just financial but also involved the credibility of the company. For years, Enron had been cagey with the details of its partnership arrangements and not entirely clear on where its income was generated. Other news was also disturbing because with the telecommunications industry in a slump, there was little demand for Enron's high-speed communications capacity trading. Also, investment in a water company had cost Enron at least $574 million.

In the end, it wasn't just the debts that were coming due that concerned Dynergy. It was the lack of clear information and the sense that more bad news could be right around the corner. The liabilities weren't all on the balance sheet. Some of them were within the corporate culture.

Source: "The Enron Debacle: Byzantine Deals Have Shattered the Energy Outfit's Credibility," *Business Week*, November 12, 2001. By Stephanie Anderson and Wendy Zellner in Dallas, with Heather Thomas in New York.

a result of the chemicals used in the dry-cleaning process. That would be a potential long-term liability for the purchaser. Are there product liability concerns that could result in lawsuits?

The Income Statement

The real value of the business is related to its ability to take assets and create a steady or increasing stream of revenue. For that reason, the potential buyer needs to examine the income statements from a few previous years to arrive at an estimated future income statement. In the list of questions on page 239 we thought about the types of changes we might make in the business operations. Those potential changes will cause us to restate the income, in hopes of coming up with a more accurate prediction.

We start at the top of the income statement with sales revenue. We asked earlier if the product mix will remain the same under our ownership or if there will be changes. In addition, we need to look at the growth trend during the past several years. Has sales volume been increasing? How solid is per unit pricing? We should look beyond the previous sales numbers however and relate them to working capital. When we examined the balance sheet, did the firm have sufficient working capital to expand the business or did cash constraints restrict its growth? Because the goal is to obtain a profitable and growing business, a thorough analysis of the current sales patterns is vital.

Cost of goods sold is often a large percent of net sales. The buyer should examine the seller's cost structure, looking for purchasing efficiencies, changes in shipping that would reduce freight charges, and manufacturing productivity. If the two firms both manufacture the same type of product and can consolidate factory capacity, both the fixed assets productivity and the cost of goods sold will improve. Calculating break-even quantities for the combined organization and comparing that to current and projected sales volume provides a tool for restating income.

Selling and administrative expenses will have to be analyzed for the first year of combined operations and successive years. In the first year there may be some overlap of personnel and expenses related to the integration of the two firms. In the second and succeeding years, overhead costs should be consolidated and the firm should be operating at a sustainable cost structure.

In the America Online-Time Warner joint proxy statement, a set of pro forma financial statements for each individual company were created. The first column showed the existing AOL figures, the second showed Time Warner, the third column showed the adjustments that would be made, and the fourth column was the final pro forma financial statement.

The purpose of presenting the documents was to demonstrate to the two companies' shareholders that the newly created corporation would be a financially sound, viable company. In our example, we have been assuming the merger or acquisition of a smaller, privately held company but the idea remains the same—assets should be restated from book value to some approximation of current market value and income streams should be adjusted for the operating plans of the acquiring company.

ASSET VALUATION

When you purchase an existing business, you are purchasing the working capital (the current assets less current liabilities) and the equipment necessary to generate income (fixed assets). Both buyer and seller could use the asset valuation method and arrive at different values for the firm. For example, both parties might be willing to add a component for goodwill, or the value of the intangibles that make this business successful, but their assessment of the value of goodwill might differ. Even something as simple as the value of fixed assets may vary between buyer and seller. The seller's concept of the market value of a retail location may differ from the buyer's perception. Whether the accounts receivable are collectible in a time frame that the buyer is comfortable with would also affect their value. The offering price for a business would therefore be constructed using the following table, but the values ascribed to each component could differ:

```
  Cash
  Accounts receivable
+ Inventory
      Current assets
- Less accounts payable and current accruals
      Net working capital
+ Capital assets (fixed assets)
+ Goodwill
      Purchase price
```

Let's look at a hypothetical example. Lucinda has been managing Starbright Gymnastics Studio for several years. The owners want to retire and have offered Lucinda the opportunity to buy the business. Because Lucinda has been running the business, she has a feel for what the costs are and how she would want to improve the operation.

STARBRIGHT GYMNASTICS
Current Balance Sheet

Assets		Liabilities	
Cash	$10,000	Current accruals	$12,000
Inventory	5,000		
Current assets	15,000		
		Mortgage	12,0000
Land	43,000	Equipment loans	15,000
Building	150,000	Vehicle loan	20,000
Equipment	40,000	Long-term debt	155,000
Vehicle	25,000		
Fixed assets	258,000	Owner's equity	106,000
Total assets	273,000	Total liabilities	273,000

STARBRIGHT GYMNASTICS
Current Income Statement

Revenue	$128,000
Cost of goods sold	8,000
Gross margin	120,000
Operating expenses	75,000
Operating income	45,000
Other expenses	
Interest	9,000
Income before taxes	36,000
Income taxes	10,800
Income after taxes	$25,200

The owners are asking $385,000 for the business, which is more than its current asset value. However, because Starbright has been in business for many years and has an excellent reputation among parents and school coaches, the owners feel that the premium is justified.

Lucinda is concerned about the cost. The owners are correct in saying that the gym has a good reputation, however, Lucinda knows that the net income is relatively low and some of the current students are looking for a facility that offers more flexible class and practice times. She feels that there are areas of improvement but they would require that she invest additional funds. For example, the gym has a small retail operation that sells gym clothes and accessories. Lucinda knows that students would like to buy their equipment at the gym, but the inventory levels are currently too low to take advantage of the opportunities. In order to expand, Lucinda would have to increase inventory, which would also increase the accounts payable. Lucinda feels that eventually the gym could make more money by offering more evening and weekend classes, which would also bring more students into the retail shop. The land and building were refinanced 5 years ago and are listed on the balance sheet at the estimated market cost at that time. Lucinda is going to adjust the values to reflect current market conditions. She estimates that the equipment is valued at close to its replacement value if she were to buy the same type of used equipment from another gym. She has added a slight increase to cover the replacement cost of newer equipment.

STARBRIGHT GYMNASTICS
Adjusted Balance Sheet

Assets			Liabilities	
Cash	$10,000		Current accruals	$12,000
Inventory	5,000	7,500		
Current assets	15,000			
			Mortgage	120,000
Land	43,000	50,000	Equipment loans	15,000
Building	150,000	175,000	Vehicle loan	20,000
Equipment	40,000	50,000	Long-term debt	155,000
Vehicle	25,000			
Fixed assets	258,000		Owner's equity	106,000
Total assets	273,000		Total liabilities	273,000

STARBRIGHT GYMNASTICS
Adjusted Income Statement

Revenue	$125,000	$130,000
Cost of goods sold	8,000	12,000
Gross margin	117,000	142,000
Operating expenses	76,000	86,000
Operating income	41,000	56,000
Other expenses		
Interest	9,000	12,000
Income before taxes	32,000	44,000
Income taxes	9,600	13,200
Income after taxes	$22,400	$30,800

Using the format we spelled out earlier, Lucinda can construct a purchase offer. The one decision she needs to make is what value she will put on goodwill. As the manager, Lucinda sees that the gym has potential, however, it has not been actively managed so she has calculated a low value for the goodwill. Her offer is $345,500.

Cash	$10,000
Accounts receivable	none
Inventory	7,500
Current assets	17,500
Less accounts payable and current accruals	12,000
Net working capital	5,500
Capital assets (fixed assets)	300,000
Goodwill	40,000
Purchase price	$345,500

The two parties could negotiate the purchase of Starbright Gymnastics and try to find a middle ground between the asking price and the offer. In fact, this is how many business transactions occur. However, in this calculation we have not used the pro forma income statement that we took such pains to construct, nor have we taken into account the risk involved in buying a business, especially since Lucinda foresees the need for change if the business is to meet her expectations.

The other thing that Lucinda needs to consider is the opportunity cost of the money she is investing. If Lucinda had $345,500 to invest, she could potentially invest in securities (a stock or bond fund) and earn 8%, which would give her $27,640 (before taxes). At the seller's offering price of $385,000, an 8% return would give Lucinda $30,800 in income. If she buys the business instead, she should expect a higher rate of return due to the risks of running the business, especially since she feels that improvements should be made. At this point in time, Starbright is generating only $32,000 in income before taxes. Is that a good enough investment? We'll come back to the question after we've looked at another valuation method.

CAPITALIZATION RATES AND BUSINESS VALUATION

Businesses are most often valued based on the income they produce. Discount or **capitalization rates** are used to convert various measures of cash flow into an estimate of value. To capitalize something means to turn it into an asset. The capitalization rate you choose is related to the discount rate but includes some assumptions about the future growth of earnings of the firm. In order to use a capitalization rate, you need to normalize the income stream. The firm's income can be assumed to increase but abnormal business occurrences must be corrected, for example, the cost of a lawsuit or costs related to an unusual event (hurricane or earthquake damage not covered by insurance, excessive draws or salaries paid to owners, and other extraordinary events).

The **value of the business** is the present value of all future cash flows and is derived by dividing the annual income by the selected capitalization rate. The capitalization rate is calculated by determining the risk adjusted discount rate and subtracting the estimated growth rate. For a firm that is not growing in excess of inflation, the discount rate and the capitalization rate will be equal. For a firm that is experiencing rapid growth, the discount rate will be different from the capitalization rate.

There are three assumptions about income growth that will affect the capitalization rate and the calculation of the firm's value. First, the firm will experience no growth beyond the level of inflation, as with rental property or a mature service business. Second, there is a constant rate of growth that exceeds inflation. Third, long-term growth is expected to grow at varying rates (as with a business in the growth stage) before settling into constant growth.

Let's look at some examples.

No growth   To value an income-producing asset with stable earnings but no growth, take the annual income and divide it by the discount rate. The discount rate will equal the capitalization rate since there is 0 growth.

A 2,550-square-foot office building on a highly visible traffic route has monthly net income $3,000. The rental market is stable and the required discount rate is 12%.

Annual income:	$36,000
Discount rate:	12%
Growth rate:	0%
Capitalization rate:	12%
Value:	$300,000

Constant growth   To establish a value, determine a risk-adjusted discount rate. Subtract the long-term growth rate from the discount rate to establish a capitalization rate. Divide the annual income by the capitalization rate.

An in-home health care company is currently experiencing 10% growth per year and expects that trend to continue. Annual income is $125,000 and the discount rate is 20%.

Annual income:	$125,000
Discount rate:	20%
Growth rate:	10%
Capitalization rate:	10%
Value:	$1,250,000

Variable growth   If the firm is expected to grow at varying rates, the computation becomes more complex. The value of the firm is the present value of the varying streams of income added to a capitalized value for the firm when it reaches a steady state.

Let's return to Lucinda now. Lucinda believes that Starbright Gym can increase revenues and income by 37.5% the first year, 10% the second year, and then show 3% constant income growth. The current income is $22,400 and Lucinda feels that an appropriate discount rate would be 25%.

LUCINDA'S DISCOUNTED CASH FLOW VALUATION

	Income growth rate	Projected income	Discounted present value
Current income		$22,400	
Year 1	37.5%	$30,800	$24,640
Year 2	10.0%	$33,880	$27,104
Present value of 2 years' income			$51,744
Terminal value to be capitalized:			
Year 3	2.0%	$34,558	
Discount	25.0%		
Growth rate	3.0%		
Capitalization rate	22.0%		
Terminal value at the end of 2 years (capitalized asset value)			$157,080
Present value of capitalized value (22%, 3 years):			$306,620
Total value			
PV of 2 years' earnings			$51,744
PV of terminal value			$306,620
Total value			$358,364

The first portion of the worksheet computes the net income in the first and second years of Lucinda's ownership, assuming the rates of growth she estimated. The income is discounted to the present using the 25% discount rate that she chose. She has not yet capitalized the ongoing value of the business, so the first 2 years' earnings are simply brought to the present. Beginning the third year, income stabilizes at a steady rate of growth and Lucinda can capitalize that constant income. The capitalization rate is the discount rate less the growth rate, or 22%. The capitalized rate begins at the end of the third year, so the capitalized value has to be brought to the present. It is discounted at the full value of the discount rate, or 25%, because that is the hurdle rate that Lucinda has set for this investment.

If Lucinda's income and expense projections are valid and her discount rate is reasonable, she should be willing to pay $358,364 for Starbright Gym. That is more than the $345,500 offer that she determined using the adjusted value of the assets but less than the $385,000 asking price by the owners. As with all of the present value computations, we need to be sure that the discount rate that Lucinda chooses reflects the risk she would incur in running this business. As the risk and discount rate increase, the price she is willing to pay for the business will decrease.

We've seen several types of financial templates and worksheets that are available on the Internet. The following two sites offer a variety of forms that might help clarify the value of a business.

If you are attempting to project future financial statements, you might want to start at the Business Owner's Toolkit (www.toolkit.cch/com/tools/). Here you will find a wide variety of business and financial planning charts, among them a New Business Cash Needs Estimate, templates for the major accounting statements, and a section that covers small business planning.

If you are specifically looking at valuing a business, go to www.cfo.com/toolbox/ and look at the Business Valuation Calculator. The calculator asks for both book value and market value for balance sheet items. It also asks for earnings information and risk assessment. The site cautions that business valuation is an imprecise science, however, the calculator gives at least a starting place when determining how much to offer for a business.

Multipliers   The final method of valuing a small business is the use of standard industry **multipliers.** Here a buyer and seller would refer to a list of suggested multiples that applies to a particular industry. Many of the factors are multiplied by gross income or total revenue, which can overstate the value of a firm if costs are not under control. Multipliers are easy to use and may serve as a rough estimate of the value of a business. However, they assume many things, most important among them that the firm will continue to be operated as it has been in the past. As we saw from Lucinda's analysis, that may not always be a valid assumption.

VALUING A PUBLICLY TRADED COMPANY

When we described the different types of business ownership, we said that corporate shareholders were in fact the owners of the company. The shareholders collectively employ the senior managers who are overseen by a Board of Directors who are acting in the shareholders' stead. In theory, the value of a publicly traded firm is the price per share of stock times the number of shares outstanding because if you could buy all of the shares of stock that existed, you would own the company. In theory, the price of stock has gyrated in the last several years, so putting a constant value on a company by using the value of its shares is difficult at best.

We will discuss equities and the stock markets in depth in Chapter 14, but it is important to remember that just as Lucinda analyzed the potential of Starbright Gym, the value of a large company's stock should reflect the underlying value of the corporation. Investors should be buying a share of the current assets of the organization and the income that will be generated by the efficient use of those assets. Technically, the capitalization rate of corporations should be the risk-adjusted discount rate less the expected growth rate. Some of the recent volatility in the price of high-tech stock may be related to unrealistically low discount rates and unrealistically high income growth expectations.

TERMS TO KNOW

Merger	Conglomerate merger	Hostile takeover
Acquisition	Synergy	Capitalization rate
Horizontal merger	Divestiture	Business valuation
Vertical merger	Leveraged buyout (LBO)	Business multipliers

TERM PAPERS AND PROJECTS

1. Examine the changes in AT&T after the breakup of the Bell Telephone System such as the creation of the "Baby Bells," AT&T's entrance into cable systems, and its decision to break itself into four entities. Is AT&T still a going concern? What has happened to the operating units that were AT&T?
2. Examine the financial statements of a company several years after it completed a significant merger or acquisition: Kellogg/Keebler, AOL/Time Warner, Daimler Benz/Chrysler are just a few examples. Try to determine whether the hoped-for efficiencies have been realized.
3. What happened to the proposed merger of Hewlett-Packard and Compaq? How well is the combined company competing in its market? What financial synergies have been realized? Are there still two personal computer lines offered by the company? What business units appear to be growing? Have any been divested?
4. Weyerhauser Inc. (a timber company headquartered in Washington State) made a hostile takeover bid for Williamette, another timber company headquartered in Portland, Oregon. Williamette did not want to sell and voted down the offer on several occasions. In late 2001, Williamette began talking to Georgia Pacific about acquiring certain of its timber and processing assets. Weyerhauser responded with "one last offer" in December 2001. In early 2002, Williamette finally relented and sold its assets to Weyerhauser. Examine the costs and profits in the timber industry, looking at Weyerhauser and some of its competitors. Remember that the time that it takes to grow marketable timber is measured in decades, not months. How would Weyerhauser have calculated the risks and benefits associated with its desired acquisition of Williamette? What synergies will be seen immediately? How many years should pass before the true effect of the merger is judged?

REVIEW QUESTIONS

1. Explain the difference between an acquisition and a merger.
2. What are the three categories of mergers? Give an example of each.
3. After an acquisition price has been established there are three basic methods a firm can use to acquire another. What are they?
4. Under what conditions would the Justice Department be involved in an acquisition or merger?

5. What is a divestiture? Why would a company divest itself of an operating unit?
6. What is a leveraged buyout?
7. What is a hostile takeover?
8. Give examples of four areas a business would want to analyze in planning assumptions.
9. What types of assets should be considered when merging with or acquiring a new company?
10. What financial statements are most revealing in a merger or acquisition?
11. What process would you use to evaluate the value of the assets you are acquiring?
12. What are two of the tools used in measuring the income a business produces? Why might a statement of cash flows be important?

CHAPTER

12

INVESTMENT OVERVIEW

LEARNING OBJECTIVES

1. Define who a lender might be.

2. Describe two ways to transfer funds to businesses.

3. Compare and contrast speculation and investment.

4. Describe the different types of investments available from a bank.

5. Discuss the services of an investment banker.

6. Describe the characteristics of equity.

7. Understand what commodities are and why one might invest in them.

8. Discuss hedging of currency as an investment strategy.

Throughout Part II we looked at individual companies and their need for financing to expand operations. One firm's need for cash provides another's investment opportunity, often with the help of a financial intermediary. Both individuals and companies invest excess cash in hopes of earning a positive rate of return within an acceptable range of risk. In Part III we will examine investment opportunities that result from the financing decisions of individual firms. This first chapter provides an overview of the types of investment vehicles that exist and their characteristics. Chapters 13 and 14 describe the types of bonds available and the mechanics of issuing, trading, and analyzing stock, respectively.

FINANCIAL INTERMEDIARIES

One of the main purposes of financial intermediaries is to transfer assets between lenders and borrowers. In this discussion, the term *lenders* is not synonymous with a bank or savings institution. **Lenders,** in this case, are those individuals or institutions that find themselves with an excess of cash. The process of transferring excess capital from one source to another results in a wide array of financial products that are created and administered by any number of financial intermediaries.

There are two basic methods for transferring funds to businesses. The first is a direct transfer from a lender to a borrower. This occurs when individuals invest in partnerships or buy securities (stocks or bonds) directly from the issuing company. Direct transfer can also be a privately funded mortgage contract or promissory note. Unless a single investor has enough excess cash to fund the needs of the borrower, this becomes a cumbersome process. The borrower needs to find enough investors with sufficient capital to fund the expansion. If the investment is in the form of a loan, the borrower would need to make payments to each of the lenders. The process becomes more complex as the amount of financing increases. For the investor, having a significant amount of capital invested in a single entity increases risk.

A second strategy for transferring funds is to pool the excess capital of many savers and transfer it to one or many borrowers. In this case, a financial intermediary is involved. For a fee the intermediary will ensure that the necessary funds are available, draw up terms and contracts, and arrange for the administration of the investment pool. The borrower has access to larger sums of money and individual lenders can diversify their risk.

SPECULATION VERSUS INVESTMENT

A **speculator** is someone who buys a security because of a belief that it will experience a significant increase in value during a very short time period, sometimes even in the space of hours. Speculators attempt to take advantage of pricing fluctuations that occur over short periods of time. The profit from speculation is not the long-term growth in value of the asset but capturing its short-term volatility.

An **investor** is someone who buys a security or puts money into a bank account, with the expectation that the value of the asset will increase over time and generate an appropriate rate of return. The time horizon can be as short as several months or as long as many years. There is less risk for an investor than a speculator because the expected time horizon is longer and the timing of the sale of the asset can be adjusted for short-term price fluctuations. If the buyer has researched the investment, it should be clear what the underlying risks are, what stream of income is likely to be produced over what time period, and what the risk-return relationship should be.

For most firms speculation is too risky. In Chapter 10, San Nicolas Manufacturing needed a warehouse to expand its operations. Until the firm had enough capital to make a purchase offer, the excess funds that it had accumulated might very well be invested in another asset such as a certificate of deposit or short-term corporate bond. But to speculate on the daily or hourly movements of stock prices or commodities might cost San Nicolas money they could ill afford to lose. With that in mind, we will be looking at investment opportunities rather than speculative ventures.

> ## Read More About It

Warren Buffett is one of the richest men in America. He is the Chairman and CEO of Berkshire Hathaway, a holding company for his investments. Berkshire Hathaway owns property and casualty insurance companies, shoe companies, jewelry stores, and the candy company, Sees. The company also has large stakes in corporations including American Express, Gillette, Coca-Cola, and Wells Fargo.

Buffett's strategy is to buy companies that have fundamental strength because of tight operating controls, strong brand loyalty, dominant market share, or clear strategic vision. Whether or not it is a direct quote, his investment philosophy is that if you aren't going to hold a stock for 10 years, you shouldn't buy it for 10 minutes. He is the antithesis of a day trader!

As chairman of Berkshire Hathaway, Buffett writes the annual letter to the shareholders. Each year the letter is a gem, explaining the thinking that preceded that year's acquisitions and is full of humor, often self-deprecating. The letter truly is written to the shareholders who are invited to the annual meeting that is held every April in Omaha, Nebraska. The meeting is actually a shareholder's *weekend* where Buffett and his vice chairman and partner, Charlie Munger, meet with shareholders and answer questions from 9:30 until 3:30 in the afternoon, with a short break for lunch! There are opportunities for shareholders to buy from vendors representing various divisions of the company and a chance to play bridge (Buffett's passion), backgammon, or baseball.

Even if you are not a shareholder (shares trade at thousands of dollars per share), you can learn from Buffett and enjoy the benefit of his musings by viewing the most recent annual report at www.berkshirehathaway.com.

SAVINGS ACCOUNTS

We have looked at financial intermediaries earlier in this book when we examined financial institutions such as banks, credit unions, and savings and loans. We have also mentioned several different kinds of accounts that are available to borrowers. For investors, banks provide several basic types of vehicles. Some of the accounts are insured up to $100,000 by the FDIC, which means that there is no risk for those funds. Although they are safe, they do not offer high returns.

Checking accounts, also called demand deposits, allow firms to withdraw money on demand (hence the name) but do not pay interest. Most depositors pay for the checking account either through monthly fees or by maintaining a minimum monthly balance. The use of a checking account is essential for a business, however, from the standpoint of maximizing the return on excess cash, it is not a good *investment* choice.

Some financial institutions offer interest-bearing checking accounts, also known as negotiable order of withdrawal (NOW) accounts. **NOW accounts** pay interest but often require a higher monthly balance. Most NOW accounts offer relatively low interest, so the firm would need to determine whether the interest earned on the NOW account was sufficient to justify leaving the minimum balance invested. If the firm could obtain a NOW account for the same minimum balance that a non-interest-bearing checking account required, the firm would have a net gain. However, this is still not a place to invest large sums of excess capital.

A **savings account,** also called a time deposit, offers a slightly higher rate of interest but does not allow you to write checks. The rate of interest is guaranteed for a specified period of time. In order to withdraw the money, you must go to the bank and, technically, a bank can require a grace period before it releases the money to you. For that reason, the savings account is less liquid and has a slightly higher risk. Although savings accounts offered by an insured financial institution are guaranteed by the FDIC, there is a risk factor involved in the time that it may take for you to convert the deposit into cash.

Money market deposit accounts (MMDAs) are an alternative to savings accounts offered by many banks. The interest rate for a money market account is not guaranteed; it varies with the current market rate of interest. In general, money market rates are slightly higher than the rate earned on savings accounts. Some money market deposit accounts allow you to write a limited number of checks per month, but they are not substitutes for checking accounts since the number of checks allowed is few, often three per month.

MMDAs often carry a higher monthly minimum balance than a regular savings account. If the balance falls below the minimum, service fees are charged. Depending on the level of cash that a firm wishes to keep, a money market deposit account may not be flexible enough, given its relatively low rate of interest.

A **certificate of deposit (CD)** is a savings account that pays a higher fixed rate of return for keeping your funds on deposit for a set period of time, ranging from 30 days to several years. In general, higher rates of return are offered for certificates of longer duration and often require a higher minimum investment. If general market interest rates fall during the CD's term, you still receive the agreed-upon amount. There is a risk that interest rates will rise during the time that the money is invested, in which case the investor has missed an opportunity to earn more. Money in a CD can be withdrawn before the term elapses, however, the investor will incur a penalty for early withdrawal. Rates on certificates of deposit vary from one institution to another and also vary from region to region. If you invest in a distant financial institution, you should also consider any fees that are imposed for wire transfer of money.

One of the benefits of a certificate of deposit is that it allows a firm to invest excess cash for a short period of time with no risk of capital loss. For a small business with relatively little excess cash, CDs can provide an important cash management tool.

In addition to the accounts that are insured, some banks offer money market mutual funds, which are different from money market deposit accounts. **Money market mutual funds** pool money from many individuals and firms and invest in very large, creditworthy notes (debt financing) issued by the government or large corporations. Because they hold the assets of many individual investors, the funds are able to buy notes in large denominations, which tend to carry higher rates of return. Mutual funds are run by investment professionals and carry an investment management fee. The investor earns interest, minus an administrative fee, which is posted to the account on a regular basis. Money market mutual funds may be issued through a bank and allow you check writing privileges, but they are not insured by the bank nor the FDIC. Banks that offer money market mutual funds are required to notify the investor that the funds carry an investment risk, including the possibility of lost principal.

DEBT AND ITS CHARACTERISTICS

Checking accounts yield no interest and savings accounts yield very little. During some periods, the interest earned on savings accounts has not kept pace with inflation. Money invested lost purchasing power even though it was earning interest. Some investors prefer to own the debt of another institution. We discuss different types of debt instruments and their valuation in Chapter 13. Here we will discuss why an investor might choose to hold debt and some of the intermediaries involved.

When an investor buys a **debt instrument,** he or she is buying a stream of interest payments as well as the promise to repay in full the principal that was borrowed. Debt obligations can be short term, such as commercial paper, or long-term obligations such as mortgages. Most debt instruments have a face value, (the amount that is being borrowed), a stated interest rate, and a maturity date. If the investor holds the debt from issue date to maturity, he or she will know precisely what the income per period will be as well as how the principal is being repaid—either in periodic increments such as a mortgage or in a lump sum at the end such as a bond. If the investor does not sell the debt before its maturity date, the risk of the investment is twofold: the investor has missed an opportunity to invest at a higher rate and the issuer will default. The interest rate on debt instruments varies depending on the length of the loan and the quality of the borrower. In many cases, the original owner of the debt can sell the investment if he or she needs cash, however, this not only involves transaction costs but the risk that another investor might not readily be found.

If the borrower does enter bankruptcy, creditors have an earlier claim on the firm's assets than equity holders (or shareholders). Debt, whether it is short or long term, is listed closer to the top of a balance sheet, illustrating its greater liquidity.

There are many places where a company or individual can buy debt. U. S. treasury bills, or T-bills, are issued by the federal government with maturities ranging from 3 months to 12 months. T-bills do not pay interest directly; instead, they are sold at a discount and pay face value at the maturity date.

Debt

An obligation that the firm assumes in order to fund its operations.

Debt instruments can be as simple as accounts payable, a form of trade credit, or as complex as sophisticated bond issues.

Most debt instruments include a promise to pay interest along with the repayment of principal.

Debt and its characteristics.

Knowing the term of the note and its implied interest rate, the investor can calculate the initial dollar cost of the T-bill. They can be purchased directly from the Federal Reserve Bank branches, however, the minimum denomination is $10,000, which effectively puts them out of reach of many small businesses.

Another debt instrument that is readily available but carries a smaller initial investment is a U.S. Series EE savings bond. The face value of Series EE bonds ranges from $50 to $10,000, but like T-bills, the bond is discounted so that it yields its face value at maturity. Savings bonds are very liquid. They can be redeemed at many banks before their maturity date for their current value, which would include any accrued interest.

Both of these forms of debt are issued by the U.S. government and are assumed to have no risk of default. An added benefit is that the income is exempt from state and local taxes.

Debt can be purchased directly from the issuer. Although we usually refer to it as accounts receivable, a retail jewelry store that finances its own sales is holding the debt of the issuer, in this case its customers. Manufactured home companies could set up finance subsidiaries and hold debt from customers. Collection agencies buy distressed debt at a discount and then attempt to turn it into cash. Private investors run advertisements in the classified section of the newspaper, offering to buy privately issued mortgages or promissory notes. However, most of the debt that companies buy is in the form of bonds issued by other companies or municipalities. They can buy directly from the corporation or through the intermediary of an investment banker.

INVESTMENT BANKERS

Unlike commercial banks, investment banks are not depository financial institutions. **Investment bankers** assist corporations in raising money by issuing securities, both bonds and stock. There are several steps in the process, which is supervised by the Securities and Exchange Commission.

First, the investment bank identifies a company that may want to sell securities and attempts to sell its services to that company. There are many investment bankers and they compete intensely for each bond or stock issue. Once an agreement is reached, the investment bank makes a detailed study of

---

The Many Roles of an Investment Banker

- Examine the creditworthiness of the client
- Determine the nature of financing: stock or bonds
- Determine an interest rate on bond issues
- Recommend an initial selling price
- Help find buyers for the securities
- Provide an estimate, or in some cases guarantee, of the net proceeds from the sale of the securities

---

These are among the many jobs of an investment banker. In light of some of the scandals of the last few years, the role of investment bankers is being reexamined.

the financial conditions of the client company. This report is called due diligence and is used to construct the company's offering.

Developing a new offering usually requires performing the following tasks:

- Determine whether the company should be issuing bonds, preferred stock, or common stock.
- If the company and its advisors decide on a bond issue, what is the prevailing interest rate for bonds of this quality?
- If the company is issuing stock, what is the initial public offering price? Will that yield the amount of capital that the firm needs?
- Select the features of the issue. Should the bond be callable or convertible? If the offerer is a municipality, will the bond be tax exempt? Will a certain number of bonds be retired each year or will the whole issue be redeemed at the maturity date?
- When will the issue be released? Whether it is a stock or bond issue, the timing of issue may be important. When does the client need the proceeds? Is there a competitive issue that will compete with this one and lower the proceeds?
- What fees will be charged for these services? Is the investment bank willing to underwrite the issue? Will they guarantee a threshold of capital for the issuer regardless of the volume of bonds or stock that is sold?

Once the type of offer has been determined, the investment banker draws up a prospectus. A **prospectus** clearly describes the issuer's finances and the risks associated with the offering. The material contained in the prospectus is strictly regulated by the Securities and Exchange Commission, if the securities are issued by a national company and expected to trade nationally. For a small company that does business in a limited area, the prospectus is usually supervised by the secretary of state. In every case, it is the responsibility of the issuer to fully disclose any facts that would materially affect the value of the investment.

Once the prospectus has been written, the investment banker attempts to find buyers for the securities. In some cases, major corporations such as insurance companies or large pension funds with significant sums of cash will buy large blocks of securities offerings. In other cases, the investment banker has to find a larger number of small investors. Sometimes the investment banker will underwrite the issues, which means to assume some of the risk of selling the securities. In an underwriting agreement, the investment bank agrees to purchase the securities at an agreed-upon price, called a *firm commitment price*. The issuing company has been assured of a certain level of funding and the investment banker is free to sell the issue at what is called the *offer price*. The difference between the firm commitment price and the offer price allows the investment bank to cover its costs. The issuing corporation has put the risk of not selling the securities onto the investment banker.

Bonds often have face value of $1,000 or $5,000, making them more affordable for a small investor. However, marketing costs are high enough that an investment bank is not likely to sell a single bond; they would prefer to sell large lots. Most small investors buy bonds from a local stockbroker, an investment firm, or from an on-line brokerage.

EQUITY AND ITS CHARACTERISTICS

When we talk about equity or equities, what springs to mind is the stock of publicly traded companies. But equity is any ownership portion of a company. Investing in a limited liability partnership is equity. Buying a membership in a grain co-op or even a local food co-op gives you equity rights.

In general, equity is the least liquid form of investment. If the equity is half of a partnership, it may be impossible to withdraw without disbanding the business. In a small corporation, there may be a limited market for shares. Equity holders have a residual claim on the assets of an organization; in case of bankruptcy or liquidation, they are the last to be reimbursed and have the highest risk of not being paid.

As owners, equity holders have the right to the profits of the organization. If all of the profits were paid out, however, the firm would not grow. For that reason, most balance sheets show several descriptions under the equity heading including retained earnings. Retained earnings are the profits that have been reinvested in the company. As such, they belong to the shareholders and are listed as part of the equity section. Retained earnings are not synonymous with cash, however. They may have been reinvested in the form of inventory or equipment or research and development.

There are many avenues by which a company can invest in equity. Some successful entrepreneurs provide seed capital to other small business start-ups. These individuals are often called angel investors. In return for an initial investment, the "angel" receives an ownership share of the company. The terms of the investment are negotiated between the two parties and are as individual as the parties who sign them.

Other forms of equity are the shares of public or privately held corporations. A privately held corporation does not sell stock to the public, however, it does have ownership shares. Many small biotechnology firms started as privately held corporations, funded initially by investment companies. Shares in the firm were assigned to the investment company as well as to the scientists who would provide the knowledge base for the firm. In order to reward employees for long hours and sometimes low pay, the companies issued stock. There was no outside market for the stock; it was hoped that these firms would be successful and would register with the Securities and Exchange Commission and go public

---

Equity

Equity represents an ownership interest in an organization.

Equity is the least liquid form of investment.

The issuer is not obligated to repurchase equity.

In theory, equity holders have rights to the profits from the business. In practice, those profits are often reinvested and do not get distributed to shareholders.

In case of bankruptcy, equity holders are paid only after the creditors' claims are settled.

Equity and its characteristics.

What do you *do* with retained earnings? When I was in accounting classes, it used to frustrate me no end to see all of that lovely money sitting in retained earnings! If only I could take it and *do something* with it!

Retained earnings and shareholders' equity describe money that is already, in a sense, spent. The liability and equity side of the balance sheet describes how the assets on the other side of the ledger have been funded (or financed). Sometimes there is debt associated with the assets, for example, the amount of inventory that is still not paid for because the accounts payable are not yet due. Or the office building that I bought that still has a mortgage lien against it. That form of financing is pretty clear.

During the course of the business year, the proceeds from the firm are reinvested in inventory or hiring personnel or purchasing trucks, warehouses, or computer systems. If the funds have been invested with no corresponding debt, the increase in business has been funded by the owners and will show up as part of retained earnings. The earnings have been retained and used to further the growth of the firm. Those profits have already been put to work.

At the end of the financial year, the accountant takes the net income figure (the amount of money earned by the firm, not paid out in dividends) and adds it to the retained earnings account. As a matter of fact, the money has already been added to the asset side of the balance sheet during the course of the year and the year-end entry merely squares the record.

I have to admit that I still don't like that retained earnings account! I'm not an accountant. There's a reason I teach finance instead of accounting—I look at the retained earnings entry and see a black hole. Lots of money just sort of gets posted to the account at the end of the fiscal year and I haven't seen it.

If only I could get my hands on that money. What I could do with it!

If and when they did, the stock would be valued by public markets and the original employees would be rewarded for the investment of their time and talent. A private investor who picked the "right" biotech company could have made money. There were, of course, high risks to this investment.

Many firms invest in equities through a stockbrokerage, whether with a personal stockbroker or through the use of electronic trading. We'll look at the mechanics of this in Chapter 14.

INVESTING AND SPECULATING IN OTHER ITEMS

Commodities are items such as corn, sugar, fuel oil, and metals like copper and zinc. Investors can buy a contract for the future delivery of a set amount of a certain quality of commodity through one of several commodities markets. The Chicago Board of Trade handles future contracts for agricultural products such as corn, wheat, and soybeans. The Coffee, Sugar, and Cocoa Exchange in New York City handles those items and others. Companies that use significant quantities of agricultural products invest in long-term commodities contracts in order to smooth the effect of fluctuating prices. Long before the coffee harvest is complete, companies that produce large quantities of ground coffee need to ensure that they will have the raw material they need at a predictable price. On any given day, a commodities trader might be able to get a contract for less than the long-term price that the company has locked in, however, the goal of the coffee roaster is not to always get the lowest price but to get the lowest consistent price for its raw materials inventory.

Some speculators brag about the money they have made trading commodities, and, indeed, the commodities market is an exciting spectacle. Traders wearing brightly colored coats wave frantically in order to attract the attention of whoever is buying or selling a contract that they want. Commodities trading is a specialized form of investment that would not be appropriate for a firm that needed a short-term working capital investment.

The New York Mercantile Exchange is the largest physical commodities trading center in the world. In the pits of the New York Merc, gold, copper, silver, gas, oil, sugar, cocoa, and other commodities are bought and sold. The New York Mercantile Exchange has a Web site (www.nymex.com) where they give information about trading commodities, buying a seat on the exchange, and visiting when you are in New York. You can also download educational publications including one titled "Why Do They Need to Yell and Make Funny Gestures?" That would be fun to read!

The Chicago Board of Trade (www.cbot.com) acts as the trading location for buyers and sellers of certain types of commodities. Many of the commodities traded at the Chicago Board of Trade are agricultural, which is logical when you think about where it is located—in the heart of the nation's farming regions. The Board of Trade provides a good introduction in their frequently asked questions section. One of the questions asked is: "How much of what is traded actually gets delivered?" The answer: typically 4% or less is actually delivered!

Like many of the contracts traded on the Board of Trade, trades made on the Chicago Mercantile Exchange (www.cme.com) are often not delivered. The Chicago Mercantile Exchange sells futures contracts, often called "derivatives" because their value derives from change in the value of the security that underlies the contract. For example, some of the futures contracts deal with foreign exchange products. Remember that we said that a firm engaged in foreign trade might want to **hedge** their exposure to foreign currency fluctuation by setting the value of a certain number of British pounds in terms of Korean won for delivery at a certain date. In that case, the firm would carry out the transfer of won for pounds. In other cases, traders will buy and sell future currency settlements if the price of the underlying currency fluctuates.

That's a complicated enough concept, however, what about buying "heating-degree days"? If you go to the Chicago Mercantile Exchange information page, they will explain that weather can destroy a company's

(Continued)

(Continued)

profits. We know that from experience. If a heat wave hits just as farmers need the rain to water new crops, the crops can be destroyed. A colder than expected winter will tax the production of power. California faced rolling power outages in the summer of 2001 when electrical generation capacity in the western region fell below demand. Prices soared and the two main power providers, Pacific Gas and Electric and Southern California Edison, were faced with huge power bills that they could not pass along to consumers. They would have liked to have put that risk off onto another party.

CME offers futures and options based on indices of heating and cooling degree-days in selected areas that experience significant weather-related risks. The derivatives allow firms to protect revenues in times of decreased demand or increased costs due to weather conditions. A full explanation of the weather futures and options can be found at the CME Web site under Weather Products.

To be honest, the idea of a degree-day strikes me as rather odd. I wonder if it is a "commodity" that will last for long or whether one of Chicago's famous gusts of wind will (figuratively) blow it off the Merc trading floor?

Real estate is a popular investment, both as undeveloped land and in the form of income-producing properties. A company might buy land with the expectation that it would be needed in the future. If the price of land were increasing at a higher rate than the cost of buying and holding the land, the company would be wise to buy the land. A company might also look at buying a warehouse or office building that could be leased until such time as the company needed the space if the revenue generated by the property met the company's discount rate. The warehouse or office building becomes a long-term asset whose present value can be calculated.

Real estate is also an attractive investment for a construction company. A residential builder might buy property in expectation that the growth of the market area would create future demand for homes. Having a parcel of land would allow the builder to create a housing development that could be built as a unified project. Working in one large tract would reduce the travel time for laborers and supervisors and create efficiencies. Buying property in advance of the region's population growth would be a logical long-term investment for this type of company.

In the News

Although our currency is not based on the gold standard, people still consider gold a valuable investment, especially when times are unsettled.

In November 2001, the World Gold Council ran an advertisement in the *Wall Street Journal*. The headline was "Be Prepared. Whatever the Forecast." The advertisement went on to say that gold was a "solid" investment alternative. (It *is* solid—when I was at the Federal Reserve

(Continued)

(Continued)

Bank of New York, our tour guide showed us dents in the concrete floor that were made when gold bars fell off the trolleys as they were being moved from one cage to the next!) The ad also states that gold helps stabilize an investment portfolio when "conventional" assets fluctuate.

There are several interesting facets to this advertisement. First, at the time that it ran, the country was in the first recession in a decade and was fighting a war against terrorism in Afghanistan. Consumer confidence had fallen to a very low level, and although the stock market had rebounded from its September lows, it was still volatile. For years, some of my students have told me that they would like to have a few gold coins hidden away somewhere, "just in case." I've always had my little bit of savings in the bank or an investment fund. It had never occurred to me to invest in gold, but it has always seemed safer and more secure to a certain group of my students than the mutual funds that we talk so easily about in class.

Second, the ad contrasts gold with "conventional" assets. What would conventional assets be? Historically speaking, it wasn't long ago that gold was a conventional asset for many people. Until recently, stocks and bonds were only for the wealthiest Americans. Mutual funds, which pool money and allow smaller investors to participate in the gains of the stock and bond markets, are relatively recent inventions. Land has always been an investment, but it is easier to sell precious metal than a small portion of a farm in eastern Oregon or central Nebraska.

Last, the ad says that you can sell gold coins and bars almost anywhere in the world. Gold can be exchanged for any form of currency, wherever you are. I could put gold coins in my suitcase and go!

For more information, the ad suggests that you contact the World Gold Council at www.gold.org.

Some investors prefer to buy commodities or items that they believe have intrinsic value. (Getty Images, Inc.)

TERMS TO KNOW

Lender	Money market	Debt instrument
Speculator	deposit account	Investment banker
Investor	(MMDA)	Prospectus
Negotiable order of	Certificate of deposit	Commodities
withdrawal (NOW)	(CD)	Hedging
account	Money market mutual	
Savings account	fund	

CLASS PROJECT: BUILD YOUR OWN MUTUAL FUND

Each student should choose one company that is publicly traded. The mutual fund will arbitrarily purchase 100 shares of the companies' stock for the beginning balance of the portfolio.

During the duration of the class, students should research their own company just as a mutual fund analyst would do. Analysis should include financial statement examination and an assessment of the strategic position of the company. News about each firm should be shared with the class.

The instructor or the class can decide whether they are willing to buy and sell shares from the fund during the academic period. If they decide to trade, they will have to determine criteria such as

- Will the person who first chose the stock have the right to veto its sale?
- Does there have to be a majority consensus to sell or replace a stock?
- Does the portfolio need to be balanced between certain types of stock holdings or can it be a mixed portfolio?

Keep track of the market as a whole during the time period that you have the mutual find. Assess how well your picks did versus the market.

Note: There are several on-line services that will track closing prices for a stock portfolio. Some of them have limits on the number of stocks that can be held in the portfolio. If that is the case, an excel spreadsheet can be created and each student be held responsible for monitoring their own stock price.

TERM PAPERS

1. Write a book report. There is a book whose title fascinates me, but that I have not read. It is *How Wall Street Captured a Nation: J. P. Morgan, Teddy Roosevelt, and the Panama Canal* by Ovidio Diaz Espino. Knowing that Teddy Roosevelt did not particularly like J. P. Morgan makes this title all the more intriguing!

2. Warren Buffet takes long-term stakes in companies. Compare his views on the economy (as found in his letter to the shareholders of Berkshire Hathaway) with those of the chairman of the Federal Reserve System.

3. Work with an investment advisor to set up a savings and investment plan given your age, financial situation, and savings goals. Evaluate the

different investment options available to you and discuss the risks and
potential rewards of several strategies.

4. Research the types of commodities that can be bought and sold on the different exchanges. Watch price fluctuations and determine what underlies
the volatility. Determine which companies might be interested in hedging
rather than speculating in these futures.

REVIEW QUESTIONS

1. Describe the two methods of transferring funds to businesses.
2. Differentiate between speculation and investing.
3. What is the difference between a NOW account and a checking account?
4. How are money market deposit accounts different from money market
   mutual fund accounts?
5. Why would a CD be an important cash management tool for small businesses?
6. What is a debt instrument? Give an example of a short-term debt instrument and a long-term debt instrument.
7. How do investment banks differ from commercial banks?
8. How does an investment bank operate?
9. What is meant by equity?
10. What are commodities? Why can they be risky as an investment?

13 TYPES OF BONDS AND THEIR VALUATION

LEARNING OBJECTIVES

1. Describe what form of financing is represented by bonds.
2. Describe the information necessary on a bond and what it means.
3. Discuss the types of covenants that a bond might carry.
4. Explain the meaning of bond ratings.
5. Describe the types of risk associated with owning bonds.
6. Name the most common types of bonds.
7. Discuss the difference between a revenue bond and a general obligation bond.
8. Describe alternative ways of paying back a bond issue.
9. Calculate the price you should be willing to pay for a bond.
10. Discuss why bonds would trade at a discount or a premium.
11. Calculate the current yield for a bond.

In Chapter 12 we looked at investment philosophies and the general characteristics of differing types of investment vehicles. In this chapter we will look specifically at the types of bonds available and the method of valuing them.

WHAT ARE BONDS?

Bonds are a form of long-term debt. They are liabilities that carry a specified **principal value,** usually $1,000 or $5,000, and a maturity date by which the principal must be repaid. The principal is also referred to as **face value,** the value printed on the face of the bond, or **par value.** The bond's price is quoted as a percentage of its par value. For example, if the bond trades at 97½

Stocks and bonds are types of securities. Bonds are specifically a form of debt which must be repaid. (Getty Images, Inc.)

it is worth 97.5% of the face value. For a $1,000 bond, that would be $975. For a $5,000 bond, the price would be $4,875. Quoting value in relationship to the par value allows buyers to see whether the bond is selling at a premium or a discount.

Bond owners receive interest that is stated on the face of the bond. Interest is also referred to as yield and is expressed in one of two ways: current yield or yield to **maturity,** both of which are explained later in the chapter. Many years ago, bonds were issued with coupons that the bondholder cut from the bond and redeemed for the interest. If the coupon was not cut and taken to the authorized agent, the interest went unpaid. Interest on bonds does not compound, so a delay in redeeming the coupon could be costly. Interest is expressed as simple annual interest and most often disbursed in semiannual payments. Today, many bondholders do not even take physical possession of the bond, let alone cut coupons, however, you will still hear the interest rate referred to as a **"coupon rate."**

BOND TERMS AND CONDITIONS

Each debt instrument has terms that the debtor must meet. The terms, also called **covenants,** are stated in a legal document called an indenture and vary based on the financial condition of the borrower. One of the most common requirements is collateralization of the debt, that is, pledging tangible assets in order to secure the loan. For example, a mortgage is collateralized by the land or property that was purchased with the loan. If the borrower is unable to meet the terms of the loan, it is said to be in default and the lender can seize the property and sell it to recoup the principal, unpaid interest, and administrative costs incurred.

Covenants are designed to protect the bondholders from risk that the company could incur after the bonds are issued. Systemic risk cannot be averted but financial risk can be mitigated through use of restrictions on the future financial behavior of the company. Following are some examples of covenants that bondholders can request:

- Limits on dividend payments or stock buybacks if the cash outflow would reduce the firm's ability to make future principal and interest payments
- Limits on the issuance of additional debt
- The requirement to periodically retire portions of the debt
- A restriction on issuing lower-cost bonds to retire the current issue
- A description of the minimum financial ratios the firm must maintain

This list is by no means exhaustive but serves to illustrate the type of protection investors might seek.

The bond is said to be in default if the issuer does not make the required interest or principal payment, or if it violates one of the covenants spelled out in the indenture. If the issuer defaults, the indenture states what actions the investors can take.

While it is important to be aware of the terms of the bond issue and monitor the performance of the company, in practical terms it is difficult for the buyers to exercise that type of constant oversight. For that reason, a trustee is appointed for each publicly held bond. The trustee's job is to see that the terms of the indenture are met and to work with the company in cases where intervention is needed. Large banks often act as trustees for major corporate bond issues.

Chapter 2 examined the different types of risk that occur. Four types are of particular importance to this discussion: the risk of default, the risk that the price of the bond will decline, the risk that inflation will increase, and the risk that the company will call the bond before maturity.

Two rating services, Moody's and Standard & Poor's, have developed rating charts that describe the level of risk for each bond issue. High-quality debt, which has the lowest risk of default, receives a triple A rating (AAA), while the lowest-quality debt receives lower ratings. The two charts have slight variations in lettering but both serve the bond buyer by evaluating risk.

The rating of the bond issue has a significant impact on its original offering terms, as well as the subsequent resale value of the debt. Even companies that have very poor financial prospects can issue bonds, however, they will be required to meet stricter covenants and pay higher interest rates to compensate the buyers for the increased possibility of default. They may also find it more difficult to sell the initial offering since some investors will not purchase bonds that carry a low credit rating. The rating on a bond issue can change over the life of the bond if there are changes in the business or financial risk of the company. For example, the difference between an AA rating and an A rating is the possibility that future payments may be affected by adverse effects. Sales at an automotive company are susceptible to cyclical downturns in the economy. If consumer confidence falls, unemployment rises, and automobile sales decrease markedly, the credit rating of the company's bonds will be lowered even if the company has been making the required payments on time and in full. The ratings reflect not just current behavior but future expectations, especially for bonds that still have a long time until maturity.

Bond rating chart

S&P	Interpretation	Moody's	Interpretation
AAA	Highest rating	Aaa	Prime quality
AA	Very strong capacity to pay	Aa	High-grade
A	Strong capacity to pay; somewhat susceptible to changing business conditions	A	Upper-medium grade
BBB	More susceptible than A rated bonds	Baa	Medium grade
BB	Somewhat speculative	Ba	Somewhat speculative
B	Speculative	B	Speculative
CCC	Vulnerable to nonpayment	Caa	Poor standing; may be in default
CC	Highly vulnerable to nonpayment	Ca	Highly speculative; often in default
C	Bankruptcy petition filed or similar action taken	C	Lowest rated; extremely poor chance of ever attaining real investment standing
D	In default		

Standard and Poor's (S&P) and Moody's are agencies that rate the creditworthiness of firms. Although the ratings differ somewhat in appearance, the underlying rating criteria are strongly related.

In the News

AT&T issued $10.09 billion of bonds in November 2001, even though bond buyers were worried about the company's prospects. Bond rating agencies had downgraded the company in the weeks before the offering, worried about the debt load that the company already carried.

In order to successfully sell its bonds, the company had to offer enticing premiums. The 5-year bonds sold with an interest rate of 6.504%, which was 2.58% above the 5-year treasury bonds. Ten-year bonds sold for 7.35%, or 2.78% above the treasury bills. The 30-year AT&T bonds sold with a coupon rate of 8.096%, or 2.95% higher than the treasury bonds. Note that the premium continues to increase the further out the AT&T bonds are sold. The higher interest rate on the longer-term bonds demonstrates the risk inherent in lengthening the time until maturity. The interest rate also takes into account concerns that AT&T will not be able to service the debt.

Source: "AT&T sells $10.09 Billion of Corporate Bonds as Investors Line Up, Lured by Enticing Yields," *Wall Street Journal*, November 16, 2001, by Gregory Zuckerman and Richard A. Bravo.

Debt also carries the risk of price fluctuations if the holder sells the debt before maturity. The price of the bond can be affected by a reduction in the quality of the bond, but it is also subject to market conditions. Bonds carry a fixed interest rate. If market interest rates increase, the value of the bond will decrease since the investor can now get a similarly risky investment at a higher rate of return. The price of the bond on the secondary market will fall until it reaches a point that the interest earned on the capital invested matches the prevailing market interest rate. By contrast, when interest rates fall, as happened in early 2001 when the Federal Reserve attempted to stimulate the economy and stave off recession, the price of existing bonds will rise because investors cannot get the same rate of return as they did previously. The closer the bond is to maturity, the less its price will fluctuate because the bondholder will soon be receiving the principal, which must be repaid in full.

The third risk is that **inflation** will occur during the life of the bond and decrease the purchasing power of the interest earned and the principal repayment. If investors believe that inflation will be a factor during the life of the bond, they will add a premium for the length of the bond and their perception of the inflation risk.

Call risk occurs when a company reserves the right to repurchase bonds at specific intervals for a specific price. The company is attempting to manage its interest expenses by giving itself the option of retiring high interest bonds and replacing them with lower interest debt. The issuer benefits from the callable bond; the buyer incurs the risk. If the bond carries a call provision, it should also carry a higher rate of interest in order to offset call risk.

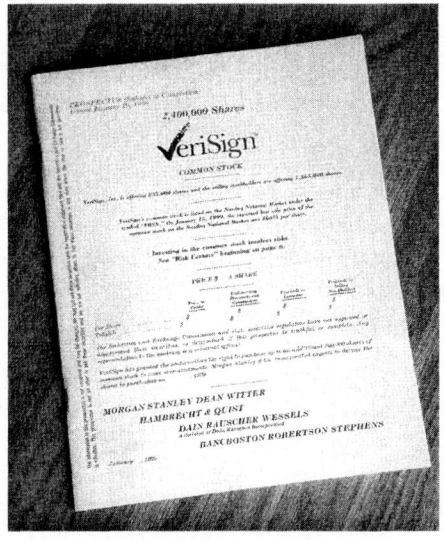

The prospectus outlines the rights and responsibilities of both borrower (the issuer of the bond) and the lender (the bond holder). (PhotoEdit)

COMMON TYPES OF BONDS

There are many types of corporate bonds and each has characteristics that differentiate it from the others. While each company's bonds are rated based on the underlying business and financial risk associated with the company, the type of bond also figures into the risk calculation.

Secured bonds are backed by company-owned property. Mortgages are perhaps the most familiar type of secured bond and are backed by real estate assets. Other forms of collateral depend on the nature of the business that is issuing them. An airline company would have bonds backed by its airplanes, a shipping company could collateralize its containers, manufacturers could issue bonds tied to equipment, and a retailer could pledge accounts receivable from its credit card operation. If the firm defaults on its bond, the bondholders, represented by the trustee, could seize the asset and sell it to settle the debt. They could also take possession of the asset and put it to use. In the case of a warehouse, the bondholders could accept the property and become the lessor. While collateralized bonds are the least risky, the bondholders do not want to take possession of the asset. The investors choose bonds because they want to earn the interest, not because they want to operate an airline or shipping company. In addition, if the bondholders were forced to sell the underlying asset, they might receive liquidation value rather than market value, and there is no guarantee that the sale would cover the company's indebtedness. Under a worst case scenario, the collateralized bonds of a bankrupt firm will be the first ones paid. For that reason, they are the safest and carry the lowest interest rate of the bonds issued by the firm.

Debentures are unsecured long-term bonds of a corporation. Debentures are more risky than secured debt because, in the case of liquidation, debentures are paid after the secured bondholders have been satisfied. Firms with more than one set of debentures often describe the hierarchy of payment in the indenture that accompanies the bond issue. Bonds that are lower in the payment hierarchy are called subordinated debentures, and they increase in risk as their position on the balance sheet descends. Because of the increased risk subordinated debentures require that the firm pay a higher rate of interest.

In spite of the higher interest rate, debentures may be preferred to secured debt because they do not encumber the underlying asset. Suppose that San Nicolas Manufacturing buys the property and warehouse that they were considering in Chapter 10, financing it with a mortgage bond. If San Nicolas sells the warehouse, their first responsibility is to settle with the mortgage bond holders, leaving them with less cash. If they have sold the property with the intention of buying a parcel that better suits their needs, they will need to reapply for financing and will run the risk that the new bond will carry a higher rate of interest than the previous one. Additionally, if there is a lag between the sale of the first piece of property and the purchase of the second, San Nicolas loses the opportunity to invest the entire proceeds in an interest-bearing account. The secured debt carries a lower interest rate but allows the firm less flexibility.

One strategy that a firm can use to lower the interest on its subordinated debentures is to add a convertibility feature. **Convertible bonds** are technically debt; that is, they have a stated maturity value and coupon rate, but they offer the investor the opportunity to convert the debt to equity at stated periods of time. For example, Green Manufacturing could offer a $1,000, 10-year bond that was convertible into 20 shares of common stock during a 2 month window during the fifth year. The value of this bond would depend on the investors' assessment of Green Manufacturing's risk profile as well as expectations that the common stock value would increase. The convertible bond allows the bondholder two earning opportunities. If the common stock is worth $10 on the conversion date, the bondholder would keep the bond rather than exchange it since the conversion value is $200 (20 shares at $10 apiece). The company must continue to honor the bond, paying the periodic interest and retiring it at full face value upon maturity. However, if the stock value has increased to $75 per share, the bondholder would convert the $1,000 bond into $1,500 (20 shares at $75) of common stock. The principal would have increased by 50%, and the bondholder would also have received 5 years of interest at the stated interest rate.

The firm benefits from the conversion feature because convertible bonds carry a lower rate of interest than subordinated bonds without the conversion feature. The conversion rate is set above the price of common stock at the issuing date so that if the company has to redeem the bond for shares, it issues fewer than it would have on the origination date. The company's management hopes that the stock price appreciates enough that the bondholders do convert to stock. Bonds require that the company not only pay interest but also redeem the bond for cash upon maturity. If the stock price appreciates, a long-term liability is converted to equity. The bondholder receives cash value for the shares from a third-party investor, not the corporation. On the balance sheet, the value of the bond has moved from liability to equity, which reduces the debt-to-equity ratio. Once the firm has converted the bond, it has increased its ability to issue new debt and maintain a favorable amount of leverage.

MUNICIPAL BONDS

When voters approve a tax levy to fund local schools, a library, or airport improvements, they have authorized their local taxing authority to issue one of many types of municipal bonds. **Municipal bonds** are issued by states, counties, cities, and authorized public authorities such as school boards, highway commissions, and port districts. The funds appropriated by the citizens will be paid over a period of time as stated in the levy proposal, but it allows the agency to sell bonds immediately to fund the covered projects. Municipal bonds are able to offer a lower rate of interest than corporate bonds because the interest income is exempt from federal income taxes. In addition, if you buy a municipal bond issued by the city or state in which you live, it is exempt from city and state taxes as well. The purchase of municipal bonds is often promoted to individuals who pay high marginal tax rates, especially those in locations that have city, state, and federal income tax.

There are two types of municipal bonds: general obligation and revenue bonds. **General obligation bonds** are backed by the full faith and credit of the issuer. Because it is assumed that the municipality is able to raise taxes as needed, the bond is backed by tax revenue, often property taxes. **Revenue bonds** derive their funds from the income stream produced by the funded asset. For example, voters were asked to approve revenue bonds for a swimming pool in a neighboring community. The principal and interest payments would come from the receipts earned each summer minus the cost of operating the facility.

> ---⟨ **Now You Know** ⟩---
>
> I've always wondered how the local school board sells its bonds. Who buys them? Through what selling agent? I know I pay taxes to fund the "bond issues," but who is getting that money?
>
> *The Olympian* (Olympia, Washington) ran an advertisement on Sunday, November 11, 2001, sponsored by the City of Tacoma Finance Department. They were offering the opportunity to purchase tax-free minibonds with a $1,000 face value. Investors could purchase up to $10,000 and the proceeds would go to fund environmental services. The interest rate was not stated in the newspaper ad, although it did say that interest would be paid twice annually beginning on June 1, 2002.
>
> While this may not be the most traditional way to sell bonds, you could have contacted the City of Tacoma Finance Department who would have sent you a prospectus detailing the costs, benefits, and risks of these municipal bonds. But the time for buying them was short: November 5–16, 2001.

Because the revenue bond has a stated interest rate and maturity date (as all bonds do), a revenue shortfall could cause the issuer to default.

Although municipal bonds are issued by a government entity, they are not risk-free. Unlike the federal government, local municipalities do not have the authority to print or issue money. If the tax or revenue receipts are not sufficient to repay the bond, it will default. Although defaults are uncommon, they do occur.

One of the difficulties with municipal bonds is the illiquid nature of the investment. Although there is an active secondary market for corporate bonds, for a small town or school district there may not be a large pool of investors.

INTEREST RATES AND MATURITY VALUES

All bonds carry a stated interest rate and a **maturity value.** A standard bond promises that in return for lending the face value, the bondholder will receive semiannual interest payments and a return of the principal at maturity. Zero coupon bonds carry a stated interest rate but use it to discount the maturity value thus determining the present value of the bond. Interest accrues to the bond during its life, and the full face value, which is paid at the maturity date, is the original loan plus the value of the accrued interest. Zero-coupon bonds are an attractive investment for people who want a specific amount of capital at a given point in time but do not need the periodic interest income. Zero-coupon bonds can be issued by corporations, municipalities, or the federal government. For the issuer, the initial cash inflow from a $1,000,000 zero-coupon bond issued at its discounted value is less than the same issue of interest-bearing bonds. The issuer would need to decide whether the working capital benefits of not having to pay periodic interest would be outweighed by the lower level of capital infusion into the firm. The buyer would have to decide if it were worth forgoing the cash interest payments in order to take advantage of lower out-of-pocket investment costs.

JUNK BONDS

Entire books have been written about junk bonds, also known as high-yield securities. "Junk" is the name given to bonds that are rated less than investment grade, which is below BBB or Baa. Early junk bonds were also called "fallen angels," which in some ways describes their fate. The bonds were originally issued by companies with sound financial situations and carried an investment grade rating. However, due to the financial or business misfortunes that had befallen the issuer, the bonds had become highly speculative or had technically defaulted. As the companies' fortunes declined, the market value of their bonds also decreased to the point that they traded significantly below face value. The market value was minimal, which made them worth about as much as junk, hence the name.

Because of their riskier profile, junk bonds must pay higher interest than safer bonds. The higher interest rate that the "fallen angels" earned was a result of the loss that original bondholders incurred when they sold the bond. If you had invested in a 10-year, 10%, $1,000 bond that was rated AA upon origination, continued to hold the bond when it fell to B, and were lucky enough to get all of your interest and principal at the end of 10 years, you would have received the promised 10% return on your original investment. If you were uncomfortable with the deteriorating financial picture and sold the bond, the subsequent investor would not have been willing to pay the $1,000 par value because the risk demanded a higher return. Since the semiannual interest payment was fixed at $50 (10% × 1,000 × ½), the second investor would bid down the price until it reached a level where the $50 semiannual interest payment equaled perhaps 13% or 14% of the newly determined market price. In the process, the seller lost part of his or her principal.

In the News

Just because a company has declared bankruptcy does not mean that its bondholders will go unpaid and its bonds become junk. Regal Cinemas, Inc., is the largest movie theater chain in America. On October 11, 2001, Regal filed bankruptcy, but it went into court with a reorganization plan that was backed by 95% of its creditors.

The reorganization was expected to take 3 months at the most. Between 20 and 25 older theaters would be closed, leaving the firm with more than 300 locations.

Creditors were in favor of the reorganization plan because they will receive full payment of their accounts. The only parties that will lose money are the leveraged buyout firms of Kohlberg Kravis Roberts & Co., and Hicks, Muse, Tate & Furst, Inc., who purchased the firm for $1 billion in a leveraged buyout. Under the reorganization they will emerge with nothing.

Source: The Olympian, Sunday, October 13, 2001, by Olympian Staff, News Services.

In the 1980s, a new type of junk bond emerged in response to the financing needs of leveraged buyout groups and hostile takeover participants. A prevalent strategy was to use massive amounts of debt in order to buy out the existing shareholders and obtain control of the corporation. The level of debt was so high in proportion to the equity that was created in the transaction that there was no possible rating for these bonds other than "speculative." Of course, each management group believed that it could quickly sell nonperforming assets to pay down debt, reduce operating expenses to generate increasing cash flows, and streamline formerly moribund organizations, turning them into dynamos that would attract a whole new infusion of equity capital with which to retire even more of the debt. Sometimes it worked. However, there were plenty of examples of LBOs and takeovers that ended in bankruptcy.

The structure of this new junk bond differed from the original "fallen angels" in that it had never been a high-quality issue. The interest rate on its face was designed to compensate investors for the risks inherent in the financing strategy.

Junk bonds have always been a speculative investment, whether they have lost credit standing or whether they were originally issued as high-yield securities. Investors who hold high-yield bonds have to assume that some will default. Each company that issues them doesn't plan to be the one that does.

In the News

The value of distressed debt that is available for sale rose dramatically between 1998 and the first quarter of 2001. Less than $150 billion of debt was available for sale in 1998. In the first quarter of 2001 alone, there was nearly $600 billion of defaulted and downgraded debt on the market.

Who would buy it? *Business Week* described three types of vultures: the Baron Vultures, Fast-Buck Vultures, and Last-Hope Vultures.

The Baron Vultures hope to pick up distressed debt and swap it for equity. These investors want the assets of the company that is in disarray in order to build a larger organization.

Fast-Buck Vultures buy troubled loans of debt-plagued companies at a sizeable discount. Most of the Fast-Buck Vultures want senior debt so that in any reorganization their claim will be the first paid. More senior debt also allows the investor to have a say in how the reorganization will progress. Although this group is called "Fast-Buck," there is an incredible commitment of time to negotiate the price that will eventually be paid on the defaulted bonds. Even with time and energy committed to the reorganization process, the strategy has risks and even senior bonds do default.

The Last-Hope Vultures are usually mutual funds or investment banks that originally purchased bonds at par and have seen them deteriorate to junk status. These "vultures" are not buying bonds; they already own them. Their strategy is to attempt to intervene in the bankrupt organization and enforce some sort of discipline on the company to stem future losses.

Source: "The Return of the Wall Street Vulture," *Business Week,* September 10, 2001, by Emily Thornton in New York, with Christopher Palmeri in Los Angeles and Mara De Hovanesian and Susan Rutledge in New York.

ISSUING BONDS

In Chapter 12 we talked in general about the services that an investment banker provides. When a company is issuing bonds, they will turn to an investment banker to facilitate the process. Investment bankers charge fees for the various services that they provide to companies during the financing process. The level of fees will depend on the complexity of the bond offering and the number of services the issuer requires. Fees and services provided are negotiable, so the company should check with different bankers before settling on one. As we look at issuing bonds in this section, we will ignore the investment banking fees and other transaction costs associated with the primary bond offering. From the practical standpoint, this perspective is unrealistic because the fees can be significant. However, since the fees and services are so variable even for the same company at different times, we will simply restate the fact that they exist and the firm should negotiate terms and conditions.

The firm should determine how much capital they would like to generate with the bond issue and the cost of borrowing. The bond issue can be tested for its effect on the balance sheet and income statement by creating pro forma financial statements and changing the interest rate and principal assumptions for the bond. The firm will also need to decide if it will retire a certain portion of the bond issue each year, or whether it plans to repay the entire principal at the maturity date. If the firm retires debt at a steady pace, it will lose the use of the money it has borrowed. However, if interest rates fall during the life of the bond, the firm can issue new debt at a lower rate. Retiring debt also releases the firm from the obligation to pay interest on the bonds that no longer exist. The firm has to weigh the costs of each of these choices.

Even if the firm plans to keep the principal for the duration of the bond's life, it will still have to plan for the eventual retirement of debt. Most firms would prefer to set up a disciplined savings plan in anticipation of the maturity date rather than having to use a substantial portion of cash in the maturity year. The firm can also take advantage of the effects of compound interest by setting up a sinking fund to which it makes regular contributions. However, the bond repayment assumptions will affect the amount of money invested in the sinking fund.

Green Manufacturing is planning to issue $100,000 of debentures with a coupon rate of 10% and maturity value of 10 years in order to expand its operations. Green plans to spend part of the issue's proceeds to buy new equipment, but does not want to secure the bond to the equipment because it feels that an unsecured issue gives more flexibility. Green's credit rating is good, so it has confidence that the bond will sell. Nan Green, the company's treasurer, has developed two alternatives for paying back the interest and principal.

The first option is to repay the entire amount of principal on the maturity date. The company would have use of the $100,000 for a full 10 years but would also have to pay interest to the bondholders for that time. Nan has proposed setting up a sinking fund to which the company would contribute every year in anticipation of the debt repayment. The future value of the sinking fund is predicated on needing $100,000 in 10 ten years. Nan estimates that the sinking fund could be invested to earn an 8% return.

The second option that Nan has looked at is a schedule that would call for the repayment of the bond in five equal installments of $20,000 beginning at the end of the second year. In this case, the interest owed would decrease based on the amount of the bond issue still outstanding. Nan has assumed that the sinking fund contributions should fund the 2-year, $20,000 debt repayment cycle with no additional use of company funds. At the end of each 2-year cycle the beginning balance of the sinking fund would be zero, but it would be funded to meet a lower payout. The fund would still return 8%.

Even with the assumptions Nan has made, there are many questions about each of the alternatives. However, to start a discussion, Nan has developed the following spreadsheet that demonstrates the present value of each set of assumptions. The present value is calculated at 10% because Nan is assuming that that is the firm's cost of capital. Note that they can invest funds at less than the cost to borrow or use them. That is not an inconsistent assumption.

GREEN MANUFACTURING: BOND RETIREMENT CALCULATIONS

	Option 1: Retire all debt at the end of 10 years			Option 2: Retire 20% of debt per year		
Assumptions:						
Bond's coupon rate	10%			10%		
FV of sinking fund	$100,000			$20,000		
Earnings on sinking fund	8%			8%		
Firm's cost of capital	10%			10%		
	Outstanding principal	Interest on debt	Sinking fund payment to retire debt	Outstanding principal	Interest on debt	Sinking fund payment to retire debt
Year 1	$100,000	$10,000	$6,903	$100,000	$10,000	$9,615
Year 2	$100,000	$10,000	$6,903	$100,000	$10,000	$9,615
Year 3	$100,000	$10,000	$6,903	$80,000	$8,000	$9,615
Year 4	$100,000	$10,000	$6,903	$80,000	$8,000	$9,615
Year 5	$100,000	$10,000	$6,903	$60,000	$6,000	$9,615
Year 6	$100,000	$10,000	$6,903	$60,000	$6,000	$9,615
Year 7	$100,000	$10,000	$6,903	$40,000	$4,000	$9,615
Year 8	$100,000	$10,000	$6,903	$40,000	$4,000	$9,615
Year 9	$100,000	$10,000	$6,903	$20,000	$2,000	$9,615
Year 10	$100,000	$10,000	$6,903	$20,000	$2,000	$9,615
PV@8%		$61,446	$42,415		$41,479	$59,082
Total PV		$103,861			$100,562	

Note the effect of some of Nan's assumptions: Option 1 calls for repayment at the end of the life of the bond. Interest remains constant at $10,000 per year, reflecting the 10% coupon and full value of the principal outstanding. The present value of interest for this option is higher because the interest does not decrease over time. However, the sinking fund contribution is far lower, even though the future value of the sinking fund is five times that of Option 2. The sinking fund payment shows the value of compound interest. Payments made in the first 2 years will earn interest for 7 or 8 years. Using the rule of 72, the value of the first 2 years' payments will more than double during the life of the sinking fund. Option 2 depletes the fund every 2 years. The first 2 years' payments will not have to cover a lower payment but also will not have the chance to accrue a sizeable amount of interest earnings.

The difference between the present value of the two options is relatively small. In the absence of any other information, Nan should recommend that the firm follow the repayment plan outlined in Option 2 since it has the lowest present value. However, there are issues that have not yet been addressed by her analysis.

- Taxes. Interest payments to bondholders reduce taxable income and interest earned on the sinking increases taxable income. Nan will have to adjust the sinking fund payments to reflect the taxes paid on earnings. She will also be able to adjust the interest payments to reflect their true cost to the firm (the interest payments are an outflow, but the taxes not paid as a result of interest expense are considered a cash inflow).
- The use of the money. Green Manufacturing is borrowing money to expand its operations. Does it believe that the cash generated by the business expansion will be sufficient to meet working capital needs and allow it to repay the bond as quickly as Option 2 assumes?
- The overall financing of the firm. The bond that Green Manufacturing issues is not the only form of debt that it has on the balance sheet, and the costs and benefits of the different forms need to be seen in combination. If repaying the bond results in Green having to increase short-term borrowing, the interest cost of short-term loans might exceed the interest rate on the bond, making Option 2 more expensive overall.
- The risk profile of the company or industry. In order to obtain a more favorable coupon rate, Green might have to agree to retire the debt at regular intervals. Retiring the principal in stages reduces the risk of the overall issue. Nan's analysis might include a higher rate for Option 1, which in turn would affect its present value.
- The stability of future interest rates. Green is obligating itself to pay 10% for the next 10 years and has estimated that it can earn 8% on the sinking fund. If interest rates fall and Green has not locked in the 8% rate, it will have to increase sinking fund payments to offset the lower interest earnings. Of course, if interest rates rise, Green will earn more on the sinking fund investment. In addition, Green may be able to buy the bonds in the secondary market for less than face value, thus lowering its cash outflow.

Clearly, Green Manufacturing has many decisions relating to the issue of this bond that only they can answer. Present value analysis provides a starting point for evaluating the effect of other assumptions.

BUYING A BOND

If a bond carries the appropriate level of interest based on its risk, it should always sell at par value regardless of where in its life cycle the investor purchases it. While this may not seem intuitive, we will look at several time horizons in order to prove the statement. The key to the explanation returns us to the time value of money.

Green Manufacturing is issuing a 10-year, 10% debenture in $1,000 denominations. Because interest is paid on the face or par value of the bond, the investor can expect to receive $100 in interest per year. To simplify the calculations, we will assume that interest is paid once per year at the end of the year. We could assume that the interest was paid semiannually, in which case the investor would receive $50 per period (10% × $1,000/2). The result would remain the same. Assuming the investor purchased the bond on its issue date, here is the present value of all future cash flows from the bond:

	Interest	PV @ 10%	PV
Year 1	$ 100.00	0.909091	$ 90.91
Year 2	$ 100.00	0.826446	$ 82.64
Year 3	$ 100.00	0.751315	$ 75.13
Year 4	$ 100.00	0.683013	$ 68.30
Year 5	$ 100.00	0.620921	$ 62.09
Year 6	$ 100.00	0.564474	$ 56.45
Year 7	$ 100.00	0.513158	$ 51.32
Year 8	$ 100.00	0.466507	$ 46.65
Year 9	$ 100.00	0.424098	$ 42.41
Year 10	$ 100.00	0.385543	$ 38.55
Maturity value	$1,000.00	0.385543	$ 385.54
Present value of cash flows			$1,000.00

The present value of the principal repayment is less than $400. Remember that the purpose of present value analysis is to determine what you would be willing to pay today for money received in the future. If the investor had $385.54 today and could invest for 10 years at 10%, the principal would be worth $1,000. The difference between $385.54 and the $1,000 price the investor will pay for this bond is the value of the interest received over the course of 10 years.

The closer the bond comes to maturity, the more the investor would be willing to pay for the lump sum payment. Assume that the 10% coupon rate is still valid, given the risk. If the investor bought Green Manufacturing's bond after 6 years had passed, the present value of the $1,000 principal would be $683.01, much higher than it was when the bond was issued. If the investor put

How a Bond is Valued

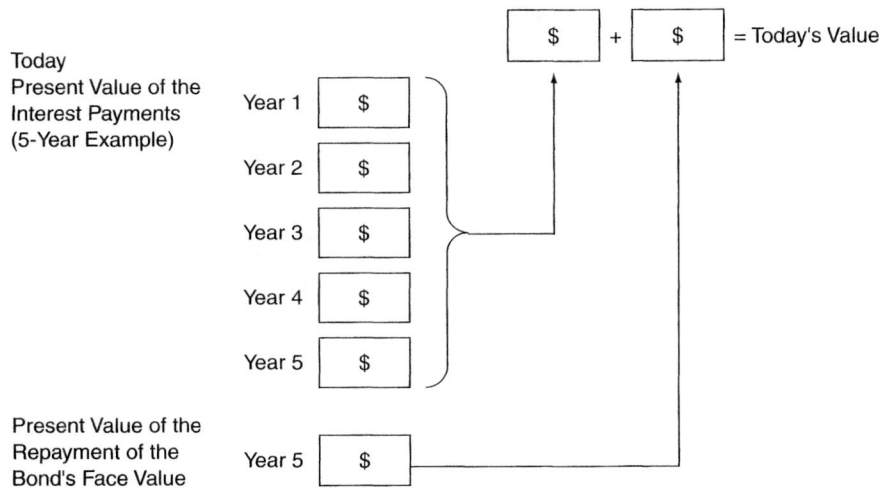

A bond is priced such that the present value of the interest earnings and the present value of the principal repayment accurately reflect the risk of the security and existing economic conditions.

that sum into a certificate of deposit that yielded 10%, he or she would have $1,000 at the end of 4 years, which is what the bond has remaining before repayment. There will be only 4 years' worth of interest payments, so the proportion of par value that is attributable to interest has decreased as the present value of the principal increases.

	Interest	*PV @ 10%*	*PV*
Year 7	$ 100.00	0.909091	$ 90.91
Year 8	$ 100.00	0.826446	$ 82.64
Year 9	$ 100.00	0.751315	$ 75.13
Year 10	$ 100.00	0.683013	$ 68.30
Maturity value	$1,000.00	0.683013	$ 683.01
Present value of cash flows			$1,000.00

Perhaps the clearest comparison of the time value of principal between a certificate of deposit and Green's bond can be seen if the investor chose to buy the bond in its last year. The cash the investor will receive at the end of the year is worth the same as a $909.09 investment in a 1-year certificate of deposit. The investor is paying $90.91 more for the bond because that represents the value of the interest that will be paid at the end of the tenth year. Using present value, you can see that the value of the bond will always be its par value if the coupon rate remains appropriate for the level of risk involved with the bond.

	Interest	PV @ 10%	PV
Year 10	$ 100.00	0.909091	$ 90.91
Maturity value	$1,000.00	0.909091	$ 909.09
Present value of cash flows			$1,000.00

Let's review that last statement: The bond will sell at par assuming the coupon rate remains appropriate for the level of risk. It contains a huge assumption. Even the interest on debt issued by the U. S. Treasury, which carries no risk of default, varies based on inflation fears, general economic conditions, and the government's monetary policy. Add to that the possibility of financial or business risk, and you can see that the value of corporate bonds does not stay constant at par.

BONDS AT A DISCOUNT

Six years have passed since Green Manufacturing issued its bond. The company has made every interest payment and the business continues to show steadily increasing profits. The bond rating has remained constant during the period, and there is no reason to believe that it won't continue to do so. However, the country has entered an inflationary period. Bonds with the same rating as Green's that are currently being issued carry a coupon rate of 12%. Clearly, an investment of $1,000 will now provide $120 annual interest instead of the $100 that Green's bonds pay, so they will not trade at par value. The bond's price in the secondary market is the present value of the cash flow using a 12% discount instead of the previous 10%.

	Interest	PV @ 12%	PV
Year 7	$ 100.00	0.892857	$ 89.29
Year 8	$ 100.00	0.797194	$ 79.72
Year 9	$ 100.00	0.71178	$ 71.18
Year 10	$ 100.00	0.635518	$ 63.55
Maturity value	$1,000.00	0.635518	$ 635.52
Present value of cash flows			$ 939.25

The current market price for this bond should be $939.25, which means that the holder of the bond has suffered a $60.75 capital loss. The bonds are now being sold at a discount. Green itself is not directly affected by the change in market value of this particular bond. The decrease in value is based on economic conditions outside Green's control, not the creditworthiness of the firm. It must still repay the full principal at the end of year 10, and the interest expense is $100 per bond outstanding. Green can benefit from the lower market value if it chooses to buy bonds on the secondary market and retire them since they are trading at less than maturity value. However, if Green were to need additional debt funding in the near future, it might incur the higher prevailing interest rates.

Debentures also trade at a discount if the company's financial condition deteriorates. Illusion Enterprises issued 10%, 10-year bonds with a par value of $1,000. Over the course of 6 years, Illusion lost market share as a result of quality control difficulties and incurred substantial costs due to lawsuits. Although the company believes it can recover, in order to compensate for the increased level of risk, investors are requiring a 24% rate of return. With 4 years remaining until maturity, Illusion's bonds currently trade at $663.30.

	Interest	PV @ 24%	PV
Year 7	$ 100.00	0.806	$ 80.60
Year 8	$ 100.00	0.650	$ 65.00
Year 9	$ 100.00	0.524	$ 52.40
Year 10	$ 100.00	0.423	$ 42.30
Principal	$1,000.00	0.423	$ 423.00
Present value of cash flows			$ 663.30

Notice how sharply the present value of the interest declines from year 7, the first year that the investor holds the bond, to year 8. Because of the uncertainty surrounding Illusion's future viability, investors do not feel that the future interest payment is worth much. Compare the value of the $100 to be paid by Illusion with the $100 interest to be paid by Green Manufacturing under the same purchase time frame. Because Green is a solid company, the present value of next year's interest is $79.72 compared with Illusion's $65.00. The present value of the principal payment alone is greater for Green than the entire value of Illusion's bond. Changes in business condition can have a drastic effect on the market value of debt.

BONDS AT A PREMIUM

A change in economic conditions could cause the value of existing bonds to rise. If interest rates decrease, the value of existing bonds will increase because investors cannot get as attractive a rate of return on newly issued debt. Instead of an inflationary cycle, let's assume that interest rates have fallen in the 6 years since Green issued its notes. The current market rate for bonds of the same quality is now 8.5%. In order to earn $100 per year interest, the investor would have to commit more current dollars. As a result, the value of Green's bonds will rise. Investors will bid up the price until it reaches equilibrium, where the interest earned (which is fixed by the coupon rate and the par value) matches the price the investor has paid.

⟨ **Looking Back** ⟩

The Confederate States of America began its existence with no currency. Its chief commodity was cotton, which it exported to England. Cotton accounted for a sizeable portion of the exports of the United States before the Southern states seceded. The Confederacy thought that the importance of its cotton sales to European buyers would bring diplomatic recognition and hard currency to the Southern states.

In order to fund the war with the Union, the Confederate States issued bonds. Each bond was printed with coupons attached and signed by hand. A coupon was cut off every 6 months and redeemed at the CSA Treasury.

One morning as I was window-shopping downtown, I saw a strange item in the window of a little antique store. It was a Confederate bond with some of the coupons still attached. The bond was authorized by an Act of Congress, C.S.A., on August 19, 1861. The face value of the bond is $500 and it carries 8% interest.

Although the bond was authorized in 1861, it was not entered until February 24, 1863, and signed on March 6.

What is curious to me is that there are not enough coupons left on the bond! If Robert E. Lee surrendered to the Union forces on April 14, 1863, it would seem to have been the end of the sovereignty of the Confederate States. However, all of the coupons prior to July 1873 are gone. Where did the 10 years' worth of coupons go? Did the Confederacy have enough money to pay some of the interest? Or did a child take one or several to school for show-and-tell?

Perhaps it is time for me to do some research!

	Interest	PV @ 8.5%	PV
Year 7	$ 100.00	0.921659	$ 92.17
Year 8	$ 100.00	0.849455	$ 84.95
Year 9	$ 100.00	0.782908	$ 78.29
Year 10	$ 100.00	0.721574	$ 72.16
Maturity value	$1,000.00	0.721574	$ 721.57
Present value of cash flows			$1,049.13

The present value of both the interest stream and the principal repayment have increased, and the current holder of the bond should expect a premium over the face value.

Bond prices are quoted as a percent of par value. Therefore, the bond above would be priced at 104.913, meaning that it trades at 4.913% over its par value. The bond is being sold at a premium. The percent pricing method allows investors to compare the return of bonds with different denominations.

YIELD

Interest earned from a bond is often called its yield. There are two different types of yield, current yield and yield to maturity, and both use the market price of the bond in the calculation.

Bond prices are listed in many newspapers. An investor could check to see if his bonds were selling at par, a premium, or at a discount. (Digital Vision Ltd.)

Current yield is the simplest to calculate. It is the percentage that an investor earns annually based on the price paid for the security. If Green Manufacturing's bond is trading for $1,049.13 and earns $100 per year interest, the current yield is

$$\text{Current yield} = \frac{\text{Annual interest payment}}{\text{Price of the bond}}$$

$$= \frac{\$100}{\$1,049.13}$$

$$= 9.53\,\%$$

The current yield is less than the 10% face value but more than the 8.5% interest rate that we used to discount the note. One weakness of the current yield is that it ignores the change in principal value that occurs when the bond is purchased for a discount or premium. The current yield is higher than the 8.5% discount, but the principal repayment will not be today's purchase price of $1,049.13. The current interest payments offset the loss of principal that occurs at the end of the bond.

The opposite occurs if the bond is sold at a discount. The current yield for Illusion's bond, which is trading at a 24% discount is

$$\text{Current yield} = \frac{\$100}{\$663.30}$$

$$= 15.08\,\%$$

When the bond matures, the principal repayment will be approximately 50% higher than the price paid for the bond. The current yield does not capture that increase in value of the lump sum payment.

Yield to maturity considers not only the current yield but the value of the increase in capital when it is held to maturity. Because we discounted the Illusion bond, we know that the yield is 24%. However, there is no simple way to calculate the yield to maturity by hand because we are dealing with a current income stream and an increase (or decrease) in lump sum value. One way to set up the equation is to set the left side equal to the market price and using guess and check, find a discount rate for the interest and principal that sets the right side equal. Some financial analysis software programs contain preprogrammed formulas that allow you to calculate yield to maturity. Financial calculators can also compute the value.

TERMS TO KNOW

Bonds
Principal value
Face value
Par value
Coupon rate
Covenants
Inflation risk

Call risk
Secured bonds
Debentures
Convertible bonds
Municipal bonds
General obligation
  bonds

Revenue bonds
Maturity value
Bonds sold at
  a discount
Bonds sold at
  a premium

TERM PAPERS AND PROJECTS

1. Compare bonds of investment grade quality with junk bonds. What company strengths and risks led to each valuation? What is the interest premium for junk bonds?
2. The Treasury Department announced in November 2001 that it would no longer sell a 30-year treasury bill. Who bought the bills? Why was the T-bill discontinued? What other investments will be used to replace the T-bill in investment portfolios?
3. Municipal bonds and school bonds are issued locally. What are the mechanics of issuing bonds? Who is in charge of paying the interest and retiring the debt?
4. Construct a 10-year laddered bond portfolio and describe the differences in yield over time. State the assumptions you have made. Did you invest in the same risk class of security? If not, how much of the difference in interest was due to the quality of the bonds and how much was due to the time horizon?
5. Investigate the value of bonds issued by the Confederate States of America. Did the coupon rate offered at the time match the rate offered by U.S. bonds? Were any of the bonds redeemed after the South surrendered? How many of the bonds were sold abroad? What happened to whatever money was left in the CSA's Treasury? Note: The same project could be completed with any government bonds from a nonexistent government entity.
6. Investigate the types of bonds and bills offered by the United States. Include savings bonds and treasury securities. Explain the difference in face value and coupon rate and describe what type of investor might be interested in each type of security.
7. Compare interest rates on different types of mortgage loans. Assess the difference in rates based on the length of the loan and who accepts the risk of interest rate fluctuations.

REVIEW QUESTIONS

1. What is a bond? How does it differ from stock?
2. Give three examples of covenants that bondholders may request regarding future behavior of the bond issuer.
3. What are bond ratings and how do they affect bond rates?
4. Should a bond that has a call risk carry a higher or lower interest rate? Explain.
5. What are secured bonds?
6. What are debentures?
7. Why would it be advantageous for a firm to issue debentures rather than secured bonds?
8. What is a convertible bond? What is an advantage to the buyer of this type of bond issue? How does the seller benefit?
9. What are municipal bonds?
10. What are junk bonds? Why do they pay a higher interest rate?
11. Would a present value analysis be valuable in determining bond prices? Why?

286 CHAPTER 13 *Types of Bonds and Their Valuation*

12. What is meant by a bond premium or bond discount?
13. How is current yield computed for a bond?

REVIEW PROBLEMS

1. A 10-year bond issued 3 years ago had a face value of $10,000 and a coupon rate of 7%. Interest rates on comparably risky bonds have decreased to 5%. What should the investor be willing to pay for the bond?

2. The Amalgamated Andiron Company has declared bankruptcy and its bonds have been downgraded to junk status. You bought a 10-year $5,000 bond yielding 8% interest 5 years ago. The current discount rate on the bond is 25%. What will you get if you try to sell the bond today?

3. A $1,000 Zorro Bond has a coupon rate of 8.25% and a current price of 87½. What is the current yield?

14

EQUITY

LEARNING OBJECTIVES

1. Describe the distinction between securities and stock.
2. Describe the process for issuing stock.
3. Explain the features of preferred stock.
4. Discuss how common stock differs from preferred stock.
5. Describe the rights that common stockholders have.
6. Calculate earnings per share.
7. Describe different types of stock such as blue chip and defensive stocks.
8. Discuss why companies buy shares of their own stock and what they do with it.
9. Calculate the value of stock using several tools.
10. Describe how stock is bought and sold on exchanges.
11. Explain the value of market indices.
12. Describe how mutual funds work and what benefit they bring to investors.
13. Explain net asset value and how it is calculated.

Throughout this book we have referred to stock and equity when discussing the ownership structure of firms. In this chapter we will look at the mechanics of issuing stock, how it is traded on the public exchanges, and methods for analyzing stock prices. We start by more fully explaining the vocabulary that stock buyers and sellers use.

WHAT DO ALL THESE TERMS MEAN?

More individuals are investing in stock, either as part of a personal investment plan or through a company-sponsored pension fund. As in other industries, there is an entire vocabulary that can seem like a foreign language until you untangle it.

Securities is the word used to describe a wide variety of investments: bonds, stock, options, commodities, and others. Many securities can be traded on primary or secondary markets, but there is no "security" that they will retain their value.

Stock represents an ownership stake in a company and is listed at the bottom of the balance sheet as owner's equity. Like creditors, shareholders have a claim on the company's assets, however all of the creditors have prior claim, even holders of unsecured, subordinated debentures. In the case of liquidation, shareholders have a residual claim and may receive nothing.

Stockholders in a corporation are owners of that firm, however unlike sole proprietorships or partnerships, the stockholders do not have personal liability for the debts of the firm. Because the corporation itself is a legal entity, stockholders have limited liability in case of bankruptcy. The most they can lose is the value of their investment in the firm.

The number of shares of stock that a company issues depends on the amount of money it needs and the price it will receive for each share it issues. The firm's managers meet with the Board of Directors to determine the financing needs of the company and how much stock to sell. Once the Board of Directors has agreed with management's plans, the firm will seek an investment bank to help draw up the prospectus. Stock issues do not require the firm to write an indenture because that is specific to bonds, however, the firm must

---

A Fairy Tale

As I wrote in an earlier chapter, shares of stock used to be traded using prices expressed in eighths. This is the story that I was told to explain the anomaly:

Once upon a time, a long, long time ago, there lived a navigator, Christopher Columbus by name, who believed that the Earth was round. He didn't really care if he proved that fact; what he wanted to do was find a shortcut to the Spice Islands and he believed that his route would be shorter. Unfortunately, he was poor and couldn't afford to hire a boat for the voyage.

Believing that the Queen was wealthy, he petitioned her to fund his venture. The Queen he appealed to was Isabella of Spain who had just finished fighting a war that had lasted for over 700 years (she didn't fight for the whole time!). She was probably not as rich as he thought, but she agreed to fund the voyage. In return for investing in his expedition, she would receive a *share* of the profits. (See, one of the words has shown up.) Since much of what was traded were goods available for sale, what she was getting was a *share* of the *stock* (inventory) that would be coming in on the boat. (Aha!) At that point in time, Spanish coins were pieces of eight and it would have made sense to value the shares of stock in some denomination that included eighths!

Although the United States has never used eighths, there is an old song about "Shave and a haircut, two bits!" Two bits is another word for a quarter. Therefore, "one bit," if there were such a thing, would be an eighth!

disclose its plans for the money and the anticipated risks that a shareholder will incur. In addition, the **prospectus** describes dividend policies, biographies of the founders and directors, voting rights, how the proposed stock issue will affect the existing ownership structure, and who the transfer agent is. A **transfer agent** is the coordinator for paying dividends and registering changes of ownership in the corporation. A transfer agent is often a major bank. The preliminary prospectus must be submitted to the **Securities and Exchange Commission** (SEC) for their approval. The SEC reviews the prospectus to ensure that it complies with the disclosure requirements. If the issue is approved, the SEC authorizes the firm to sell up to a certain number of shares of stock. Stock that has never been issued before is considered a primary market transaction and the firm receives the proceeds of the sale, minus investment banking fees.

If the firm has never sold stock before, the transaction is called an **initial public offering (IPO).** IPOs are often quite exciting because it is difficult to tell how much people will be willing to pay for stock in a newly public company. Investment bankers try to price the stock at what they believe is a reasonable estimate of its value, but often the stock issue is more desirable than the underwriter had anticipated and the price is bid up. Other times the price that the company would like to obtain is higher than investors are willing to pay. In that case, the company may choose to delay the offering until it feels that market conditions have improved.

A stock issue by a company that already has stock traded in the market is called a seasoned new issue. The specific shares have not been traded before and the proceeds go to the issuer, but the issue price is less volatile since there are existing shares to provide a benchmark.

Stock can carry a par value. However, it is not equivalent to a bond's par value, which is the sum that will be paid to the bondholder at the maturity date. When par value is assigned to a stock, it is for bookkeeping purposes or, for certain kinds of stock, used to calculate dividends. It is not an indication of market value, even the value that the firm expects to receive on its issue date.

The firm does not have to sell all of the **authorized shares** at one time. The shares that are authorized and sold are called **issued stock**; the shares that have been authorized but not yet sold are called unissued stock. In the future, the firm could sell the unissued stock without having it reauthorized by the SEC. Only the issued shares are listed on the firm's balance sheet because they are the only ones that have a claim on the assets. Treasury stock is the name given to issued shares that have been repurchased by the firm. They are listed on the balance sheet after retained earnings.

Unlike bonds, which come in many different types, there are only two forms of stock: preferred stock and common stock.

PREFERRED STOCK

Preferred stock is a form of equity that also has some of the characteristics of bonds. Compared with common stock, it has a "preferred" claim on the assets and earnings of the firm. Although it is not secured, it is less risky than common stock. Unlike common stockholders, preferred stockholders do not have voting rights.

Preferred stock usually carries a par value per share with a fixed dividend rate. The dividend is paid from the firm's earnings and, if the preferred stock has a par value, is calculated as the dividend rate times the par value, not the current market value. Some preferred stock issues carry a specifically stated dividend rather than par value and dividend rate. In either case, the dividend is predictable.

The **dividend** is promised by the issuer, as is the coupon rate on a bond; however there is no maturity date on which the firm will redeem the stock. In addition, if the firm does not have earnings, it can choose not to declare dividends that year. If the firm does not pay dividends, it is said to be in arrears. If the preferred stock is cumulative preferred stock, the arrears must be made up before any dividends can be paid to common stockholders. Most preferred stock is cumulative, however, there are some issues that are non-cumulative preferred stock, in which case arrears do not have to be made up. For a company in financial distress, the type of preferred stock may be irrelevant. The firm could choose to pay dividends even if it shows no profit, but that would drain cash from an already struggling firm, which would not be in its best interests. Although preferred stock is higher in a liquidation payment hierarchy than common stock, it still represents an ownership stake in the firm, and the goal of the "owners" should be to ensure that the firm continues as a going concern. There is no guarantee, however, that any arrears will be made good.

One benefit to issuing preferred stock rather than bonds is the perpetual nature of equity. The firm is under no obligation to retire stock. The firm maintains use of the money in exchange for a set payment, in the form of dividends. That, however, can also be the drawback—the use of the money is perpetual, as is the fee for using it. A firm that issues preferred stock can include a call feature that would allow the firm to call in the preferred stock. The call feature is included in the prospectus when the stock is originally sold. The basic structure of the call allows the firm to redeem the stock at its discretion. The redemption price is specified in the prospectus and usually includes a bonus to the shareholder in the form of an extra year of dividends or a lump sum payment. At the end of a specified period of time, shares that have not been surrendered by the shareholder will cease to earn dividends, which is an incentive for the holder to submit the shares.

Preferred shares are designated by a *pf* in stock listing pages. Many firms have more than one issue of preferred stock and each will be listed separately and identified alphabetically, for example, pfA for the first issue. Each issue carries its own dividend rate and place in the order of payment.

COMMON STOCK

Common stock has none of the hybrid qualities of preferred stock. For the investor, it is the riskiest form of investment in a firm. For the firm, it is perhaps the most flexible since it carries no promised dividend or repayment obligation. Common stockholders have a final claim on the earnings of the firm. If the firm is bankrupt, there may be no final value. However, if a firm is successful, the common stockholders receive the rewards. The rewards are often demonstrated by the increase in the firm's stock price.

Many of the old stock certificates are ornately decorated with scenes depicting the type of work done by the issuing company. Today most stockholders have an electronic account and do not take possession of a paper certificate. (New York Stock Exchange, Inc.)

If a firm were small, and all of the owners lived or worked near the business, important decisions could be handled at a weekly meeting with the owners sitting around a conference table. However, major corporations have far too many "owners" to allow this type of decision making. For example, at the end of 2000, General Electric Corporation had 9,932,006,000 shares of stock outstanding! Even allowing for the fact that many investors own blocks of stock, there is no practical way for investors-owners to participate in the day-to-day management of the firm. As a result, common stockholders have **voting rights.** Typically, each share of common stock is allowed one vote, however, there are some cases where a company has different classes of stock that carry different voting rights.

RIGHTS OF COMMON STOCKHOLDERS

The common stockholders hire the members of the **Board of Directors** who are charged with the responsibility for acting on behalf of the shareholders and supervising the management of the firm. The firm usually submits a slate of directors, although shareholders can nominate candidates. If stockholders are comfortable with the direction that the company has taken, the company's suggested directors tend to be elected. However, when the company has experienced difficulty, election to the Board of Directors becomes more contentious. In some cases, groups of dissatisfied shareholders have worked together to change the composition of a board.

Common stockholders not only have the right to vote for the board but they also must approve any changes in the rules that govern the corporation.

In addition to voting on management proposals, shareholders are also entitled to propose amendments to the corporate charter. Shareholder activists have proposed rules that would restrict investment in certain foreign countries, require human rights monitoring in overseas factories, and limit the amount of executive compensation. What is more important than whether an individual amendment passes is the fact that shareholders do have an avenue for expressing their concerns about the company they own.

Shareholders may attend the annual meeting and vote their shares in person or they can vote by proxy. A **proxy** is a legal agreement that designates a third party, usually the firm's independent auditor, to vote the shares according to the shareholder's instructions. Shares not voted in person or by proxy can be voted by management. This is an important point to remember: Members of the Board of Directors are representatives of the owners (shareholders), while the Chief Executive Officer and other senior managers are the employees of the firm. By not actively voting, the shareholder has not expressed his or her opinion and given the Board of Directors the collective weight of opinion in order to guide management.

If the firm's business is stable, a shareholder may receive only one proxy package a year, just prior to the firm's annual meeting. However, if the firm is being pursued by an acquirer or if management takeovers or restructurings are threatened, proxy fights may occur. A proxy fight is a battle for the proxy votes of shareholders. For example, in the case of a hostile takeover, the firm's management would send out documents stating why they believe the firm should remain independent and solicit the shareholders' votes in support of the existing structure. The potential acquirer would send information detailing its purchase offer for shares of stock or its desire for a merger. During a prolonged and active proxy battle, shareholders might receive numerous proxies, each of which could be voted. The last proxy signed by the shareholder is the final vote counted.

Some stockholders have preemptive rights. **Preemptive rights** allow the existing stockholders to maintain their proportionate share in the firm if it chooses to issue more stock in the future. If the company issues new stock, it must first offer it to the existing shareholders. This stock sale is called a rights offering. If the shareholder wishes to maintain the same proportion, she or he will buy the shares. If not, the shareholder must release them so that others can buy them. Rights offerings are more expensive for a corporation because it has to go through two steps in marketing new shares. Even without a specific rights offering, existing shareholders can purchase shares in any new issue to maintain their investment or increase it. Many corporations have asked their shareholders to change the bylaws requiring rights offerings, arguing that the costs of a rights offering outweigh the benefits to the shareholders.

Common stockholders are entitled to the profits of the organization. Some companies choose to pay dividends to common stockholders. If dividends are paid, they are issued quarterly and must be approved by the Board of Directors. On the declaration date, the amount of dividends per share is announced along with the date on which they will be paid. Imagine the time it would take to determine who owned all of General Electric's more than 9 billion shares! Because companies need to have time to determine who owns the shares and then process the dividends, there is also an ex-dividend date. Shareholders of record before the ex-dividend date will receive the just declared dividend. Shares that trade after the ex-dividend date will trade without the dividend. Checks are mailed on the payment date.

⌐ **In the News** ⌐

Shareholders are not just individuals who have a few hundred shares of their employer's stock. Shareholders can also be large institutional investors. One of the largest is CALPERS, the California state pension fund. When a proxy fight is launched, every investor gets a proxy to vote, with the number of votes corresponding to the number of shares they hold. For the large investor, the proxy vote counts for a lot.

Sam Wyly is a Texas financier who wanted to make radical changes to Computer Associates, a software company headed by its founder Charles B. Wang. Wyly originally planned to overthrow the chairman and the entire 10-member Board of Directors.

The key to this story is that Wyly's moves were seen as too radical by "two influential firms that advise shareholders on proxy fights" according to a *Business Week* article. When he changed his list of demands and reduced the number of nominees to the board to four, the advisors threw their weight behind his proposal.

Even a large institutional investor with a whole staff of analysts seeks the advice of a proxy advisor. Imagine how confusing proxy fights can be for the individual investor who has to sift through competing statements from the company and the challengers.

Source: "If At First You Don't Succeed . . . ," *Business Week*, September 3, 2001, by Andrew Park.

EARNINGS PER SHARE

Earnings per share (EPS) represents the amount of earnings per share of common stock outstanding. Earnings per share represents the amount of earnings that would be allocated to common stockholders if all profits were disbursed, and it is calculated by taking net income less the dividends paid to preferred stockholders.

$$\text{EPS} = \frac{\text{Net income} - \text{preferred stock dividends}}{\text{Number of shares of common stock outstanding}}$$

Companies use earnings per share to describe their profitability from year to year. EPS is not the same as dividends and does not obligate the firm to pay dividends.

CLASSIFICATIONS OF COMMON STOCK

As noted earlier, there are only two types of equities: preferred stock and common stock. However, stock market analysts often refer to stock by different classifications such as "blue chip" stock or "growth" stock. The description does not differentiate aspects of stock but attempts to categorize the company that has issued the stock.

Blue chip stocks are issued by large nationally known corporations with sound credit history and firm financial footing. Blue chip stock prices tend to be stable even in difficult economic times because they have a history of steady growth and solid dividend payments. An example of a blue chip stock would be General Electric or Procter & Gamble.

Growth stocks are issued by companies that have earnings and sales growth greater than their industry average. They can be small companies that have developed new products or markets, or companies that continually innovate. Most growth companies do not pay dividends but choose to retain earnings to fund future growth opportunities.

Income stocks pay relatively high dividends. They are in mature industries with little increase in earnings above inflation. Utility companies are an example of income stocks because they pay a stable rate of return and have little or no expected revenue growth.

Speculative stocks carry higher risk than the general market. Start-up companies in new industries are speculative. Companies that have fallen into financial disarray could also be considered speculative stocks. The risk for both of these categories is high and stock prices tend to be volatile.

Cyclical stocks are those belonging to companies whose sales are tied to economic fluctuations. When the economy grows, these companies prosper. In more difficult economic environments, sales slump and earnings are pressed. Durable goods manufacturers, automakers, and the housing industry are all examples of cyclical stocks.

Defensive stocks may offset the swings of cyclical stocks. When the economy weakens, homeowners may turn to remodeling or repair projects rather than trade up to a new home. Hardware stores or home improvement stores may not suffer even if contractors buy less, since consumers may pick up the slack.

Large cap, mid cap, and small cap describe the market capitalization of the firm. Capitalization is the number of shares multiplied by the price per share. The largest companies, with the most shares outstanding and a high total value, are called large cap. As the value of their shares increases, small-cap companies can grow into mid-cap companies and mid-cap companies can become large-cap companies.

MANAGING STOCK

Firms are sensitive to the type of liabilities that they carry on the balance sheet. We've looked at the importance of managing current liabilities in order to maximize working capital. Debt, whether secured or debentures, obligates the firm to pay interest, and the covenants in an indenture can limit the firm's future financing actions. Companies are also interested in managing shareholders' equity.

One sign of a healthy, growing company is an increase in the price of its stock and good sales volume. Sometimes the share price becomes high enough that management is concerned that smaller investors will not be able to afford shares. To keep the price within a range that encourages trading, companies split the stock. A **stock split** takes the existing number of shares and increases it by some factor. For example, a company that had 1,000 shares outstanding with a closing price of $250 per share might split 2-for-1. After the end of the business day, each share of stock would split in half—there would be two "new" shares for every one that had existed before. The next morning, there would be 2,000 shares of stock and the opening price would be adjusted to $125 per share. Existing shareholders would have the same percent ownership in the firm and the same total investment value. However, the lower trading price might increase interest in the stock, and newly released demand could push the price slightly higher.

STOCK BUYBACKS AND TREASURY STOCK

On occasion the Board of Directors authorizes management to buy back shares of the company from the public. This is a called stock buyback. The stock that is purchased is still issued stock; it does not become unissued stock simply because the firm owns it. It is carried on the balance sheet as **treasury stock.** Although the shares are still issued, they are not counted as outstanding shares.

There are several reasons that a company would buy its own shares. If the firm believes that the current market price does not reflect the underlying value, it might use the purchase to signal that opinion. If the price does rise in the future, the company can sell its shares and reap the profit. Buying shares also reduces the number of shares outstanding and is a way for the company to improve earnings per share, even if the earnings themselves are not significantly higher. If earnings are spread over fewer outstanding shares, the profits to the individual shareholders will appear higher. Treasury stock can also be used as a cash management tool. Shares that are owned by the company can be given to employees as performance incentives without reducing the working capital of the firm.

There has been a lot of discussion over the past several years about whether companies should substantially increase the dividends paid to common stockholders. Start-up companies are expected to retain what earnings they have to grow their business into the growth or maturity phase. Organizations with net losses do not have earnings to distribute. The debate focuses around profitable companies with a stable revenue stream and few exponential growth opportunities. Profitable companies that don't pay dividends argue that they increase shareholder value by reinvesting the profits in the company, thus expanding their business and generating further profits. They argue that the stock market rewards this decision by pushing up the price of the company's stock. As long as the company can sustain earnings growth in excess of the corresponding discount rate, the decision is theoretically valid. In a rational market, a shareholder who wishes to capture the added value can sell shares of stock at a higher price than he or she paid for them. The shareholder would also punish an inefficient company by driving down the price of its shares.

Of course, there are many aspects to this issue. If the company retained earnings sufficient to fund the business but issued the remaining profits in the form of dividends, shareholders could decide how to allocate those earnings. If they believed that the firm had growth potential that exceeded their alternate uses of the money, shareholders would reinvest in the same organization. If however, the firm had not demonstrated that the earnings it achieved were superior to the other investments available, given a corresponding risk factor investors would reward more profitable firms by investing in their shares. Theoretically, capital would be directed to the most efficient uses. Some contend that by automatically reinvesting profits in their own firm, companies will accept investments with a lower rate of return than an efficient market would require

VALUING STOCK

After the volatility of the last several years, it might be easiest to state that stock is simply worth whatever anyone is willing to pay for it. However, that statement disregards the fact that stock represents collective ownership of a specific set of assets that should be expected to produce a stream of income now and into the future. We will return to the emotional aspects of stock valuation, but for now we will examine three mathematical approaches.

Book Value

If the company's balance sheet were continually updated to reflect market value of all assets and liabilities, valuation would be simple. The liabilities could be subtracted from the assets and the remaining value divided by the number of shares outstanding.

$$\text{Assets (at true market value)} - \text{liabilities} = \text{equity}$$

$$\text{Price per share} = \frac{\text{Equity}}{\text{Number of shares outstanding}}$$

In fact, balance sheets often reflect historic costs for long-term assets. If the replacement cost is higher than the balance sheet, the stock should trade above **book value.** However, if the value of assets has declined, book value will overstate the price that investors should pay.

Book value also addresses only the assets owned by the firm, not the uses to which they are being put. Using book value as a way to establish share price could result in a higher stock valuation for a firm with newly acquired assets and lower income than a firm in the same industry with older equipment and higher earnings per share.

Price-Earnings Ratio

The **price-earnings (PE) ratio** is a measure of a stock's value relative to the market as a whole and competitors in its industry. It is simple to calculate.

$$\text{PE ratio} = \frac{\text{Price per share}}{\text{Earnings per share}}$$

The price an investor is willing to pay per share of stock should increase as earnings per share increase. For example, a firm that has steady earnings that are growing at just about the country's growth rate would not have the same increase in share price as a company whose earnings were growing twice the rate of the economy.

The price-earnings ratio has been used to compare companies within a specific industry. Companies have been said to be "good buys" if their PE ratio is lower than the prevailing rate in the industry. But who sets that base level? PE ratios for the stock market as a whole climbed during the 1990s, reflecting investor confidence in the economy. In general, industries that are experiencing growth will have a higher PE ratio than low-growth industries because investors are basing their decision on not just one year but the expectation that growth will continue into the future. In that sense, the price-earnings ratio is very much like the discounted cash flow method of evaluating the cost of acquiring a business. Like the capitalization rate, PE ratios should take into account not only the current growth rate but also reasonable expectations for growth in perpetuity. The PE ratio should also consider whether the firm is susceptible to economic fluctuations. If so, earnings will be less stable, risk will increase, and the PE ratio should be adjusted accordingly.

Remember that this calculation looks at earnings, not revenue. If the company has no earnings, either because it is in its infancy or because it has sustained a net loss for the year, there is no earnings per share ratio.

Discounted Dividend Valuation Method

The **discounted dividend valuation method** calculates a share price based on the expectation of future dividends. This method uses the same theory as the capitalization rate, which states that the capitalized value of the income stream is what we will pay for the stock. In this case, the income stream is dividends. The investment risk is reduced by the rate of growth in dividends, which is assumed to be steady.

$$\text{Stock price} = \frac{\text{Current yearly dividend}}{\text{Required rate of return} - \text{assumed growth rate}}$$

Let's assume that Terra, Inc., pays $1.60 per year in dividends. They are a stable company that will grow 2% per year. Our required rate of return on this company is 12%.

$$\text{Stock price} = \frac{\$1.60}{12\% - 2\%} = \frac{\$1.60}{10\%} = \$16.00$$

This method works only if the firm pays dividends, so its application is limited.

Mathematical Models

Institutional investors such as pension funds, insurance companies, and educational and charitable endowments have sophisticated computer programs that attempt to predict changes in the price of stock in order to buy stock when it is undervalued and sell it for a good return. The model they have created are proprietary, belonging to them, and reflect their ris tolerance and any restrictions imposed by the nature of their business suc as the payments they must fund from investments (insurance claims, retire ment benefits, etc.). Even with access to reams of historic data and tren analysis, these large investors can be surprised by the actual prices pai for stock.

OTHER FACTORS THAT AFFECT STOCK VALUE

Interest rates have an inverse relationship with stock prices. As interest rate rise, the firm's cost of borrowing increases, thus reducing the amount of rev enue that is available for shareholders. Earnings per share fall as a result o higher debt costs, which pushes down the price of stock. Added to this is th fact that as interest rates rise, investors can obtain higher earnings at lower ris by investing in bonds or insured accounts.

The health of the individual company can affect its share price, even in a expanding market. A company that has sustained losses or not met its revenue projections will see its share price fall, sometimes precipitously. Investors per ceive that the company's risk has increased, and the lower share price reflect the risk-related adjustment.

Although it would be nice to quantify stock prices and create predictable sustainable valuation models, investors are human and emotions affect stoc prices. Optimism, greed, and fear can cause a market rally or slump. If con sumer confidence is high, spending follows. New homes sell, which mean more washing machines, refrigerators, and other durable goods move off th production line. Retailers sell carpet, lumber for new decks, paint fo bedrooms, and new sheets and curtains. The economy as a whole is expandin and with it come higher prices for stocks. Optimism (faith that the econom will continue to expand) pushes stock prices upward in reaction to the eco nomic growth that consumers are fueling.

As long-term investors begin to reap the rewards of increasing stoc prices, new investors jump into the market and demand pushes stock price still higher. Sometimes optimism causes investors to forget fundamental valu ation theories.

In the 1990s, investors became caught up in the excitement of the Inter net revolution. Computer ownership increased and more households ha Internet access. In addition to information, the Internet provided opportuni ties for shopping, which many companies attempted to capture. Investor rushed to buy "dotcom" companies (companies that had a commercial Inter net address, such as anycompany.com) because they believed that the ne medium was a gold mine. Demand caused stock prices to increase dramatic ally, even though the companies were start-ups with high expenses and n revenue. In addition, the firms were attempting to gain sales in an undevelope marketplace. However, the allure was undeniable. Early investors were able t realize profits by buying dotcom stock when it was first issued, holding it unti it reached their personal threshold, and selling it for sizeable profits. Storie about the gains made from trading Internet stocks caused optimism to slip into greed. Greed (the desire for profit) pushes stock prices up when they are already rising, but fear can cause all of the gains to evaporate.

Long-term investors know that there are economic cycles; stock prices will not always increase. If the economy slows or international events cause concern in domestic markets, stock prices will fall on expectations of lower future growth and income. As securities prices fall, some investors become nervous and want to sell their holdings, which adds to the downturn. When the supply of securities for sale exceeds demand, prices fall further. Falling prices cause more fear, which exaggerates the economic difficulties.

So what price is valid for stock? In a rational market, the price should reflect the earnings capability of the firm and the risk factors specific to its industry, its financial structure, and the state of the economy. In an irrational market, stock prices are anyone's guess.

PUBLICLY TRADED STOCK

When a company issues stock, it receives the proceeds of the sale minus investment banking fees. Securities that have been previously issued are traded on a secondary market. Secondary markets can either be an organized exchange where buyers and sellers meet face-to-face in a physical location or an over-the-counter market where transactions are handled over the phone or via computer.

The New York Stock Exchange is the largest secondary market in the United States. The NYSE, also called the "Big Board," is the oldest of all of the organized exchanges. In order to be listed on the New York Stock Exchange, firms must meet strict regulations concerning size, profitability, market value, and equity ownership structure. If a company fails to maintain the minimum membership levels, it can be delisted from the exchange.

In order to actually trade shares on the exchange you need to be a member and buy a "seat." There is no physical seat; the term denotes membership in the exchange. The number of seats is limited and when seats become available they are sold at the price agreed upon by buyer and seller. Seats can be purchased by individuals or brokerage firms.

BUYING AND SELLING STOCK AT AN ORGANIZED EXCHANGE

The New York Stock Exchange operates on the **open outcry method** of trading. Only members can trade on the floor, so individuals who want to buy or sell shares need to use an intermediary.

I live in Washington State, on the opposite coast and three time zones away from New York City. If I wanted to purchase shares of an NYSE-listed company, my first step would be to contact a broker whose firm had a seat on the exchange. I could arrange the trade in person, over the telephone, or via Internet. But no matter what communication medium I used, a broker would be executing my trade.

My order to buy shares would be communicated to a floor broker located at the edge of the trading floor. Upon receipt of the order, the broker would proceed to a trading desk on the floor of the exchange where transactions in that stock take place. Buyers and sellers brandish paper that is color-coded to indicate whether they are buying, selling, or merely checking the current bid or ask price for the stock. Each stock has a specialist assigned to it to ensure that trading in the stock is orderly and fair. If there are sufficient bids and offers to keep the stock trading smoothly, the specialist does not intervene. However if there is a mismatch, the specialist steps in and buys or sells from his or her own account to keep the market moving.

The order I just placed was a market order. I authorized the broker to buy shares at the best price he or she could get in the market. If I had wanted to specify the price I was willing to pay for those shares, I would have placed a limit order. As a buyer, I would specify the highest price I was willing to pay for the shares. A seller could place a limit order stating the lowest price the seller would accept. If the limit price cannot be met, the order goes into the specialist's book until a match can be made.

Millions of shares of stock are held in electronic form—ownership is recorded electronically and the shares are held in computerized form in the owner's account at a stockbrokerage. Companies will mail stock certificates upon request, but like many other financial transactions, most of the transfers are done via computer. Just as it is simpler for money to be transmitted using electronic funds transfer than to carry or mail a check from one business to the other, it is easier for the stockholder to authorize the sale of his or her digitally encoded stock than to take the stock certificate to the local broker's office. Electronic buying and selling of stock can take place even when the stockbroker's office is closed, which would not be the case if the transaction were dependent on surrendering a paper stock certificate.

BUYING STOCK ON MARGIN

Stock that is purchased through a stockbroker can either be paid for in full at the time of the transaction or can be bought on margin. If the stock is bought on margin, the customer pays for a certain percentage of the stock and finances the rest through the brokerage. Let's assume that I want to buy 100 shares of a company that is trading at $54 per share. The total cost of my purchase is $5,400. I pay the brokerage firm 20% of the value of the stock ($1,080) and the rest of the stock is in my margin account. I will, of course, pay a fee for the loan and the shares of stock will be the collateral. As long as the value of the stock stays above the amount of the loan I have outstanding, the shares will remain in the stockbroker's account in my name. If the price of the shares falls below the value of my loan, the stockbroker has the right to sell the shares and recoup his or her loan to me.

One of the causes of the 1929 stock market crash was the fact that so many investors had bought on margin and, as stock prices tumbled, more and more stock from margin accounts was added to the system, pushing prices lower yet. In order to stop panic from ensuing again, the New York Stock Exchange instituted breaker points, rules that determined at what level of loss stock trading would halt. If the market falls by more than a certain percent or number of points, trading is suspended in order to calm market fears. If the free fall continues, the market can be closed for the day.

To keep markets calm in the first few days following the reopening of stock trading in September 2001, Federal Reserve officials, brokerage houses, and the New York Stock Exchange agreed that stock would not be sold to cover margins. There was no way of knowing how the markets would react in the first days and weeks, so the decision was made not to add any extra stress to the system. As we now know, the market tumbled the first week but by the end of the year, it had regained stability and stayed at or around the September 10 levels.

THE AMERICAN STOCK EXCHANGE AND REGIONAL STOCK EXCHANGES

Historically, the American Stock Exchange (AMEX) was the second most important exchange. Companies that were not quite large enough to trade on the New York Stock Exchange traded on the American Stock Exchange. In recent years, the American Stock Exchange has been eclipsed by the over-the-counter market known as NASDAQ. There are also active regional stock exchanges such as the Pacific Stock Exchange in Los Angeles and San Francisco and the Philadelphia Exchange (in Philadelphia and Miami). Regional stock exchanges trade in securities of local or regional interest that have strong management and financial strength.

NASDAQ

NASDAQ is the commonly used name for one of the over-the-counter stock trading systems. The over-the-counter (OTC) market does not have a specific physical location like the NYSE, AMEX, or regional stock exchanges. It is the linking of dealers who trade in certain stock issues. There is no need to buy a seat on this exchange.

Depending on the volume of trading activity, pricing information will be communicated in one of several ways. Thinly traded stocks are priced daily and the information mailed to traders. Because there is so little trading volume and there is a time lag between the quote and its receipt, it may be more difficult for shareholders to make quick trades at the most competitive price. For the most actively traded stocks, traders are linked by high-speed computers as part of the NASDAQ system. NASDAQ is not a location, it is the acronym for National Association of Securities Dealers Automated Quotations system. Dealers are allowed to post bid and ask prices in an attempt to match buyers and sellers. The bid price is the price at which a buyer is willing to purchase stock. The ask price is the selling price the owner is willing to accept. Dealers match buyers and sellers and make their profit by taking advantage of the spread between the bid and ask prices. It is not a leisurely pursuit. Bid and ask prices scroll rapidly down screens as traders try to make the best matches. Often a trader will be watching a televised computer screen and be on one of many phones to another dealer, attempting to capture the bid or ask price that is scrolling down the screen and match it to a client's order.

In terms of number of companies, there are more stocks listed on the over-the-counter market than the New York Stock Exchange. However, due to the size of companies listed on the NYSE, it is responsible for a majority of the dollar value of stock trades that occur in the United States. Many of the companies whose stock is traded in the OTC market are smaller and less capitalized than the companies that trade on the New York Stock Exchange, thus they trade at lower prices and volumes. There are obvious exceptions such as Microsoft and Intel. Many high-tech companies that would qualify for listing on the NYSE have chosen to remain part of the over-the-counter market.

INDICES—HOW DID THE MARKET DO?

Stock prices fluctuate based on the performance of the issuer as well as in response to general market conditions. Indices like "The Dow" or the S&P500 give an indication of the direction of the market as a whole. No one index can give the entire picture, nor will it give the performance of an individual stock. Investors rely on indices to give them a snapshot of market activity.

A typical newcast may report: "The Dow closed up 50 points today on active trading with gainers outnumbering losers 5 to 3." There's a fair amount of information in that statement. "The Dow" refers to the Dow Jones Industrial Average (DJIA), an index of stock from 30 large, well-established companies. Because the DJIA focuses on larger companies, it is less susceptible

Options based on indices such as the DJIA can also be traded. Investors are betting that the market basket of stocks represented by the index will rise or fall. (Index Stock Imagery, Inc.)

to the volatility that would be experienced by a growth company or nascent industry. The index is widely used to gain a sense of overall market sentiment. "Active trading" indicates that there was enough volume to facilitate fair trading and enable the market to clear buy and sell orders, but the word does not indicate a frenzy. On an especially light trading day, the spread between bid and ask prices could increase and closing prices might not give as much of an indication of the "market's sentiment." A day with heavy trading could indicate uncertainty in the markets and perhaps even panic selling. The ratio of gainers to losers further indicates the direction of the market. In my example, less than 63% of the shares gained value while 37% lost value. A more positive day would have seen gainers outnumbering losers 4 to 1! On that day, 80% of the stocks traded would have gained in value while only 20% declined.

There are other indices in addition to the Dow Jones Industrial Average. The Standard & Poor's 500, also known as the S&P500 is based on the movement of 500 shares of stock, not 30. The companies in the S&P500 trade mostly on the New York Stock Exchange, but it also includes shares from the AMEX and NASDAQ. Because it is broader based, it may be more indicative of the stock market as a whole rather than just large-cap or blue chip stocks. NASDAQ has an index that charts the direction of stock traded over the counter. Because the stocks traded through the NASDAQ system are often issued by smaller firms with less financial wherewithal than NYSE companies, the NASDAQ index tends to be more volatile than the Dow or the S&P500. Not one of the indices predicts future earnings or describes the underlying value of the companies whose shares are tracked. The indices do serve to indicate general trends and the level of investor confidence.

You Should Know

Stock prices are subject to supply and demand, just as any other commodity. If there is terrific news about a company and everyone wants to own a piece of it, the stock price will climb. By the same token, if too many shares are available, the price will fall.

Too many shares may be available because investors are bailing out of a poorly performing company, or it could simply be that a large investor is liquidating its holdings. In late 2001, the price of Disney shares fell after the Bass brothers, wealthy Texas investors, were forced to sell their holdings to cover their margin call.

Another group who can move the market are institutional investors who hold large blocks of stock. If they attempt to sell a large quantity of stock at one time, they will drive the price of the stock downward. In fact, that's allegedly what contributed to the steep drop in prices when the stock market reopened in September 2001. Individual investors sat still and didn't panic. It was reported that institutional investors sold large volumes of shares as soon as the market opened, pushing prices down.

MUTUAL FUNDS

Stock prices rise and fall daily and over the course of months and years. Speculators try to quickly time their purchases to take advantage of temporary price discrepancies. Most institutional and individual investors take a longer-term approach to stock purchases. Although they would be thrilled to stumble across a fast-growing, highly profitable company whose share price does nothing but appreciate, they realize that the best way to choose companies in which to invest is to do a thorough analysis of the company, its market, the competitors, and its financial stability. Unfortunately, there is a limit to the amount of time the firm or individual has to devote to analyzing companies.

Mutual funds allow small investors to pool their resources and buy a mix of securities, either stocks, bonds, or a combination. There are mutual funds with a wide variety of investment parameters and risk levels. Some funds invest in the strongest firms in a specific industry such as mining, biotech, or retail. There are funds that mimic the movement of the market as a whole by investing in the stocks that comprise the S&P500. Risk-tolerant investors can invest in distressed stock or junk bonds.

Investment companies that offer mutual funds hire analysts who are trained to do the type of financial and market research that we have described. They choose the companies they believe will perform best and continue to monitor the company's financial condition after the stock or bond is purchased. Analysts can be generalists or specialize in a certain industry or type of security. Actively managed mutual funds regularly adjust their holdings based on the quality of the securities they hold, selling the stock or bonds that are not performing according to the fund's standards and replacing them with higher-quality issues.

Buying a share of a mutual fund rather than individual stocks and bonds allows smaller investors to diversify their holdings. A $1,000 investment in a single company's stock may be far riskier than a $1,000 investment in a mutual fund that holds a wider variety of shares. The larger number of companies held by a mutual fund smooths the effect of a single company's poor performance.

In the News

First Eagle Fund of America is a mutual fund with holdings of $400 million. Harold Levy, the fund manager, likes to invest in companies that are "in a state of flux." He wants to invest in companies that are about to change because he believes that change of the right sort creates value for the investor. One type of change that Levy looks for includes the hiring of a new chief executive. New management tends to shake up the status quo and creates value for the fund.

First Eagle does not limit itself to one industry. It looks for change and growth opportunities across a wide range of companies.

Source: "First Eagle Looks for Companies 'in Flux,'" *Wall Street Journal*, November 28, 2001, by Adam L. Freeman.

Some funds consciously attempt to adjust for economic risk by holding both cyclical stocks and defensive stocks. If the economy is growing, cyclical stocks will increase in value. If the economy slows and the price of cyclical stock softens, the lower price should be offset or mitigated by the increase in value of defensive stocks. It would be difficult for a small investor to get that type of diversity by purchasing shares of individual companies.

Buying a mutual fund can reduce transaction costs. Because mutual funds buy and sell such large quantities of securities, their commissions are lower per share. If the mutual fund is an index fund and if it mirrors the S&P500, NASDAQ, or another index, there should be no trading costs to speak of since there will be very little change in the holdings.

Buying a mutual fund also provides investment management services such as systems that invest an automatic payroll deduction, transfer money from one fund to another, or allow checks to be drawn against the investment.

Although transaction costs can be lower for a fund than for individual shares, there are significant costs involved in managing a mutual fund. Those costs are passed on to the investor. A load fund is one that charges a sales commission either when you buy or sell the fund. Load funds are often sold by a third party such as a bank or financial planner who does not manage the fund but sells investments in funds managed by others. A mutual fund that does not charge a sales fee is called a no-load fund; most no-load funds are purchased directly from the investment company. In addition to sales commissions, management fees are subtracted from the fund's earnings. High fees can reduce a fund's attractiveness by reducing the amount of earnings that the investor receives. Management fees are usually expressed as an expense ratio, that is, the ratio of expenses to total assets. Investment management firms are required to report the expense ratio to fund holders.

NET ASSET VALUE

A mutual fund is not a share of stock and does not trade in the same way that individual shares do. The price you pay for one unit of a mutual fund is based on the net asset value of the fund. **Net asset value** is calculated by adding the current value of the holdings in that fund, subtracting the liabilities, and dividing by the number of shares outstanding.

$$\text{Net asset value} = \frac{\text{Total market value of all securities} - \text{liabilities}}{\text{Number of shares outstanding}}$$

If you sell your shares in a mutual fund, the fund will pay you the net asset value based on the prices at the close of business on the day you sold the shares. The fund will usually not give you an exact price for your shares until the securities markets have closed because that determines the market value.

Most mutual funds are open-end investment companies. There is no limit to the number of shares they can issue. If there is a balance between fund buyers and sellers, the mutual fund will buy back shares and resell them. If more buyers want to own shares, the investment firm will use the cash inflow to buy securities that meet the investment goals of the fund, increasing the number of shares accordingly. However, if the fund experiences a net loss in investor capital, it may be forced to liquidate its holdings to satisfy the requirements of its shareholders.

There is no security in securities!

TERMS TO KNOW

Securities	Common stock	Stock split
Stock	Voting rights	Stock buyback
Prospectus	Board of Directors	Treasury stock
Transfer agent	Proxy	Book value
Securities and Exchange Commission (SEC)	Preemptive rights	Price-earnings (PE) ratio
	Earnings per share (EPS)	Discounted dividend valuation ratio
Initial public offering (IPO)	Blue chip stock	
	Growth stock	Open outcry market
Authorized shares	Income stock	NASDAQ
Issued shares	Speculative stock	Mutual funds
Preferred stock	Cyclical stock	Net asset value
Dividend	Defensive stock	

TERM PAPERS AND PROJECTS

1. Dotcoms were the latest get rich quick scheme. Not all of the share prices could be justified using standard valuation techniques. How were they able to sell at such high prices so quickly? What did investors think they saw that would justify the high prices they paid?

2. Follow an initial public offering during the course of the term. What price was charged on the first day of trading and how did the price change during the weeks that you observed it? What are the prices of companies in the same industry? Does the EPS reflect industry price-earnings ratios or is there a premium or discount? If so, what do you believe caused the difference?

3. How do small companies issue shares? How do they trade? Interview a small company that has issued shares of stock. Why did they choose equity financing rather than debt?

REVIEW QUESTIONS

1. From an investment and profit point of view, why would it be better to be a stockholder rather than an owner or partner in a failing firm?

2. What are the two basic factors in determining the number of shares of stock a company can issue?

3. What is preferred stock? Why might it be a better investment than bonds?

4. What rights are associated with common stock? How does it differ from preferred stock?

5. What does EPS mean and how is it calculated?
6. What is a blue chip stock? A growth stock? An income stock? Give examples of each.
7. What is a cyclical industry? What major companies are members of cyclical industries?
8. What are defensive stocks and why would you hold them?
9. Why might a firm split its stock?
10. What is treasury stock? How might a company use stock that it holds as treasury stock?
11. What is a price-earnings ratio? How would it be used in evaluating stock?
12. Describe three factors that would affect stock value.
13. How is stock purchased?
14. Why are mutual funds advantageous to small investors?

TIME VALUE OF MONEY CHARTS

Table A-1 Compound Interest

Formula: $FV = PV(1+i)^n$

Interest Rate (i)

Periods (n)	1%	2%	3%	4%	5%	6%	7%	8%	9%	10%	11%	12%	13%	14%	15%	16%	17%	18%	19%	20%
1	1.0100	1.0200	1.0300	1.0400	1.0500	1.0600	1.0700	1.0800	1.0900	1.1000	1.1100	1.1200	1.1300	1.1400	1.1500	1.1600	1.1700	1.1800	1.1900	1.2000
2	1.0201	1.0404	1.0609	1.0816	1.1025	1.1236	1.1449	1.1664	1.1881	1.2100	1.2321	1.2544	1.2769	1.2996	1.3225	1.3456	1.3689	1.3924	1.4161	1.4400
3	1.0303	1.0612	1.0927	1.1249	1.1576	1.1910	1.2250	1.2597	1.2950	1.3310	1.3676	1.4049	1.4429	1.4815	1.5209	1.5609	1.6016	1.6430	1.6852	1.7280
4	1.0406	1.0824	1.1255	1.1699	1.2155	1.2625	1.3108	1.3605	1.4116	1.4641	1.5181	1.5735	1.6305	1.6890	1.7490	1.8106	1.8739	1.9388	2.0053	2.0736
5	1.0510	1.1041	1.1593	1.2167	1.2763	1.3382	1.4026	1.4693	1.5386	1.6105	1.6851	1.7623	1.8424	1.9254	2.0114	2.1003	2.1924	2.2878	2.3864	2.4883
6	1.0615	1.1262	1.1941	1.2653	1.3401	1.4185	1.5007	1.5869	1.6771	1.7716	1.8704	1.9738	2.0820	2.1950	2.3131	2.4364	2.5652	2.6996	2.8398	2.9860
7	1.0721	1.1487	1.2299	1.3159	1.4071	1.5036	1.6058	1.7138	1.8280	1.9487	2.0762	2.2107	2.3526	2.5023	2.6600	2.8262	3.0012	3.1855	3.3793	3.5832
8	1.0829	1.1717	1.2668	1.3686	1.4775	1.5938	1.7182	1.8509	1.9926	2.1436	2.3045	2.4760	2.6584	2.8526	3.0590	3.2784	3.5115	3.7589	4.0214	4.2998
9	1.0937	1.1951	1.3048	1.4233	1.5513	1.6895	1.8385	1.9990	2.1719	2.3579	2.5580	2.7731	3.0040	3.2519	3.5179	3.8030	4.1084	4.4355	4.7854	5.1598
10	1.1046	1.2190	1.3439	1.4802	1.6289	1.7908	1.9672	2.1589	2.3674	2.5937	2.8394	3.1058	3.3946	3.7072	4.0456	4.4114	4.8068	5.2338	5.6947	6.1917
11	1.1157	1.2434	1.3842	1.5395	1.7103	1.8983	2.1049	2.3316	2.5804	2.8531	3.1518	3.4785	3.8359	4.2262	4.6524	5.1173	5.6240	6.1759	6.7767	7.4301
12	1.1268	1.2682	1.4258	1.6010	1.7959	2.0122	2.2522	2.5182	2.8127	3.1384	3.4985	3.8960	4.3345	4.8179	5.3503	5.9360	6.5801	7.2876	8.0642	8.9161
13	1.1381	1.2936	1.4685	1.6651	1.8856	2.1329	2.4098	2.7196	3.0658	3.4523	3.8833	4.3635	4.8980	5.4924	6.1528	6.8858	7.6987	8.5994	9.5964	10.6993
14	1.1495	1.3195	1.5126	1.7317	1.9799	2.2609	2.5785	2.9372	3.3417	3.7975	4.3104	4.8871	5.5348	6.2613	7.0757	7.9875	9.0075	10.1472	11.4198	12.8392
15	1.1610	1.3459	1.5580	1.8009	2.0789	2.3966	2.7590	3.1722	3.6425	4.1772	4.7846	5.4736	6.2543	7.1379	8.1371	9.2655	10.5387	11.9737	13.5895	15.4070
16	1.1726	1.3728	1.6047	1.8730	2.1829	2.5404	2.9522	3.4259	3.9703	4.5950	5.3109	6.1304	7.0673	8.1372	9.3576	10.7480	12.3303	14.1290	16.1715	18.4884
17	1.1843	1.4002	1.6528	1.9479	2.2920	2.6928	3.1588	3.7000	4.3276	5.0545	5.8951	6.8660	7.9861	9.2765	10.7613	12.4677	14.4265	16.6722	19.2441	22.1861
18	1.1961	1.4282	1.7024	2.0258	2.4066	2.8543	3.3799	3.9960	4.7171	5.5599	6.5436	7.6900	9.0243	10.5752	12.3755	14.4625	16.8790	19.6733	22.9005	26.6233
19	1.2081	1.4568	1.7535	2.1068	2.5270	3.0256	3.6165	4.3157	5.1417	6.1159	7.2633	8.6128	10.1974	12.0557	14.2318	16.7765	19.7484	23.2144	27.2516	31.9480
20	1.2202	1.4859	1.8061	2.1911	2.6533	3.2071	3.8697	4.6610	5.6044	6.7275	8.0623	9.6463	11.5231	13.7435	16.3665	19.4608	23.1056	27.3930	32.4294	38.3376
21	1.2324	1.5157	1.8603	2.2788	2.7860	3.3996	4.1406	5.0338	6.1088	7.4002	8.9492	10.8038	13.0211	15.6676	18.8215	22.5745	27.0336	32.3238	38.5910	46.0051
22	1.2447	1.5460	1.9161	2.3699	2.9253	3.6035	4.4304	5.4365	6.6586	8.1403	9.9336	12.1003	14.7138	17.8610	21.6447	26.1864	31.6293	38.1421	45.9233	55.2061
23	1.2572	1.5769	1.9736	2.4647	3.0715	3.8197	4.7405	5.8715	7.2579	8.9543	11.0263	13.5523	16.6266	20.3616	24.8915	30.3762	37.0062	45.0076	54.6487	66.2474
24	1.2697	1.6084	2.0328	2.5633	3.2251	4.0489	5.0724	6.3412	7.9111	9.8497	12.2392	15.1786	18.7881	23.2122	28.6252	35.2364	43.2973	53.1090	65.0320	79.4968
25	1.2824	1.6406	2.0938	2.6658	3.3864	4.2919	5.4274	6.8485	8.6231	10.8347	13.5855	17.0001	21.2305	26.4619	32.9190	40.8742	50.6578	62.6686	77.3881	95.3962
26	1.2953	1.6734	2.1566	2.7725	3.5557	4.5494	5.8074	7.3964	9.3992	11.9182	15.0799	19.0401	23.9905	30.1666	37.8568	47.4141	59.2697	73.9490	92.0918	114.4755
27	1.3082	1.7069	2.2213	2.8834	3.7335	4.8223	6.2139	7.9881	10.2451	13.1100	16.7386	21.3249	27.1093	34.3899	43.5353	55.0004	69.3455	87.2598	109.5893	137.3706
28	1.3213	1.7410	2.2879	2.9987	3.9201	5.1117	6.6488	8.6271	11.1671	14.4210	18.5799	23.8839	30.6335	39.2045	50.0656	63.8004	81.1342	102.9666	130.4112	164.8447
29	1.3345	1.7758	2.3566	3.1187	4.1161	5.4184	7.1143	9.3173	12.1722	15.8631	20.6237	26.7499	34.6158	44.6931	57.5755	74.0085	94.9271	121.5005	155.1893	197.8136
30	1.3478	1.8114	2.4273	3.2434	4.3219	5.7435	7.6123	10.0627	13.2677	17.4494	22.8923	29.9599	39.1159	50.9502	66.2118	85.8499	111.0647	143.3706	184.6753	237.3763
31	1.3613	1.8476	2.5001	3.3731	4.5380	6.0881	8.1451	10.8677	14.4618	19.1943	25.4104	33.5551	44.2010	58.0832	76.1435	99.5859	129.9456	169.1774	219.7636	284.8516
32	1.3749	1.8845	2.5751	3.5081	4.7649	6.4534	8.7153	11.7371	15.7633	21.1138	28.2056	37.5817	49.9471	66.2148	87.5651	115.5196	152.0364	199.6293	261.5187	341.8219
33	1.3887	1.9222	2.6523	3.6484	5.0032	6.8406	9.3253	12.6760	17.1820	23.2252	31.3082	42.0915	56.4402	75.4849	100.6998	134.0027	177.8826	235.5625	311.2073	410.1863
34	1.4026	1.9607	2.7319	3.7943	5.2533	7.2510	9.9781	13.6901	18.7284	25.5477	34.7521	47.1425	63.7774	86.0528	115.8048	155.4432	208.1226	277.9638	370.3366	492.2235
35	1.4166	1.9999	2.8139	3.9461	5.5160	7.6861	10.6766	14.7853	20.4140	28.1024	38.5749	52.7996	72.0685	98.1002	133.1755	180.3141	243.5035	327.9973	440.7006	590.6682
36	1.4308	2.0399	2.8983	4.1039	5.7918	8.1473	11.4239	15.9682	22.2512	30.9127	42.8181	59.1356	81.4374	111.8342	153.1519	209.1643	284.8991	387.0368	524.4337	708.8019

Table A-2 Daily Compound Interest

$FV = PV\,(1 + i/365)^{\text{number of days}}$

Time	2.0%	4.0%	5.0%	5.5%	6.0%	6.5%	7.0%	7.5%	8.0%	8.5%	9.0%	10.0%	12.0%	15.0%	18.0%	21.0%
1 day	1.00005	1.00011	1.00014	1.00015	1.00016	1.00018	1.00019	1.00021	1.00022	1.00023	1.00025	1.00027	1.00033	1.00041	1.00049	1.00058
2 days	1.00011	1.00022	1.00027	1.00030	1.00033	1.00036	1.00038	1.00041	1.00044	1.00047	1.00049	1.00055	1.00066	1.00082	1.00099	1.00115
3 days	1.00016	1.00033	1.00041	1.00045	1.00049	1.00053	1.00058	1.00062	1.00066	1.00070	1.00074	1.00082	1.00099	1.00123	1.00148	1.00173
4 days	1.00022	1.00044	1.00055	1.00060	1.00066	1.00071	1.00077	1.00082	1.00088	1.00093	1.00099	1.00110	1.00132	1.00164	1.00197	1.00230
5 days	1.00027	1.00055	1.00069	1.00075	1.00082	1.00089	1.00096	1.00103	1.00110	1.00116	1.00123	1.00137	1.00164	1.00206	1.00247	1.00288
6 days	1.00033	1.00066	1.00082	1.00090	1.00099	1.00107	1.00115	1.00123	1.00132	1.00140	1.00148	1.00164	1.00197	1.00247	1.00296	1.00346
1 week	1.00038	1.00077	1.00096	1.00106	1.00115	1.00125	1.00134	1.00144	1.00154	1.00163	1.00173	1.00192	1.00230	1.00288	1.00346	1.00403
2 weeks	1.00077	1.00154	1.00192	1.00211	1.00230	1.00250	1.00269	1.00288	1.00307	1.00327	1.00346	1.00384	1.00461	1.00577	1.00693	1.00808
3 weeks	1.00115	1.00230	1.00288	1.00317	1.00346	1.00375	1.00404	1.00432	1.00461	1.00490	1.00519	1.00577	1.00693	1.00867	1.01041	1.01215
1 month	1.00167	1.00334	1.00418	1.00459	1.00501	1.00543	1.00585	1.00627	1.00669	1.00711	1.00753	1.00837	1.01005	1.01258	1.01511	1.01765
2 months	1.00334	1.00669	1.00837	1.00921	1.01005	1.01089	1.01173	1.01258	1.01342	1.01427	1.01511	1.01680	1.02020	1.02531	1.03045	1.03561
3 months	1.00501	1.01005	1.01258	1.01384	1.01511	1.01638	1.01765	1.01892	1.02020	1.02147	1.02275	1.02531	1.03045	1.03820	1.04602	1.05389
4 months	1.00669	1.01342	1.01681	1.01850	1.02020	1.02190	1.02361	1.02531	1.02702	1.02874	1.03045	1.03389	1.04080	1.05126	1.06182	1.07249
5 months	1.00837	1.01681	1.02105	1.02318	1.02531	1.02745	1.02959	1.03174	1.03389	1.03605	1.03821	1.04254	1.05126	1.06448	1.07786	1.09141
6 months	1.01005	1.02020	1.02531	1.02788	1.03045	1.03303	1.03562	1.03821	1.04081	1.04341	1.04602	1.05126	1.06183	1.07787	1.09415	1.11068
9 months	1.01511	1.03045	1.03821	1.04211	1.04602	1.04995	1.05390	1.05786	1.06183	1.06582	1.06982	1.07787	1.09416	1.11905	1.14450	1.17053
1 year	1.02020	1.04081	1.05127	1.05654	1.06183	1.06715	1.07250	1.07788	1.08328	1.08871	1.09416	1.10516	1.12747	1.16180	1.19716	1.23360
2 years	1.04081	1.08328	1.10516	1.11627	1.12749	1.13882	1.15026	1.16182	1.17349	1.18528	1.19719	1.22137	1.27120	1.34978	1.43320	1.52178
3 years	1.06183	1.12749	1.16182	1.17938	1.19720	1.21529	1.23365	1.25229	1.27122	1.29042	1.30992	1.34980	1.43324	1.56817	1.71578	1.87727
4 years	1.08328	1.17350	1.22139	1.24606	1.27122	1.29690	1.32309	1.34982	1.37708	1.40489	1.43327	1.49174	1.61595	1.82189	2.05407	2.31581
5 years	1.10517	1.22139	1.28400	1.31650	1.34983	1.38399	1.41902	1.45494	1.49176	1.52951	1.56823	1.64861	1.82194	2.11667	2.45906	2.85679
10 years	1.22140	1.49179	1.64866	1.73318	1.82203	1.91543	2.01362	2.11684	2.22535	2.33942	2.45933	2.71791	3.31946	4.48031	6.04696	8.16124
15 years	1.34985	1.82206	2.11689	2.28174	2.45942	2.65094	2.85736	3.07986	3.31968	3.57817	3.85678	4.48077	6.04786	9.48335	14.86983	23.31494
20 years	1.49181	2.22544	2.71810	3.00392	3.31979	3.66887	4.05466	4.48100	4.95216	5.47286	6.04831	7.38703	11.01883	20.07316	36.56577	66.60584
25 years	1.64870	2.71813	3.49004	3.95467	4.48114	5.07768	5.75364	6.51956	7.38744	8.37083	9.48510	12.17832	20.07564	42.48834	89.91734	190.27879
30 years	1.82209	3.31990	4.48123	5.20633	6.04875	7.02747	8.16453	9.48554	11.02028	12.80330	14.87478	20.07729	36.57659	89.93396	221.11190	543.58624

311

Table A-3 Present Value

Formula: $PV = FV \left[\dfrac{1}{(1+i)^n} \right]$

Interest Rate (i)

Periods (n)	1%	2%	3%	4%	5%	6%	7%	8%	9%	10%	11%	12%	13%	14%	15%	16%	17%	18%	19%	20%
1	0.9901	0.9804	0.9709	0.9615	0.9524	0.9434	0.9346	0.9259	0.9174	0.9091	0.9009	0.8929	0.8850	0.8772	0.8696	0.8621	0.8547	0.8475	0.8403	0.8333
2	0.9803	0.9612	0.9426	0.9246	0.9070	0.8900	0.8734	0.8573	0.8417	0.8264	0.8116	0.7972	0.7831	0.7695	0.7561	0.7432	0.7305	0.7182	0.7062	0.6944
3	0.9706	0.9423	0.9151	0.8890	0.8638	0.8396	0.8163	0.7938	0.7722	0.7513	0.7312	0.7118	0.6931	0.6750	0.6575	0.6407	0.6244	0.6086	0.5934	0.5787
4	0.9610	0.9238	0.8885	0.8548	0.8227	0.7921	0.7629	0.7350	0.7084	0.6830	0.6587	0.6355	0.6133	0.5921	0.5718	0.5523	0.5337	0.5158	0.4987	0.4823
5	0.9515	0.9057	0.8626	0.8219	0.7835	0.7473	0.7130	0.6806	0.6499	0.6209	0.5935	0.5674	0.5428	0.5194	0.4972	0.4761	0.4561	0.4371	0.4190	0.4019
6	0.9420	0.8880	0.8375	0.7903	0.7462	0.7050	0.6663	0.6302	0.5963	0.5645	0.5346	0.5066	0.4803	0.4556	0.4323	0.4104	0.3898	0.3704	0.3521	0.3349
7	0.9327	0.8706	0.8131	0.7599	0.7107	0.6651	0.6227	0.5835	0.5470	0.5132	0.4817	0.4523	0.4251	0.3996	0.3759	0.3538	0.3332	0.3139	0.2959	0.2791
8	0.9235	0.8535	0.7894	0.7307	0.6768	0.6274	0.5820	0.5403	0.5019	0.4665	0.4339	0.4039	0.3762	0.3506	0.3269	0.3050	0.2848	0.2660	0.2487	0.2326
9	0.9143	0.8368	0.7664	0.7026	0.6446	0.5919	0.5439	0.5002	0.4604	0.4241	0.3909	0.3606	0.3329	0.3075	0.2843	0.2630	0.2434	0.2255	0.2090	0.1938
10	0.9053	0.8203	0.7441	0.6756	0.6139	0.5584	0.5083	0.4632	0.4224	0.3855	0.3522	0.3220	0.2946	0.2697	0.2472	0.2267	0.2080	0.1911	0.1756	0.1615
11	0.8963	0.8043	0.7224	0.6496	0.5847	0.5268	0.4751	0.4289	0.3875	0.3505	0.3173	0.2875	0.2607	0.2366	0.2149	0.1954	0.1778	0.1619	0.1476	0.1346
12	0.8874	0.7885	0.7014	0.6246	0.5568	0.4970	0.4440	0.3971	0.3555	0.3186	0.2858	0.2567	0.2307	0.2076	0.1869	0.1685	0.1520	0.1372	0.1240	0.1122
13	0.8787	0.7730	0.6810	0.6006	0.5303	0.4688	0.4150	0.3677	0.3262	0.2897	0.2575	0.2292	0.2042	0.1821	0.1625	0.1452	0.1299	0.1163	0.1042	0.0935
14	0.8700	0.7579	0.6611	0.5775	0.5051	0.4423	0.3878	0.3405	0.2992	0.2633	0.2320	0.2046	0.1807	0.1597	0.1413	0.1252	0.1110	0.0985	0.0876	0.0779
15	0.8613	0.7430	0.6419	0.5553	0.4810	0.4173	0.3624	0.3152	0.2745	0.2394	0.2090	0.1827	0.1599	0.1401	0.1229	0.1079	0.0949	0.0835	0.0736	0.0649
16	0.8528	0.7284	0.6232	0.5339	0.4581	0.3936	0.3387	0.2919	0.2519	0.2176	0.1883	0.1631	0.1415	0.1229	0.1069	0.0930	0.0811	0.0708	0.0618	0.0541
17	0.8444	0.7142	0.6050	0.5134	0.4363	0.3714	0.3166	0.2703	0.2311	0.1978	0.1696	0.1456	0.1252	0.1078	0.0929	0.0802	0.0693	0.0600	0.0520	0.0451
18	0.8360	0.7002	0.5874	0.4936	0.4155	0.3503	0.2959	0.2502	0.2120	0.1799	0.1528	0.1300	0.1108	0.0946	0.0808	0.0691	0.0592	0.0508	0.0437	0.0376
19	0.8277	0.6864	0.5703	0.4746	0.3957	0.3305	0.2765	0.2317	0.1945	0.1635	0.1377	0.1161	0.0981	0.0829	0.0703	0.0596	0.0506	0.0431	0.0367	0.0313
20	0.8195	0.6730	0.5537	0.4564	0.3769	0.3118	0.2584	0.2145	0.1784	0.1486	0.1240	0.1037	0.0868	0.0728	0.0611	0.0514	0.0433	0.0365	0.0308	0.0261
21	0.8114	0.6598	0.5375	0.4388	0.3589	0.2942	0.2415	0.1987	0.1637	0.1351	0.1117	0.0926	0.0768	0.0638	0.0531	0.0443	0.0370	0.0309	0.0259	0.0217
22	0.8034	0.6468	0.5219	0.4220	0.3418	0.2775	0.2257	0.1839	0.1502	0.1228	0.1007	0.0826	0.0680	0.0560	0.0462	0.0382	0.0316	0.0262	0.0218	0.0181
23	0.7954	0.6342	0.5067	0.4057	0.3256	0.2618	0.2109	0.1703	0.1378	0.1117	0.0907	0.0738	0.0601	0.0491	0.0402	0.0329	0.0270	0.0222	0.0183	0.0151
24	0.7876	0.6217	0.4919	0.3901	0.3101	0.2470	0.1971	0.1577	0.1264	0.1015	0.0817	0.0659	0.0532	0.0431	0.0349	0.0284	0.0231	0.0188	0.0154	0.0126
25	0.7798	0.6095	0.4776	0.3751	0.2953	0.2330	0.1842	0.1460	0.1160	0.0923	0.0736	0.0588	0.0471	0.0378	0.0304	0.0245	0.0197	0.0160	0.0129	0.0105
26	0.7720	0.5976	0.4637	0.3607	0.2812	0.2198	0.1722	0.1352	0.1064	0.0839	0.0663	0.0525	0.0417	0.0331	0.0264	0.0211	0.0169	0.0135	0.0109	0.0087
27	0.7644	0.5859	0.4502	0.3468	0.2678	0.2074	0.1609	0.1252	0.0976	0.0763	0.0597	0.0469	0.0369	0.0291	0.0230	0.0182	0.0144	0.0115	0.0091	0.0073
28	0.7568	0.5744	0.4371	0.3335	0.2551	0.1956	0.1504	0.1159	0.0895	0.0693	0.0538	0.0419	0.0326	0.0255	0.0200	0.0157	0.0123	0.0097	0.0077	0.0061
29	0.7493	0.5631	0.4243	0.3207	0.2429	0.1846	0.1406	0.1073	0.0822	0.0630	0.0485	0.0374	0.0289	0.0224	0.0174	0.0135	0.0105	0.0082	0.0064	0.0051
30	0.7419	0.5521	0.4120	0.3083	0.2314	0.1741	0.1314	0.0994	0.0754	0.0573	0.0437	0.0334	0.0256	0.0196	0.0151	0.0116	0.0090	0.0070	0.0054	0.0042
31	0.7346	0.5412	0.4000	0.2965	0.2204	0.1643	0.1228	0.0920	0.0691	0.0521	0.0394	0.0298	0.0226	0.0172	0.0131	0.0100	0.0077	0.0059	0.0046	0.0035
32	0.7273	0.5306	0.3883	0.2851	0.2099	0.1550	0.1147	0.0852	0.0634	0.0474	0.0355	0.0266	0.0200	0.0151	0.0114	0.0087	0.0066	0.0050	0.0038	0.0029
33	0.7201	0.5202	0.3770	0.2741	0.1999	0.1462	0.1072	0.0789	0.0582	0.0431	0.0319	0.0238	0.0177	0.0132	0.0099	0.0075	0.0056	0.0042	0.0032	0.0024
34	0.7130	0.5100	0.3660	0.2636	0.1904	0.1379	0.1002	0.0730	0.0534	0.0391	0.0288	0.0212	0.0157	0.0116	0.0086	0.0064	0.0048	0.0036	0.0027	0.0020
35	0.7059	0.5000	0.3554	0.2534	0.1813	0.1301	0.0937	0.0676	0.0490	0.0356	0.0259	0.0189	0.0139	0.0102	0.0075	0.0055	0.0041	0.0030	0.0023	0.0017
36	0.6989	0.4902	0.3450	0.2437	0.1727	0.1227	0.0875	0.0626	0.0449	0.0323	0.0234	0.0169	0.0123	0.0089	0.0065	0.0048	0.0035	0.0026	0.0019	0.0014

Source: Adelman/Marks. Entrepreneurial Finance: Finance for Small Business, 2/e. © 2000 Pearson Prentice Hall, Upper Saddle River, NJ.

Table A-4 Sinking Fund

(n)	1%	1½%	2%	2½%	3%	4%	5%	6%	8%	10%	12%
1	1.00000	1.00000	1.00000	1.00000	1.00000	1.00000	1.00000	1.00000	1.00000	1.00000	1.00000
2	0.49751	0.49628	0.49505	0.49383	0.49261	0.49020	0.48780	0.48544	0.48077	0.47619	0.47170
3	0.33002	0.32838	0.32675	0.32514	0.32353	0.32035	0.31721	0.31411	0.30803	0.30211	0.29635
4	0.24628	0.24444	0.24262	0.24082	0.23903	0.23549	0.23201	0.22859	0.22192	0.21547	0.20923
5	0.19604	0.19409	0.19216	0.19025	0.18835	0.18463	0.18097	0.17740	0.17046	0.16380	0.15741
6	0.16255	0.16053	0.15853	0.15655	0.15460	0.15076	0.14702	0.14336	0.13632	0.12961	0.12323
7	0.13863	0.13656	0.13451	0.13250	0.13051	0.12661	0.12282	0.11914	0.11207	0.10541	0.09912
8	0.12069	0.11858	0.11651	0.11447	0.11246	0.10853	0.10472	0.10104	0.09401	0.08744	0.08130
9	0.10674	0.10461	0.10252	0.10046	0.09843	0.09449	0.09069	0.08702	0.08008	0.07364	0.06768
10	0.09558	0.09343	0.09133	0.08926	0.08723	0.08329	0.07950	0.07587	0.06903	0.06275	0.05698
11	0.08645	0.08429	0.08218	0.08011	0.07808	0.07415	0.07039	0.06679	0.06008	0.05396	0.04842
12	0.07885	0.07668	0.07456	0.07249	0.07046	0.06655	0.06283	0.05928	0.05270	0.04676	0.04144
13	0.07241	0.07024	0.06812	0.06605	0.06403	0.06014	0.05646	0.05296	0.04652	0.04078	0.03568
14	0.06690	0.06472	0.06260	0.06054	0.05853	0.05467	0.05102	0.04758	0.04130	0.03575	0.03087
15	0.06212	0.05994	0.05783	0.05577	0.05377	0.04994	0.04634	0.04296	0.03683	0.03147	0.02682
16	0.05794	0.05577	0.05365	0.05160	0.04961	0.04582	0.04227	0.03895	0.03298	0.02782	0.02339
17	0.05426	0.05208	0.04997	0.04793	0.04595	0.04220	0.03870	0.03544	0.02963	0.02466	0.02046
18	0.05098	0.04881	0.04670	0.04467	0.04271	0.03899	0.03555	0.03236	0.02670	0.02193	0.01794
19	0.04805	0.04588	0.04378	0.04176	0.03981	0.03614	0.03275	0.02962	0.02413	0.01955	0.01576
20	0.04542	0.04325	0.04116	0.03915	0.03722	0.03358	0.03024	0.02718	0.02185	0.01746	0.01388
21	0.04303	0.04087	0.03878	0.03679	0.03487	0.03128	0.02800	0.02500	0.01983	0.01562	0.01224
22	0.04086	0.03870	0.03663	0.03465	0.03275	0.02920	0.02597	0.02305	0.01803	0.01401	0.01081
23	0.03889	0.03673	0.03467	0.03270	0.03081	0.02731	0.02414	0.02128	0.01642	0.01257	0.00956
24	0.03707	0.03492	0.03287	0.03091	0.02905	0.02559	0.02247	0.01968	0.01498	0.01130	0.00846
25	0.03541	0.03326	0.03122	0.02928	0.02743	0.02401	0.02095	0.01823	0.01368	0.01017	0.00750
26	0.03387	0.03173	0.02970	0.02777	0.02594	0.02257	0.01956	0.01690	0.01251	0.00916	0.00665
27	0.03245	0.03032	0.02829	0.02638	0.02456	0.02124	0.01829	0.01570	0.01145	0.00826	0.00590
28	0.03112	0.02900	0.02699	0.02509	0.02329	0.02001	0.01712	0.01459	0.01049	0.00745	0.00524
29	0.02990	0.02778	0.02578	0.02389	0.02211	0.01888	0.01605	0.01358	0.00962	0.00673	0.00466
30	0.02875	0.02664	0.02465	0.02278	0.02102	0.01783	0.01505	0.01265	0.00883	0.00608	0.00414
31	0.02768	0.02557	0.02360	0.02174	0.02000	0.01686	0.01413	0.01179	0.00811	0.00550	0.00369
32	0.02667	0.02458	0.02261	0.02077	0.01905	0.01595	0.01328	0.01100	0.00745	0.00497	0.00328
33	0.02573	0.02364	0.02169	0.01986	0.01816	0.01510	0.01249	0.01027	0.00685	0.00450	0.00292
34	0.02484	0.02276	0.02082	0.01901	0.01732	0.01431	0.01176	0.00960	0.00630	0.00407	0.00260
35	0.02400	0.02193	0.02000	0.01821	0.01654	0.01358	0.01107	0.00897	0.00580	0.00369	0.00232
36	0.02321	0.02115	0.01923	0.01745	0.01580	0.01289	0.01043	0.00839	0.00534	0.00334	0.00206
37	0.02247	0.02041	0.01851	0.01674	0.01511	0.01224	0.00984	0.00786	0.00492	0.00303	0.00184
38	0.02176	0.01972	0.01782	0.01607	0.01446	0.01163	0.00928	0.00736	0.00454	0.00275	0.00164
39	0.02109	0.01905	0.01717	0.01544	0.01384	0.01106	0.00876	0.00689	0.00419	0.00249	0.00146
40	0.02046	0.01843	0.01656	0.01484	0.01326	0.01052	0.00828	0.00646	0.00386	0.00226	0.00130
41	0.01985	0.01783	0.01597	0.01427	0.01271	0.01002	0.00782	0.00606	0.00356	0.00205	0.00116
42	0.01928	0.01726	0.01542	0.01373	0.01219	0.00954	0.00739	0.00568	0.00329	0.00186	0.00104
43	0.01873	0.01672	0.01489	0.01322	0.01170	0.00909	0.00699	0.00533	0.00303	0.00169	0.00092
44	0.01820	0.01621	0.01439	0.01273	0.01123	0.00866	0.00662	0.00501	0.00280	0.00153	0.00083
45	0.01771	0.01572	0.01391	0.01227	0.01079	0.00826	0.00626	0.00470	0.00259	0.00139	0.00074
46	0.01723	0.01525	0.01345	0.01183	0.01036	0.00788	0.00593	0.00441	0.00239	0.00126	0.00066
47	0.01677	0.01480	0.01302	0.01141	0.00996	0.00752	0.00561	0.00415	0.00221	0.00115	0.00059
48	0.01633	0.01437	0.01260	0.01101	0.00958	0.00718	0.00532	0.00390	0.00204	0.00104	0.00052
49	0.01591	0.01396	0.01220	0.01062	0.00921	0.00686	0.00504	0.00366	0.00189	0.00095	0.00047
50	0.01551	0.01357	0.01182	0.01026	0.00887	0.00655	0.00478	0.00344	0.00174	0.00086	0.00042

n = number of periods in annuity; i = interest per period

Source: Kindsfather/Parish. *Business Mathematics.* © 2003 Pearson Prentice Hall, Upper Saddle River, NJ.

313

Table A-5 Present Value of an Annuity Due

Formula: $PV = A\left[\left[\dfrac{(1+i)^{(n-1)} - 1}{i(1+i)^{(n-1)}}\right] + 1\right]$

Interest Rate (i)

Periods (n)	1%	2%	3%	4%	5%	6%	7%	8%	9%	10%	11%	12%	13%	14%	15%	16%	17%	18%	19%	20%
1	1.0000	1.0000	1.0000	1.0000	1.0000	1.0000	1.0000	1.0000	1.0000	1.0000	1.0000	1.0000	1.0000	1.0000	1.0000	1.0000	1.0000	1.0000	1.0000	1.0000
2	1.9901	1.9804	1.9709	1.9615	1.9524	1.9434	1.9346	1.9259	1.9174	1.9091	1.9009	1.8929	1.8850	1.8772	1.8696	1.8621	1.8547	1.8475	1.8403	1.8333
3	2.9704	2.9416	2.9135	2.8861	2.8594	2.8334	2.8080	2.7833	2.7591	2.7355	2.7125	2.6901	2.6681	2.6467	2.6257	2.6052	2.5852	2.5656	2.5465	2.5278
4	3.9410	3.8839	3.8286	3.7751	3.7232	3.6730	3.6243	3.5771	3.5313	3.4869	3.4437	3.4018	3.3612	3.3216	3.2832	3.2459	3.2096	3.1743	3.1399	3.1065
5	4.9020	4.8077	4.7171	4.6299	4.5460	4.4651	4.3872	4.3121	4.2397	4.1699	4.1024	4.0373	3.9745	3.9137	3.8550	3.7982	3.7432	3.6901	3.6386	3.5887
6	5.8534	5.7135	5.5797	5.4518	5.3295	5.2124	5.1002	4.9927	4.8897	4.7908	4.6959	4.6048	4.5172	4.4331	4.3522	4.2743	4.1993	4.1272	4.0576	3.9906
7	6.7955	6.6014	6.4172	6.2421	6.0757	5.9173	5.7665	5.6229	5.4859	5.3553	5.2305	5.1114	4.9975	4.8887	4.7845	4.6847	4.5892	4.4976	4.4098	4.3255
8	7.7282	7.4720	7.2303	7.0021	6.7864	6.5824	6.3893	6.2064	6.0330	5.8684	5.7122	5.5638	5.4226	5.2883	5.1604	5.0386	4.9224	4.8115	4.7057	4.6046
9	8.6517	8.3255	8.0197	7.7327	7.4632	7.2098	6.9713	6.7466	6.5348	6.3349	6.1461	5.9676	5.7988	5.6389	5.4873	5.3436	5.2072	5.0776	4.9544	4.8372
10	9.5660	9.1622	8.7861	8.4353	8.1078	7.8017	7.5152	7.2469	6.9952	6.7590	6.5370	6.3282	6.1317	5.9464	5.7716	5.6065	5.4506	5.3030	5.1633	5.0310
11	10.4713	9.9826	9.5302	9.1109	8.7217	8.3601	8.0236	7.7101	7.4177	7.1446	6.8892	6.6502	6.4262	6.2161	6.0188	5.8332	5.6586	5.4941	5.3389	5.1925
12	11.3676	10.7868	10.2526	9.7605	9.3064	8.8869	8.4987	8.1390	7.8052	7.4951	7.2065	6.9377	6.6869	6.4527	6.2337	6.0286	5.8364	5.6560	5.4865	5.3271
13	12.2551	11.5753	10.9540	10.3851	9.8633	9.3838	8.9427	8.5361	8.1607	7.8137	7.4924	7.1944	6.9176	6.6603	6.4206	6.1971	5.9884	5.7932	5.6105	5.4392
14	13.1337	12.3484	11.6350	10.9856	10.3936	9.8527	9.3577	8.9038	8.4869	8.1034	7.7499	7.4235	7.1218	6.8424	6.5831	6.3423	6.1183	5.9095	5.7147	5.5327
15	14.0037	13.1062	12.2961	11.5631	10.8986	10.2950	9.7455	9.2442	8.7862	8.3667	7.9819	7.6282	7.3025	7.0021	6.7245	6.4675	6.2293	6.0081	5.8023	5.6106
16	14.8651	13.8493	12.9379	12.1184	11.3797	10.7122	10.1079	9.5595	9.0607	8.6061	8.1909	7.8109	7.4624	7.1422	6.8474	6.5755	6.3242	6.0916	5.8759	5.6755
17	15.7179	14.5777	13.5611	12.6523	11.8378	11.1059	10.4466	9.8514	9.3126	8.8237	8.3792	7.9740	7.6039	7.2651	6.9542	6.6685	6.4053	6.1624	5.9377	5.7296
18	16.5623	15.2919	14.1661	13.1657	12.2741	11.4773	10.7632	10.1216	9.5436	9.0216	8.5488	8.1196	7.7291	7.3729	7.0472	6.7487	6.4746	6.2223	5.9897	5.7746
19	17.3983	15.9920	14.7535	13.6593	12.6896	11.8276	11.0591	10.3719	9.7556	9.2014	8.7016	8.2497	7.8399	7.4674	7.1280	6.8178	6.5339	6.2732	6.0333	5.8122
20	18.2260	16.6785	15.3238	14.1339	13.0853	12.1581	11.3356	10.6036	9.9501	9.3649	8.8393	8.3658	7.9380	7.5504	7.1982	6.8775	6.5845	6.3162	6.0700	5.8435
21	19.0456	17.3514	15.8775	14.5903	13.4622	12.4699	11.5940	10.8181	10.1285	9.5136	8.9633	8.4694	8.0248	7.6231	7.2593	6.9288	6.6278	6.3527	6.1009	5.8696
22	19.8570	18.0112	16.4150	15.0292	13.8212	12.7641	11.8355	11.0168	10.2922	9.6487	9.0751	8.5620	8.1016	7.6870	7.3125	6.9731	6.6648	6.3837	6.1268	5.8913
23	20.6604	18.6580	16.9369	15.4511	14.1630	13.0416	12.0612	11.2007	10.4424	9.7715	9.1757	8.6446	8.1695	7.7429	7.3587	7.0113	6.6964	6.4099	6.1486	5.9094
24	21.4558	19.2922	17.4436	15.8568	14.4886	13.3034	12.2722	11.3711	10.5802	9.8832	9.2664	8.7184	8.2297	7.7921	7.3988	7.0442	6.7234	6.4321	6.1668	5.9245
25	22.2434	19.9139	17.9355	16.2470	14.7986	13.5504	12.4693	11.5288	10.7066	9.9847	9.3481	8.7843	8.2829	7.8351	7.4338	7.0726	6.7465	6.4509	6.1822	5.9371
26	23.0232	20.5235	18.4131	16.6221	15.0939	13.7834	12.6536	11.6748	10.8226	10.0770	9.4217	8.8431	8.3300	7.8729	7.4641	7.0971	6.7662	6.4669	6.1951	5.9476
27	23.7952	21.1210	18.8768	16.9828	15.3752	14.0032	12.8258	11.8100	10.9290	10.1609	9.4881	8.8957	8.3717	7.9061	7.4906	7.1182	6.7831	6.4804	6.2060	5.9563
28	24.5596	21.7069	19.3270	17.3296	15.6430	14.2105	12.9867	11.9352	11.0266	10.2372	9.5478	8.9426	8.4086	7.9352	7.5135	7.1364	6.7975	6.4919	6.2151	5.9636
29	25.3164	22.2813	19.7641	17.6631	15.8981	14.4062	13.1371	12.0511	11.1161	10.3066	9.6016	8.9844	8.4412	7.9607	7.5335	7.1520	6.8099	6.5016	6.2228	5.9697
30	26.0658	22.8444	20.1885	17.9837	16.1411	14.5907	13.2777	12.1584	11.1983	10.3696	9.6501	9.0218	8.4701	7.9830	7.5509	7.1656	6.8204	6.5098	6.2292	5.9747
31	26.8077	23.3965	20.6004	18.2920	16.3725	14.7648	13.4090	12.2578	11.2737	10.4269	9.6938	9.0552	8.4957	8.0027	7.5660	7.1772	6.8294	6.5168	6.2347	5.9789
32	27.5423	23.9377	21.0004	18.5885	16.5928	14.9291	13.5318	12.3498	11.3426	10.4790	9.7331	9.0850	8.5183	8.0199	7.5791	7.1872	6.8371	6.5227	6.2392	5.9824
33	28.2696	24.4683	21.3888	18.8736	16.8027	15.0840	13.6466	12.4350	11.4062	10.5264	9.7686	9.1116	8.5383	8.0350	7.5905	7.1959	6.8437	6.5277	6.2430	5.9854
34	28.9897	24.9886	21.7658	19.1476	17.0025	15.2302	13.7538	12.5139	11.4644	10.5694	9.8005	9.1354	8.5560	8.0482	7.6005	7.2034	6.8493	6.5320	6.2462	5.9878
35	29.7027	25.4986	22.1318	19.4112	17.1929	15.3681	13.8540	12.5869	11.5178	10.6086	9.8293	9.1566	8.5717	8.0599	7.6091	7.2098	6.8541	6.5356	6.2489	5.9898
36	30.4086	25.9986	22.4872	19.6646	17.3742	15.4982	13.9477	12.6546	11.5668	10.6442	9.8552	9.1755	8.5856	8.0700	7.6166	7.2153	6.8582	6.5386	6.2512	5.9915

Source: Adelman/Marks. Entrepreneurial Finance: Finance for Small Business, 2/e. © 2000 Pearson Prentice Hall, Upper Saddle River, NJ.

Table A-6 Present Value of an Ordinary Annuity

Formula: $PV = A\left[\dfrac{(1 + i)^n - 1}{i(1 + i)^n}\right]$

Interest Rate (i)

Periods (n)	1%	2%	3%	4%	5%	6%	7%	8%	9%	10%	11%	12%	13%	14%	15%	16%	17%	18%	19%	20%
1	0.9901	0.9804	0.9709	0.9615	0.9524	0.9434	0.9346	0.9259	0.9174	0.9091	0.9009	0.8929	0.8850	0.8772	0.8696	0.8621	0.8547	0.8475	0.8403	0.8333
2	1.9704	1.9416	1.9135	1.8861	1.8594	1.8334	1.8080	1.7833	1.7591	1.7355	1.7125	1.6901	1.6681	1.6467	1.6257	1.6052	1.5852	1.5656	1.5465	1.5278
3	2.9410	2.8839	2.8286	2.7751	2.7232	2.6730	2.6243	2.5771	2.5313	2.4869	2.4437	2.4018	2.3612	2.3216	2.2832	2.2459	2.2096	2.1743	2.1399	2.1065
4	3.9020	3.8077	3.7171	3.6299	3.5460	3.4651	3.3872	3.3121	3.2397	3.1699	3.1024	3.0373	2.9745	2.9137	2.8550	2.7982	2.7432	2.6901	2.6386	2.5887
5	4.8534	4.7135	4.5797	4.4518	4.3295	4.2124	4.1002	3.9927	3.8897	3.7908	3.6959	3.6048	3.5172	3.4331	3.3522	3.2743	3.1993	3.1272	3.0576	2.9906
6	5.7955	5.6014	5.4172	5.2421	5.0757	4.9173	4.7665	4.6229	4.4859	4.3553	4.2305	4.1114	3.9975	3.8887	3.7845	3.6847	3.5892	3.4976	3.4098	3.3255
7	6.7282	6.4720	6.2303	6.0021	5.7864	5.5824	5.3893	5.2064	5.0330	4.8684	4.7122	4.5638	4.4226	4.2883	4.1604	4.0386	3.9224	3.8115	3.7057	3.6046
8	7.6517	7.3255	7.0197	6.7327	6.4632	6.2098	5.9713	5.7466	5.5348	5.3349	5.1461	4.9676	4.7988	4.6389	4.4873	4.3436	4.2072	4.0776	3.9544	3.8372
9	8.5660	8.1622	7.7861	7.4353	7.1078	6.8017	6.5152	6.2469	5.9952	5.7590	5.5370	5.3282	5.1317	4.9464	4.7716	4.6065	4.4506	4.3030	4.1633	4.0310
10	9.4713	8.9826	8.5302	8.1109	7.7217	7.3601	7.0236	6.7101	6.4177	6.1446	5.8892	5.6502	5.4262	5.2161	5.0188	4.8332	4.6586	4.4941	4.3389	4.1925
11	10.3676	9.7868	9.2526	8.7605	8.3064	7.8869	7.4987	7.1390	6.8052	6.4951	6.2065	5.9377	5.6869	5.4527	5.2337	5.0286	4.8364	4.6560	4.4865	4.3271
12	11.2551	10.5753	9.9540	9.3851	8.8633	8.3838	7.9427	7.5361	7.1607	6.8137	6.4924	6.1944	5.9176	5.6603	5.4206	5.1971	4.9884	4.7932	4.6105	4.4392
13	12.1337	11.3484	10.6350	9.9856	9.3936	8.8527	8.3577	7.9038	7.4869	7.1034	6.7499	6.4235	6.1218	5.8424	5.5831	5.3423	5.1183	4.9095	4.7147	4.5327
14	13.0037	12.1062	11.2961	10.5631	9.8986	9.2950	8.7455	8.2442	7.7862	7.3667	6.9819	6.6282	6.3025	6.0021	5.7245	5.4675	5.2293	5.0081	4.8023	4.6106
15	13.8651	12.8493	11.9379	11.1184	10.3797	9.7122	9.1079	8.5595	8.0607	7.6061	7.1909	6.8109	6.4624	6.1422	5.8474	5.5755	5.3242	5.0916	4.8759	4.6755
16	14.7179	13.5777	12.5611	11.6523	10.8378	10.1059	9.4466	8.8514	8.3126	7.8237	7.3792	6.9740	6.6039	6.2651	5.9542	5.6685	5.4053	5.1624	4.9377	4.7296
17	15.5623	14.2919	13.1661	12.1657	11.2741	10.4773	9.7632	9.1216	8.5436	8.0216	7.5488	7.1196	6.7291	6.3729	6.0472	5.7487	5.4746	5.2223	4.9897	4.7746
18	16.3983	14.9920	13.7535	12.6593	11.6896	10.8276	10.0591	9.3719	8.7556	8.2014	7.7016	7.2497	6.8399	6.4674	6.1280	5.8178	5.5339	5.2732	5.0333	4.8122
19	17.2260	15.6785	14.3238	13.1339	12.0853	11.1581	10.3356	9.6036	8.9501	8.3649	7.8393	7.3658	6.9380	6.5504	6.1982	5.8775	5.5845	5.3162	5.0700	4.8435
20	18.0456	16.3514	14.8775	13.5903	12.4622	11.4699	10.5940	9.8181	9.1285	8.5136	7.9633	7.4694	7.0248	6.6231	6.2593	5.9288	5.6278	5.3527	5.1009	4.8696
21	18.8570	17.0112	15.4150	14.0292	12.8212	11.7641	10.8355	10.0168	9.2922	8.6487	8.0751	7.5620	7.1016	6.6870	6.3125	5.9731	5.6648	5.3837	5.1268	4.8913
22	19.6604	17.6580	15.9369	14.4511	13.1630	12.0416	11.0612	10.2007	9.4424	8.7715	8.1757	7.6446	7.1695	6.7429	6.3587	6.0113	5.6964	5.4099	5.1486	4.9094
23	20.4558	18.2922	16.4436	14.8568	13.4886	12.3034	11.2722	10.3711	9.5802	8.8832	8.2664	7.7184	7.2297	6.7921	6.3988	6.0442	5.7234	5.4321	5.1668	4.9245
24	21.2434	18.9139	16.9355	15.2470	13.7986	12.5504	11.4693	10.5288	9.7066	8.9847	8.3481	7.7843	7.2829	6.8351	6.4338	6.0726	5.7465	5.4509	5.1822	4.9371
25	22.0232	19.5235	17.4131	15.6221	14.0939	12.7834	11.6536	10.6748	9.8226	9.0770	8.4217	7.8431	7.3300	6.8729	6.4641	6.0971	5.7662	5.4669	5.1951	4.9476
26	22.7952	20.1210	17.8768	15.9828	14.3752	13.0032	11.8258	10.8100	9.9290	9.1609	8.4881	7.8957	7.3717	6.9061	6.4906	6.1182	5.7831	5.4804	5.2060	4.9563
27	23.5596	20.7069	18.3270	16.3296	14.6430	13.2105	11.9867	10.9352	10.0266	9.2372	8.5478	7.9426	7.4086	6.9352	6.5135	6.1364	5.7975	5.4919	5.2151	4.9636
28	24.3164	21.2813	18.7641	16.6631	14.8981	13.4062	12.1371	11.0511	10.1161	9.3066	8.6016	7.9844	7.4412	6.9607	6.5335	6.1520	5.8099	5.5016	5.2228	4.9697
29	25.0658	21.8444	19.1885	16.9837	15.1411	13.5907	12.2777	11.1584	10.1983	9.3696	8.6501	8.0218	7.4701	6.9830	6.5509	6.1656	5.8204	5.5098	5.2292	4.9747
30	25.8077	22.3965	19.6004	17.2920	15.3725	13.7648	12.4090	11.2578	10.2737	9.4269	8.6938	8.0552	7.4957	7.0027	6.5660	6.1772	5.8294	5.5168	5.2347	4.9789
31	26.5423	22.9377	20.0004	17.5885	15.5928	13.9291	12.5318	11.3498	10.3426	9.4790	8.7331	8.0850	7.5183	7.0199	6.5791	6.1872	5.8371	5.5227	5.2392	4.9824
32	27.2696	23.4683	20.3888	17.8736	15.8027	14.0840	12.6466	11.4350	10.4062	9.5264	8.7686	8.1116	7.5383	7.0350	6.5905	6.1959	5.8437	5.5277	5.2430	4.9854
33	27.9897	23.9886	20.7658	18.1476	16.0025	14.2302	12.7538	11.5139	10.4644	9.5694	8.8005	8.1354	7.5560	7.0482	6.6005	6.2034	5.8493	5.5320	5.2462	4.9878
34	28.7027	24.4986	21.1318	18.4112	16.1929	14.3681	12.8540	11.5869	10.5178	9.6086	8.8293	8.1566	7.5717	7.0599	6.6091	6.2098	5.8541	5.5356	5.2489	4.9898
35	29.4086	24.9986	21.4872	18.6646	16.3742	14.4982	12.9477	11.6546	10.5668	9.6442	8.8552	8.1755	7.5856	7.0700	6.6166	6.2153	5.8582	5.5386	5.2512	4.9915
36	30.1075	25.4888	21.8323	18.9083	16.5469	14.6210	13.0352	11.7172	10.6118	9.6765	8.8786	8.1924	7.5979	7.0790	6.6231	6.2201	5.8617	5.5412	5.2531	4.9929

Source: Adelman/Marks. *Entrepreneurial Finance: Finance for Small Business*, 2/e. © 2000 Pearson Prentice Hall, Upper Saddle River, NJ.

Table A-7 Future Value of an Annuity

Formula: $FV = A\left[\dfrac{(1+i)^n - 1}{i}\right]$

Interest Rate (i)

Periods (n)	1%	2%	3%	4%	5%	6%	7%	8%	9%	10%	11%	12%	13%	14%	15%	16%	17%	18%	19%	20%
1	1.000	1.000	1.000	1.000	1.000	1.000	1.000	1.000	1.000	1.000	1.000	1.000	1.000	1.000	1.000	1.000	1.000	1.000	1.000	1.000
2	2.0100	2.0200	2.0300	2.0400	2.0500	2.0600	2.0700	2.0800	2.0900	2.1000	2.1100	2.1200	2.1300	2.1400	2.1500	2.1600	2.1700	2.1800	2.1900	2.2000
3	3.0301	3.0604	3.0909	3.1216	3.1525	3.1836	3.2149	3.2464	3.2781	3.3100	3.3421	3.3744	3.4069	3.4396	3.4725	3.5056	3.5389	3.5724	3.6061	3.6400
4	4.0604	4.1216	4.1836	4.2465	4.3101	4.3746	4.4399	4.5061	4.5731	4.6410	4.7097	4.7793	4.8498	4.9211	4.9934	5.0665	5.1405	5.2154	5.2913	5.3680
5	5.1010	5.2040	5.3091	5.4163	5.5256	5.6371	5.7507	5.8666	5.9847	6.1051	6.2278	6.3528	6.4803	6.6101	6.7424	6.8771	7.0144	7.1542	7.2966	7.4416
6	6.1520	6.3081	6.4684	6.6330	6.8019	6.9753	7.1533	7.3359	7.5233	7.7156	7.9129	8.1152	8.3227	8.5355	8.7537	8.9775	9.2068	9.4420	9.6830	9.9299
7	7.2135	7.4343	7.6625	7.8983	8.1420	8.3938	8.6540	8.9228	9.2004	9.4872	9.7833	10.0890	10.4047	10.7305	11.0668	11.4139	11.7720	12.1415	12.5227	12.9159
8	8.2857	8.5830	8.8923	9.2142	9.5491	9.8975	10.2598	10.6366	11.0285	11.4359	11.8594	12.2997	12.7573	13.2328	13.7268	14.2401	14.7733	15.3270	15.9020	16.4991
9	9.3685	9.7546	10.1591	10.5828	11.0266	11.4913	11.9780	12.4876	13.0210	13.5795	14.1640	14.7757	15.4157	16.0853	16.7858	17.5185	18.2847	19.0859	19.9234	20.7989
10	10.4622	10.9497	11.4639	12.0061	12.5779	13.1808	13.8164	14.4866	15.1929	15.9374	16.7220	17.5487	18.4197	19.3373	20.3037	21.3215	22.3931	23.5213	24.7089	25.9587
11	11.5668	12.1687	12.8078	13.4864	14.2068	14.9716	15.7836	16.6455	17.5603	18.5312	19.5614	20.6546	21.8143	23.0445	24.3493	25.7329	27.1999	28.7551	30.4035	32.1504
12	12.6825	13.4121	14.1920	15.0258	15.9171	16.8699	17.8885	18.9771	20.1407	21.3843	22.7132	24.1331	25.6502	27.2707	29.0017	30.8502	32.8239	34.9311	37.1802	39.5805
13	13.8093	14.6803	15.6178	16.6268	17.7130	18.8821	20.1406	21.4953	22.9534	24.5227	26.2116	28.0291	29.9847	32.0887	34.3519	36.7862	39.4040	42.2187	45.2445	48.4966
14	14.9474	15.9739	17.0863	18.2919	19.5986	21.0151	22.5505	24.2149	26.0192	27.9750	30.0949	32.3926	34.8827	37.5811	40.5047	43.6720	47.1027	50.8180	54.8409	59.1959
15	16.0969	17.2934	18.5989	20.0236	21.5786	23.2760	25.1290	27.1521	29.3609	31.7725	34.4054	37.2797	40.4175	43.8424	47.5804	51.6595	56.1101	60.9653	66.2607	72.0351
16	17.2579	18.6393	20.1569	21.8245	23.6575	25.6725	27.8881	30.3243	33.0034	35.9497	39.1899	42.7533	46.6717	50.9804	55.7175	60.9250	66.6488	72.9390	79.8502	87.4421
17	18.4304	20.0121	21.7616	23.6975	25.8404	28.2129	30.8402	33.7502	36.9737	40.5447	44.5008	48.8837	53.7391	59.1176	65.0751	71.6730	78.9792	87.0680	96.0218	105.9306
18	19.6147	21.4123	23.4144	25.6454	28.1324	30.9057	33.9990	37.4502	41.3013	45.5992	50.3959	55.7497	61.7251	68.3941	75.8364	84.1407	93.4056	103.7403	115.2659	128.1167
19	20.8109	22.8406	25.1169	27.6712	30.5390	33.7600	37.3790	41.4463	46.0185	51.1591	56.9395	63.4397	70.7494	78.9692	88.2118	98.6032	110.2846	123.4135	138.1664	154.7400
20	22.0190	24.2974	26.8704	29.7781	33.0660	36.7856	40.9955	45.7620	51.1601	57.2750	64.2028	72.0524	80.9468	91.0249	102.4436	115.3797	130.0329	146.6280	165.4180	186.6880
21	23.2392	25.7833	28.6765	31.9692	35.7193	39.9927	44.8652	50.4229	56.7645	64.0025	72.2651	81.6987	92.4699	104.7684	118.8101	134.8405	153.1385	174.0210	197.8474	225.0256
22	24.4716	26.8704	30.5368	34.2480	38.5052	43.3923	49.0057	55.4568	62.8733	71.4027	81.2143	92.5026	105.4910	120.4360	137.6316	157.4150	180.1721	206.3448	236.4385	271.0307
23	25.7163	28.8450	32.4529	36.6179	41.4305	46.9958	53.4361	60.8933	69.5319	79.5430	91.1479	104.6029	120.2048	138.2970	159.2764	183.6014	211.8013	244.4868	282.3618	326.2369
24	26.9735	30.4219	34.4265	39.0826	44.5020	50.8156	58.1767	66.7648	76.7898	88.4973	102.1742	118.1552	136.8315	158.6586	184.1678	213.9776	248.8076	289.4945	337.0105	392.4842
25	28.2432	32.0303	36.4593	41.6459	47.7271	54.8645	63.2490	73.1059	84.7009	98.3471	114.4133	133.3339	155.6196	181.8708	212.7930	249.2140	292.1049	342.6035	402.0425	471.9811
26	29.5256	33.6709	38.5530	44.3117	51.1135	59.1564	68.6765	79.9544	93.3240	109.1818	127.9988	150.3339	176.8501	208.3327	245.7120	290.0883	342.7627	405.2721	479.4306	567.3773
27	30.8209	35.3443	40.7096	47.0842	54.6691	63.7058	74.4838	87.3508	102.7231	121.0999	143.0786	169.3740	200.8406	238.4993	283.5688	337.5024	402.0323	479.2211	571.5224	681.8528
28	32.1291	37.0512	42.9309	49.9676	58.4026	68.5281	80.6977	95.3388	112.9682	134.2099	159.8173	190.6989	227.9499	272.8892	327.1041	392.5028	471.3778	566.4809	681.1116	819.2233
29	33.4504	38.7922	45.2189	52.9663	62.3227	73.6398	87.3465	103.9659	124.1354	148.6309	178.3972	214.5828	258.5834	312.0937	377.1697	456.3032	552.5121	669.4475	811.5228	984.0680
30	34.7849	40.5681	47.5754	56.0849	66.4388	79.0582	94.4608	113.2832	136.3075	164.4940	199.0209	241.3327	293.1992	356.7868	434.7451	530.3117	647.4391	790.9480	966.7122	1,181.8816
31	36.1327	42.3794	50.0027	59.3283	70.7608	84.8017	102.0730	123.3459	149.5752	181.9434	221.9132	271.2926	332.3151	407.7370	500.9569	616.1616	758.5038	934.3186	1,151.3875	1,419.2579
32	37.4941	44.2270	52.5028	62.7015	75.2988	90.8898	110.2182	134.2135	164.0370	201.1378	247.3236	304.8477	376.5161	465.8202	577.1005	715.7475	888.4494	1,103.4960	1,371.1511	1,704.1095
33	38.8690	46.1116	55.0778	66.2095	80.0638	97.3432	118.9334	145.9506	179.8003	222.2515	275.5292	342.4294	426.4632	532.0350	664.6655	831.2671	1,040.4858	1,303.1253	1,632.6698	2,045.9314
34	40.2577	48.0338	57.7302	69.8579	85.0670	104.1838	128.2588	158.6267	196.9823	245.4767	306.8374	384.5210	482.9034	607.5199	765.3664	965.2698	1,218.3684	1,538.6878	1,943.8771	2,456.1176
35	41.6603	49.9945	60.4621	73.6522	90.3203	111.4348	138.2369	172.3168	215.7108	271.0244	341.5896	431.6635	546.6808	693.5727	881.1702	1,120.7130	1,426.4910	1,816.6516	2,314.2137	2,948.3411
36	43.0769	51.9944	63.2759	77.5983	95.8363	119.1209	148.9135	187.1021	236.1247	299.1268	380.1644	484.4631	618.7493	791.6729	1,014.3457	1,301.0270	1,669.9945	2,144.6489	2,754.9143	3,539.0094

APPENDIX

B

MACRS DEPRECIATION SCHEDULE

Table B-1 MACRS Recovery Periods

Recovery Period	Type of Assets
3 year	Certain types of horses
5 year	Automobiles, light trucks, typewriters, calculators, copiers, computers
7 year	Office furniture and fixtures
10 year	Vessels, barges, tugs, and similar water transportation equipment
15 year	Telephone distribution plant
20 year	Municipal sewers
27.5 year	Residential rental property
31.5 year	Nonresidential real property

Source: Cain/Carman. *Mathematics for Business Careers,* 5/e. © 2001 Pearson Prentice Hall, Upper Saddle River, NJ.

Table B-2 MACRS Depreciation Rates

Recovery Year	Recovery Period					
	3-Year	5-Year	7-Year	10-Year	15-Year	20-Year
1	33.33%	20.00%	14.29%	10.00%	5.00%	3.750%
2	44.45%	32.00%	24.49%	18.00%	9.50%	7.219%
3	14.81%	19.20%	17.49%	14.40%	8.55%	6.677%
4	7.41%	11.52%	12.49%	11.52%	7.70%	6.177%
5		11.52%	8.93%	9.22%	6.93%	5.713%
6		5.76%	8.92%	7.37%	6.23%	5.285%
7			8.93%	6.55%	5.90%	4.888%
8			4.46%	6.55%	5.90%	4.522%
9				6.56%	5.91%	4.462%
10				6.55%	5.90%	4.461%
11				3.28%	5.91%	4.462%
12					5.90%	4.461%
13					5.91%	4.462%
14					5.90%	4.461%
15					5.91%	4.462%
16					2.95%	4.461%
17						4.462%
18						4.461%
19						4.462%
20						4.461%
21						2.231%

Source: Cain/Carman. *Mathematics for Business Careers,* 5/e. © 2001 Pearson Prentice Hall, Upper Saddle River, NJ.

INDEX